W9-BCF-377

PUBLIC ADDRESSES, LETTERS AND PAPERS OF WILLIAM BRADLEY UMSTEAD

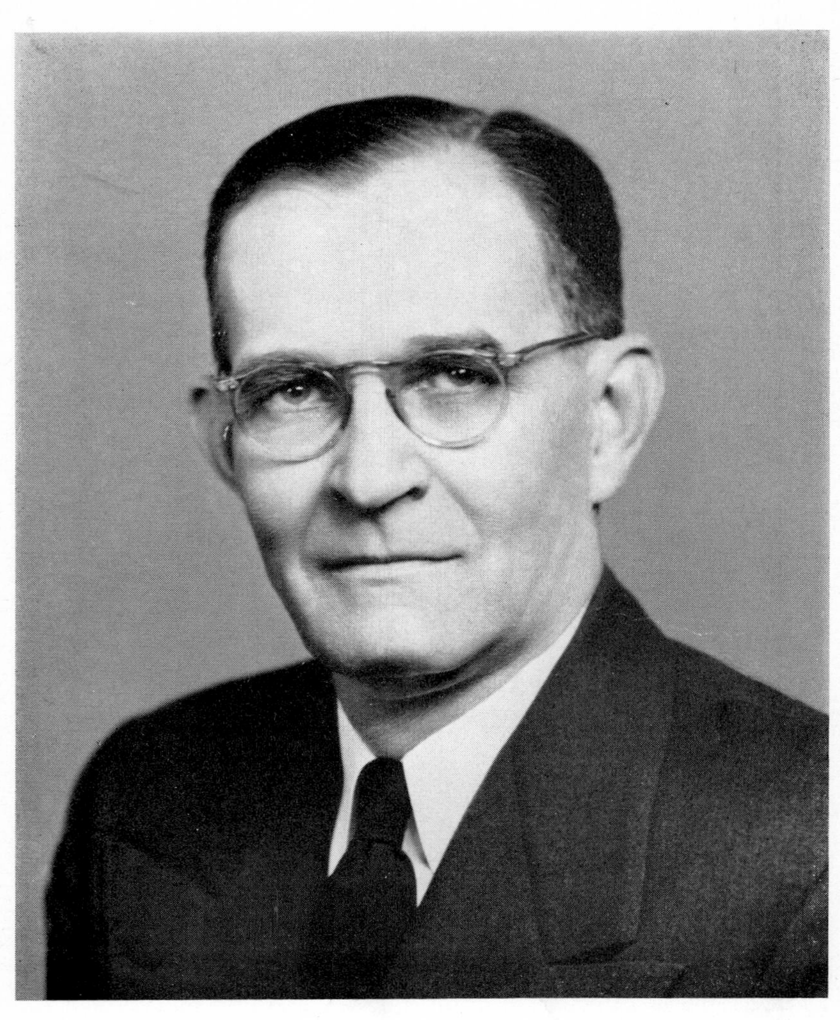

William B Umstead

PUBLIC ADDRESSES, LETTERS, AND PAPERS of WILLIAM BRADLEY UMSTEAD

GOVERNOR OF NORTH CAROLINA 1953-1954

Edited by
David Leroy Corbitt
Editor, Division of Publications
STATE DEPARTMENT OF ARCHIVES AND HISTORY

Raleigh
Council of State
State of North Carolina
1957

FOREWORD

For approximately thirty-five years the State of North Carolina has published the public addresses and papers of the governors after they retired from the governor's office. All governors prior to Governor Umstead whose papers have been published served a four-year term and their published material covered a four-year period. Governor Umstead, however, was stricken with a heart attack two days after his inauguration and was either in the hospital or confined to his bed at the Mansion much of the term he served. He was unable to complete his term of office, having died November 7, 1954.

This volume of messages to the General Assembly, proclamations, addresses, statements, and articles for the press are arranged as the material in the letter books of previous governors. The material in this volume was either written by Governor Umstead or issued from his office during the time he served as governor.

A number of pictures of important persons or events connected with some phase of the activities and duties of his administration are included. It is hoped that these pictures will add interest and value to the work.

Governor Umstead, who was ill most of his term, did not make as many addresses as some previous governors. When he did make an address, he frequently spoke without manuscript. This explains why we do not have more of his addresses. In some instances we found that tape recordings were made of his addresses, and we were able to obtain copies from these recordings. We have included all of his addresses—short or long—if we could locate them. We are aware of the fact that we did not find all of them.

In compiling the appointments, an effort has been made to list the names, the addresses, and the terms of the appointees, on the several boards and commissions, and to give citations to the laws authorizing these appointments. It is believed that this is pertinent and valuable information.

The sketch "William Bradley Umstead" was written by Edward L. Rankin, Jr., Governor Umstead's private secretary.

The funds for printing this volume have been provided by the Council of State as has been the custom in previous volumes.

The State Department of Archives and History authorized my services for the purpose of arranging the papers, writing the headings, preparing the table of contents, compiling the index, and supervising the printing and mailing of the volumes.

In some instances I have found it necessary to change the capitalization, punctuations, phraseology, and sentence arrangement, but in all cases I have endeavored to retain the original meaning.

Mrs. Catharine Coppersmith assisted in selecting the material and typed all except the index. She also compiled the appointments including the footnotes. Miss Beth Crabtree, an editorial assistant in the Department, read the proof and compiled the index. Other persons such as the staff of the State Library, the staff of the State News Bureau, and others have rendered valuable assistance. To all who have assisted me, I wish to express my appreciation.

D. L. Corbitt.

November 1, 1957.
Raleigh, N. C.

WILLIAM BRADLEY UMSTEAD *

By Edward L. Rankin, Jr.

The date was Thursday, January 8, 1953—an overcast, damp day in the City of Raleigh where inaugural ceremonies were under way for a new Governor, William Bradley Umstead of Durham. It was a great day for the winner of a hard-fought political campaign, and great crowds of his friends, supporters, and well-wishers were on hand to witness the event. It was a moving tribute to a candidate who had won without making a single campaign promise of reward to any individual.

In keeping with the pomp and circumstance, William Umstead was dressed in top hat and morning clothes—the traditional garb for a new Governor but certainly not characteristic of the lean, serious-minded man who wore them. With his family at his side, the incoming Governor rode in the procession to Memorial Auditorium, along with Governor W. Kerr Scott, whose term was ending.

There William Umstead was administered his oath of office in solemn and moving ceremonies witnessed by the joint session of the North Carolina General Assembly and a large public gathering. Then came the forceful, precisely-worded inaugural speech over which the new Governor had labored so many weeks, rewriting, changing, amending and rephrasing. It was a long speech because it described in detail a far-reaching program for North Carolina; plans designed to touch and stir every part of state government and our economic way of life. The program called for progress and advancement in many fields—public education, industrial development, agriculture, highway safety, governmental reorganization, prison reform, mental hospitals, paroles and probation, to mention a few. It called for large expenditures of public funds in the areas of greatest need, much to the surprise of some of the Governor's more conservative friends. A few were deeply shocked.

Yet the ideas, the policies, the plans all followed in detail the clearcut primary platform of William Umstead, the candidate.

* For more information on Governor Umstead's life see pages 381-389. This memorial address by R. Percy Reade, was delivered March 15, 1955, before a joint session of the General Assembly.

Rarely has any candidate for Governor had a more complete or specific platform. These were his objectives for North Carolina, and he would not have dreamed of changing his stand now that he was elected and faced with the responsibility of leadership.

The Governor spoke with vigor and conviction and received an ovation at the conclusion of his address. His administration was under way. Strangely enough, delivering the address had tired him, and he sank into his chair with relief.

The customary mammoth luncheon at the Executive Mansion followed immediately with hundreds of guests to meet and to greet. In the rush and confusion, the Governor had no lunch. He did not mind a bit because he was with his family and friends and the many reunions were joyful. Few governors have ever had more devoted, loyal friends. They knew him as a man of highest character, integrity, and honor, and above all, a man to be trusted under any circumstances. It really did not matter whether they first knew him as a farm boy at Bahama, a student at Chapel Hill, public school teacher, comrade-at-arms in France, lawyer, solicitor, Democratic Party leader, Congressman, or United States Senator; William Umstead cherished his friendships and his friends. Many of his closest friends were fellow classmates of the class of 1916 at the University of North Carolina. Reunions with these friends always led to much good talk, laughter, and banter. While a student at the University, the Governor was noted for his debating prowess, ability in student politics, Sunday afternoon hiking and poetry-quoting. He was also known to sing such old favorite songs as:

I was born about ten thousand years ago
There ain't nothing ever happened I don't know
I saw Jonah swallow the whale, and
I pulled the lion's tail, and
I'll lick the man who says it isn't so!

The traditional public reception at the Executive Mansion that evening brought in thousands to shake his hand, and for over four hours he and Mrs. Umstead, a quiet-spoken and gracious First Lady, stood in the official receiving line greeting people from all over the State. By the time they were able to slip away to attend the Inaugural Ball, it was almost midnight and the tiring pace was beginning to tell on the Governor. He was showing signs of strain, looked wan and gray; but he made his appearance at the Ball, led the Grand March, and then was called upon for an unexpected harmonica solo. It was far into the morning when the Umsteads were able to retire.

Friday, January 9, quickly passed as hundreds of well-wishers called at the Governor's Office. It was an exhausting day. There was no opportunity to organize the newly assembled staff or get any work accomplished. The desks and the file cabinets were still arranged as left by the outgoing Governor and his staff. At the close of the day, Governor Umstead made a list of the many things to be done the next week. He was eager to get his legislative program under way, and happy at the prospect of having as his Legislative Counsel, W. Frank Taylor of Goldsboro, an able, conscientious legislative veteran and former Speaker of the House of Representatives.

The Governor returned to his home in Durham that evening, and spent the next morning in his law office closing out some business affairs. He retired early that night and found it difficult to sleep because of a persistent cough. Finally, the cough became so severe and racking that his physician, Dr. Ralph Fleming, had to be summoned. Dr. Fleming found more than a bad cough. He found a feverish man with deep chest congestion and signs of more serious trouble.

This diagnosis was confirmed within hours at Watts Hospital, where it was discovered that the Governor had suffered a heart attack and was verging on pneumonia. By early Sunday morning, Mrs. Umstead had telephoned me the shocking news and it was my sad duty to notify the news media.

Television and radio flashed the news to the people of the State, and newspapers followed with front-page headlines. This was the first time in over half a century that a Chief Executive of North Carolina had become seriously ill. The news deeply moved the people of the State and messages of best wishes, sympathy and concern poured in from every corner of North Carolina. Many telephone calls came from legislative leaders and old friends. The unspoken question was: "How bad was the attack?" Dr. Fleming described it as "mild," but could add little in predictions on recovery time.

So began the administration of Governor William Bradley

Umstead, a dedicated public servant with great plans and aspirations for North Carolina. This sudden and completely unexpected illness came as a terrific blow. The General Assembly was in session and awaited his legislative program. There had been no time for conferences with department and agency heads. There was the unfinished matter of a Budget Message to prepare and deliver. Administrative leaders in the Legislature awaited instructions and advice.

This was the situation and these were the facts. What was to be done? For a few uncertain weeks, no one knew. Everything depended upon the Governor's ability to recover sufficiently to make the necessary decisions. During this time, Representative John W. Umstead, the Governor's brother, Frank W. Taylor, and I made many anxious trips to Durham to confer with Dr. Fleming and speak a word of comfort and encouragement to the State's No. 1 patient. It was good to note that Governor Umstead accepted his fate calmly and set out, in his own deliberate way, to do the best he could under the circumstances.

Meanwhile, it was my duty as Private Secretary to set up the organization of the Governor's Office and to work with Legislative Counsel Taylor and with members of the General Assembly. Fortunately, Governor Umstead had selected an experienced office staff, many of whom had served with him in past campaigns, or in Washington, while he was a member of the United States Senate. These staff members included Mrs. Elizabeth J. Duke, Mrs. Rachel W. Spears, Miss Margaret Scott, Miss Betty Carter, Mrs. Claire Eastman Nickels, Mrs. Susan Lobinger, Sgt. Harold Minges and J. Edward Massenburg. Their loyalty, diligence, experience and understanding helped us across a difficult and troubled time.

Governor Umstead won the fight with his serious illness after nearly six weeks in the hospital, and was permitted to return to the Executive Mansion on the condition that he remain in bed and follow a carefully regimented schedule. Despite the handicaps and limitations, the Governor did not complain but set out to make the best use of the few hours each day he could use to direct his program to a successful conclusion.

He was greatly cheered when his many friends in the General Assembly quickly rallied around him, and held fast in their loyalty and their support for him and the program and principles for which he stood. They did this without urging and with an unshaken faith in his ability and judgment to accomplish his legislative goals. It would not be easy, because such results usually require a free exchange of ideas, suggestions and strategy with the Chief Executive. Yet these legislators had to accept the restricting circumstances, make the best of hurried bedside conferences and move ahead on relayed instructions from an invalid Governor. To make matters more complicated, the Governor's doctors hovered nearby and kept a tight rein over his daily schedule, watching carefully the pressures exerted by legislative problems.

Governor Umstead, as might be expected, met each problem with calm deliberation. To offset the problem of how to communicate with the legislators, he set up a system of conferences with groups of legislators who were brought from the Capitol by car and gathered around his bedside on the second floor of the Executive Mansion. Here the Governor put forth his greatest effort in a forceful presentation of his program and what it meant for North Carolina. Even those who did not agree with some of the legislation in question were greatly impressed with the Governor's grasp and knowledge of the state government problems involved. Despite the handicap of not being able to talk at length with individual legislators, his leadership could not be denied and the 1953 General Assembly began to move ahead after a shaky beginning.

The legislative process is always a stern test for any governor and his leadership. It demands the utmost in skill and ability in dealing with legislators, governmental departments and agencies, various economic groups and organizations, the press and other news media, and of course, the ever-shifting winds of public opinion. It also requires a keen understanding of people, places and events, past and present. As the weeks passed, it became increasingly clear that William Umstead would pass his legislative test with flying colors. Again and again administrative bills came from committees or passed readings on the floor of the House and Senate with the cry of Umstead supporters: "Sail on! Sail on!."

This was a tribute to a frail but determined Governor who would not let illness stand in his way. It was also a sound victory for his friends and legislative leaders. Few people, however, ever knew the toll it took on Governor Umstead as he directed his forces from his bedside at the Executive Mansion. Conscientious to a painful degree, he spent many wakeful hours at night grappling with the many problems which faced him.

On May 21, more than four months after his heart attack, the Governor returned to his office for the first time. With the General Assembly behind him, he was confronted immediately with the usual flood of appointments which had to be made. Pressure had already picked up, letters of endorsement came by the hundreds, and candidates across the State planned their campaigns for various appointments. In the midst of all this, scarcely after the close of the General Assembly, came the sudden tragic death of United States Senator Willis Smith. This meant that the Governor was faced with the grave responsibility of appointing a successor to fill out the term of the Senator until the next General Election. Immediately across the State there formed groups behind certain candidates and vigorous campaigns were undertaken to influence the Governor to appoint their choice. Unless seen firsthand, it is inconceivable to imagine the pressure which can be exerted by political groups desiring appointment of a candidate to high public office. Governor Umstead took this responsibility in his usual stride, confiding completely in no one except himself, but conferring daily with dozens of his friends and associates. He was careful to hear as many groups and delegations as his strength would permit and the weeks dragged on while he searched for the right man. The final decision: Alton A. Lennon of Wilmington, a surprise candidate who was named to complete the term of Senator Smith. Governor Umstead then went on to complete his major appointments to get the Umstead administration rolling full speed ahead. This included, for example, a new fourteen-man State Highway Commission.

By mid-summer, he was working full time in the office and undertaking a busy schedule with the exception of outside speeches and appearances. It was a well-known fact that Governor Umstead had never served as a member of the General Assembly of North Carolina, and so many department heads and other veterans of state government service were amazed to find the tremendous understanding and detailed knowledge of administration problems which the Governor had. He was a patient listener, and a deliberate and careful administrator. At the same time, he did not hestitate to move into situations which he believed needed correcting; and his forthright manner won him the respect, if not always the admiration, of many.

One of the basic characteristics of William Umstead was the fact that he "wore no man's collar" and operated as a public official with a deep sense of public responsibility for the common good and common welfare of all the people. A studious and able lawyer, Governor Umstead's primary problem in administration of his many duties was delegation of responsibility to staff members and department heads. Despite the fact that he was the Chief Executive of a multi-million-dollar governmental operation, he found it difficult to relinquish any responsibilities which were his. He made a valiant effort to see all who had business with him, to answer as much mail as humanly possible, and according to his capacity, to serve to the fullest as Chief Executive, administrator, policy-maker, political leader and Commander-in-Chief of the National Guard.

Meanwhile, life at the Executive Mansion had settled into a comfortable routine under the direction of Mrs. Umstead and with the help of her hostess, Miss Laura Reilley. Public entertainment was held to a minimum, of course, but Mrs. Umstead was kept busy with the many social duties and appearances of a First Lady. Merle Bradley, the attractive ten-year-old daughter of the Umsteads, quickly adjusted to her new surroundings and brought in her girl friends to play in the huge rooms and on the broad lawn. The sounds of their activity and laughter was a cheerful and somewhat unexpected note for the old Mansion.

By Fall the Governor was well enough to attend his first Southern Governors' Conference, which was held at Hot Springs, Virginia. Here he had an opportunity to meet with his fellow governors from the Southern States and to discuss the multitude of problems and opportunities in state government. One of his old friends there was Governor John S. Battle of Virginia, whom Governor Umstead had known for many years. As might be expected, Governor Umstead attended each session of the Governors' Conference, listened carefully, made notes and had little to say. He showed great interest in the problems of public schools, as well as the need for more industrial development throughout the

South. He also followed carefully all the discussions on mental hospitals and mental care, and was pleased to note that his program to furnish more state funds for public schools and mental hospitals kept North Carolina among the leaders in these fields.

Governor Umstead returned to Raleigh and a busy schedule which carried him through the remaining months of 1953. Always fond of college football, the Governor managed to see as many home games at Chapel Hill as possible. He also spent considerable time with such regular responsibilities as the Council of State, Board of Buildings and Grounds, Executive Committee of the University Trustees. As titular head of the Democratic Party, he kept in close touch with all political developments.

One of his great interests was the reorganization of the State Board of Paroles which he had successfully pushed through the 1953 General Assembly. He conferred frequently with the three-man board and upheld the new policies stressing uniform and fair parole consideration for all prisoners, which were instituted by this board. He was also vitally interested in the work of the Department of Conservation and Development, especially the industrial development of the State. As he said in his inaugural address: "One of the most important things at this time is to bring to our State new industry and new types of industry. We should encourage also the expansion of industries which we now have. Large segments of industry are now moving South, and North Carolina should make every possible effort to get its share. This would provide employment for thousands of our people, and would increase our per capita income and our revenues. It would enable us to keep at home thousands of young men and women, educated at the expense of the State, who leave our borders each year to find opportunities elsewhere."

When the Conservation and Development Board held its quarterly meetings, the Governor actively participated as Chairman, showed great interest in the work of each division and continually challenged board and staff members alike to better efforts. As he often pointed out, progress *anywhere* in North Carolina helped the entire State. The establishment of a Speakers' Bureau in the Department to spread the story of progress and development received his hearty approval.

In early February, the Governor, upon the advice of his doctors, took a week's vacation in Florida and returned rested and ready to go back to work. With all the vigor at his command, he plunged into his daily activities and devoted more and more hours of hard work to administration problems of every kind. As a means of stimulating industrial development, he traveled to New York City for several conferences there with groups of industralists who had North Carolina connections. Several months later the Governor and Mrs. Umstead went to Washington, D. C., to attend a conference of governors called by the President of the United States. During the first week of June the Governor took up the traditional task of delivering commencement addresses at the state institutions of higher learning and also at Duke University. He also began to take on more outside speaking engagements and appearances, such as an annual farmers day, the opening or dedication of a new state building, a convention of state employees, safety meetings and community forums on industrial development.

Perhaps one of his greatest thrills was the evening he returned to Mangum School at Bahama, Durham County, to deliver the commencement address for the graduating class there. Bahama was his home community and this visit must have stirred the many memories of his childhood.

He probably thought of Robbie, a little black mare who shared thirty-three years of his life. This was a little-known story of devotion and hard work which reflected the warm and human side of a North Carolina farm boy.

It all began one day in 1904 when a trim black colt was born on a tobacco farm of the late John W. Umstead, Sr., in the northern part of Durham County. To the world this was no special event; but to the Umstead family, and especially to William, a slender, sandy-haired lad of nine, it was a day of great excitement.

As William expected, the long-legged colt was given to him to raise as his own horse. He promptly named her Robbie, in honor of a favorite school teacher whose first name was Roberta.

Under William's loving care, Robbie grew into a compactly built little horse with a gentle disposition and a stout heart.

She proved to be a fine saddle horse, buggy horse, and yet could work long hours plowing in the fields or doing any other work required of a work animal on the farm. When the mare was old enough to ride, William bought a new black McClellan saddle with matching black bridle and soon became a familiar sight in the neighborhood as he and his swift-footed mount galloped over the fields and countryside.

By scrimping and saving like most farm boys with little cash income, William managed to buy a black, rubber-tired buggy, which Robbie pulled with an effortless trot that covered miles of dusty Durham County roads.

Yet all was not play for the farm boy and his horse. Like most farms, life on the Umstead tobacco farm required long hours of work. Always an industrious lad, William did not mind the work; but he was anxious to see that no one else handled Robbie, so he hurried home each day from his country school to make certain that he alone worked the little mare.

Years passed, William completed high school with a good record and entered the University of North Carolina. He did well at Chapel Hill, and at the close of his freshman and sophomore years, returned home to the farm to team up with Robbie and make a tobacco crop so he could pay his way through school the next year. Robbie also provided transportation during the summer days for social outings and picnics. This arrangement worked fine until the summer before the boy's last year. His father was growing old and had been unable to put in a tobacco crop, so William returned home for the summer faced with the serious problem of making enough money to replace the tobacco cash income and complete his college education.

His equipment consisted of Robbie and himself—an alert, serious-minded young man with an inherited and acquired capacity for hard work. Then William heard that a road construction gang was planning to build a concrete bridge on a state highway nearby, so he went over to see the construction superintendent about a job.

"What can you do?" the superintendent asked, looking him up and down.

"Anything," replied the boy, showing more confidence than he felt.

"Do you have a team and wagon? We are going to need lots of rock and sand hauled."

William's face brightened. "I have a fine horse and I can borrow my father's one-horse wagon."

While the superintendent did not think a one-horse team could keep up the work, he agreed to let William try it. The boy appeared next day with Robbie and the wagon. Assigned to hauling crushed rock, the sturdy little horse and boy labored several days to supply the labor force with enough stone. Realizing then that he and Robbie could not do it alone, William rented a small gray horse and borrowed enough money from an old friend of the family to buy a new two-horse wagon in Durham.

With his two-horse team and wagon, William was given the back-breaking task of hauling sand from the river bottom to the bridge site. Working steadily from dawn until dusk six days a week, the boy and his team soon proved to the superintendent that they could handle the job.

One week before school resumed at Chapel Hill, William and Robbie and the new horse completed the job. It meant six days a week of grueling labor under the summer sun from a week after school closed in May until the first week of September; but, accustomed to hard work, William had hauled sand every day, except Sundays, for his entire summer vacation and made enough money to send him back to Chapel Hill for his senior year.

Following graduation from the University in 1916 with an excellent record and winner of the coveted Mangum Medal, William went to Kinston to teach school, and Robbie, then twelve years old, was moved into the village of Bahama where William's father had gone to live because Mr. Umstead was getting too old to farm.

In the years that followed, William Umstead left his teaching job to serve overseas during World War I, returned to earn his law degree at Trinity College, now Duke University, and began his record of public service which was to carry him to the highest positions of public trust. Robbie remained in good hands in Bahama. While the busy life of a public official prevented many rides on his horse, William Umstead never considered the possibility of selling Robbie. In 1932 he began his career as a Congressman, and was re-elected in 1934 and 1936. This meant that he had to move to Washington, but still he saw Robbie when he visited Durham County between Congressional sessions. The little mare was showing signs of age, but lived well under the care of a relative of the Congressman.

Then one day in 1937 William Umstead received word that Robbie was ill. When he got there the little black mare was down in her stall. William saw that she would never rise again and death came several days later to the faithful little horse. She was buried nearby.

The years passed, but the Governor never forgot his horse, Robbie. She shared thirty-three years of his life and he would talk about her as if it were only yesterday when, clad in faded overalls, he would leap upon her sturdy back and gallop away across the fields of Durham County.

By the Spring of 1954, the Umstead Administration was in full swing, and the Governor was deeply absorbed in his many responsibilities. It became apparent, however, that the daily demands upon him were draining steadily his small reservoir of physical strength. The Governor rarely mentioned his health problem or complained about physical limitations which would naturally frustrate such a vigorous, active person.

United States Senator Clyde R. Hoey died suddenly in May, and again the Governor was faced with the need to appoint a new member of the United States Senate. Rarely, if ever, has a Governor of North Carolina had to make two such appointments in one term. Political activity was soon at fever-pitch as candidates and their supporters sought favorable consideration from the Governor. Within a week after Senator Hoey's death, the Honorable Forrest H. Shuford, Commissioner of Labor, died unexpectedly. This left a vacancy on the Council of State which had to be filled.

The Governor moved much faster with his Senatorial appointment this time, and named the Honorable Sam J. Ervin, Jr., of Morganton to fill the seat of Senator Hoey. He selected Frank Crane of Union County as the man to replace Forrest H. Shuford. Both appointments were well received and later both men went on to win their positions by vote of the people.

Events continued to move rapidly and the Governor was confronted with still another crisis of immense proportions. On May 17, 1954, the Supreme Court of the United States held that a state may not deny to any person, on account of race, the right to attend any school that it maintains. This decision overturned the law of the land as it had been stated previously by this same Court for some sixty years. North Carolina's public school system, of course, had been built on a basis of legally requiring separate schools for the children of different races.

North Carolina and the other Southern States were stunned by the Court decision. The outcry from many states was immediate and angry, especially from public officials. Governor Umstead was shocked with the action of the Court, but he withheld public comment until he had time to read the language of the decision and confer with Attorney General Harry McMullan, Superintendent of Public Instruction Charles F. Carroll and others. Chief Justice M. V. Barnhill of the Supreme Court of North Carolina, attended the first conference at the request of the Governor, not as a representative of the Court, but rather as a trusted friend of the Governor.

The calm reaction of Governor Umstead and other state leaders to the segregation decision was in the best North Carolina tradition of reasoned moderation. While people generally felt very deeply about the issues involved, they responded to the Governor's leadership; and this explosive moment in the State's history passed without wild, irresponsible, and intemperate statements or actions.

The Governor's first comprehensive statement on the Court decision was made on May 27 when he reviewed the legal history of the decision, told of North Carolina's progress toward equal school facilities for all, and then clearly outlined the "complications and difficulties of immeasurable extent" which faced North Carolina as a result of this decision.

Then he said: "However, the Supreme Court of the United States has spoken. It has reversed itself and has declared segregation in public schools unconstitutional. In my opinion its previous decisions of this question were correct. This reversal of its former decisions is, in my judgment, a clear and serious invasion of the rights of the sovereign states. Nevertheless, this is now the latest Supreme Court interpretation of the Fourteenth Amendment.

"Overnight, this decision has brought to our State a complex problem—the wise solution of which will require the calm, careful, and thoughtful study of all of us. This is no time for rash statements or the proposal of impossible schemes. The problem is too big for any one person to decide. I shall seek the advice of the Attorney General, the Superintendent of Public Instruction, the State Board of Education, Legislators and other citizens of this State as to the course we shall pursue and the character of the program we should follow in the light of the recent Supreme Court decision."

On June 10, the Governor, accompanied by a small group of state officials, flew to Richmond, Virginia, to attend a conference with other Southern governors on the school segregation problem. He listened intently to the different viewpoints represented at this conference, but did not commit himself or North Carolina to any course of action. William Umstead was not implusive by nature, and wanted to think through each step of a problem before he finally decided to take that step.

After considerable study and discussion, he announced the appointment of a "Governor's Special Advisory Committee on Education," which would make a study of the school situation in North Carolina and then make recommendations for consideration of the 1955 General Assembly. The Honorable Thomas J. Pearsall of Rocky Mount was named chairman of a group consisting of nineteen men and women, including three Negroes. This Committee was continued by Governor Luther H. Hodges, and later reconstituted by the 1955 General Assembly as the "Advisory Committee on Education."

By August the doctors called for a rest and the Governor went to Nags Head for four days, then later took a week at Morehead City. This was an effort to build up his strength in preparation for the hearings of the Advisory Budget Commission which were to consume a great deal of the month of September. He insisted on sitting through each day of the hearings and listened carefully as each department head or agency made his presentation and request for budgets. With his deep interest in governmental problems, he did not hesitate to cross-examine various department heads on their problems, their needs and their requests.

Looking back upon the days spent in hearings and conferences with the Advisory Budget Commission, it is clear that the toll on his physical strength was simply too great for the Governor. On October 3, the Governor entered Watts Hospital for a period of treatment and rest and remained there until October 25. Even in the hopsital, he could not relinquish the grave responsibilities of his office. On October 15, the great "Hurricane Hazel" struck the coast of North Carolina, moved inland and roared across the State, leaving a trail of great damage and desolation. From his hospital bed, the Governor sent a wire to the President of the United States, asking for aid in time of emergency and natural disaster. The President responded to this request by declaring North Carolina a major disaster area and the vast job of rehabilitation got under way.

Governor Umstead returned to his office with a slower step, a thinner face, but with all the determination to continue in his job and to meet every responsibilty of his office. Long conferences followed and the day's calendar was soon full with visitors, groups, and state department heads.

The year between sessions of the General Assembly is always a busy period of budget study and recommendations for the next session. So, in the summer of 1954, the Governor and Advisory Budget Commission began their intensive work on hearings, preparation and recommendations. Despite all the other major problems on hand, the Governor made it clear that he expected to devote as much time as possible to every phase of the Commission's work.

He also showed great interest in the work of the State Commission on Government Reorganization and attended several meetings of this commission. In early July, the Governor and a small party flew to Lake George, New York, where he attended his first national Governors' Conference. He attended every session, discussed mutual problems with many fellow governors, and returned with a number of ideas for consideration.

On Thursday, November 4, 1954, the Governor left his office to attend another conference of the Advisory Budget Commission. He was not well that day, although those of us in the office did not realize the seriousness of his condition. He stayed in the meeting until lunch time and then doggedly returned to the meeting following his lunch. By mid-afternoon the Governor's failing strength would not permit him to remain, and reluctantly he returned to the Mansion and to bed. After a brief examination, the doctors ordered the Governor back to Watts Hospital in Durham for rest and treatment. It was explained to the press that the Governor had a severe cold which had failed to respond to treatment and this condition had aggravated his heart condition.

Before he left for the hospital, I had a thirty-minute conference with the Governor to handle a number of details, including several appointments which he wanted to announce. The Governor sat up in bed, a blanket around his shoulders, while we talked. He was completely exhausted, unable to over come his physical ailments; but the determined spirit of the man shone through his clear eyes, firm voice and complete command of what he was discussing. His instructions to me were as precise and thorough as ever. We parted with a firm handshake and unspoken words of warm affection.

Following the procedure used during earlier hospitalizations, the Governor's Office began to issue medical bulletins on the Governor's condition two or three times a day. On Friday, November 5, the Governor's condition continued serious and no improvement was shown. On Saturday, November 6, the Governor was reported some better in the morning. Early Sunday morning, November 7, Dr. Fleming reported that the Governor had pneumonia and there was no improvement. Mrs. Umstead and daughter, Merle Bradley, were called early Sunday morning and advised to come to the hospital. They were at the bedside when the Governor expired quietly and suddenly at 9:10 a.m. The cause of the death was congestive heart failure.

After learning that Mrs. Umstead and Merle Bradley had been summoned to Durham, I hurried to the hospital, arriving about 10:00 a.m. It was then my sad duty to pick up the telephone at 10:15 a.m. and inform the press that the Governor of North Carolina was dead. My next telephone call was to the Lieutenant Governor of North Carolina, the Honorable Luther H. Hodges of Leaksville, to notify him officially that he was the new Governor of North Carolina.

It was a stunned and shocked North Carolina that received the news of the Governor's death on Sunday morning, November 7. Many people heard the news while attending church. Friends of the Governor, who knew his determination to complete his term of office, could not believe that he was gone.

Since the State had not experienced the loss of a Chief Executive in modern times, there was no precedent for handling the ceremony of succession. The Constitution simply specified that the Lieutenant Governor succeeded to office upon the death of the Governor. There was no precedent for a State funeral and all these details and decisions had to be worked out with the Council of State and with Mrs. Umstead and members of the Umstead family. Monday, November 8, was devoted to plans for the funeral and a motorcade was setup for state officials to attend the funeral in a group.

At 11:30 a.m., Tuesday, November 9, last rites were held for Governor Umstead at Trinity Methodist Church in Durham, where he had been an active member and lay leader for many years. Burial followed in the little Mount Tabor Methodist Church graveyard near Bahama. This had been the church of his ancestors. Thousands of friends from across the State attended the funeral and the graveside services. The funeral procession reached miles out into the county as it moved toward the Governor's final resting place.

At 4:00 p.m. that afternoon, Luther H. Hodges formally took his oath of office as the Governor of North Carolina. A huge crowd jammed into the Capitol's Hall of the House of Representatives to watch the brief, solemn ceremonies.

William Umstead literally laid down his life in the performance of his duties as Governor. Although he was proud of his record in many high public offices, he cherished the governorship above all else and was determined, beyond description, to serve out his term of office and to complete the program he had planned for a *Better Tomorrow* in North Carolina.

This conscientious attention to duty was dramatically illustrated by one of his final acts in life.

The day after the funeral, I was approached by a lawyer who had been working for a special State Commission preparing a report and recommendations on the judicial redistricting of North Carolina. He explained that the final report of this Commission had been given to the Governor several days before he entered the hospital for the last time, and that the report was needed immediately since it was the only complete, corrected copy in existence.

After searching the office without success, I went to the Executive Mansion and looked around Governor Umstead's bedroom. There was his big easy chair with a reading lamp and a small table covered with reports, journals, newspapers and other reading material. This was where he did most of his reading and studying. A careful search of all this material did not uncover the report.

The Governor's maid, Margaret, was then asked if she had any idea where the report might be found. She did not remember seeing the document, and stood undecided for a moment. Then her glance fell on the worn, old-fashioned leather suitcase which the Governor had taken with him to the hospital.

Moving quietly, she opened the bag carefully and began to remove the few personal articles it contained. There, at the bottom of the bag, neatly folded under a pair of pajamas, was the missing report.

Gravely ill, William Umstead had not gone to the hospital empty-handed. Conscientious always, he had carried with him this copy of a redistricting plan in which he was deeply interested because it dealt with a subject close to his heart—law and the courts. He had carried the report with him because he expected to study it at his very first opportunity.

This was typical of a brave man who struggled against greater odds and greater handicaps than any other Governor in the last half century. He accepted his handicaps without complaint, and was willing to go every step of the way necessary to carry out the duty and responsibilities given him by the vote of the people of North Carolina.

CONTENTS

EXECUTIVE ORDERS: *Page*

1953

1954

PUBLIC ADDRESSES:

1953

1954

STATEMENTS AND ARTICLES FOR THE PRESS:

1953

Page

LIST OF ILLUSTRATIONS

MESSAGES TO THE GENERAL ASSEMBLY

Courtesy of the Herald Sun

Governor Umstead, Mrs. Umstead and their daughter, Merle, leaving their home in Durham for the inauguration in Raleigh, January 8, 1953.

INAUGURAL ADDRESS

Delivered in Memorial Auditorium
Raleigh
January 8, 1953

Mr. President, Mr. Speaker, Members of the General Assembly of North Carolina:

It is with a mixture of humility and pride that I assume the office of Governor of North Carolina. Within the powers and sovereignty of the people of the State there is no greater honor, and with it there goes a responsibility of which I am keenly aware. With a proper reverence for the past, confidence in the present, and faith in tomorrow, I dedicate myself to the discharge of this high trust.

Civilization never stands still. It either moves forward or backward. In its inescapable tide it carries to and fro the failures, accomplishments, faith, hopes, and aspirations of all mankind. It has been said that civilization is a covenant between the dead, the living and the yet unborn. Those who are selected by the people to manage and direct their affairs assume the obligation of keeping that covenant.

Today we look with pride and deep appreciation upon the records made by those who have preceded us in this Commonwealth, and to them we give thanks. Due to their sacrifices, courage, and far-sightedness, ours is a wonderful heritage. Our obligation to them and those yet unborn requires that we in this hour use what we have in such a manner as to keep the covenant. This requires complete dedication by those who have been selected to pilot the course of our government.

To you and the people of North Carolina, I express my profound thanks and appreciation for this high honor. Let us remember that no one should be permitted to affect selfishly or adversely the best interests of our people, and that which affects one part of our State affects all of the State. I seek your sympathetic understanding, and want your advice, help, and counsel. Let us work together for the State we all love. With confidence in your patriotic devotion to the task ahead of us, and the knowledge that in the life stream of North Carolina there is a strength which endureth and a determination which cannot be subdued, I enter upon the office of Governor, and I now submit to you and to the people of the State some of my views and recommendations.

PUBLIC EDUCATION

It has been said that "The history of civilization is being daily written, to a large degree, in the classrooms of the world." The truth of this statement is fully understood by all of us. We are justly proud of the progress we have made in public education. There is still much to do. Although North Carolina ranks forty-fourth among the states in per capita annual income, it ranks thirtieth among the states in the amount of money spent for public education. This means that we are determined to have, and are willing to make sacrifices for, the best system of public schools we can possibly afford. Until we are able to increase the per capita income of our people, we shall necessarily be limited in the amount of money we can spend for education.

Some months ago I advocated the reduction of the teacher load from 31.7 to 30. The State Board of Education, out of unexpended funds, arranged to make this reduction during the present school term. I recommend that the General Assembly continue this reduction during the next biennium. We should further reduce the teacher load as rapidly as finances will permit. I recommend that sufficient funds be provided to employ properly qualified attendance personnel sufficient in number to enforce effectively the school attendance law;

That sufficient funds be made available to provide such additional clerical assistance, services, and supplies as may be found necessary due to the growth of our school system;

That the transportation of our children be made as safe as humanly possible;

That every effort be made to improve the inspection requirements now employed;

And that the driver training and safety education classes be made available to high school boys and girls throughout the State.

I recommend a ten per cent salary increase for school teachers and other school personnel, retroactive to July 1, 1952, and that as much increase in the salaries of public school teachers be made during the next biennium as can be provided with available revenues.

The proper agencies should thoroughly study the possibilty of a more comprehensive program of vocational education in public schools. Such a program will no doubt involve long-range planning, and in my opinion now is the time to begin such planning. We should continue to encourage the program of agricultural vocational education.

We should continue the physical examination of children to determine defects which, unless remedied in time, result in handicaps through life, and provision should be made to provide means for correcting the defects.

There is a shortage of elementary teachers in North Carolina and in most sections of the country. It is my belief that this shortage is not due entirely to our salary scale. I am told that the requirements and regulations for elementary teachers are so rigorous and complicated as to deter young people from seeking to become elementary teachers, and in some instances make it exceedingly difficult for them to do so. If this is true, it should be remedied at once. The General Assembly, the State Board of Education, and the State Department of Public Instruction should give immediate and thorough consideration to this problem and take such action as may be necessary to solve it.

While admitting the shortcomings in our school system, I feel that we should devote less time and publicity to emphasizing its weakest points and more time and publicity to emphasizing its strongest points. It is not necessary always to dwell on the worst in order to move steadily toward the attainment of the best.

Since 1933, when the State took over the operation of our public schools, the local school units have gradually lost control. There should be some proper way to restore some degree of local control without injuring our state system. I think that a fuller recognition of local school units would strengthen our school system.

The question of further consolidation of schools is largely one of administration. However, it can be carried too far. The human element should be considered, and if the State Board of Education does not now have sufficient discretionary power to enable it, in any given situation, to consider the human element, such power should be given it by the enactment of proper amendments to the school law.

I suggest that the General Assembly provide for the codification of the State School Law in order that it may be readily usable by those who need it.

We have constructed in North Carolina a great many school buildings during the past few years. The need has not been met. Our school population is rapidly increasing, and in order to protect and preserve our public school system we must supply the necessary facilities. Under our State Constitution we must provide equal school facilities for our children, without discrimination. This, in my judgment, can be done only by grants-in-aid to the counties which are unable to provide such facilities. I, therefore, recommend that the proper committees of the General Assembly, as soon as practicable, conduct hearings to determine the amount of money necessary to provide such aid, and that it submit to the people of the State a bond issue to secure funds to provide the necessary aid to the counties for the construction of school facilities for all of our children, and that the funds be granted by the State Board of Education to the counties on the basis of need and the ability to pay. This is not intended to relieve the counties of the primary responsibility to provide adequate school facilities, without discrimination.

Institutions of Higher Learning

North Carolina is justly proud of its institutions of higher learning. They are essential to our intellectual, social, economic, cultural, and spiritual development, and merit the continued support of our people. Every effort should be made to see that these institutions understand the needs of the State, and that they seek always to meet these needs.

During the past few years there has been a tremendous building program for our institutions of higher learning, and other permanent improvements are now and will continue to be needed. However, the lack of available funds makes any large scale building program for these institutions impossible at this time. The buildings must be maintained and repaired. This alone is a large program, and must be done for the preservation of the investment already made.

SCHOOLS FOR THE BLIND AND DEAF

Our schools for the blind and deaf serve a worthy purpose, are doing splendid work, and should be encouraged in their efforts.

EDUCATIONAL TELEVISION

Some months ago the Federal Communications Commission allocated to, or reserved for, North Carolina eight television channels for educational purposes. Sufficient time has not elapsed since the perfection of this modern method of communication to determine its probable effect in the field of individual, group, or mass education. Certainly its importance is sufficient to place upon the State, through its proper officials, the serious obligation of a thorough investigation, to the end that we may avoid, if possible, becoming involved in an unwise venture, if it is determined to be that; and, in order that we may take full advantage of an opportunity in the field of education, if it is determined to be wise and proper.

In this matter we shall be plowing in new ground, and it will require the talents, the time, and the wisdom of able men and women to determine what course we should follow. I recommend that the General Assembly authorize a commission to be appointed by the Governor to study this important matter and report its findings to this session of the General Assembly.

ROADS

Since 1921 we have developed a state-wide system of public roads in which there are some 66,000 miles, including about 26,000 miles of hard-surfaced roads.

Good roads are a modern necessity. On our main roads the traffic load is large and rapidly will become larger. Our industrial and agricultural output will increase year by year. Our tourist trade depends largely on good primary roads.

Many of our main roads are in very bad condition and are being worn out as rapidly as we are building them. In addition to the over-all traffic load, the tremendous increase in heavy commercial traffic is taking its toll and adding tremendously to the cost of maintenance of our primary roads.

We must continue to maintain, improve, and build roads. It is a task which is never finished. We should strive to make every road in North Carolina usable to motor vehicles at all times. We must maintain our entire road system and the 200 million dollar secondary road program will place upon the State an unknown cost of maintenance, depending in a large measure upon the durability of these roads.

There will not be, within the forseeable future, from existing gasoline revenues, after the cost of maintenance and other expenses are deducted, adequate funds left with which to build primary roads. I, therefore, recommend that the General Assembly look into our entire road situation and determine, if possible, a long-range primary road building program, and that it determine what, if anything, should be done to increase our current revenue by a more equitable distribution of the cost of the use of our highways, and further, consider what measures, if any, should now be taken to protect our highways against usages which contribute to their rapid deterioration.

Ours is a state highway system, and we should endeavor to restore unified control and at the same time try to bring highway administration closer to the people.

As I have stated, there are some 66,000 miles of roads under the jurisdiction of the Highway and Public Works Commission, of which about 26,000 miles are hard-surfaced. We now have ten Highway Divisions and ten Commissioners. Ten Commissioners, on a part-time, per diem basis, cannot now properly look after our expanded road system. I, therefore, recommend that the General Assembly amend existing laws to increase the number of Divisions and Commissioners to fifteen. In my judgment this would make for efficiency and economy.

HIGHWAY SAFETY

In the final analysis, the reduction of the slaughter and injury of our citizens and the destruction of property on our highways depend in a large measure upon the citizenship of our State. When fully aroused, the people of North Carolina can do much to make our highways safer. The General Assembly should seriously consider this gravely important matter, and I recommend:

That it enact a common sense measure providing effective mechanical inspection of all motor vehicles operating in North Carolina;

That a drivers' training program be established in every public high school in the State;

That it be made unlawful for any person to change or alter the manufacturers' specifications of the motor or other mechanical parts, features or design of any vehicle with the purpose or intent of increasing its speed, and that any vehicle so altered or changed shall not be allowed to operate on the streets or highways of the State;

That the hit-and-run statute be amended to provide that any person who collides with a motor vehicle parked or unattended on the streets or highways of North Carolina shall be guilty of a misdemeanor, unless he immediately notifies the owner of the car or the police authorities of the incident.

It is well known that in many instances traffic laws are not properly enforced. I call upon the State Highway Patrol, all peace officers, and the courts for an effective enforcement of such laws.

AGRICULTURE

Agriculture is still the pride of our State. More people work on farms in North Carolina than in any state in the Union—about one-third of our population. The cash income from farm crops is now about $900,000,000 per year, and is an important part of our State's economy.

The improvement in agriculture during the past fifteen years is obvious on every hand. We must continue this improvement and endeavor to raise the average per capita income of the people working on our farms in North Carolina. The large number of agricultural workers accounts in a large measure for our low per capita income. Contrary to the views of many people, the majority of those who make a living on the farm are not getting rich. The Federal Farm Program, the Extension Service, State College, the Experiment Stations, Vocational Agricultural Teachers, teachers of Home Economics, the State Department of Agriculture, the Rural Electrification Authority, the Production and Marketing Administration, the Forest Service, the Soil Conservation Service, the Farm Home Administration, the Farm Credit Administration, and other agricultural agencies make a mighty team for the advancement and improvement of agriculture in North Carolina. I commend the Farm Bureau and the Grange for their splendid efforts for agriculture. It shall be my purpose to work with all of these agencies, and I recommend and suggest the following:

We should have a co-operative movement on the part of the appropriate agencies, the farmers, cities and towns and all of our people, for a unified and effective effort to stop erosion of soil.

We need more improved pasture land, more dairy and beef cattle and more poultry. There should be a greater utilization of our forest resources and a comprehensive and effective forestry program, including adequate fire protection, and a wider use of recommended forest improvement practices.

We need more effective methods of protecting and using our water resources and our wildlife.

We need additional processing plants for agricultural products, and we should develop better and expanding marketing facilities for our poultry, fruit, vegetables, and livestock.

Every effort should be made to eliminate such inequalities in freight rates affecting agriculture in North Carolina as may now exist.

We should expand our program of agricultural research. My belief in the value of agricultural research is of long standing, and I will support such a program. We have learned from industry that research is essential to progress. This is true also of agriculture. A greater effort should be made to carry to the farmers the splendid results of our research program.

Every effort should be made by the State and every agency involved, and by all of our people, to conserve, enrich, and

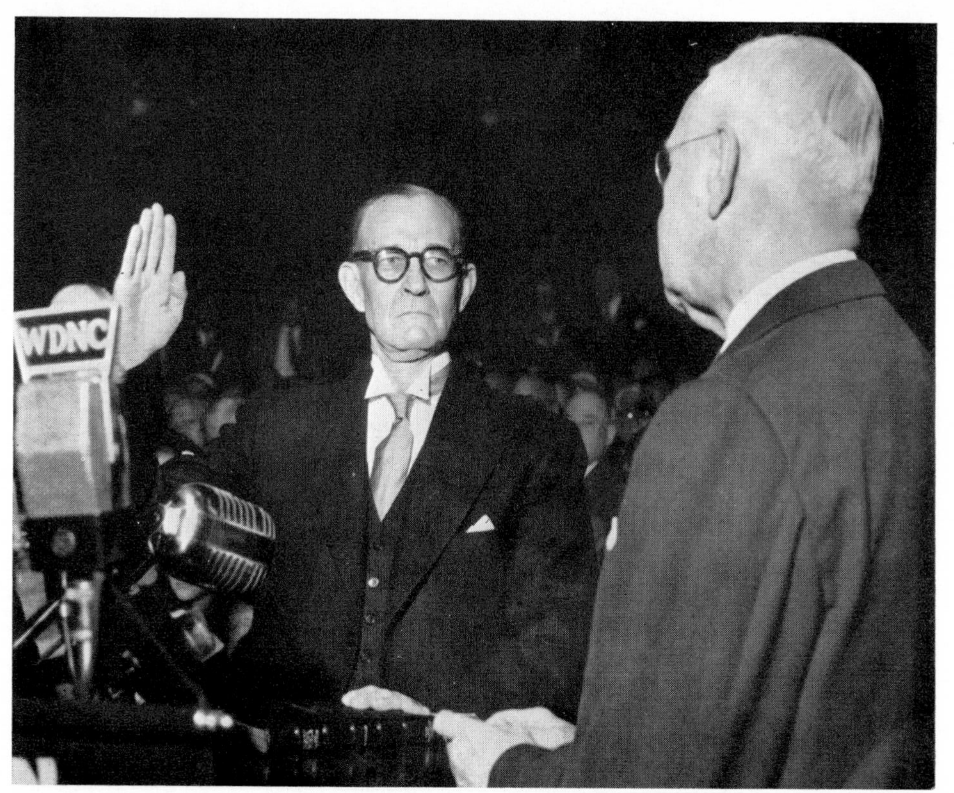

Photo courtesy Herald Sun

Chief Justice W. A. Devin administering the oath of office to Governor Umstead, January 8, 1953.

use properly God's good earth, which with its water, trees, and grasses, has supported all the generations before us, to the end that it will be able to continue to support, feed, and clothe the generations yet to come.

CONSERVATION AND DEVELOPMENT

The words "Conservation and Development" include many things so important to the development of North Carolina.

One of the most important things at this time is to bring our State new industry and new types of industry. We should encourage also the expansion of industries which we now have. Large segments of industry are now moving south, and North Carolina should make every possible effort to get its share. This would provide employment for thousands of our people, and would increase our per capita income and our revenues. It would enable us to keep at home thousands of young men and women, educated at the expense of the State who leave our borders each year to find opportunities elsewhere.

If we continue to improve the state services now being rendered, it will be necessary to have more tax dollars. In my opinion, it is better to obtain new taxpayers than to increase taxes on the taxpayers we now have. In this effort we shall need the assistance of all of our people, and particularly in the effort to create a friendly and wholesome atmosphere which will appeal to those we shall endeavor to bring here. I shall seek the active assistance of a substantial number of our citizens to supplement the efforts of the existing state agencies in this vitally important matter.

We must encourage the further development of our sea food industry. I am told that we have actually lost ground in this industry in recent years. With our long shore line and our bountiful and diversified supply of sea food, it should be possible for our fishermen in larger numbers to find it increasingly profitable again to "go down to the sea in ships." I recommend that the General Assembly carefully examine the laws pertaining to our fishing industry and make such changes as may be necessary.

We have now completed two fine ports, one at Morehead City and one at Wilmington. I have been interested in these projects for years. However, the port facilities as such cannot, and will not, bring to us a substantial export and import trade. This trade must be developed. This will require skilled specialists and considerable time. I recommend that the General Assembly make it possible to pay to the necessary skilled specialists salaries in line with similar types of work at other ports so that these gateways to the shipping lanes of the world may be profitable and important in the development of our economy. Furthermore, I recommend that the Ports Authority Act be re-examined and amended so as to make possible the development of small inland ports.

We have a splendid inland waterway which runs through our State. All along its rambling course, opportunities exist which should be developed.

Our State is rich in mineral resources, and the General Assembly should take such action as may be necessary to encourage the further development of these resources.

A substantial amount of income in North Carolina is derived from our tourist trade. Our recreational and scenic facilities are outstanding. Our hunting and fishing areas are the equal of those to be found anywhere. Our historical points are sufficient to arouse the interest of all lovers of our state and national heritage. Our outdoor historical pageants are unsurpassed in the Nation. Our beaches, our mountains, our sandhills, and our piedmont offer to tourists practically every known form of recreation. In this matter of bringing additional tourists to our State, every town, city and county can play an important part. We must provide them with clean, comfortable and pleasant accommodations at reasonable prices. Courtesy and kindness should be extended to every tourist. I invite the co-operation of every citizen in this matter.

I am glad to call attention to the splendid contribution of the North Carolina Recreational Commission. It is seeking to aid the various communities in our State in the more effective use of recreational facilities and is helping to educate our people to use some of their leisure time in forms of recreation which contribute to the enrichment of their lives. This program can also make a contribution toward our efforts to bring additional tourists to our State and to keep them here a while longer.

The topographic mapping program now underway should be continued because of its value to conservation, agriculture, and road building.

The last session of the General Assembly passed an act dealing with stream pollution. Some progress has been made, but it has been rather slow. In many places in the Inland Waterway, the water is polluted. Attention should be given to this. I suggest that such other and further steps be taken as may be necessary, in keeping with wise and fair procedures, to avoid and eliminate stream pollution in North Carolina.

The program of advertising North Carolina has been a good investment. It should be continued and enlarged, and additional funds should be provided for this purpose.

HEALTH

Our Public Health Department has made a great contribution to our State. Its work must be encouraged and continued within the limits of available revenues.

In 1945 the General Assembly initiated a unique system of medical care, involving all the necessary factors without violating any of our basic democratic principles. It included a co-ordinated and balanced system of medical training, teaching, and healing. Under the Medical Care Commission this program has proceeded orderly and efficiently. Needy sick have been assisted. Many hospitals have been constructed. At Chapel Hill, the Health Center, with its teaching hospital has been established. This program is of basic importance, and must be maintained and operated in such manner as to translate the original concept of the Medical Care Plan into a reality of service to people in all parts of our State. It is, I hope, an effective answer to the advocates of socialized medicine, to which I am strongly opposed.

The splendid results being accomplished by the State Tuberculosis Sanatoriums, the Orthopaedic Hospital, and the Hospital for Cerebral Palsy patients, are outstanding. These institutions should have the continued sympathetic support of our State.

STATE INSTITUTIONS FOR THE MENTALLY ILL

One of our greatest obligations is to our mentally ill. During the last few years great progress has been made in their treatment and care. Much remains to be done, and continued emphasis should be placed upon the curing of our mentally ill.

We call the institution at Kinston The Caswell Training School. It is not now and never has been a "training school." It is and has been a detention home for feeble-minded children, who grow into feeble-minded men and women, and there they stay through the years. There has never been a place which has even been called a training school for feeble-minded children of the Negro race.

There is not sufficient room in our institutions for the adults who need attention. The need is so urgent that it can be met adequately only by the proceeds from a bond issue. I recommend, therefore, that the General Assembly submit to the people of the State a bond issue in an amount sufficient to provide funds for not only training schools for the feeble-minded white and Negro children of our State, but also for the construction and equipment of sufficient facilities to meet the needs of adults now and for some years to come. We have worked at it in piece-meal fashion long enough. We must make every effort to cure both children and adults, where such is within the capacity of medical science, and sufficient trained personnel must be provided. These people have no spokesmen except those whose hearts have been touched by the condition of those affected by this program.

Along with the establishment of training schools for feeble-minded children, proper provisions should be made for a co-ordinated study of the causes of feeble-mindedness and to seek the most practical and best known methods of preventing it.

WELFARE

Regardless of the degree of prosperity we may attain, there are always those among us who need assistance. The welfare program in North Carolina is broad and comprehensive and is important to many of our people. It is an expensive item in our budget. Ever-increasing numbers on the welfare rolls, with the

Left to right: Mrs. Umstead, Governor Umstead, Merle Umstead, and Governor Scott in the reviewing stand at Governor Umstead's inauguration, January 8, 1953.

greatly increased costs, make it mandatory that those charged with the administration of this program carefully investigate each case involved. Special emphasis and attention should be given to the rehabilitation of those who obtain assistance. There should be close co-operation with the Employment Service. We should not take pride in the number of people on our relief rolls. We should take pride in the number we can properly remove from our relief rolls. Whether the money comes from county, city, state or federal government, it should be carefully used and directed toward the rebuilding of useful citizens.

REORGANIZATION OF STATE GOVERNMENT

Much has been said and written about the reorganization of state government in North Carolina and elsewhere. Many states have studied this problem with satisfactory results. Every effort should be made looking to the sufficient and economical administration of each function of the state government.

As our population has increased and as more state services have become necessary, from time to time additional state agencies have been created, frequently operating as separate units. In many instances old units of the government have greatly expanded. Our government has become big business, reaching into all parts of the State. I am not prepared to offer a plan of reorganization. An effective plan will require serious, careful and extended study. I, therefore, recommend that the General Assembly authorize a commission to be appointed by the Governor to study this matter and report its findings and recommendations to the Governor by December 1, 1954. The Institute of Government is now studying this problem and its studies will be made available to the commission.

PRISON SYSTEM

North Carolina is one of the few states where the Prison System is under the control of the Public Works and Highway Department. In recent months and years there has been much criticism of the administration of our Prison System. Every effort should be made to rehabilitate and save from a life of crime every offender sentenced to prison. At the same time it should be understood that confirmed, hardened criminals cannot be coddled and that discipline and order in a prison system are essential and must be maintained at any cost. It is perhaps desirable to separate the Prison System from the Public Works and Highway Commission. There are, however, difficult administrative and financial problems to overcome which will require careful study and wise planning. If separation were made without such study and planning, the situation would probably be worse than it is now. I, therefore, recommend that this matter be thoroughly considered by the commission which has been recommended and be included in its report.

PAROLES COMMISSION

I think that people generally appreciate the need for, and the value of, our Parole System. The number of prisoners has grown to the point where it is impossible for one commissioner to conduct adequately the affairs of the parole office. I, therefore, recommend that the General Assembly rewrite the statute dealing with the parole system, make such changes as it deems necessary for its improvement, and create a Paroles Commission consisting of three commissioners, and provide that one shall be designated as chairman and that they be appointed by, and hold office subject to the will of, the Governor.

It has been suggested that the Probation Department should be combined with the Paroles Department. I am not prepared to make any recommendation as to this. The matter, however, should be given careful study by the commission which has been recommended and be included in its report.

STATE EMPLOYEES

There are now approximately 66,000 people on the payroll of the State. In most instances they are conscientious and hardworking, and I am proud of them. They have the right to expect of the State a fair wage and proper treatment. The State has a right to expect from them an honest day's work for a day's pay. Dissatisfied employees who constantly engage in unjustified complaining would render themselves and the State a good service by seeking employment elsewhere.

Due to the increase in the cost of living, I have heretofore announced that I would favor a 10 per cent increase in the salary and wages of all state employees, retroactive to July 1, 1952, and now recommend that this be done.

I should like for all those who work for North Carolina, however humble their job may be, to be proud that they work for the State. I should like for each of them to be courteous, not only to their fellow citizens, but also to all those who may come into or pass through our State from elsewhere. I should like for them to feel that they are a part of the state government, and I seek their sympathetic understanding of the problems of our State, and their assistance in making it a better place in which to live.

When the State Retirement System was initiated, many people had been working for the State for years who, because of age, had to be retired soon after its beginning. Many of these draw relatively small amounts and are frequently referred to as "hardship cases." I recommend that all those who had been in the employ of the State for not less than twenty years at the time the Retirement System was created, now receiving retirement benefits, be paid not less than $50.00 per month. This will not remove all the hardships and inequities, but in my judgment this much should be done.

PUBLIC UTILITIES

The importance of public utilities is recognized by all. Electric power, telephones, railroads, motor freight, and passenger carriers, and other public utilities are essential to our growth and development.

Due to the efforts of the REA and private power companies, about 90 per cent of the farms and rural establishments in North Carolina have electricity. There is a growing demand and need for telephones in our rural areas. It will be my purpose to encourage to the fullest extent the continuation of both of these splendid programs. They are not state functions, and never have been. The State has never furnished any power and has never installed a telephone. It can, through the Utilities Commission, in proper cases, see that those who hold franchises furnish these utilities. In these matters I shall seek the co-operation of both private industry and our federal government.

The public has come to depend upon the services rendered by railroads and motor freight and passenger carriers. All of these are essential to the continued growth and development of our State. The holder of a franchise assumes a public obligation which should be fulfilled, and they subject themselves to governmental regulation and control, and this should be fair to them and to the public.

The increased industrial expansion of North Carolina will require an abundance of electric power. The power companies in this State have greatly increased the output of their plants during the past years. The federal government also has made additional electric power available. Every effort will be made to have power in sufficient quantities to meet the requirements of the people and of our expanding industry.

The work of the Utilities Commission has increased, both in volume and importance. It should be provided with sufficient clerical and expert assistance to enable it to render the service expected of it.

LABOR

The relation between those who work in, and those who manage and control our industries generally has been good. I congratulate the State Department of Labor for its effective work in the field of industrial relations. Employers and employees are mutually dependent upon each other. The less friction there is, the better it is for both. The importance and the right of collective bargaining is fully recognized, and it should be used to settle any difficulties which may arise, and the rights of all parties should be carefully protected and preserved.

Every citizen of North Carolina has the right to work and to go to work wherever his job may be. Every person restrained of his liberty is entitled to a remedy. While I am Governor of this State I shall endeavor to see that the laws are enforced which

Photo Courtesy Herald Sun

Virginia governors attending the inauguration of Governor Umstead, January 8, 1953. *Front left to right:* Governor Umstead; William M. Tuck, Governor of Virginia 1946-1950; John S. Battle, Governor of Virginia, 1950-1954; and W. Kerr Scott, Governor of North Carolina, 1949-1953.

protect every citizen in his right to go to his job unmolested by anyone.

We have a Federal Wage and Hour Law which provides for minimum wages and maximum hours. This law applies only to employees engaged in interstate commerce, as that term is now liberally construed. There are many industrial and service employees in North Carolina who do not come within the provisions of the Federal Wage and Hour Law. In my opinion it would be beneficial to the State to have a minimum wage law and, therefore, I recommend that the General Assembly enact such a law, bearing in mind that it should be reasonable and fair to employees, employers, and to the public. It should provide for proper and necessary exemptions and safeguards.

I should like to have the help of industrial leaders and industrial workers in a broad effort to bring additional industry to North Carolina. In this, the relationship and record of cooperation between these two groups will play an important part.

COURTS

The profound respect which the people have always had for our courts and the judicial system has been a powerful factor for good in the life of our State.

Our population increased from about two and a half million in 1920 to over four million in 1950, and some of our towns have experienced rapid growth. In spite of this increase of about 60 per cent in population, there has been only one Judicial District added since 1913. It is true that in the thirties provision was made for the appointment of eight special judges. Even with the special judges, the work of the Superior Courts has grown until it is beyond the capacity of our judges to perform properly their duties. In my judgment, no Superior Court judge should be required to hold more than forty weeks of court in any calendar year. Forty weeks of court, plus the many other and important judicial duties which have to be performed, together with the fact that every judge needs time to study the constant changes in the law, will place upon them a heavy work load. It has been suggested that additional Superior Court Districts be created. This would be difficult from a practical and political standpoint. Furthermore, there appears to be no pressing need for additional solicitors. The need for additional judges is imperative. I, therefore, recommend that the General Assembly provide for additional regular Superior Court judges.

REFERENDUM

Since the act was first passed legalizing the sale of intoxicating liquor in those counties in North Carolina which voted in favor of it, there has existed a wide difference of opinion on this question. In the minds of many people it seems to have come to be a question of revenue. Even though the amount of money collected in taxes from the sale of intoxicating liquor in North Carolina has come to constitute an important part of our revenue, the issue should not be disposed of on the basis of taxation. It is a moral question and should be treated as such.

Prior to 1948, and in that year, and again in 1952, I publicly stated that I favored a referendum on the liquor question. I now favor it, and therefore, recommend that the General Assembly submit this issue to the people of North Carolina.

REDISTRICTING FOR SENATORS AND REPRESENTATIVES

The Constitution of North Carolina declares that the General Assembly, at the first session after the return of every enumeration by order of Congress, shall redistrict the State so that each Senate District shall contain, as nearly as may be, an equal number of inhabitants. It also provides for the re-allocation of certain members of the House of Representatives. The 1951 General Assembly did not comply with this requirement. I, therefore, recommend that this General Assembly carry out the clear mandate of the Constitution of North Carolina.

TAXES

The General Assembly of 1951 appropriated from the General Fund about 175 million dollars for this fiscal year. If the 10 per cent additional pay is granted to all state employees, retroactive to July 1, 1952, as recommended, it will add about thirteen million dollars to the General Fund expenditures for this fiscal year, making a total of about one hundred and eighty-eight million dollars. This is ten million more than was collected during the last fiscal year and about six million more than the estimate for this year. It is within about four million of the estimated revenue for the first year of the next biennium, and within about six million of the estimate for the second year. In other words, appropriations about equal revenues, with no provisions for normal increases in existing state services, additional children attending school, reasonable increase in salaries of public school teachers, or for other purposes. Some of these needs should be met.

Federal taxes are high and burdensome, and our state taxes are relatively high in comparison with adjoining states. I would consider new taxes or increased rates unwise and detrimental to the further development of our State. We must operate on a balanced budget to preserve our credit and standing.

If the General Assembly finds that a realistic estimate of revenues for the next biennium will not be sufficient to meet properly the essential needs of the State, including a reasonable increase for our teachers, then instead of new taxes or increased rates, I suggest that the schedule of exemptions under the sales tax be revised.

CONCLUSION

There are other matters which I shall, no doubt, desire to present for your consideration later in the session. In these and all other things which merit our attention I seek your sympathetic co-operation. I shall not forget that you have been elected by the people in your respective counties and your duty is to them. I know, too, that you will remember that you represent the entire State. All that we do should be motivated by a desire to achieve in our State a higher level of intellectual, cultural, economic, and spiritual attainment.

Every administration from Governor Aycock to Governor Scott, inclusive, has made substantial contributions to the continued development of our Commonwealth. The patriotic members of the General Assemblies through the years, with wisdom and courage, and in spite of all difficulties, have wisely and sanely builded. Near the beginning of the second fifty years of the century, we are in a position to take full advantage of the combined contributions which have heretofore been made. We have the talent and tools. This is an hour of great responsibility for you and for me. I have complete confidence in your patriotic devotion to North Carolina. Ahead of us there will be new and unpredictable problems. Let us not be afraid. Let us meet with a courage that is characteristic of our people the uncertainties of a swiftly moving future.

The processes of government must meet changing conditions and when new problems arise, we must find solutions without violating our fundamental principles. Let us see to it that North Carolina remains a land of opportunity and adventure. Let us discourage, always, the idea that any form of security is an adequate substitute for opportunity. Let us rekindle in the hearts of the citizens of the State a passion for individual liberty under the law.

If we plow deep into the soil and search deep into the soul of North Carolina, we can say, amidst the storms which may come, "In every high and stormy gale, my anchor holds within the vale."

If we co-operate and work together, without dissension but with understanding and in harmony, for the best interest of the State, we can and will attain marvelous advancement in the days ahead.

Relying upon the guidance and direction of Divine Providence, I now dedicate myself, and invite you to dedicate yourselves to the service of North Carolina for a *Better Tomorrow.*

SALARY INCREASE FOR STATE EMPLOYEES

SPECIAL MESSAGE [1]

February 12, 1953

Mr. President, Mr. Speaker and
Members of the General Assembly:

I am informed that there has been considerable discussion as to whether or not a separate bill should be introduced authorizing immediate payment of the 10 per cent salary increase, retroactive to July 1, 1952, and the press has recently published an article to the effect that such a bill was being contemplated and would probably be introduced within the next day or two.

In order that all state employees and members of the General Assembly may fully understand the situation, I shall appreciate it if you will read this letter so that it may be fully publicized throughout the State.

There is in the Budget Appropriation Bill, which is now under consideration by the Appropriation Committee, provision for this 10 per cent retroactive increase and I feel confident that the bill will be enacted without this provision being changed. The amount of the increase for the current year is exactly in accordance with the recommendations I have made. However, Section 143-15 of the *General Statutes* (this being a part of the Executive Budget Act) reads as follows:

"The provisions of this article shall continue to be the legislative policy with reference to the making of appropriations and shall be treated as rules of both branches of the General Assembly until and unless the same may be changed by the General Assembly either by express enactment or by rule adopted by either branch of the General Assembly.

"The General Assembly may reduce or strike out such item in the Budget Appropriation Bill as it may deem to be to the interest of the public service, but neither House shall consider further or special appropriations until the Budget Appropriation Bill shall have been enacted in whole or in part or rejected, unless the Governor shall submit and recommend an emergency

[1] This message was not delivered in person but read before the House and Senate.

appropriation bill or emergency appropriation bills, which may be amended in the manner set out herein, and such emergency appropriation bill, or bills when enacted, shall continue in force only until the Budget Appropriation Bill shall become effective, unless otherwise provided by the General Assembly."

This means, of course, that neither House of the General Assembly should consider any special appropriations until the Budget Appropriation Bill shall have been enacted in whole or in part or rejected, unless the Governor shall submit and recommend an emergency appropriation bill. A salary increase under the circumstances now existing cannot, in my opinion, be construed as an "emergency appropriation bill." While I would like to see this 10 per cent increase paid to all employees at the earliest possible date, I could not, of course, ask the Appropriation Committee to proceed in a manner contrary to law, and I feel that the employees who are to be the beneficiaries of this increase and the General Assembly will wholeheartedly agree with me in this respect.

BUDGET REPORT

SPECIAL MESSAGE [1]

February 24, 1953

Mr. President, Mr. Speaker and
Members of the General Assembly:

For your consideration I herewith transmit my views concerning The Budget Report for the coming biennium.

In compliance with the *Public Laws of 1929,* Chapter 100, you have already received The Budget Report of the Director of the Budget and the Advisory Budget Commission together with two appropriation bills referred to in the Budget Report.

The Budget Report was signed by the Director of the Budget and all the members of the Commission. They gave careful consideration to the requests of the many institutions and agencies of the State and apportioned the money in accordance with their

[1] This message was not delivered in person but read before the House and Senate.

best judgment. I commend them for their unselfish and devoted service in behalf of the State of North Carolina.

It was not my privilege to attend all the hearings before the Commission nor to be present when the estimates were determined, thus, you will understand that this budget is not the work of this administration, and that it is my duty to advise you of changes which I deem necessary.

I recommend that there be included in the Maintenance Appropriation Bill:

Some additional pay for public school teachers in addition to the 10 per cent increase now in the bill;

Funds to employ attendance officers sufficient in number to enforce effectively the school attendance law, and for such additional clerical assistance, services, and supplies as may be necessary due to the growth of our school system;

Necessary funds for driver training and safety education classes in the high schools throughout the State;

Additional funds for vocational education and for the operation of the office of the State Superintendent of Public Instruction;

Funds for the payment of at least $50 per month to those employees who had been in the employ of the State for not less than twenty years at the time the Retirement System went into effect and who are now receiving retirement payments;

Additional funds for the operation of the mental institutions. This is absolutely necessary, both from a humanitarian standpoint and from the standpoint of saving the State tremendous amounts of money in the years to come;

Additional money for the operation of the North Carolina Ports Authority. Unless import and export trade is developed at the Morehead and Wilmington ports, there will continue to be annual deficits which will have to be paid by the State. To develop this trade, skilled personnel and advertising are absolutely necessary;

Funds for making an engineering study for the development and utilization of inland ports and waterways in Eastern North Carolina.

Such additional funds as may be necessary to carry on essential agricultural research and for an effective forestry program, including adequate fire protection;

Funds for the additional revenue agents, auditors, and necessary personnel required by the State Department of Revenue;

Such additional funds as may be necessary to carry on effectively the state program with reference to stream pollution.

There are other important items which have been requested that deserve your careful attention.

CASH OPERATING FUND

I call your attention to the Cash Operating Fund of about $17,500,000 in the Appropriation Bill. This is less than 5 per cent of the General Fund appropriations already recommended for the next two years. In my judgment, this fund is essential, in view of the uncertainty of future conditions. In addition to the wisdom of having money available at all times to meet the obligations of the State, this fund is a guarantee, to the extent of the amount involved, that the teachers and all other state employees will receive their pay in full and on time, and that all the functions of the state government can continue without interruption.

FISCAL SITUATION

No amendments to the Revenue Bill were recommended by the Advisory Budget Commission. It is, therefore, necessary for me to present my views on the fiscal policy of the State for the next two years.

We are under legal compulsion to operate under a balanced budget. Such General Fund surplus now anticipated to be available on June 30, 1953 has been accounted for in the recommendations of the Advisory Budget Commission and incorporated in the Appropriations Bills; therefore, appropriations for the next biennium must be within the limits of available revenue. In my opinion, under present conditions, the estimates of anticipated revenue under the present tax structure for the next biennium are realistic and as high as we can safely go.

Courtesy Herald Sun

During the inauguration of Governor Umstead, January 8, 1953. *Left to right:* Lieutenant Governor H. P. Taylor; Governor W. Kerr Scott; Governor Umstead; Merle Umstead; and Lieutenant Governor Luther H. Hodges.

PUBLIC SCHOOL BONDS

We have constructed in North Carolina many school buildings during the past few years. The need has not yet been met. Our school population is rapidly increasing, and in order to protect and preserve our public school system we must aid in providing the necessary facilities. Under the provisions of our State Constitution and the decisions of the courts, we must provide equal school facilities for the children of North Carolina, without discrimination. After careful consideration I recommend that a bond issue be submitted to the people in the sum of $50,000,000 for grants-in-aid to our school units, and that a sound formula be worked out for its distribution which will be fair and at the same time meet the requirements of need and ability to pay. This amount may not be sufficient to provide all the facilities that are necessary; however, I believe it is as much as can be expended wisely during the next two years and, if properly used, will no doubt result in the expenditure of large additional sums by the counties and towns of our State to provide school facilities. I emphasize that this proposal for grants-in-aid to the counties is not intended to relieve the counties of their primary responsibility to provide adequate school facilities, without discrimination.

MENTAL INSTITUTIONS

I have heretofore stated that adequate funds are not available to provide training schools for feeble-minded white and Negro children, nor do we have money available to construct necessary facilities at the various mental institutions.

I have carefully investigated these needs and from the best information available to me the sum of $22,000,000 will be required to provide the necessary facilities. I, therefore, recommend that the General Assembly submit a bond issue to the people for this amount. I have had prepared a list of the necessary facilities and the estimated cost to be provided by funds from this bond issue, a copy of which list is attached hereto for your examination and consideration. I am recommending about a million dollars less than the total estimated cost.

INSTITUTIONAL BUILDING BONDS

I stated in my message to the General Assembly on January 8 that the lack of available funds would prohibit any large-scale building program at the institutions of higher learning and other state institutions at this time. However, after careful investigation I have found that there are some pressing and essential needs which should be provided now. The total cost of these needs will approximate $15,000,000. I, therefore, recommend that bonds in this amount be authorized by the General Assembly for the purpose of meeting these essential needs, and I submit herewith a list of the items, showing the estimated cost, for your examination and consideration.

Included in The Budget Permanent Improvement Appropriation Bill are items which total approximately $5,700,000 for improvements at the mental institutions. These items have been included in the recommended bond program for mental institutions. Therefore, if you approve the bond issue for mental institutions, you will have the sum of $5,700,000 available for other purposes during the next biennium.

The total sum of the three bond issues herein recommended is $87,000,000. I am advised that after the bonds are issued about $4,600,000 each year will be required for debt service on these bonds. If you find that this sum, together with the cost of the other additional items I have recommended in this message and other items which you may find necessary, cannot be financed with funds estimated to be available for the next biennium, then I call your attention to the statement made in my message to you on January 8 with reference to taxes.

CONCLUSION

I have previously stated, and I repeat, that I have complete confidence in your patriotic devotion to North Carolina. I present to you and to the people of North Carolina the clear-cut issue of some of the pressing needs of the State as I have outlined them in this message. I earnestly seek your support of this program which I feel is imperative to meet the requirements of a growing State during the next two years.

Our responsibility cannot be avoided. Near the beginning of the second fifty years of this century we must not only use the talents and the tools which we have, but we must continue to increase our talents and our tools for the further sound development of North Carolina.

URGENTLY NEEDED PERMANENT IMPROVEMENT PROJECTS OTHER THAN MENTAL INSTITUTIONS

Exhibit 1

EDUCATIONAL INSTITUTIONS

University of North Carolina:		
Institute of Government Building and Equipment	$ 500,000	
Renovation of Dormitories	196,000	
Renovation Bingham Hall— Building and Equipment	41,000	
Excavation Basement Peabody Hall	36,000	
Division of Health Affairs—		
Equipment for Cancer Research	10,000	
To complete 4th floor of Dental School Building	143,000	
Equipment South Wing Medical School	50,000	
To renovate 3rd floor of Medical School	25,000	
Sub-total		$ 1,001,000
State College of Agriculture and Engineering—		
Addition to Brooks Hall (Old Library for School of Design)	465,000	
Renovate Dairy Manufacturing Building and Equipment	150,000	
Renovate Syme, Gold, and Welch Dormitories	125,000	
To complete Nuclear Reactor Building	120,000	
Pulp Laboratory Building and Equipment	200,000	
Agricultural Engineering Building and Equipment	400,000	
Fencing and screening railroad and pedestrian grade crossings with seeing-eye gates	85,000	
Sub-total		$ 1,545,000

Item	Amount	Total
Agricultural Experiment Station—		
Land Purchase—McCullers Station	50,000	
Woman's College—		
Additional Funds to Complete Renovation Old Library	100,000	
To Repair and Renovate Music Building	185,000	
Sub-total		285,000
Total University of North Carolina		$ 2,881,000
East Carolina College:		
Dormitory for Women (Building and Equipment)	830,000	
Dormitory for Men (Building and Equipment)	830,000	
Completion of Interior New Library	50,000	
Convert Wright Building Basement into Student Union	55,000	
Convert Existing Library into Classroom Building and Equipment	65,000	
Extension of Roads and Walks	25,000	
Rewiring Austin Building	25,000	
Total		$ 1,880,000
Agricultural and Technical College:		
Boys' Dormitory	700,000	
Classroom Building and Equipment	500,000	
Agricultural Building and Equipment	800,000	
R.O.T.C. Administration Building	90,000	
Total		$ 2,090,000
Western Carolina Teachers College:		
Physical Education Building	400,000	
Sewage Disposal Plant	250,000	
Walks, Drives, and Ground Improvements	40,000	
Total		$ 690,000
Appalachian State Teachers College:		
Supplemental Funds for Elementary Demonstration School Building and Equipment	214,000	
Library Building Enlargement	100,000	
Gymnasium—Supplemental	250,000	
Renovation and Equipment—Cafeteria	100,000	
Total		$ 664,100
Winston-Salem Teachers College:		
Renovation of Workshop Building	75,000	
Total		$ 75,000

Mrs. Franklin D. Roosevelt and Mrs. William B. Umstead on the occasion of Mrs. Roosevelt addressing the Sir Walter Cabinet, February 3, 1953.

Elizabeth City State Teachers College:		
Girls' Dormitory and Equipment	250,000	
Dormitory for Women Teachers	200,000	
Total		$ 450,000
Fayetteville State Teachers College:		
Renovation Vance Hall	105,000	
Enlargement Mechanical Arts Building	79,400	
Total		$ 184,400
North Carolina College at Durham:		
Education Building	600,000	
Commerce Building	600,000	
Biology Building	600,000	
Total		$ 1,800,000
North Carolina School for the Deaf:		
Renovate Goodwin Hall	94,500	
Total		$ 94,500
Total Educational Institutions		$10,809,000

NORTH CAROLINA SANATORIA

North Carolina Sanatorium at McCain:		
Center Part Negro Division	$ 175,000	
		$ 175,000
Eastern North Carolina Sanatorium at Wilson:		
South Wing Addition including Equipment	$ 500,000	
Remodel Existing Colored Wing including Equipment	65,000	
2 Residences for Medical Staff	35,000	
Total Eastern North Carolina Sanatorium		$ 600,000
Total North Carolina Sanatoria		$ 775,000

CORRECTIONAL INSTITUTIONS

State Home and Industrial School for Girls:		
School Building and Equipment	$ 100,000	
Morrison Training School:		
Freezing Unit	$ 30,000	
Total Correctional Institutions		$ 130,000

OTHER ITEMS

Board of Public Buildings and Grounds:		
Health Building Addition 4th and 5th Floors	300,000	
For Purchase of Land	340,000	
Renovation of Old Highway Building for Art Gallery	200,000	
Department of Agriculture Additions and Betterments—Test Farms (See Exhibit 1-a)	86,500	
Sub-total		$ 926,500
North Carolina State Commission for the Blind:		
Pre-conditioning Center at Butner—		
Staff House for White Employees and Equipment	55,000	
Staff House for Colored Employees and Equipment	55,000	
Roads, Walks, Drives, etc.	10,000	
Sub-total		$ 120,000
North Carolina Armory Commission:		
For Construction of Armories (matching federal funds on basis of 3-1 ratio)	239,500	
Total others		$ 1,286,000
Total		$13,000,000
Medical Care Commission		2,000,000
Grand Total		$15,000,000

DEPARTMENT OF AGRICULTURE

Additions and Betterments—		
Details of Projects Recommended:		
Coastal Plain Test Farm—		
2 Laborers' Dwellings	$	11,000
Mountain Test Farm—		
1 Laborer's Dwelling		5,500
Tidewater Test Farm—		
1 Laborer's Dwelling		5,500
Upper Coastal Plain Test Farm—		
Truck and Tractor storage		5,000
Upper Mountain Test Farm—		
Hay Storage Shed		2,000
1 Laborer's Dwelling		5,500
Storage Buildings for Dwellings		3,000

Peanut Test Farm—		
Machinery Shed and Shop	6,000	
2 Laborers' Dwellings	12,000	
Superintendent's Residence	14,000	
Crops Drying Building	2,000	
State Museum—		
New Exhibits and Equipment	15,000	
Total		$ 86,500

Exhibit 2

MENTAL INSTITUTIONS

State Hospital at Raleigh:		
1. Renovation of Harvey Building for Convalescent Women	$ 63,000	
2. Renovation of Royster Building for Convalescent Men	135,000	
3. Addition to Dobbin Infirmary	250,000	
4. Male Epileptic Building Addition	250,000	
5. Female Epileptic Building Addition	250,000	
6. Renovation of Male Wing	1,500,000	
7. Renovation of Erwin Apartments	93,000	
8. Employees' Cottages	400,000	
9. Addition to Williams Hall Attendants' Building	200,000	
10. Living Quarters for Resident Physicians	100,000	
11. Addition to Nurses' Home	302,000	
12. New Truck Drives and Repairs to Existing Roads	100,000	
13. Fire Protection Facilities	18,000	
14. Toilet Facilities at Recreation Field	16,000	
15. Cold Storage Building	65,000	
16. Renovation of Male Patients' Dining Room and Employees' Cafeteria	200,000	
17. Renovation of Female Dining Room Building	75,000	
18. Completion of Renovation to Main Kitchen Building	26,250	
19. Renovation of Toilet and Bathrooms in Eight Buildings	94,500	
20. Chapel	173,000	
21. Office and Stock Room for Plant Engineer and Superintendent of Buildings and Grounds	5,000	
22. Incinerator and Garbage Equipment	25,000	
23. Farm Buildings (Barns, Sheds, Silos and Feed House)	57,200	
Total State Hospital at Raleigh		$ 4,398,450

State Hospital at Morganton:		
1. Hospital and Admissions Building— Building and Equipment	$ 2,000,000	
2. Remodel Present Kitchen for Employees and Staff Cafeteria—Building and Equipment	75,000	
3. Renovation of N Ward— Building and Equipment	70,000	
4. Renovation of T and U Wards— Building and Equipment	105,000	
5. Renovation of V and W Wards— Building and Equipment	105,000	
6. Reworking Harper Building— Building and Equipment	85,000	
7. Addition to Male Employees' Building— Building and Equipment	100,000	
8. Additional Warehouse Facilities and Space	50,000	
9. Renovation of R and S Wards— Building and Equipment	105,000	
10. Roads, Walks and Parking Areas	40,000	
11. Seventeen Miles of Access Truck Trails and Fire Breaks on Watershed	20,000	
12. Outside Lighting System	15,000	
13. Firehouse	5,000	
14. Fifteen Employees' Cottages	75,000	
15. Five Staff Cottages	65,000	
16. Renovation of Staff House	10,000	
Total State Hospital at Morganton		$ 2,925,000
State Hospital at Goldsboro:		
1. School for Feeble-minded Negro Children	$ 4,500,000	
2. Completion of the Criminal Insane Building	250,000	
3. Nurses' Home and Dormitory for Single Attendants	150,000	
4. Ten 5-Room Cottages for Personnel	60,000	
5. Ten 8-Room Duplex Houses for Attendants	90,000	
Total State Hospital at Goldsboro		$ 5,050,000
Caswell Training School:		
1. Enlargement of Staff Dormitory for Single Women	$ 180,000	
2. Enlargement of Staff Dormitory for Married Couples	180,000	
3. Recreational Building and Equipment	168,000	
4. Dormitory for Boys	620,000	
5. Roads and Parking Areas	40,000	
6. One Staff House (Doctor—6-Room)	15,000	

7. One Staff House (Educational Director—6-Room)	12,500	
8. Eight Staff Houses (6-Room)	100,000	
9. Twenty Houses for Attendants (4-Room)	100,000	
10. Fifteen Houses for Maintenance Personnel	90,000	
11. Incinerator	8,500	
Total Caswell Training School		$ 1,514,000
State Hospital at Butner:		
1. Renovation of Ward Buildings	$ 4,000,000	
2. Construction of Second Floor Corridor on Barrack Lane	100,000	
3. Detention Screens for Windows in Second Floor of Admission Center	10,890	
4. Pasteurization	50,000	
5. Porch for Administration Building and Minor Alterations on Interior	15,000	
6. Hospital Detention Fence	14,250	
7. Staff Houses	84,000	
8. Employee Cottages (5-Room)	40,000	
9. Nurses' Offices—Male and Female	5,000	
10. Dormitory for Colored Employees	175,000	
11. Connect Administration Building to Surgery	53,410	
12. Renovation of Old Post Headquarters Building	35,000	
Total State Hospital at Butner		$ 4,582,550
Training School for Feeble-minded White Children		$ 4,500,000
Total Mental Institutions		$22,970,000

SUPPLEMENTAL APPROPRIATION FOR MEMORIAL HOSPITAL

SPECIAL MESSAGE [1]

March 16, 1953

Mr. President, Mr. Speaker and
Members of the General Assembly:

The General Assembly has designated the North Carolina Memorial Hospital at the University in Chapel Hill as a continuing memorial to those North Carolinians who have given their lives, and who may hereafter give their lives, as members of the Armed Forces, in protecting the freedom and common welfare of their fellow citizens. Down through the years, it will become a great health center for all of the people of our State.

The beginning operation of the North Carolina Memorial Hospital has placed heavy responsibility on the persons in charge and has presented many difficult problems. The time of opening the hospital was established many months ago on the basis of a conservative construction schedule set by the architects and builders. The appointments of faculty members to the Schools of Medicine and Nursing and the acceptance of students in these schools and of interns and residents for the hospital were carried out according to this scheduled opening.

Unavoidable construction delays, chiefly due to the Korean War, took place after many faculty appointments were made and students accepted for the various programs. Consequently, the staff has been assembled and the student program scheduled for activation more rapidly than patient space was completed. It developed, therefore, that the new teaching and service programs were started in an incomplete hospital building with shortages of equipment. Beginning operation has accordingly been inordinately expensive.

The problems of construction, equipment and supplies, the recruitment of certain personnel and the establishment of smooth-working operating programs in the presence of highly complicated

[1] This message was not delivered in person but read before the Senate and House of Representatives.

teaching and research programs have made the activation of the North Carolina Memorial Hospital slower than had been hoped. Accordingly, total activation costs during 1952-1953 will be greater than anticipated.

The hospital operating program to date and the projected program for the remainder of 1952-1953 has been given intense study during the past few weeks by the University officials and Budget Bureau representatives. An emergency supplemental appropriation of $341,155 will be necessary to cover the operating costs for 1952-1953.

A bill, therefore, is being introduced in the Senate entitled an act "to provide an emergency supplemental appropriation to the North Carolina Memorial Hospital Division of Health Affairs at the University of North Carolina." I recommend and request that this bill be approved by the Appropriations Committee and passed by the General Assembly without delay so that the necessary operating funds will be available for the remainder of the fiscal year 1952-1953.

RADIO AND TELEVISION PROGRAM

SPECIAL MESSAGE [1]

April 7, 1953

Mr. President, Mr. Speaker and
Members of the General Assembly:

The State Educational Radio and Television Commission which was appointed pursuant to Joint Resolution No. 10, adopted at the beginning of this session of the General Assembly, has filed with me a report of its activities and recommendations as provided for in section 7 of said resolution. A copy of the report, embodying the recommendations of the Commission, is submitted to you for your consideration.

---

[1] This message was not delivered in person but was read before the House.

I recommend that necessary legislation be enacted to comply with the recommendations embodied in the Commission's report. A bill entitled "an Act to continue the North Carolina Educational Radio and Television Commission created by Joint Resolution No. 10 of the 1953 General Assembly to authorize counties and municipalities to contribute funds to said Commission and to appropriate twelve thousand dollars to said Commission for the biennium 1953-1955"; and, a resolution "requesting the Federal Communications Commission to continue its reservation of educational television channels in this State and to allocate additional educational television channels beyond those presently located in North Carolina," have been prepared for introduction in the Senate to accomplish this purpose and are being offered for your consideration.

APPOINTMENTS TO BOARDS

SPECIAL MESSAGE [1]

April 29, 1953

To The President and the
Honorable Senate of North Carolina:

I have the honor to transmit herewith a list of appointments to certain boards which, under the law, must be transmitted to the Senate for confirmation at this session, as follows, to wit:

1. Board of Directors of Sanatoriums for Treatment of Tuberculosis—*General Statutes* 131-62.

Charles A Cannon, Concord	Term 6 years Expiring April 29, 1959
Dr. M. A. Pittman, Wilson	Term 6 years Expiring April 29, 1959
Carl C. Council, Durham	Term 6 years Expiring April 29, 1959
E. A. Rasberry, Snow Hill	Term 6 years Expiring April 29, 1959

[1] This message was not delivered in person but read before the Senate.

2. Board of Trustees, Teachers' and State Employees' Retirement System—*General Statutes* 135-6.

Sam J. Burrow, Jr., Asheboro To complete unexpired term of Arnold Davis (resigned)	Expiring April 5, 1956
Clyde Gordon, Burlington To succeed J. W. Byrd	Term 4 years Expiring April 5, 1957

PROCLAMATIONS

RED CROSS MONTH

Executive Department
Raleigh

A Proclamation by the Governor
March 11, 1953

Whereas, the people of North Carolina are served by the neighborly, humanitarian services of the American Red Cross, and one of the first responsibilities of which is assistance to servicemen, veterans, and their families in personal and family problems, and

Whereas, the Red Cross in North Carolina continues to be responsible for collecting large quantities of blood for the military forces and for civilian hospital emergencies, and at the request of the Office of Defense Mobilization, the Red Cross is expanding its blood collections for the production of gamma globulin, which helps prevent paralysis in poliomyelitis, and which will be allocated in North Carolina by the Department of Public Health to communities hit by polio, and

Whereas, skilled and experienced volunteers in Red Cross chapters, augmented where needed by disaster staffs from the national organizations, use these skills and the necessary financial and material aid to assist families who are victims of floods, tornadoes, fires, and other natural catastrophes, and are engaged in the training of thousands of citizens in health and safety skills for their own protection and that of their families in time of emergency, and above all, help to keep alive in the minds and hearts of people the elements of service, sacrifice, love, and mercy:

Now, therefore, I, William B. Umstead, Governor of the State of North Carolina, do hereby designate March, 1953, as Red Cross Month, and I urge that in these times of major emphasis on strengthening the military forces and home-front defenses, every citizen give support to their Red Cross in its 1953 Fund Campaign, so that this humanitarian organization may adequately meet its defense and normal community responsibilities, and help arouse in mankind everywhere faith in the good that comes from doing good.

(Seal) In witness thereof, I have hereunto set my hand and caused the Great Seal of the State of North Carolina to be affixed. Done at the City of Raleigh this 11th day of March, in the year of our Lord, nineteen hundred and fifty-three.

William B. Umstead, *Governor.*

By the Governor:
Edward L. Rankin, Jr., *Private Secretary.*

CANCER CONTROL MONTH

Executive Department
Raleigh

A Proclamation by the Governor
April 1, 1953

Whereas, in North Carolina in 1952 about 3,411 people died of cancer, and the number will probably be larger in 1953, and in order to combat this widespread disease, it is necessary to have the concerted effort of government, the medical profession, scientists, and all of our citizens, and

Whereas, through programs of education, research, and science, many lives have been saved, and many more can be saved, and

Whereas, the President of the United States has proclaimed April as a month for special effort regarding this serious problem:

Now, therefore, I do hereby proclaim the month of April as Cancer Control Month, and I urge every citizen of the State, during the month of April to learn as much about the disease of cancer as possible and to support the 1953 Crusade of the American Cancer Society.

(Seal) In witness thereof, I have hereunto set my hand and caused the Great Seal of the State of North Carolina to be affixed. Done at the City of Raleigh, this 1st day of April, in the year of our Lord, nineteen hundred and fifty-three.

William B. Umstead, *Governor.*

By the Governor:
Edward L. Rankin, Jr., *Private Secretary.*

RULES ABOUT ANTHRAX

EXECUTIVE DEPARTMENT
RALEIGH

A PROCLAMATION BY THE GOVERNOR
[May 12, 1953]

Whereas, from both a public health and a livestock standpoint Anthrax is a disease against which every necessary means of suppression should be exercised, and

Whereas, North Carolina is not an enzootic Anthrax area, and

Whereas, one human case of Anthrax has occurred in a manufacturing plant in North Carolina, and

Whereas, manufacturing material containing imported goat hair and the premises and the plant have been found to be highly contaminated with Anthrax organisms, including spores, by competent state and federal agencies, and

Whereas, there is no known method of sterilization of soil when contaminated with Anthrax spores:

Now, therefore, I, William B. Umstead, Governor of North Carolina, under and by virtue of the authority contained in *General Statutes* 106-304, -305, -306, as amended, do hereby authorize the Commissioner of Agriculture to make rules and regulations either forbidding or controlling the importation of any feed stuffs or any other article of material dangerous to livestock as a carrier of infectious or contagious disease from any area outside of the State. This shall also include any and all materials imported for manufacturing purposes or for any other use, which have been tested by any state or federal agency competent to make such tests and found to contain living infectious and contagious organisms known to be injurious to the health of man or livestock.

William B. Umstead, *Governor.*

(Seal)
By the Governor:
Edward L. Rankin, Jr., *Private Secretary.*

NORTH CAROLINA BONDS

EXECUTIVE DEPARTMENT
RALEIGH

A PROCLAMATION BY THE GOVERNOR
July 21, 1953

Pursuant to the provisions of Chapter 1148 of the *1953 Session Laws of North Carolina* entitled:

An Act to authorize the issuance of twenty-two million dollars in bonds of the State to provide for urgently needed permanent improvements at the State's mental institutions, subject to a vote of the people of the State.

and the provisions of Chapter 1046 of the *1953 Session Laws of North Carolina* entitled:

An Act to authorize the issuance of fifty million dollars in bonds of the State to provide for urgently needed funds to be used for the construction and improvement of school plant facilities in the counties of the State, subject to a vote of the people of the State.

the undersigned, William B. Umstead, Governor of the State of North Carolina, does hereby fix Saturday,

October 3rd, 1953,

as the date for the holding of the elections authorized by said acts at which there shall be submitted to the qualified voters of the State of North Carolina the following questions:

1. Shall the State of North Carolina contract a new debt on behalf of the State by issuance of not exceeding $22,000,000 State of North Carolina Mental Institutions Bonds under the provisions of Chapter 1148 of the *1953 Session Laws of North Carolina,* such new debt to be in excess of two-thirds of the amount by which the State's outstanding indebtedness shall have been reduced during the biennium next preceding the contracting of such new debt and in addition to all other debts heretofore or hereafter authorized to be contracted on behalf of the State?

2. Shall the State of North Carolina contract a new debt on behalf of the State by the issuance of not exceeding $50,000,000

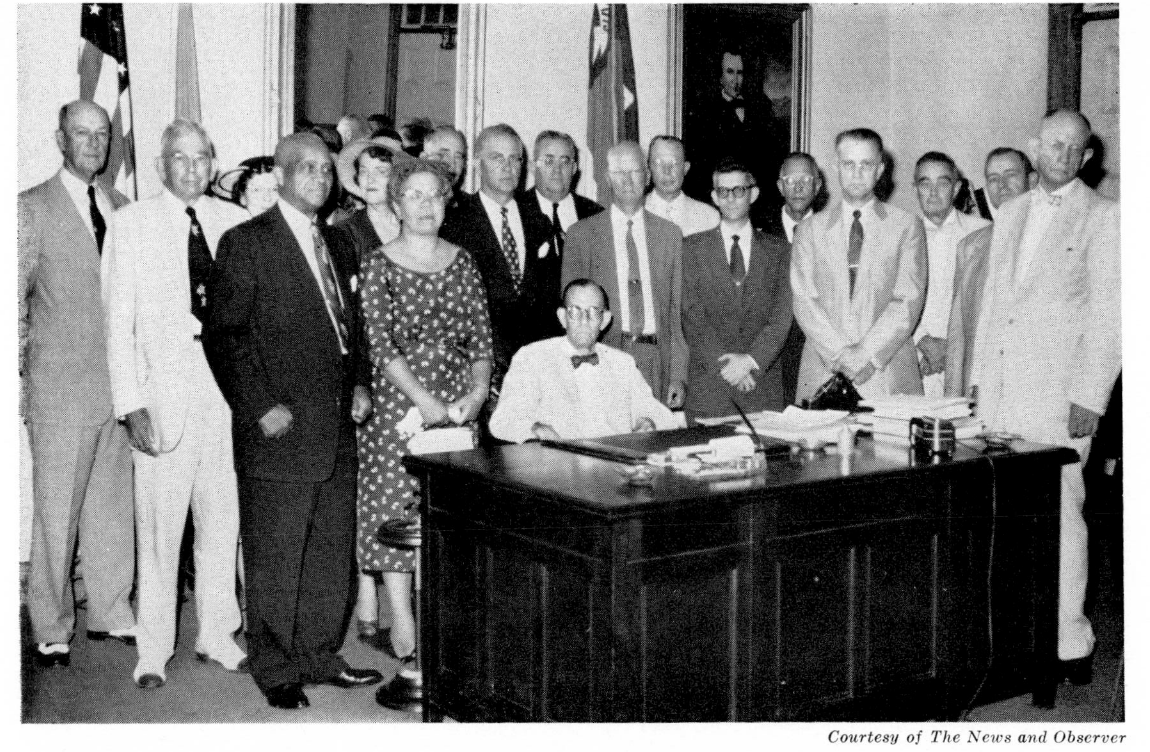

Courtesy of The News and Observer

Advisory Committee on Public Education appointed following the decision of May 17, 1953 by the Supreme Court abolishing segregation in the public schools. *Left to right:* J. H. Clark, Elizabethtown; Dr. Clarence Poe, Raleigh; Mrs. Helen S. Kafer, New Bern; Dr. F. D. Bluford, Greensboro; Ruth Current, Raleigh; Mrs. Hazel Parker, Tarboro; I. E. Ready, Roanoke Rapids; Chairman Thomas J. Pearsall, Rocky Mount; Holt McPherson, High Point; R. O. Huffman, Morganton; James C. Manning, Williamston; Dallas Herring, Rose Hill; Dr. J. W. Seabrook, Fayetteville; Fred B. Helms, Charlotte; W. T. Joyner, Raleigh; Paul A. Reid, Cullowhee; and Judge L. R. Varser, Lumberton. Gordon Gray, Chapel Hill and Arthur D. Williams of Wilson are not in the picture.

State of North Carolina School Plant Construction and Improvement Bonds under the provisions of Chapter 1046 of the *1953 Session Laws of North Carolina,* such new debt to be in excess of two-thirds of the amount by which the State's outstanding indebtedness shall have been reduced during the biennium next preceding the contracting of such new debt and in addition to all other debts heretofore or hereafter authorized to be contracted on behalf of the State?

Said elections shall be held in accordance with the provisions of the general election laws of the State of North Carolina, except that no absentee ballots will be allowed in said elections.

I do hereby call upon the State Board of Elections, the County Boards of Election in the several counties of the State of North Carolina and all other duly constituted election officials to proceed to hold the said elections on the date so fixed in accordance with the said acts of the General Assembly.

Done at Raleigh, in the County of Wake, this 21st day (Seal) of July, 1953.

William B. Umstead, *Governor.*

By the Governor:
Edward L. Rankin, Jr., *Private Secretary.*

EMPLOY THE PHYSICALLY HANDICAPPED WEEK

EXECUTIVE DEPARTMENT
RALEIGH

A PROCLAMATION BY THE GOVERNOR
September 18, 1953

Whereas, opportunities for suitable and gainful employment are the hope and ambition of all workers, and the American system of free choice of occupations, consistent with each worker's abilities and interests, is best suited to provide such opportunities; and

Whereas, a great many physically handicapped workers presently employed have proven their competence when they have been rehabilitated or otherwise properly prepared for suitable jobs; and

Whereas, there is a continuing need for greater understanding of effective methods for the placement of physically handicapped workers in suitable occupations, and community participation in educational and promotional programs can best accomplish this purpose; and

Whereas, the Congress, by a joint resolution approved August 11, 1945 (59 Statutes 530), designated the first week in October of each year as National Employ the Physically Handicapped Week, and requested the President to issue a proclamation calling public attention to the need for nation-wide support of and interest in the employment of otherwise qualified but physically handicapped men and women:

Now, therefore, I, William B. Umstead, Governor of the State of North Carolina, do hereby call upon the people of our State to observe the week beginning October 4, 1953, as National Employ the Physically Handicapped Week, and to co-operate with the State Committee on Employment of the Physically Handicapped in carrying out the purposes of the aforementioned joint resolution of Congress.

I also request the mayors of municipalities, other public officials, leaders of industry and labor, and members of religious, civic, veterans, agricultural, women's, handicapped persons, and fraternal organizations and all other groups and individuals to take part in the observance of the designated week, in order to enlist the widest possible support of programs designed to increase opportunities in employment for the physically handicapped.

(Seal) In witness whereof, I have hereunto set my hand and cause the Great Seal of the State of North Carolina to be affixed. Done at the City of Raleigh this 18th day of September, in the year of our Lord, nineteen hundred and fifty-three.

William B. Umstead, *Governor.*

By the Governor:
E. L. Rankin, Jr., *Private Secretary.*

STATE-WIDE FARM BUREAU WEEK

EXECUTIVE DEPARTMENT
RALEIGH

A PROCLAMATION BY THE GOVERNOR
September 28, 1953

Whereas, the North Carolina Farm Bureau Federation has contributed much to the progress, prosperity and happiness of the people of this State, and I am confident it will continue its splendid service during the period of readjustment in which we find ourselves, when sound thinking is demanded of our leaders, and when all segments of our economy are affected by their decisions; and

Whereas, this organization can do more effective and constructive work and render greater service to our State by substantially increasing the membership in each of the 100 counties; and

Whereas, it is essential that our farm people co-ordinate their interests in support of the program so ably outlined by the chosen leaders of the North Carolina Farm Bureau Federation:

Now, therefore, I, William B. Umstead, Governor of the State of North Carolina, do hereby proclaim and set aside September 28th to October 4th as State-Wide Farm Bureau Week, and call upon the people of our State to work together for the best interests of our State and Nation.

(Seal) In witness whereof, I have hereunto set my hand and caused the Great Seal of the State of North Carolina to be affixed. Done at the City of Raleigh this 28th day of September, in the year of our Lord, nineteen hundred and fifty-three.

William B. Umstead, *Governor.*

By the Governor:
Edward L. Rankin, Jr., *Private Secretary.*

SELECTIVE SERVICE ACT

EXECUTIVE DEPARTMENT
RALEIGH

A PROCLAMATION BY THE GOVERNOR
September 29, 1953

Whereas, Public Law 759 of the 80th Congress, also known as the Selective Service Act of 1948, as amended by Public Law 51, 82nd Congress, known as Universal Military Training Act, provides in Sec. 6 (c) (2) A that in any case in which the governor of any state determines and issues a proclamation to the effect that the authorized strength of any organized unit of the National Guard cannot be maintained by enlistment or appointment of persons who are not liable for training and service under such act, or any persons who served honorably on active duty between September 16, 1940, and June 24, 1948, for a period of ninety days or more but less than twelve months in the Army, the Air Force, the Navy, the Marine Corps, the Coast Guard, the Public Health Service, or the Armed Forces of any country allied with the United States in World War II prior to September 2, 1945, any person, who prior to attaining the age of 18 years and six months, and prior to the issuance of orders for him to report for induction, enlists or accepts appointment in any such organized unit shall be deferred from training and service under this act so long as he continues to serve satisfactorily as a member of such organized unit; and

Whereas, I have determined that the authorized strength of certain organized units of the North Carolina National Guard cannot be maintained by the enlistment or appointment of persons in the categories referred to above:

Now, therefore, I, William B. Umstead, Governor of North Carolina, in order that the North Carolina National Guard may as amended by Public Law 51, 82nd Congress, and by virtue of the authority vested in me as Governor of the State of North Carolina, in order that the North Carolina National Guard may discharge its responsibility to the security of the Nation, do hereby proclaim that the authorized strength of certain organized units of the North Carolina National Guard cannot be maintained through the enlistment or appointment of persons referred to in Sec. 6 (c) (2) A.

And I hereby direct the Adjutant General of North Carolina to maintain a current list of those organized units of the North Carolina National Guard which have not reached or cannot be maintained at their authorized strengths as designated from time to time by the Adjutant General under my direction.

I also invite young men from the age of 17 to 18 years and six months to enlist in those organized units of the North Carolina National Guard which are not at authorized strength and thus meet their obligation of service to their country while at the same time they continue their education or employment.

(Seal) In witness whereof, I have hereunto set my hand and cause the Great Seal of the State of North Carolina to be affixed. Done at the City of Raleigh this 29th day of September, in the year of our Lord, nineteen hundred and fifty-three.

William B. Umstead, *Governor.*

By the Governor:
Edward L. Rankin, Jr., *Private Secretary.*

UNITED NATIONS DAY

EXECUTIVE DEPARTMENT
RALEIGH

A PROCLAMATION BY THE GOVERNOR
October 22, 1953

Whereas, the United Nations is an organization created for the purpose of affording a means for the settlement of international disputes and is our greatest hope for international peace; and

Whereas, the General Assembly of the United Nations has declared October 24 as United Nations Day and has suggested that on that day efforts be made to inform the people of the world of the achievements and aims of the United Nations to the end that such efforts will encourage and bring hope to all those everywhere interested in world peace based upon freedom and justice; and

Whereas, the President of the United States has issued a proclamation asking the people of the United States to observe Saturday, October 24, 1953, as United Nations Day:

Now, therefore, I, William B. Umstead, Governor of the State of North Carolina, do hereby urge the citizens of this State to observe Saturday, October 24, 1953, as United Nations Day, and I call upon the officials of the state and local government units and all of our citizens to co-operate in appropriate observance of this day in the support of the United Nations in its efforts to increase its usefulness and to encourage its work in behalf of peace throughout the world and the prevention of aggression.

(Seal) In witness whereof, I have hereunto set my hand and caused the Great Seal of the State of North Carolina to be affixed. Done at the City of Raleigh this twenty-second day of October in the year of our Lord, nineteen hundred and fifty-three.

William B. Umstead, *Governor.*

By the Governor:
Edward L. Rankin, Jr., *Private Secretary.*

A DAY OF PRAYER FOR RAIN

EXECUTIVE DEPARTMENT
RALEIGH

A PROCLAMATION BY THE GOVERNOR
October 30, 1953

Whereas, the prolonged and widespread drought has become so grave that countless citizens of North Carolina are facing serious financial difficulties, crop losses have been extensive, feed stocks are depleted, herds of livestock are being liquidated, the agricultural resources of the State are in jeopardy and the entire economy of the State is seriously effected; and

Whereas, the lack of rain has created a serious problem in public water supply for many municipalities in North Carolina, forcing some communities to ration water and rely on auxiliary reservoirs for essential water supplies; and

Whereas, the governors of the several drought-stricken states have joined together in this effort to urge the people of these states to pray for rain, and in as much as we believe that Almighty God in His mercy sends rain upon the just and unjust and we are encouraged as His children to come to Him for the supplying of our needs, I am moved to take this action:

Now, therefore, I, William B. Umstead, Governor of the State of North Carolina do hereby proclaim Sunday, November 1, 1953, to be a day of prayer for rain and on that day I request that all Christian people who gather for worship, petition, in penitence and faith, our Father for relief from the prevailing drought, if it be His will. In the event of His having sent this relief in His grace by such a time, I then urge that upon this day His people shall express their thanksgiving for this blessing which we so badly need.

(Seal) In witness whereof, I have hereunto set my hand and caused the Great Seal of the State of North Carolina to be affixed. Done at the City of Raleigh this thirtieth day of October in the year of our Lord, nineteen hundred and fifty-three.

William B. Umstead, *Governor.*

By the Governor:
Edward L. Rankin, Jr., *Private Secretary.*

HUNTING, FISHING, AND TRAPPING FORBIDDEN

EXECUTIVE DEPARTMENT

RALEIGH

A PROCLAMATION BY THE GOVERNOR

November 10, 1953

Under and by virtue of the authority vested in the undersigned William B. Umstead as Governor of the State of North Carolina, by Chapter 305 of the *Session Laws of 1953,* upon the joint recommendations of Honorable Ben E. Douglas, Director of the Department of Conservation and Development, and Honorable

Clyde P. Patton, Director of the North Carolina Wildlife Resources Commission, on account of the long period of protracted drought and other hazardous fire conditions which now threaten certain portions of the forests and water resources of the State and which now appear to require extraordinary precautions,

It Is Hereby Proclaimed And Declared

All of the woodlands and inland waters of the counties of:

Alexander	Cherokee	McDowell	Surry
Alleghany	Clay	Macon	Swain
Ashe	Cleveland	Madison	Transylvania
Avery	Graham	Mitchell	Yadkin
Buncombe	Haywood	Polk	Yancey
Burke	Henderson	Rutherford	Watauga
Caldwell	Jackson	Stokes	Wilkes
Catawba			

of the State are hereby closed to hunting, fishing, and trapping for the period of the emergency, and all persons, for the period of the emergency, are forbidden to build camp fires or burn brush, grass or other debris within five hundred (500) feet of any woodland in any of the counties of the State.

Fishing is not prohibited in the said inland waters which is done entirely from boats and in connection with which no camp on land is built, maintained or used.

The emergency will be deemed to continue until this proclamation is annulled, as authorized by Chapter 305 of the *Session Laws of 1953,* when I am satisfied the period of emergency has passed. Attention is called to the fact that said act makes violation of this proclamation a misdemeanor and persons convicted are subject to punishment by fine or imprisonment, in the discretion of the court.

I respectively request that this proclamation be published in its entirety at least one time in all the newspapers in or circulating said counties of the State, as a public service.

This proclamation shall become effective twenty-four (24) hours after the time of its issue.

(Seal) Done and issued at Raleigh, this the tenth day of November, 1953, at 4:30 o'clock, P. M.

William B. Umstead, *Governor.*

By the Governor:
Edward L. Rankin, Jr., *Private Secretary.*

THANKSGIVING DAY

EXECUTIVE DEPARTMENT
RALEIGH

A PROCLAMATION BY THE GOVERNOR
November 18, 1953

Whereas, it is one of the best-loved traditions of America that we set aside each year in November one day when we pause in our labors and return thanks for all the blessings bestowed upon us; and

Whereas, Thanksgiving Day is a truly American day which began in the fall of 1621 when Governor William Bradford of the Plymouth Colony asked his people to give thanks in gratitude for the first harvest in the new world; and

Whereas, in this year 1953 we in America enjoy the blessings of a free people with individual liberty under the law, in contrast to various areas of the world which are blighted by totalitarian forms of government; and

Whereas, Thanksgiving Day offers us the opportunity to reaffirm our beliefs in democracy, in the inherent dignity of every man and woman, and by which we have gained strength and vigor through the years:

Therefore, I, William B. Umstead, Governor of North Carolina, do hereby proclaim Thursday, November 26, a legal holiday in North Carolina and a day of general thanksgiving and I call upon all people on that day humbly to express thanks to the Giver of every good and perfect gift and prayerfully seek divine blessings, care, and guidance in the days ahead.

In witness whereof, I have hereunto set my hand and caused the Great Seal of the State of North Carolina to (Seal) be affixed. Done at the City of Raleigh this eighteenth day of November in the year of our Lord, nineteen hundred and fifty-three.

William B. Umstead, *Governor.*

By the Governor:
Edward L. Rankin, Jr., *Private Secretary*

DROUGHT EMERGENCY MEASURES

EXECUTIVE DEPARTMENT
RALEIGH

A PROCLAMATION BY THE GOVERNOR
November 19, 1953

Under and by virtue of the authority vested in the undersigned William B. Umstead as Governor of the State of North Carolina, by Chapter 305 of the *Session Laws of 1953,* upon the joint recommendation of Honorable Ben E. Douglas, Director of the Department of Conservation and Development, and Honorable Clyde P. Patton, Director of the North Carolina Wildlife Resources Commission, on account of the long period of protracted drought and other hazardous fire conditions which now threaten certain portions of the forests and water resources of the State and which now appear to require extraordinary precautions,

It Is Hereby Proclaimed And Declared

All of the woodlands and inland waters of the counties of:

Alamance	Davie	Iredell	Randolph
Anson	Durham	Lincoln	Rockingham
Cabarrus	Forsyth	Mecklenburg	Rowan
Caswell	Gaston	Montgomery	Stanly
Chatham	Granville	Orange	Union
Davidson	Guilford	Person	

of the State, in addition to the counties in which a similar proclamation was heretofore made, are hereby closed to hunting, fishing, and trapping, for the period of the emergency, and all persons, for the period of the emergency, are forbidden to build camp fires or burn brush, grass or other debris within five hundred (500) feet of any woodland in any of the said counties of the State.

Fishing is not prohibited in the said inland waters which is done entirely from boats and in connection with which no camp on land is built, maintained or used.

The emergency will be deemed to continue until this proclamation is annulled, as authorized by Chapter 305 of the *Session Laws of 1953,* when I am satisfied the period of emergency has passed. Attention is called to the fact that said act makes violation of this proclamation a misdemeanor and persons convicted are subject to punishment by fine or imprisonment, in the discretion of the court.

I respectfully request that this proclamation be published in its entirety at least one time in all the newspapers published in or circulating said counties of the State, as a public service.

This proclamation shall become effective twenty-four (24) hours after the time of its issue.

Done and issued at Raleigh, this the nineteenth day of
(Seal) November, 1953, at 8:30 o'clock, A.M.

William B. Umstead, *Governor.*

By the Governor:
Edward L. Rankin, Jr., *Private Secretary.*

HUNTING AND FISHING PROCLAMATION REVOKED

EXECUTIVE DEPARTMENT
RALEIGH

A PROCLAMATION BY THE GOVERNOR
November 23, 1953

Whereas, on the 10th day of November, 1953, at 4:30 o'clock, P.M., under and by virtue of the authority vested in the undersigned William B. Umstead as Governor of the State of North Carolina, by Chapter 305 of the *Session Laws of 1953,* a proclamation was issued closing to hunting, fishing and trapping, for the period of the emergency therein set out, all of the woodlands and inland waters of the counties of Stokes, Caldwell, Rutherford, Transylvania, Yadkin, Catawba, Polk, Swain, Surry, Cleveland, Yancey, Macon, Alleghany, Burke, Madison, Graham, Ashe, Avery, Buncombe, Cherokee, Wilkes, Mitchell, Henderson, Clay, Watauga, McDowell, Haywood, Jackson and Alexander, and

Whereas, on the 19th day of November, 1953, at 8:30 o'clock, A.M., a similar proclamation was issued, closing to hunting, fishing and trapping, for the period of the emergency, all of the woodlands and inland waters of the counties of Granville, Chatham, Stanly, Mecklenburg, Person, Montgomery, Union, Davie, Caswell, Anson, Forsyth, Iredell, Alamance, Rockingham, Davidson, Lincoln, Orange, Guilford, Rowan, Gaston, Durham, Randolph and Cabarrus, and

Whereas, both the proclamations referred to herein contained provisions forbidding the building of camp fires or burning brush, grass or other debris within five hundred (500) feet of any woodland in any of the said counties of the State, and

Whereas, it has been made to appear satisfactorily to me, upon the joint recommendation of Honorable Ben E. Douglas, Director of the Department of Conservation and Development, and Honorable Clyde P. Patton, Executive Director of the North Carolina Wildlife Resources Commission, that the period of the emergency referred to in the former proclamations has passed:

Now, therefore, it is hereby proclaimed and declared that the proclamations hereinabove referred to are hereby annulled and declared to be of no further force and effect.

I respectfully request that this proclamation be published in its entirety at least one time in all the newspapers published in or circulating said counties of the State, as a public service.

This proclamation shall become effective immediately.

(Seal) Done and issued at Raleigh, this the 23rd day of November, 1953, at 12:30 o'clock, P.M.

William B. Umstead, *Governor.*

By the Governor:
Edward L. Rankin, Jr., *Private Secretary.*

BANKING HOLIDAY

EXECUTIVE DEPARTMENT
RALEIGH

A PROCLAMATION BY THE GOVERNOR
December 10, 1953

Whereas, December 25, 1953, Christmas Day, a state and national holiday, falls on Friday; and

Whereas, by general consent, many businesses will enjoy Saturday, December 26, 1953, as a holiday; and

Whereas, a request has been made by the North Carolina Bankers' Association that Saturday, December 26, 1953, be declared a banking holiday;

Now, therefore, I William B. Umstead, Governor of North Carolina, by and with the advice and consent of the Council of State, under and by virtue of authority of Section 53-77 of the *General Statutes of North Carolina,* do hereby designate Saturday, December 26, 1953, as a banking holiday. During such period of holiday, all of the ordinary and usual operations and business of all banking corporations, state or national, in this State, shall be suspended, and during such period no banking corporation shall pay out or receive deposits, make loans and discounts, transfer credits, or transact any other banking business whatsoever except such acts as are authorized by the aforesaid law.

(Seal) Done at our capital City of Raleigh, this tenth day of December, 1953, in the year of our Lord, one thousand nine hundred and fifty-three.

William B. Umstead, *Governor.*

By the Governor:
Edward L. Rankin, Jr., *Private Secretary.*

NATIONAL GUARD RECRUITING MONTH

EXECUTIVE DEPARTMENT
RALEIGH

A PROCLAMATION BY THE GOVERNOR
January 18, 1954

Whereas, the Departments of the Army and the Air Force are desirous that the strength of the National Guard, Army and Air Force, be materially increased as soon as possible, and

Whereas, this can be accomplished by a concentrated recruiting campaign designed to encourage enlistment of young men and men with prior military service, and

Whereas, the North Carolina Army and Air National Guard through the years have served our State and Nation long and faithfully, in time of war as well as in time of peace, and merit the wholehearted support of the entire citizenship of this State:

Now, therefore, I, William B. Umstead, Governor of North Carolina and Commander-in-Chief of the North Carolina Army and Air National Guard, in order to accomplish the assigned mission and to honor our men of the North Carolina National Guard for their services to the State and Nation in every armed conflict in which our country has been engaged, do hereby proclaim the month of February, 1954, as National Guard Recruiting Month in the State of North Carolina. I urge all citizens of this great State to support wholeheartedly the North Carolina National Guard, both Army and Air, and the citizens of each community are requested especially to assist their local unit in its recruiting campaign.

(Seal) In witness whereof, I have hereunto set my hand and caused the Great Seal of the State of North Carolina to be affixed. Done at the City of Raleigh this eighteenth day of January in the year of our Lord, nineteen hundred and fifty-four.

William B. Umstead, *Governor.*

By the Governor:
Edward L. Rankin, Jr., *Private Secretary.*

REPUBLIC OF TURKEY WEEK

Executive Department
Raleigh

A Proclamation by the Governor
February 13, 1954

Whereas, His Excellency Celal Bayar, the President of Turkey, and Madame Bayar, are now visiting the United States at the invitation of President and Mrs. Eisenhower, this being the first visit to the United States by a Turkish head of State; and

Whereas, His Excellency and Madame Bayar and party will visit North Carolina as the last stop on their nation-wide tour, arriving in Raleigh on Thursday, February 18, and departing on Friday, February 19, after visiting numerous points of interest in our State; and

Whereas, the Republic of Turkey has seven thousand years of culture to which she has added immeasurably in recent decades, increasing in economic stature in world affairs and earning well-merited recognition as a staunch ally of the free nations of the world, and as a partner in the Atlantic Pact; and

Whereas, Turkish troops fought bravely and effectively alongside American troops and others under the flag of the United Nations, this being a further demonstration of the community of ideals, co-operation and military alliance between Turkey and the United States which is mutually beneficial and a strong deterrent to unprovoked aggression:

Now, therefore, I, William B. Umstead, Governor of North Carolina, by virtue of the authority vested in me, do hereby extend a hearty and sincere welcome to His Excellency and Madame Bayar from the people of our State and do hereby proclaim February 14 to February 20 as Republic of Turkey Week in North Carolina and do urge the people of our State during this period to broaden their knowledge of the Turkish Republic and to deepen their understanding of the people of that great country.

In witness whereof, I have hereunto set my hand and caused the Great Seal of the State of North Carolina to be affixed. Done at the City of Raleigh this thirteenth day of February, in the year of our Lord, nineteen hundred and fifty-four.

(Seal)

William B. Umstead, *Governor.*

By the Governor:
Edward L. Rankin, Jr., *Private Secretary.*

THE PHYSICALLY HANDICAPPED WEEK

EXECUTIVE DEPARTMENT
RALEIGH

A PROCLAMATION BY THE GOVERNOR
October 4, 1954

Whereas, the physically handicapped of our Nation have demonstrated that they are capable workers when placed in jobs suited to their abilities, training, and experience, and therefore, as a group, constitute a valuable resource of man power; and

Whereas, there is a continuing need for greater understanding of effective methods for the placement of physically handicapped workers in suitable occupations, and community participation in educational and promotional programs can best accomplish this purpose; and

Whereas, the Congress, by a joint resolution approved August 11, 1945, designated the first week in October of each year as National Employ the Physically Handicapped Week, and requested the President to issue a proclamation calling public attention to the need for nation-wide support of programs calling for full opportunity for physically handicapped men and women in employment.

Now, therefore, I, William B. Umstead, Governor of the State of North Carolina, do hereby call upon the people of our State to observe the week beginning October 4, 1954, as National Employ the Physically Handicapped Week, and to co-operate with the State Committee of Employment of the Physically Handicapped in carrying out the purposes of the aforementioned joint resolution of Congress.

I also request the mayors of municipalities, other public officials, leaders of industry and labor, and members of religious, civic, veterans', agricultural, women's, handicapped persons', and fraternal organizations and all other groups and individuals to take part in the observance of the designated week, in order to enlist the widest possible support of programs designed to increase opportunities in employment for the physically handicapped.

Photo Courtesy Rell Clements

State Highway and Public Works Commission, May, 1953. *Left to right around the table:* Forrest Lockey, Aberdeen; James A. Gray, Jr., Winston-Salem; James A. Hardison, Wadesboro; W. Ralph Winkler, Boone; June F. Scarborough, Statesville; J. Fleming Snipes, Marion; Harry E. Buchanan, Hendersonville; R. Brooks Peeters, attorney (*standing*), Raleigh; A. H. Graham, *Chairman* (*seated*); W. H. Rogers, Jr., engineer (*standing*), Raleigh; J. Emmett Winslow, Hertford; H. Maynard Hicks, Snow Hill; C. Heide Trask, Rocky Mount: M. E. Robinson, Goldsboro; C. A. Hasty, Maxton; John Van Lindley, Greensboro; Miss Ina Ferrell (*secretary*), Raleigh. Donnie A. Sorrell, Durham, was ab-

In witness whereof, I have hereunto set my hand and cause the Great Seal of North Carolina to be affixed.
(Seal) Done at the City of Raleigh this 4th day of October, in the year of our Lord, nineteen hundred and fifty-four.

William B. Umstead, *Governor.*

By the Governor:
Edward L. Rankin, Jr., *Private Secretary.*

FIRE PREVENTION WEEK[1]

EXECUTIVE DEPARTMENT
RALEIGH

A PROCLAMATION BY THE GOVERNOR
October 7, 1954

Since the earliest days of civilization, fire has been both a blessing and threat to human life and the well-being of society. Uncontrolled fire has been one of the greatest destroyers of life and property throughout history, causing an untold amount of suffering and destruction.

Fire prevention today is still a matter of great importance to everyone, and losses through fires continue to remain a major threat to life and property. The annual loss of property resulting from fire amounts to nearly a billion dollars a year.

In view of the importance of fire prevention, it is most appropriate that one week each year be designated as Fire Prevention Week and observed throughout our State and Nation as a means of educating our people to the need for a sound fire-prevention program in every community.

I hereby designate the week beginning October 3, 1954, as Fire Prevention Week in North Carolina and urge all our citizens to co-operate in a year-round campaign against the waste caused by preventable fires. I commend the efforts of the North Carolina Insurance Department and the various fire departments across the State for their splendid efforts in the reduction of fire hazards and the consequent losses.

Done at the City of Raleigh, October 7, 1954.

William B. Umstead, *Governor.*

---

[1] From *The Transylvania Times* (Brevard), October 7, 1954.

AMERICAN RED CROSS RELIEF AGENCY[1]

EXECUTIVE DEPARTMENT
RALEIGH

A PROCLAMATION BY THE GOVERNOR
October 10, 1954

Whereas, the hurricane has brought distress and suffering to the people of our State, and

Whereas, the American National Red Cross is the nationally recognized disaster relief agency, and has demonstrated its ability to meet the needs of families and individuals who are victims of disaster, and

Whereas, the American National Red Cross has an experienced staff, capable of seeing that relief is supplied on the basis of need to all disaster-affected persons:

Now, therefore, I, William B. Umstead, by virtue of the power invested in me, as Governor of North Carolina, do hereby designate the American National Red Cross as the official disaster relief agency to deal with the problems of individuals and families affected by the hurricane, and I urge all citizens and agencies, both public and private within the State of North Carolina to give the Red Cross their full support and co-operation. And I further urge that all individuals, groups, and organizations, wherever located, desiring to make contributions send them to American National Red Cross Disaster Relief Headquarters, Community Center, Wilmington, or to their local Red Cross Chapter. All such donations will be used by the Red Cross in their humane task of caring for the needs of families and individuals who have suffered loss in the disaster and who are unable to rehabilitate themselves without assistance.

Done at the City of Raleigh, October 10, 1954.

William B. Umstead, *Governor.*

[1] Taken from *The Durham Sun,* October 23, 1954.

EXECUTIVE ORDERS

W. H. S. BURGWYN APPOINTED AN EMERGENCY JUDGE

EXECUTIVE DEPARTMENT

RALEIGH

EXECUTIVE ORDER NO. 1

July 1, 1953

W. H. S. Burgwyn, having been appointed a special judge of the Superior Court of North Carolina on the 15th day of May, 1937, by Honorable Clyde R. Hoey, Governor of North Carolina, and the said W. H. S. Burgwyn, having been reappointed to said office in 1939, 1941, 1943, 1945, 1947, 1949, and 1951, and having served as a special Superior Court judge under said appointments continuously from said time, and the said W. H. S. Burgwyn, having arrived at the age of sixty-seven years on January 22, 1953, and the said W. H. S. Burgwyn, having by letter notified the undersigned Governor of the State of North Carolina and ex officio Director of the Budget that, under the provisions of *General Statutes,* Section 7-51, he desired to retire from said office as special judge of the Superior Court at the end of his term on June 30, 1953, and thereby, under the terms and provisions of said law and *General Statute* 7-50, become an emergency judge of the Superior Court of the State of North Carolina, as therein provided.

It is now ordered and found by the undersigned William B. Umstead, Governor of the State of North Carolina and ex officio Director of the Budget, that said W. H. S. Burgwyn was entitled to retire at the end of his term on June 30, 1953, as a Special Judge of the Superior Court of North Carolina, he having attained the age of more than sixty-five years at the date of such retirement and having served continuously as a Special Superior Court Judge for more than fifteen years at the time of such retirement, and W. H. S. Burgwyn is entitled to retire and to receive all benefits and compensation provided by law as an emergency judge and to perform all the duties and responsibilities imposed by law upon him in such position as an emergency judge of the Superior Court of North Carolina.

Copy of this order shall be furnished to the Chief Justice of the Supreme Court of North Carolina and to the State Auditor.

Done at Raleigh, this the 1st day of July, 1953.

William B. Umstead, *Governor.*

ESTABLISHING SCHOOLS OF NURSING

EXECUTIVE DEPARTMENT
RALEIGH

EXECUTIVE ORDER NO. 2
July 20, 1953

By virtue of the authority vested in me by Chapter 1208 of the *Session Laws of the 1953 General Assembly* and upon the unanimous recommendation of the Committee appointed pursuant to the law to investigate, study, and make recommendations concerning the advisability and feasibility of establishing a program of nurse's training at one or more of the state-supported educational institutions, Schools of Nursing shall be established at the Negro Agricultural and Technical College in Greensboro and at Winston-Salem Teachers' College. Each of these colleges shall immediately proceed to employ a competent and qualified director for a School of Nursing and shall thereafter open its School of Nursing as soon as twenty or more students have qualified and enrolled to begin the first year of training in the Nursing School curriculum at the college. Budget details for the operation of these two Schools of Nursing will be worked out by the college administrators in co-operation with Assistant Budget Director D. S. Coltrane consistent with funds appropriated for this purpose by the 1953 General Assembly.

The recommendations of the Committee were found to be entirely acceptable, and I have adopted these recommendations in full.

Serving on the Committee were:

Senator Warren R. Williams of Lee County; Miss Ruth Council, Nursing Consultant in the State Board of Health; and

Mr. Reid Holmes, Administrator of the North Carolina Baptist Hospital at Winston-Salem. Senator Williams served as Chairman of the Committee. Dr. Elizabeth Kemble, Dean of the School of Nursing at Chapel Hill, and Dr. William Richardson of the School of Public Health at Chapel Hill, served as advisors to the Committee. This opportunity is taken to express publicly my appreciation for the careful study made by this Committee and its advisors and for the able service it has rendered the public in this matter.

Done at Raleigh, this the 20th day of July, 1953.

William B. Umstead, *Governor.*

JOHN J. BURNEY APPOINTED AN EMERGENCY JUDGE

EXECUTIVE DEPARTMENT
RALEIGH

EXECUTIVE ORDER NO. 3
December 29, 1953

John J. Burney, resident judge of the Superior Court of the Eighth Judicial District of North Carolina, having filed with the Governor and members of the Council of State of North Carolina, on November 28, 1953, a petition representing that he is now and has been, since January 1, 1939, duly elected, qualified and acting as resident judge of the Superior Court of North Carolina, for the Eighth Judicial District, and petitioning that he be retired as such judge, under authority of *G. S.* 7-51.1, which authorizes retirement of any judge of the Superior Court who, by reason of disease or accident, is totally disqualified from efficiently performing the duties of said office, upon the approval of the Governor and Council of State, acting together, and to receive, for life, two-thirds of the annual salary from time to time received by judges of the Superior Court, and

John J. Burney, resident judge of the Superior Court, as aforesaid, having filed with Honorable William B. Umstead, Governor of North Carolina, under date of November 27, 1953, his resignation as resident judge of the Superior Court, of the Eighth

Judicial District of North Carolina, effective on December 31, 1953, by reason of being totally disabled from efficiently performing the duties of said office and for the purpose of being retired, under the provisions of *G. S.* 7-51.1.

Based upon the foregoing petition, affidavits of Doctors G. B. Barefoot of Wilmington, North Carolina; W. M. Nicholson of Duke Hospital, Durham, North Carolina; and D. R. Murchison of Wilmington, North Carolina, attached to said petition, and the said resignation, the following facts are found by the undersigned Governor and Council of State of North Carolina:

First: That the petitioner, John J. Burney, will have served as a regular judge of the Superior Court of North Carolina for fifteen (15) years on December 31, 1953.

Second: That said petitioner has tendered the Governor his resignation as resident judge of the Superior Court for the Eighth Judicial District of North Carolina, because of physical disability brought about by reason of diseases.

Third: It is further found as a fact, by the unanimous vote of said Council of State (after notice and opportunity for hearing was given to said petitioner) that said John J. Burney is totally disabled by reason of physical disability and disease from efficiently performing the duties of the office of judge of the Superior Court, which said finding is fully warranted from the verified petition and supported by medical certificates attached thereto.

Upon the foregoing findings of fact, it is considered, ordered, and adjudged that the petition of John J. Burney be and the same is granted, and that he is entitled to and is, as by law provided, allowed to retire from active duty as a judge of the Superior Court, by reason of said physical disability and disease, on December 31, 1953, and is entitled to receive the retirement benefits granted by *G. S.* 7-51.1, and

It is further ordered that said petition and supporting evidence be filed with the Council of State, and that a copy of this order be entered in the minutes of the Council of State, and that a copy of this order shall be furnished to Honorable W. A. Devin, Chief Justice of the Supreme Court of North Carolina.

Done at Raleigh, North Carolina, this 29th day of December, 1953.

William B. Umstead, *Governor,*
Thad Eure, *Secretary of State,*
Edwin Gill, *Treasurer,*
Henry L. Bridges, *Auditor,*
Charles F. Carroll, *Superintendent of Public Instruction,*
Charles F. Gold, *Commissioner of Insurance,*
Forrest H. Shuford, *Commissioner of Labor.*

WILLIAM A. DEVIN APPOINTED AN EMERGENCY JUDGE

EXECUTIVE DEPARTMENT
RALEIGH

EXECUTIVE ORDER NO. 4
February 1, 1954

The Honorable William Augustus Devin, having retired from his office as Chief Justice of the Supreme Court of North Carolina, to be effective at 5 o'clock P.M. on the 30th day of January, 1954, for the purpose of assuming the status of an emergency judge of the Superior Court of North Carolina, as authorized by *General Statutes* 7-50 and 7-51, it is found as a fact by the undersigned William B. Umstead, Governor of North Carolina, that William Augustus Devin was appointed by Governor Locke Craig as judge of the Superior Court from the Tenth Judicial District and qualified for said office on the 23rd day of September, 1913, and, by virtue of successive elections to the said office, he served as judge of the Superior Court until he was appointed by Governor J. C. B. Ehringhaus as associate justice of the Supreme Court of North Carolina, succeeding Associate Justice W. J. Brogden, on November 1, 1935; that he was re-elected as an associate justice of the Supreme Court for an eight-year term on November 3, 1936, and was again re-elected for an eight-year term as associate justice of the Supreme Court on November 7, 1944; that he continued to serve said office of associate justice of the Supreme Court of

North Carolina until he resigned said position on the 17th day of September, 1951, to accept the appointment by Governor W. Kerr Scott as chief justice of the Supreme Court of North Carolina to succeed Chief Justice W. P. Stacy, whose occupancy of said office was terminated by his death; that he was duly elected as chief justice of the Supreme Court of North Carolina at the election held on the 4th day of November, 1952, and has continued to serve until the effective date of his retirement as applied for.

It is therefore ordered and found by the undersigned Governor of the State of North Carolina that William Augustus Devin is now eighty-two years of age and has served more than fifteen years as a judge of the Superior Court of North Carolina, and more than fifteen years as a justice and chief justice of the Supreme Court of North Carolina, and is therefore entitled upon his retirement from his position as chief justice of the Supreme Court of North Carolina, as a retired chief justice of said Court, to receive for life two-thirds of the annual salary from time to time received by the chief justice of the Supreme Court of North Carolina, payable monthly, and, as a retired chief justice of the Supreme Court of North Carolina, to assume the status of emergency judge of the Superior Court, as provided by *G. S.* 7-50, and to receive compensation for each regular term of court held by him as an emergency judge as provided by *G. S.* 7-51, together with his actual expenses, as therein provided.

A copy of this executive order shall be furnished to Honorable William Augustus Devin, a copy to the chief justice of the Supreme Court of North Carolina, and a copy to the State Auditor. A commission will be issued to William Augustus Devin as emergency judge of the Superior Court of North Carolina in accordance with this order.

Done at Raleigh, North Carolina, this 1st day of February, 1954.

William B. Umstead, *Governor.*

JOHN H. CLEMENT APPOINTED AN EMERGENCY JUDGE

EXECUTIVE DEPARTMENT
RALEIGH

EXECUTIVE ORDER NO. 5
March 15, 1954

The Honorable John H. Clement, having retired from his office as resident judge of the Eleventh Judicial District of North Carolina, to be effective on the 10th day of March, 1954, for the purpose of assuming the status of an emergency judge of the Superior Court of North Carolina, as authorized by *General Statutes* 7-50 and 7-51, it is found as a fact by the undersigned William B. Umstead, Governor of North Carolina, that John H. Clement was appointed by Governor Angus W. McLean as judge of the Superior Court from the Eleventh Judicial District and qualified for said office on the 2nd day of June, 1928, and, by virtue of successive elections to the said office, he served as resident judge of the Superior Court of said district until the effective date of his retirement as requested by him in a letter to the Governor, received in the executive offices on the 10th day of March, 1954.

It is therefore ordered and found by the undersigned Governor of the State of North Carolina that John H. Clement is now seventy-two years of age and has served more than fifteen years as a judge of the Superior Court of North Carolina, and is therefore entitled upon his retirement from his position as judge of the Superior Court of North Carolina, as a retired judge of said Court, to receive for life two-thirds of the annual salary from time to time received by a judge of the Superior Court of North Carolina, payable monthly, and, as a retired judge of the Superior Court of North Carolina, to assume the status of emergency judge of the Superior Court, as provided by *G. S.* 7-50, and to receive compensation for each regular term of court held by him as an emergency judge as provided by *G. S.* 7-51, together with his actual expenses, as therein provided.

A copy of this executive order shall be furnished to Honorable John H. Clement, a copy to the Chief Justice of the Supreme Court of North Carolina, and a copy to the State Auditor. A commission will be issued to John H. Clement as emergency judge of the Superior Court of North Carolina in accordance with this order.

Done at Raleigh, North Carolina, this 15th day of March, 1954.

William B. Umstead, *Governor.*

W. C. HARRIS APPOINTED AN EMERGENCY JUDGE

EXECUTIVE DEPARTMENT
RALEIGH

EXECUTIVE ORDER NO. 6
September 30, 1954

The Honorable W. C. Harris, having retired from his office as judge of the Superior Court of North Carolina and resident judge of the Seventh Judicial District of North Carolina, to be effective on the 30th day of September, 1954, for the purpose of assuming the status of an emergency judge of the Superior Court of North Carolina, as authorized by *General Statutes* 7-50 and 7-51, it is found as a fact by the undersigned William B. Umstead, Governor of North Carolina, that W. C. Harris was elected as judge of the Superior Court from the Seventh Judicial District and qualified for said office on the 1st day of January, 1927, and, by virtue of successive elections to the said office, has served as judge of the Superior Court of North Carolina until this time;

It is therefore ordered and found by the undersigned Governor of the State of North Carolina that W. C. Harris is now sixty-eight years of age and has served more than fifteen years as a judge of the Superior Court of North Carolina, and is therefore entitled upon his retirement from his position as judge of the Superior Court of North Carolina and, as a retired judge of said Court, to receive for life two-thirds of the annual salary from time to time received by a judge of the Superior Court, payable monthly, and as a retired judge of the Superior Court of North Carolina, to assume the status of emergency judge of the Superior Court, as provided by *G. S.* 7-50, and to receive compensation for each regular term of court held by him as an emergency judge as provided by *G. S.* 7-51, together with his actual expenses, as therein provided, and such other compensation as may be provided by law from time to time.

A copy of this executive order shall be furnished to Honorable W. C. Harris, a copy to the Chief Justice of the Supreme Court of North Carolina, and a copy to the State Auditor. A commission will be issued to W. C. Harris as emergency judge of the Superior Court of North Carolina in accordance with this order.

Done at Raleigh, North Carolina, this 30th day of September, 1954.

William B. Umstead, *Governor.*

PUBLIC ADDRESSES

Courtesy of the Herald Sun

Board of Conservation and Development meeting in Morehead City, July 27, 1953. *Left to right:* Cecil Morris, Atlantic; Henry Rankin, Jr., Fayetteville; Charles S. Allen, Durham; Miles J. Smith, Salisbury *(1st Vice Chairman)*; Eric W. Rodgers, Scotland Neck; Charles H. Jenkins, Ahoskie; Governor Umstead; Scroop W. Enloe, Jr., Spruce Pine; Ben E. Douglas, Director; Amos R. Kearns, High Point; W. B. Austin, Jefferson; Walter J. Damtoft, Canton *(2nd Vice Chairman)*; T. Max Watson, Spindale; Leo H. Harvey, Kinston; Carl Buchan, Jr., North Wilkesboro; Robert M. Hanes, Winston-Salem; Hugh M. Morton, Wilmington.

THE DEMOCRATIC PARTY HAS GIVEN DISTINGUISHED SERVICE

ADDRESS[1] DELIVERED AT THE JEFFERSON-JACKSON DAY DINNER HELD AT HOTEL SIR WALTER RALEIGH

February 28, 1953

Mr. Chairman, Ladies and Gentlemen:

I extend to you my greetings and best wishes. I deeply regret that I cannot be with you tonight and have the pleasure of seeing each of you in person, and of hearing your distinguished speaker.

I have known Senator Richard Russell of Georgia for many years and worked with him when I was in the House of Representatives and in the United States Senate. His ability, character and patriotic devotion to his country have made him an outstanding Senator and a recognized leader in national affairs. I have for him, not only the highest respect, but also a deep personal affection. We are honored by his presence in our State.

I congratulate you, and through you the Democrats of North Carolina, for our fine victory on November 4. The Democratic Party in North Carolina has a record of distinguished service to the people of our State. It has given sound progressive government for the past half century and will, I am sure, continue to recognize and meet its responsibilties and obligations.

This gathering tonight of Democrats from every section of the State is further evidence of the devotion of the Democratic Party to the best interests of North Carolina.

---

[1] Governor Umstead was unable to attend this meeting and this brief address was read by Lieutenant Governor Luther H. Hodges.

BEAUTY AND INSPIRATION OF POETRY

REMARKS DELIVERED AT THE CEREMONY HONORING NORTH CAROLINA'S POET LAUREATE[1]
RALEIGH
August 4, 1953

[Dr. Frontis W. Johnston, President of the State Literary and Historical Association, presided at the exercises.]

Ladies and Gentlemen:

We are ready to begin our ceremonies of the morning. We will begin immediately by presenting the Governor.

Mr. Chairman, Ladies and Gentlemen:

We meet here this morning to honor Mr. James Larkin Pearson. Since he was a boy he has loved books, and from those books he has obtained knowledge, comfort, and inspiration, and with that knowledge and inspiration, he has seen fit by the writing of poems to pour back into the lives of the people of North Carolina, and of the Nation, a quality of beauty and of inspiration which has been recognized not only within the borders of our State but throughout the United States. He is to be congratulated this morning upon his marvelous achievement, because those who write poetry somehow have to have their feet on the ground and their eyes and their hearts in the stars. From the beauty of poetry there comes the enrichment of the lives of everyone who reads the poems and who seeks to find in them the beauty put there by the writer. Therefore, this morning it is a distinct pleasure for me, under and by virtue of the authority of a law enacted by a recent session of the General Assembly, to declare Mr. James Larkin Pearson the Poet Laureate of the State of North Carolina, and to present him a commission signifying his appointment. Thank you for your service to our people and best wishes.

---

[1] When Governor Umstead appointed James Larkin Pearson Poet Laureate of North Carolina, the State Literary and Historical Association scheduled a program at which time the commission was officially presented to Mr. Pearson. The remarks of those persons participating in the program follow in the sequence of delivery.

The program was tape-recorded and later taken from the recording and typed for inclusion in this volume.

Response by James Larkin Pearson:

To Your Excellency, Governor Umstead, to Dr. Johnston, to Dr. Crittenden, who is not present this morning, to the Literary and Historical Association of North Carolina, and to all my friends over the state who have had a part in bestowing upon me this distinguished honor, I extend my most sincere and heartfelt thanks. I accept this gracious award with a mixed feeling of pleasure and deep responsibility, and I can only hope that I may be in some measure worthy of it. I think it is a fitting thing, and a very fine and encouraging thing, that our State of North Carolina has come to recognize poetry as a worthwhile commodity in our intellectual life, and I hope future generations of poets will have this as a goal set before them, inspiring them to higher achievements. For myself, during my incumbency of the office, I will try to wear the crown of laurel leaves with becoming dignity. Thanks again to everybody.

Now, I have been permitted to take just a few minutes to read at least one of my poems. The one that is most widely known and most often called for is "Fifty Acres." It has been included in several anthologies and has become so well known that three stanzas of it have gotten into *Bartlett's Familiar Quotations,* and Simon and Schuster will have out in September a new anthology in which "Fifty Acres" will appear.

FIFTY ACRES

I've never been to London,
  I've never been to Rome;
But on my Fifty Acres
  I travel here at home.

The hill that looks upon me
  Right here where I was born
Shall be my mighty Jungfrau,
  My Alp, my Matterhorn.

A little land of Egypt
  My meadow plot shall be,
With pyramids of hay stacks
  Along its sheltered lee.

My hundred yards of brooklet
  Shall fancy's faith beguile,
And be my Rhine, my Avon,
  My Amazon, my Nile.

My humble bed of roses,
  My honeysuckle hedge,
Will do for all the gardens
  At all the far world's edge.

In June I find the Tropics
  Camped all about the place;
Then white December shows me
  The Arctic's frozen face.

My wood-lot grows an Arden,
  My pond a Caspian Sea;
And so my Fifty Acres
  Is all the world to me.

Here on my Fifty Acres
  I safe at home remain,
And have my own Bermuda,
  My Sicily, my Spain.

Dr. Johnston:

It may appear to the most of you that we need to give no reasons for this appointment beyond those we already know. Yet, it seems appropriate at this time that we have some remarks by way of appreciation of Mr. Pearson and his work. There are a number of people here, and I shall call first on Miss Lucy Cherry Crisp, Director of the State Art Gallery, who will speak for the writers of North Carolina.

Miss Crisp:

That any boy born in America has the right to dream that some day he may grow up to be President was a tradition well known to a boy born more than half a century ago. This boy, I am told, sometimes heard his people speak of the poet Longfellow, and he himself can quote a few of the songs of this great poet. So, as the time went on, a dream grew in this boy's mind that some day he would run for Poet. He would rather be Poet

Dame Flora MacLeod of Dunvegan Castle, Isle of Skye, Scotland, 18th chief of the MacLeod Clan, visit Governor Umstead, September 25, 1953, at the Governor's Mansion.

than President. Thus it was that day after day, as he plowed the stubborn fields of his family's farm, now and again he stopped at the end of a row to write down in a little book he always carried with him the words that came suddenly singing through his mind. This boy nourished in his heart the dream that some day he would run for Poet.

Today we have come here to bestow upon this boy, long since grown to be a man, the office he once sought to run for, the high office of Poet of the people—the people of North Carolina. This title of Poet Laureate, Mr. Pearson, comes to you as recognition of all the long years you have spent in singing the songs of the people, the people of North Carolina, the people of your own State. The songs that many of the rest of us have heard singing in our hearts but lacked the power to gather up suitable words. The office carries with it a responsibility as well as a recognition—the responsibility we are certain you will continue to fulfill.

This is a great day for you and all the writers of the State of North Carolina, and they all rejoice with you in it. They have good reason to rejoice. It is a great day for our State as well, when the State and a representative person of its government pauses in the midst of the great rush of the so-called affairs of State to appoint officially a Poet Laureate—a poet to sing of the deepest joys and the highest yearnings of its people's hearts. There is great cause for rejoicing. The world will not be unmindful, as we here assembled are not unmindful, of the real significance of this moment. It is as though we pause to say to all the world that we here in North Carolina, being mindful that it is the things of the spirit that really matter, do here and now bestow upon one of our own the office and responsibility to keep us constantly reminded that these things are true. And I am sure that all of you here assembled share with me the conviction so simply and so adequately put into words by the writer of old, "Brethren, it is good for us to be here."

Dr. Johnston:

Speaking on behalf of the press, we have asked Mr. Sam Ragan [1] to express appreciation this morning.

---

[1] Managing editor, *The News and Observer,* Raleigh, North Carolina.

Mr. Ragan:

It is a great pleasure to join in this tribute to a fellow newspaper man, and I think it is very good that we have this official recognition of the achievement of the spiritual just as well as we recognize the achievement of material progress. Every civilization, as you know, has its poets to sing of its glory, to sing of man's aspiration and his dreams, and I think that in James Larkin Pearson we have such a poet for North Carolina. In doing honor to this true son of North Carolina, the State also does honor to itself because it recognizes the need for the singer of songs, the maker of dreams, and the man who can write and sing of a state's progress in spiritual things and of man's own dreams. Thank you.

Dr. Johnston:

On behalf of the public schools, I present Dr. Charles F. Carroll, Superintendent of Public Instruction.

Dr. Carroll:

Mr. Chairman, Governor Umstead, Ladies and Gentlemen, Mr. and Mrs. Pearson:

I bring greetings this morning from that horde of children in North Carolina, some nine-hundred-odd thousands of them, likewise from their thirty-odd-thousand teachers. I bring greetings and commendations and congratulations to you, Mr. Pearson, from this vast number who are so interested in those matters with which you deal. We in education, even at the public school level, are forever giving consideration to the question of what we shall teach. We are concerned with knowledges, with skills, with values, and in the final analysis, all so often we revert to you, the poets, because it is from you that we get our bearings so often. We look back into some of the poetry that we have observed and learned, and we see that the poet always has an insight and particularly a feeling that so many of us mortals never had. I feel that if we were uttering a prayer this morning it would be that we who are a large majority of your fellows might have and might know, and particularly that we might feel, some of the thoughts and feelings that enter into your work. You have achieved well and we are satisfied that your greatest rewards and achievements lie before you. We recall that Keats gave utterance to these words: "Beauty is truth, truth beauty. That is all we know on earth and all we need to know." We look to the poet for beauty, for genuine truth, and we remember one other poet who said, "Joyful let the poet be, because through him other men see." We hope, Mr. Pearson, that through the years we might see better, more deeply, more profoundly, more significantly, as the result of your labors and your creativeness.

Dr. Johnston:

To speak for higher education I present Dr. Harold L. Trigg, President of St. Augustine's College, Raleigh, N. C.

Dr. Trigg:

Ladies and Gentlemen:

There are certain moments of destiny in the life of a great state like ours, and this is certainly one of them. There are contributions from men and events and movements, men who are leaders in the State, like our great Governor, like Dr. Crittenden, who recommend that we have a sense of values and recognize people who have produced, men like Mr. Pearson, who have contributed greatly to the life and culture of the State. There are great events that give us opportunity to pause and re-evaluate our values. Mr. Pearson, who discovered himself—a great educational lesson—who discovered himself and his capacity to compose poetry at a very early age, and who has pursued that ability and that capacity to goals which bring him to the highest level. At present, in that area of activity, he is the bearer of the laurel of the muses.

There are events that have brought confusion, but now at the close of the war we have cause to recheck our purposes and objectives. We have gone through a period when the colleges and institutions of higher learning of the State have faced an uncontrollable desire on the part of young people to qualify for attainment in the armed forces, a technical age that has been overemphasized by the necessity of success in technology only. We have the combination of the two coming together in the recognition of the ability of this great poet. We hope that it means a challenge coming from you to the institutions of higher learning in the State of North Carolina not to abolish technology certainly, but to restore a balance between the mechanistic and the spiritual. So it is in that vein that the colleges bring felicitations to you, and I am sure that they would join me in accepting the challenge to paramount the effect of your great work and to produce the balance between the physical and the spiritual.

Dr. Johnston:

Our concluding appreciation of this program is to be made by the President of the North Carolina Library Association, Miss Jane B. Wilson:

Miss Wilson:

To speak for a people is not a gift but a hard-earned duty. To say for these people what they yearn to say for themselves, but cannot, requires keen understanding and a willingness to serve in a very personal and apathetic capacity. To say the words that lie on the surface, to sing the richer melodies of the life and soul of many folks, represents a great faith. On behalf of the members of the North Carolina Library Association, I should like to present something truly of the clay of North Carolina—something of its great beauty—a volume containing short sketches of its authors. In it may be found an autobiographical sketch of the State's poet, James Larkin Pearson, whom we honor today. With Mr. Pearson's permission, I should like to assume the privilege of presenting a copy of *North Carolina Authors* containing his autobiographical sketch, to the Governor of North Carolina. With the Governor's permission, I should like to present to Mr. Pearson a copy of the book, with deepest appreciation of the Association and the North Carolina English Teachers' Association, who were the co-editors of this book. It is North Carolina through and through, for it was written by people born in this State from one end to the other. It was edited by North Carolinians. It was printed in Charlotte, and now it is here in Raleigh to go back to Guilford County. Mr. Pearson, I am sure that I speak for all of those here this morning who have not spoken, in wishing you every success in your new position, and we wish for you many years of productive endeavor. We are sure that the State of North Carolina will always remember this hour and we are proud to have you in an official capacity as our Poet Laureate.

OUR GREATEST RESPONSIBILITY

ADDRESS[1] DELIVERED OVER A STATE-WIDE RADIO NETWORK ON BEHALF OF BOND ISSUES FOR PUBLIC SCHOOLS AND HOSPITALS FOR THE MENTALLY ILL
RALEIGH
September 10, 1953

Ladies and Gentlemen:

This is the first opportunity I have had to speak to all of the people of North Carolina since I was inaugurated Governor. First of all, I should like to express my thanks and appreciation for your kindness during the first months of this year. I am grateful for your messages, cards, letters, telegrams, and especially for your prayers, and your continued interest.

It is now my pleasure and privilege to speak to you about two subjects of vital importance. The General Assembly, last spring, after thorough consideration and with a farsightedness typical of its patriotic service, voted to submit to the people on October 3 two bond issues—one to provide for additional public school facilities, and the other to provide for additional hospital facilities for the mentally ill and for institutions for feeble-minded children. By doing so, the General Assembly placed squarely upon the conscience of the citizens of this State the duty of expressing their will as to the future development of North Carolina in these, the *two areas* of our greatest responsibility.

Civilization never stands still. It either moves forward or backward; and in its inescapable tide it carries to and fro the failure, accomplishment, faith, hope, and aspiration of all mankind. In my opinion, the passage of these two bond issues will be further evidence of North Carolina's determination to live true to its heritage and to meet the responsibilities of the hour. We cannot shirk our duty to our children or to our mentally ill.

The bond issues call for the issuance of $50,000,000 in bonds to provide funds for public school facilities and $22,000,000 to

[1] This address originated over radio station WPTF, Raleigh.

provide funds for additional mental hospital facilities and institutions for feeble-minded children.

For many years I have felt that education is the first responsibility of the State. It has been truly said that "the history of civilization is being daily written, to a large degree, in the classrooms of the world." The truth of this statement is understood by all of us, and we are proud of the progress that we have made in public education, but there remains much to be done. We have constructed in North Carolina many school buildings in the past few years, and yet the need has not been met. The increase in school population has been more rapid than the construction of school facilities. Crowded schoolroom conditions must be relieved in North Carolina if we are to do, in this generation, what should be done for the education of our children and for the development of our State. Youth cannot wait! It must be served in its day, or it will be too late!

When the public schools opened for the 1953-1954 term, parents, teachers, and pupils faced an emergency. According to the figures provided by the State Department of Public Instruction, our schools are short more than 7,000 classrooms. Two hundred and fifty thousand school children are crowded into inadequate or substandard classrooms. Libraries, shops, laboratories, and science rooms—all important parts of today's educational program—are available only to a portion of our school children.

During the depression and war years, there was, of necessity, a minimum amount of school construction and maintenance. This was caused, first by shrinking revenues, and later by shortages of materials and manpower during and immediately after the war. However, during these years North Carolina experienced a rapid increase in its birth rate. In 1933, 75,000 births were recorded. In 1952, over 112,000 were recorded. Thus in a period of 19 years the number of births in our State increased by more than 49 per cent. In addition to the rapid increase in our birth rate, more and more of our young people are taking advantage of the opportunity to continue their education until they obtain a high school diploma. For example, in 1950 there were six times as many high school graduates in North Carolina as there were in

1924. More young people are staying in school for longer periods of time. This is a splendid achievement, but it does mean that additional school facilities must be provided.

The unprecedented increase of our school population has imposed upon our counties, and upon the State, the serious duty of providing additional school facilities.

The law enacted by the 1953 General Assembly provides for the distribution of the funds to be derived from these school bonds. First, every county will receive $100,000, which amounts to $10,000,000; second, the counties will receive $15,000,000 on the basis of school population; third, the remaining $25,000,000 will be allocated according to need and ability to pay, and will be handled under a formula to be adopted by the State Board of Education, with the approval of the Governor.

This bond issue is not intended to relieve the counties of the primary responsibility to provide adequate school facilities. It must be recognized, however, that our smaller counties must be helped if the children in these counties are to receive equal school facilities. This is in keeping with the principle of the old equalization fund, and is the same principle involved in the operation of our present state-wide public school system.

Our obligation to our mentally ill is universally recognized. As medical science has learned more about mental illness, there has been a growing awareness, in North Carolina and throughout the Nation, of the need for better treatment, better care, and better facilities for the mentally ill. Great progress has been made in North Carolina during the past few years, but much remains to be done, and continued emphasis should be placed upon the treatment and cure of our mentally ill. In spite of all that has been done, we are still sadly deficient in facilities to care for our mentally ill. North Carolina was the twelfth state of the original thirteen states to establish hospital facilities for mentally disordered persons. From this slow start, we have not yet recovered. Today we lag in available beds, and are sadly behind in providing curative practices that look toward the restoration of some of these people to their families and to a normal way of life. Too much of what we have to offer is mere custodial care. Too little of it treats or cures. However, we have proven at Butner Hospital that many so-called incurables can be cured.

We have an institution at Kinston which is called the Caswell Training School. It is not now and has never been a real "training school." It is, and has been, a detention home for feeble-minded children who grow into feeble-minded men and women; and there they stay through the years. There has never been a place which has even been called a training school for feeble-minded children of the Negro race. With modern care and treatment, many feeble-minded children can be returned to a useful life. When I taught school at Kinston in 1916, I first visited the Caswell Training School. I determined then that if I should ever have the opportunity, I would undertake to do something for the feeble-minded children of North Carolina. I, therefore, plead with you to give them an opportunity to have proper treatment, which will inevitably result in the curing of a substantial percentage of those committed to these institutions.

There is not sufficient room in institutions for the adults who need attention. In 1945, we had 8,300 mental patients in state hospitals. We have now 11,300. This is an increase of 36 per cent in eight years. In the meantime, waiting lists of people urgently needing admission to these hospitals have rapidly grown. Some of these are being housed in jails and county homes as the only means of protecting them from harm to themselves and others. Your family may not have this problem today. Tomorrow it may! We have worked at this problem piece-meal fashion long enough. The mentally ill have no spokesman except members of their families and those whose hearts have been touched by the need for better facilities and treatment.

We have made great strides in North Carolina with our good health program to build new hospitals, new clinics, and provide more hospital beds for people who are physically ill. Now is the time to do more for the mentally sick who deserve and need adequate care and attention.

Our great State, with all its resources cannot longer delay providing the means of caring adequately for this group of our

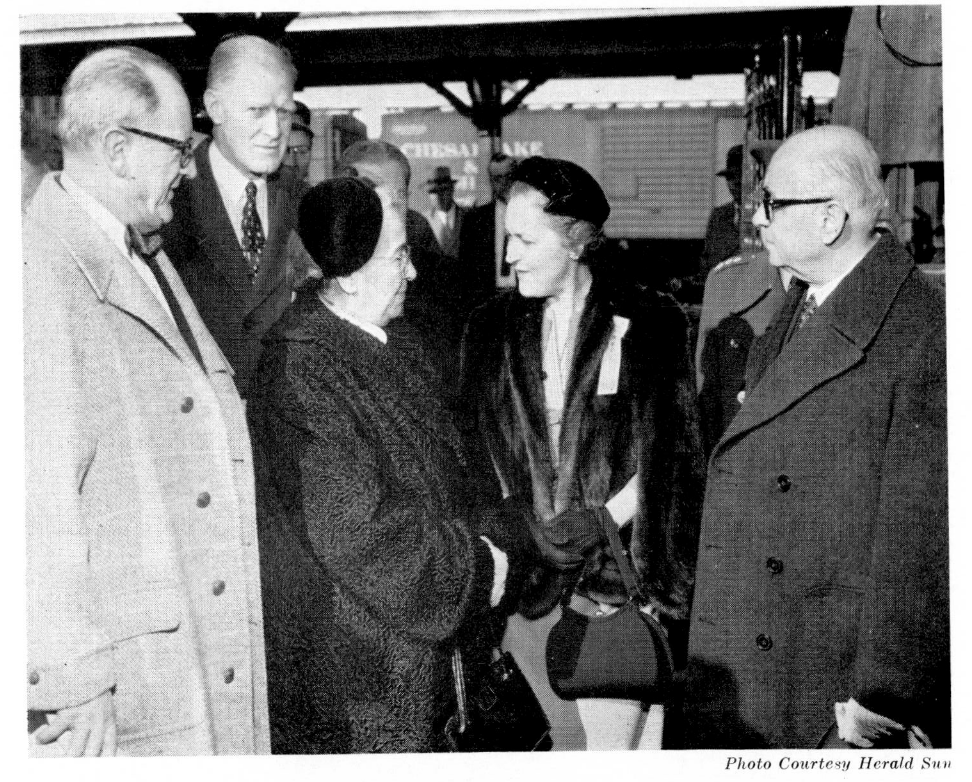

Photo Courtesy Herald Sun

Secretary of State Thad Eure and Mrs. Umstead meeting President and Madame Celal Bayar of Turkey, February 18, 1954, as they arrived in Raleigh for a visit. *Left to right:* Thad Eure, Madame Bayar, Mrs. Umstead, and President Bayar. The man next to Eure is not identified.

citizens. The $22,000,000 proposed in the mental hospitals bond issue will be used to improve and repair existing buildings, to provide new facilities more nearly in keeping with the need of the times, to bring the physical plants of these hospitals to a point where they can operate with maximum efficiency, and to provide institutions for feeble-minded children of both races.

This is also an investment in human resources—an investment which cannot be measured in terms of dollars and cents. Nevertheless, we know that each patient cured and each child saved means an economic benefit to the State. With proper facilities and trained personnel, North Carolina can accomplish great things in solving a health problem which is increasing here, and in all other states at this time. These bond issues offer a great opportunity for North Carolina. I urge every voter to support and vote for the two bond issues on October 3. It is a challenge which we must meet.

The provision of adequate school facilities, mental hospitals and institutions for feeble-minded children, is the business and responsibility of every citizen of North Carolina; and I sincerely believe that you will assume this responsibility because of your interest in humanity and in the development and progress of our State. I, therefore, call upon every citizen, every organization and group interested in the education of our youth and the welfare and care of our mentally ill, to do all in your power to persuade the voters in your respective communities to go to the polls on October 3 and give these bond issues an overwhelming vote of approval. By doing so, we can live up to the heritage of which we are so proud, and measure up to the responsibilities of today, and thereby make provisions for the necessities of tomorrow. Let us, individually and collectively, conduct a crusade from now until October 3 for these things which are good, and which will result in everlasting benefit to the people of North Carolina.

NORTH CAROLINIANS CARE FOR THEIR CHILDREN

ADDRESS[1] DELIVERED OVER RADIO STATION WPTF IN BEHALF OF THE BOND CAMPAIGN FOR PUBLIC SCHOOLS AND THE MENTALLY ILL

RALEIGH

September 30, 1953

Ladies and Gentlemen:

In my opinion, the passage of the two bond issues Saturday is essential to the future development of North Carolina. The outcome of this bond election will affect the lives of every citizen in our State, either directly or indirectly. The question is: Are you interested in adequate school facilities for the children of this State and adequate facilities for the care of the mentally ill? Do you care enough to take the necessary time to vote on Saturday for these bond issues? I believe that you do, and I do not think you will shirk your duty to our children or to our mentally ill.

As I stated sometime ago, there is no new principle involved in the school bond issue. It is the same thing applied to school facilities, which we attempted to do by the old Equalization Fund and which we are now successfully doing by our state-wide system of public education in the operation of our schools.

As the campaign for these bond issues comes to a close, there are several questions which have been asked by interested citizens across the State, such as: How much money will it take to retire these bonds? Where will the money come from and, are we voting a new tax on ourselves?

The 1953 General Assembly authorized the issuance of these bonds, if approved by a special election on October 3, and provided that the bonds shall be repaid over a period of twenty years. Careful calculations have determined that the payment on these bonds, both principal and interest, will amount to an average of about $4,600,000 a year for the next twenty years. The total debt service required for both bond issues amounts to about 2½ per cent of the current General Fund Revenue and will be paid out of the General Fund, for which appropriations have already been

[1] Arrangements were made for an appeal in support of the bond issues involving a hundred stations across the State, originating from WPTF, Raleigh.

made for two years. In view of the fact that both principal and interest amounts to only 2½ per cent of present state appropriations from the General Fund, new taxes will not be required for the purpose of retiring these bonds. It has been suggested in some parts of the State that the passage of the bonds would increase the tax on land. This is not true. There is no state levied land tax and none is proposed in connection with these bond issues.

The funds from these bonds will be an investment in human resources, which cannot be measured in terms of dollars and cents. The expenditure of these funds will be of economic benefit to the State, and their passage will be in keeping with the humane and progressive instinct which has characterized the spirit of North Carolina for the past fifty years.

Although there has been no organized opposition to the passage of the bond issues, we must not take their passage for granted. If you are interested in the development and growth of our State, in adequate school facilities for our children, and in the care of our mentally ill, then I urge you to do everything you can from now until the polls close on Saturday to insure the passage of these bonds. And, I repeat, that by doing this we can live up to the heritage of which we are so proud, measure up to the responsibilities of today, and make provisions for the necessities of tomorrow. I am confident that the people of North Carolina *do* care for their children and mentally ill and will respond to this challenge for these things which are good, and which will result in everlasting benefit to the people of our State.

NORTH CAROLINA IS PROUD OF ITS ARMED SERVICES PERSONNEL

ADDRESS DELIVERED OVER THE RADIO TO NORTH CAROLINIANS STATIONED IN THE LONG BEACH AREA OF CALIFORNIA
RALEIGH
October 14, 1953

Ladies and Gentlemen of the Armed Services:

As Governor of North Carolina, I deeply appreciate this opportunity to bring a word of greeting to all North Carolinians serving in the armed forces of the United States in the Long Beach,

California, area. I appreciate this opportunity made possible by the Long Beach Armed Services Young Men's Christian Association as a part of its weekly program on the radio, and I commend its efforts in behalf of all servicemen and servicewomen.

North Carolina is justly proud of its young men and women in the armed forces of the United States. Our State has always been among the first to provide the volunteers in time of national emergency or actual war. North Carolinians now in service are carrying on our great tradition of patriotism, and we are pleased and proud at the reports we receive concerning their contributions to our national security. I know that all of you miss being at home, and I want you to know that we here in North Carolina also miss you. I am sure that your loved ones and friends would want me to send their greetings to each of you wherever you may be stationed.

As North Carolinians and as Americans, we are deeply grateful for the end of actual combat in Korea. We hope that a permanent peace may follow the period of truce negotiations. However, there is no doubt that we must continue to guard against aggression, and we must maintain armed forces sufficient to safeguard our homes and our Nation. Every North Carolinian now in the service is making his or her own contribution to the safety of our Nation and the peace of all mankind. I hope that we will never lose sight of the necessity for patriotic service and self-sacrifice both in time of peace and in time of national emergency.

Public schools of North Carolina have opened their doors again for our young people, and our school facilities have been overwhelmed by the number of first graders. Despite the use of every available facility, there is overcrowding in many schools and our local and state education authorities are wrestling with some difficult problems. This is true not only in North Carolina but in other states as well. Our Nation's birth rate continues to rise. I am happy to report to you, however, that some relief is in sight as a result of the recent bond election, which was held on October 3, to provide funds in the amount of $50,000,000 to help our public school system. The people of North Carolina gave this bond issue an overwhelming majority at the polls. Also, the voters gave overwhelming approval to $22,000,000 in bonds which will

Photo Courtesy North Carolina News Bureau

Governor Umstead and family in the library of the Governor's Mansion, February 23, 1954. *Left to right:* Mrs. Charles D. Davis, mother of Mrs. Umstead; Mrs. Umstead; Governor Umstead; and Merle Umstead, their daughter.

be used to help our mental hospitals provide the facilities which are so badly needed for mentally ill patients. I am very proud of North Carolina and the courageous manner in which our people are meeting the challenge facing us in the proper education of our children and the proper care of our mentally ill people.

We are well into the fall here in North Carolina and our weather has been very beautiful. The highways to our mountains are busy these weekends as motorists drive up to the Smokies and the Blue Ridge to view the fall colors in all their beauty. The college football season has gotten off to a fine start and there is a great deal of interest among sports fans throughout the State. As of this time, Duke and Carolina remain undefeated among the major colleges in North Carolina.

It is my hope that you will be able to return home at least on leave sometime this fall. Meanwhile, may I extend to each North Carolinian within the range of my voice the very best wishes of the people of North Carolina. I do hope you will have a successful tour of duty, and we are looking forward to having you return home.

THE GROWTH AND DEVELOPMENT OF NORTH CAROLINA STATE COLLEGE

ADDRESS [1] DELIVERED BEFORE THE NORTH CAROLINA STATE DEVELOPMENT COUNCIL
RALEIGH
October 16, 1953

Ladies and Gentlemen:

Our North Carolina State College of today is quite different from the one brick building overlooking Pullen Forest in 1889. It has had an eventful history since those days of six teachers,

---

[1] The North Carolina State College Development Council consists of six foundations organized for the purpose of upholding the research and teaching programs of the several schools. The following foundations form the Council: North Carolina State College Foundation, Inc.; The Agricultural Foundation, Inc.; North Carolina Dairy Foundation, Inc.; North Carolina Engineering Foundation, Inc.; North Carolina Textile Foundation, Inc.; and North Carolina Architectural Foundation, Inc.

At the time of Governor Umstead's address, the six foundations listed above had raised over $2,000,000 and had spent over $900,000 in support of college functions and programs.

40-odd students, and a sixty-acre farm. It has been a magnificent journey from old Holladay, Watauga, and Pullen halls to the mammoth center of technical education, research, and extension that is now North Carolina State College of Agriculture and Engineering of the Consolidated University of North Carolina.

But more than buildings, test tubes, and hothouses, the development of State College is most vividly revealed through the thousands of citizens it has trained for the agricultural, industrial, professional, and educational development of our State. What they have done, and are doing, to make our lives more fruitful is beyond description. In addition to its seven schools teaching nearly 4,000 students on the Raleigh campus, State College has carried itself into every county through short courses, night classes, experiment stations, and extension programs. And in its great democratic tradition, it has served the hard-working farmers, businessmen, housewives, professional folks, and government officials with equal realism until today the boundaries of the State College campus are virtually the boundaries of North Carolina.

In the last twelve or fifteen years, North Carolina State College has grown in stature until now it is considered one of the best institutions of its kind in our Republic. This reputation is deserved. The record speaks for itself. It is basically a record of keeping a finger on the agricultural and industrial needs of the people. It is a record of interpreting and meeting these needs. It is a record of reaching our people with a leadership and help that is unexcelled by any institution of its kind anywhere.

I want to congratulate the College upon the formation of its Development Council and for the vision which produced its new Development Program. The purpose, as I understand it, is to co-ordinate all of the teaching, research, and extension services of the College into a more closely knit program, and to make the College and all it has to offer more available to the people, and its services more usable by them. When you think about it, these purposes conceived in the minds of men of a former generation brought North Carolina State College into being for the purpose of providing agriculture and industry with the kind of technical education and services that will help us all. And State College is doing just that, closely attuned to the everyday lives of our people, it is helping us improve our crops, our livestock, our soils, our machines, our food, and our clothing. Above all, it is helping us develop future citizens to continue this progress and improve our standards of living.

I am intensely interested in what our North Carolina State College is doing to make lighter the burden, to light the way, and to develop the horizons of our everyday lives. I respect the heritage, and endorse the mission of this great institution of the people, and I am grateful for this opportunity to encourage its future development.

COTTON AND PEANUT MARKETING QUOTAS

ADDRESS DELIVERED OVER STATE WIDE RADIO NETWORK
RALEIGH
December 8, 1953

Ladies and Gentlemen:

It is always a pleasure to have an opportunity to talk to the people of North Carolina about such important farm matters as the peanut and cotton marketing quota referendums scheduled for December 15, 1953. While my remarks concerning the referendum are primarily addressed to peanut and cotton growers in this State, I hope that all of our people will learn more about this vital part of our agricultural program and what it has meant to North Carolina. We must never forget that agriculture is still the pride of our State. One-third of our people work on farms; another third live in rural areas, and the cash income from our farms is now about $900,000,000 per year.

To understand fully the events of today, it is always wise to look back at the history of these events during past years. To understand fully what marketing quotas have meant to our farmers, we should glance back at the beginning of the farm program in 1933. It was my privilege and pleasure to be a member of Congress when most of the legislation upon which the national farm program now rests was being formulated and passed. From my own experience I knew how badly this legislation was needed. The record has clearly demonstrated that agriculture suffers first and most severely in any recession or depression following a period of inflation. It has been proven, in my judgment, that we cannot hope to enjoy in this country any sound or stable economy, unless agriculture is prosperous.

When I returned home in 1919 from military service, there was an appearance of prosperity. We soon learned how false it was. In the deflation of 1920, agriculture was first to feel the blow. In the depression of the thirties, peanuts dropped to 1 cent per pound, cotton to 5 cents, and tobacco to an average of around 10 cents. I think it is now generally admitted that the distress of agriculture from 1920 to 1933 hastened the awful day, when it became necessary to close every banking institution in America. Immediately after this, all other efforts to stabilize agriculture having failed, Congress, upon the recommendation of President Roosevelt, began the enactment of laws which have become known as our National Farm Program. Each of these laws has played an important part in giving agriculture some degree of equality with other parts of our economy.

Membership on the Sub-committee on Appropriation for the Department of Agriculture, when I was a member of Congress, gave me the opportunity to study agricultural problems as they then existed, and the various phases of our farm program. I am still proud to have had an active part in helping to formulate, support, and defend this program which has brought so many benefits to our State. The entire program is vital not only to agriculture, but to our entire economy.

As you will recall, the Agricultural Act of 1938 strengthened and broadened the Soil Conservation and Domestic Allotment Act providing for assistance in the marketing of agricultural commodities for domestic consumption and export, provided for price support loans on certain commodities, and for farm marketing quotas for tobacco, corn, wheat, cotton, and rice. In 1941 peanuts were added to the act and marketing quotas for wheat and corn were changed. In 1949 substantial changes were made in the marketing quota provisions for cotton, and in the same year the price support provisions were repealed with the enactment of the Agricultural Adjustment Act of 1949. I might point out here that the constitutional validity of the marketing quota provisions has been upheld for tobacco, cotton, and wheat.

The act, as passed by Congress, provides a means whereby our farmers themselves may keep the production of certain commodities in line with the demand for these commodities. When surpluses exist, producers of such surplus commodities may make adjustments by use of acreage allotments and marketing quotas. The law *does not* impose marketing quotas upon farmers, but provides a method whereby they may impose such quotas upon themselves, by voting in a referendum to determine whether marketing quotas will be in effect. To me, this is the heart of a great program which has been administered by the farmers themselves through community, county, and state committees. In fact, the committee system has been perhaps the greatest reason for its unparalleled success. These committeemen have served with great sacrifice to themselves, and have made a splendid contribution to the welfare of agriculture in this State.

The basic legislation passed by Congress outlines the supply level at which it is mandatory for the Secretary of Agriculture to call a referendum. When such a referendum is called, at least two-thirds of the farmers growing such commodities must approve marketing quotas for these commodities, before the quotas go into effect. Our North Carolina farmers know what it means to have marketing quotas since there have been marketing quotas on tobacco every year since 1938 with the exception of 1939. In that year, when quotas were defeated, the result was bad, and we learned that it was to the advantage of the farmer to operate within quotas, when the supply exceeds the demand. We have also had peanut marketing quotas for several years, more recently beginning in 1949. We have not had marketing quotas on cotton since 1950. By the use of these marketing quotas, North Carolina tobacco and peanut farmers have been able to improve their economic standards, and at the same time, hold prices to consumers at a reasonable level.

Since surpluses exist, the Secretary of Agriculture is required to call for a referendum on marketing quotas for cotton and peanuts. You are eligible to vote in the peanut referendum as owner, landlord, operator, tenant or sharecropper, if you shared in the 1953 crop produced on a farm having a picked or thrashed area of more than one acre. If two-thirds of the votes are favorable, quotas will be in effect for the 1954, 1955, and 1956 crops of peanuts. If more than two-thirds of the voters oppose, quotas will not be in effect for the 1954 peanut crop. In this case, another peanut referendum would be held in the fall of 1954.

The cotton referendum will be held on the same date, Tuesday, December 15, 1953, and at the same polling places, those normally used in your PMA elections. Only those persons who shared in the 1953 cotton crop will be eligible to vote in this referendum. Marketing quotas will be in effect only, if two-thirds of those voting in the referendum cast their ballots in favor of the quotas.

I think that every peanut or cotton farmer should bear these facts in mind. If marketing quotas are approved, each farmer will receive his fair share of the national allotment, and if he plants within such allotment, no penalties are involved, and he will be eligible for price support at 90 per cent of parity. If more than one-third of the farmers vote against marketing quotas, the guaranteed price support drops to 50 per cent of parity, for those who plant within their allotment. If marketing quotas are approved, any farmer who exceeds his acreage allotment will be subject to a marketing quota penalty which will be set at a later date. Producers who overplant would not be eligible for price support on either commodity. *We should remember that acreage allotments will be in effect even if the quotas are defeated.* These allotments will be necessary to determine eligibility for price support. So we see that the principal issues now involved are (1) price support level and (2) whether marketing quota penalties will be assessed on those producers who exceed their allotment. Ninety per cent of parity for cotton at present is approximately 33 cents. Fifty per cent of parity for cotton is around 18 cents. Cotton cannot be grown profitably for 18 cents per pound.

Our cotton growers have noted that acreage allotments, as already announced, provide for a severe cut for some North Carolina growers. Our farmers planted in 1953 approximately 760,000 acres of cotton and the five-year average for 1947 through 1952 (excluding 1949) was approximately 723,000 acres. The allotment for 1954 is 528,638 acres. Legislation prescribes the exact manner in which state, county and individual farm allotments are determined. This means, of course, that local committees are not allowed much leeway in determining the individual farm allotments. And because of the method of distributing county allotments to individual farms, severe cuts from past acreages have been made on many farms.

It is believed that Congress will increase the national allotment soon after it convenes in January. Efforts were made during the past session of Congress to change the legislation which would provide for a larger national allotment and a different method of distributing county allotments among farms. I am sure these efforts will be continued as soon as Congress convenes.

I hope that some of the remarks I have made properly indicate the urgent need for approving marketing quotas for cotton and peanuts in North Carolina, and I urge every eligible farmer to support actively and vote for marketing quotas in the referendums on Tuesday, December 15. I think that we should all remember that a light vote, or an unfavorable vote, may have an adverse effect upon our tobacco program. A light vote or an unfavorable vote on marketing quotas for cotton and peanuts on December 15 would be bad, in my opinion, for the growers involved, and might also endanger our entire farm program. These referendums offer the growers of peanuts and cotton an opportunity again to express effectively their views with regard to marketing quotas on our basic crops. The drought, economic factors, and the absence of a clear-cut statement of policy with reference to a farm program, have resulted in confusion and concern among farmers and those interested in farm prosperity. An overwhelming vote in favor of marketing quotas should have at least some effect, upon the attitude of those now in control with regard to the farm program. Make the vote large, and make the vote favorable.

Thank you very much!

MARCH OF DIMES

ADDRESS[1] DELIVERED OVER RADIO STATION WPTF ON OPENING THE MARCH OF DIMES CAMPAIGN RALEIGH

January 2, 1954

[Governor Umstead was introduced by Mr. Thad Eure, Secretary of State, who was Chairman of the North Carolina March of Dimes. Mr. Eure's remarks follow:]

Ladies and Gentlemen:

As Chairman of the North Carolina March of Dimes, permit me now to thank every individual in the State who has manifested an interest in the campaign to raise funds to be made available for the care of our polio patients, and for the research program which we hope will bring about the final doom of polio. This dread disease is a constant threat to us in North Carolina and to our children. We know, because we have experienced the tragedy of two state-wide epidemics in 1944 and 1948, and this year we have had severe outbreaks in several of our counties. Our good Governor is graciously serving as Honorary Chairman of the North Carolina March of Dimes, and it is my great pleasure to present him to tell you the story you will want to know as we launch our campaign this year—His Excellency, William B. Umstead, Governor of North Carolina.

Governor Umstead:

Ladies and Gentlemen:

I appreciate this opportunity to speak to you about polio and the effort which the March of Dimes is making to protect us against it. Since the March of Dimes began under the leadership of the late Franklin D. Roosevelt, the people of North Carolina have given their active support to this worthy cause. The generosity of our people is well known, and it has proved to be a good investment.

All of us remember the tragedy of the two state-wide polio epidemics in 1944 and 1948. Many of our communities and counties were hard hit by this crippling disease; and as usual, our children were the ones most often stricken. The March of Dimes meant a great deal to North Carolina during the dark days of those epidemics, and this splendid organization has worked tire-

[1] This was a state-wide broadcast originating at radio station WPTF, Raleigh.

lessly since then during other outbreaks. The record reveals that the March of Dimes has spent $6,364,000 in North Carolina on polio cases up to 1953. This means that *all* March of Dimes contributions raised in North Carolina have been made available for the care of our own polio patients. Every cent contributed to the national program to conquer this dreaded disease has been returned to our State to meet our own needs. In other words, despite the annual million dollar campaigns conducted in North Carolina for the past several years, our State has not been able to make any contributions to the National Foundation's research program.

Despite that fact, polio research is being carried on here in North Carolina. March of Dimes grants totalling over $700,000 have been made to four North Carolina institutions. During the past summer, over 30,000 children were inoculated with gamma globulin during the outbreaks of polio in Caldwell, Catawba, and Avery counties.

Today it can be said that science has made substantial progress in protecting the human body against paralytic polio. It is a fact that cases have been prevented and certain localized epidemics have actually been altered. We are entering an era of polio prevention which we sincerely hope will spell the final doom of this tragic affliction.

One of the leading factors in the prevention of polio is gamma globulin, a vital derivative which is being used in mass inoculations in many areas. Health officers have expressed the belief that this serum had a definite effect in reducing incidence of paralytic polio among those inoculated.

In 1954, as part of the new Polio Prevention Program, the National Foundation plans at least to double, or perhaps triple, the amount of gamma globulin available to the Nation and to North Carolina. This alone will cost $19,000,000 in March of Dimes funds, a figure which is more than all the appropriations for research from 1938 through 1952.

It has just been announced that a new vaccine will be introduced against polio in 1954. This is a trial vaccine and it may or may not be the answer to polio. So far, it has passed all of its preliminary laboratory tests. Starting in February somewhere in the South, the National Foundation will begin the tremendous task of vaccinating from 500,000 to 1,000,000 school children in 200 communities with this new vaccine.

If the vaccine proves effective, the conquest of polio may become a reality.

This is encouraging news for every parent in North Carolina. We can all help in this crucial campaign to make the prevention of polio a reality. I am confident that the people of North Carolina will continue their generous support of the March of Dimes. All of the dimes and dollars we can spare are needed to give the research scientists the tools they need to wipe out this crippler of mankind. Let us give generously as an expression of thanks for the progress already made and as evidence of our faith in the ultimate success of polio prevention. Thank you.

FREEDOM OF THE PRESS

ADDRESS DELIVERED AT THE CONFERENCE OF FREEDOM OF INFORMATION OF THE NORTH CAROLINA PRESS ASSOCIATION
RALEIGH
January 14, 1954

Ladies and Gentlemen:

I appreciate this opportunity to appear briefly on your program sponsored by the Freedom of Information Committee of the North Carolina Associated Press members. The subject of this Conference is a basic one in our government and way of life. Your genuine interest in the freedom of speech and the freedom of the press is a demonstration of good citizenship which is worthy of hearty commendation. This Conference is also in keeping with the best traditions of our Republic and, in itself, is an example of the subject which we discuss. If our forefathers had not wisely provided for these freedoms, perhaps we would not be meeting here today.

The right of free speech and a free press are inseparable and serve as twin guarantees of our freedom, having their roots embedded in the fundamental law of our land. These rights have withstood the storms of violence and abuse throughout our history and they have served as firm foundations upon which we have built this Nation.

Lenin, the father of Communism, once said, "Why should freedom of speech and the press be allowed? Why should a government which is doing what it believes to be right allow itself to be questioned? Ideas are more fatal things than guns. Why should any man be allowed to buy a printing press and disseminate opinions calculated to embarrass the government?" This has always been the view of a totalitarian state. On the other hand, Thomas Jefferson, one of our Nation's founders, was a consistent and active proponent of the freedom of speech and the freedom of the press. He said: "Our liberty depends on the freedom of the press and that cannot be limited without being lost. The force of public opinion cannot be resisted when permitted freely to be expressed." Jefferson also expressed the belief that "The mass of the citizens is the safest depository of their own rights." I am a firm believer that Jefferson was right. Regardless of our political philosophies, I am confident that none of us here today take exception to these basic beliefs.

Our Constitution guarantees that our Republic shall be governed by the consent of the people. This emphasizes clearly the fundamental need for an informed electorate, and free expression of public opinion. Without the unrestricted circulation of information to all the people, our Nation would never have reached its present position of greatness. The press, the radio, the periodicals, and in more recent years, television, have made it possible for our citizens to keep informed on the affairs of our government and in the day-to-day life of our people. It is difficult to describe the tremendous contribution made by the press and other media during the relatively short history of our country. We are all grateful for this contribution, however, and realize more than ever the difficulty of keeping informed in the fast-moving affairs of today.

We all agree, of course, that public business should be conducted in the open. A citizen has the recognized and legitimate right to know the results of deliberation, decisions, and official actions of those entrusted with the responsibility, duty, and power of public office. We who hold public office are indeed servants of the people and have the responsibility of performing our duties faithfully and honestly. There will always be a variance of opinion at times between the press and some public agency, or public official as to the proper interpretation of press coverage. I am sure that when such differences arise in North Carolina we can settle them in a reasonable and sensible manner.

Under our form of government, the basic rights which we have carry with them a responsibility. This is certainly true as to freedom of speech and freedom of the press. It is the duty of all of us to safeguard these freedoms. The press, radio, television and other means of communication are naturally regarded as guardians of these freedoms. They must follow carefully, yet firmly, the delicate line between reporting and interpretation in their news columns. The public depends upon the high quality of their skill for correct information. When the press and other means of communication fail to measure up to this responsibility, the freedom of speech and the press are endangered, and the public suffers injury. On the other hand, when news gathering organizations present accurate, unbiased news, free of slanted and unfair inferences, they increase the respect and support of everyone for the freedom of speech and the press. Every reporter, every radio commentator, every editor, and every person who appears on television and, in fact, every speaker, has a serious responsibility for the manner in which he protects the very right which he uses, to the end that all citizens may be properly informed and make decisions based upon accurate and reliable information.

I wish for you every success in the deliberations of your Conference and I hope that the results will be of lasting benefit not only to all who participate but to all of the citizens of North Carolina. I earnestly ask for your continued devotion to the development of North Carolina, and for your continued contributions toward the stable thinking of our people.

WHAT IS GOOD FOR ANY LOCALITY IS GOOD FOR THE STATE

Address[1] Delivered Before A Meeting of the Representatives of the Northwest North Carolina Development Association, Incorporated

Raleigh

January 21, 1954

Mr. Davis, Mr. Douglas, Ladies and Gentlemen:

I am very grateful to Mr. Douglas for his very generous introduction. I'm very happy to come over here this morning and welcome you to Raleigh, and very briefly to express my appreciation for what you have started. I think the spontaneous, voluntary organization of your group, designated as you have designated it—the Northwest North Carolina Development Association, Incorporated—is a splendid idea. I think the four things which you have determined to be your prime objectives—the further development of agriculture, of industry, of recreation and tourists, of community development—are four very fine objectives. If you can make a reasonable contribution toward each of those four objectives, you will have made a permanent contribution, not only to the nine counties embraced in your Association, but also to the State of North Carolina.

Let me say something to you which I am undertaking to say whenever I have an opportunity. The time has come in this State when every citizen of every county should, and must, understand that whatever is good for his locality and for his county, is good for the State in the final analysis; and that every contribution made to the development of North Carolina, along whatever line it may be, makes a contribution to the development of the entire State. That's one reason that I'm so glad that you have organized this Association.

---

[1] These representatives gathered in Raleigh to hear officials of the Department of Conservation and Development, the Department of Agriculture, North Carolina State College and others outline steps in a program for the general development of a nine-county (Ashe, Alleghany, Davie, Forsyth, Stokes, Surry, Watauga, Wilkes and Yadkin) area of the State. Mr. Ben E. Douglas, Director of the Department of Conservation and Development, arranged the meeting, and Mr. Archie K. Davis of Winston-Salem, gave the general objectives of the group which was formed "to promote the industrial, agricultural, and recreational welfare of the northwest. . . ."

Now the objectives which you have set for yourselves will not be attained in a week, nor a month, nor a year, nor in three years, nor in a decade. You have simply determined to do a little more about these problems, in a more effective manner, than could be done without your co-operative effort. I know something about the counties involved in this Association, and something about the citizenship. I agree with Mr. Douglas that there is no finer productive labor on earth than we have in North Carolina. The citizenship of the counties composing this Association is not only patriotic, but it is intelligent, and by proper planning I think it can achieve tremendous results; results which will help your respective counties and communities, and which, I repeat, will result in a tremendous contribution to North Carolina.

The idea of the nine counties appeals to me. When you, for instance, hear of an industry which one county may have an opportunity to get, and if it develops, when all of the surveys have been made and the data has been collected, that that isn't the place for that particular industry, then let me remind you that it will also help your community if you in turn go to another place somewhere in your area that has the particular things that the particular industry must have, even if your community does not have it. That is what we have got to do all over the State. Call upon the Board of Conservation and Development. Call upon the North Carolina Employment Service. Call upon any department of the State, Mr. Davis, that this Association feels can give it any information—can give it any assistance—and I am quite certain that the response will not only be prompt, but that it will be cheerful and willing. If it is not, you let me know and I will see if I cannot help you about it. I am quite certain that all departments of the government will be delighted to co-operate with you in every way that they can.

Now let me thank you again for coming. I think that the fact that so many of you have come here on a day like this is evidence of your determination not just to set up this organization on paper, but I think that it is evidence of your determination to make it really work in the counties embraced in this Association. I hope, as Mr. Douglas said, that it will be an incentive to other areas of this State to organize similar associations and to press toward the attainment of the objectives as rapidly as they can. There are plenty of things that can be done in a few weeks and in a few years. All of it can be done. But we are constantly reminded that in these days of changing conditions, it requires all that we can do, all of us, day by day, not only in our respective jobs, but in our efforts to make some worthwhile contribution to the State that we love, from which we all have received so much. If you will bear that in mind in your deliberations and in your efforts, if you will continually undertake to do something for North Carolina, you will be doing it when you do something for your own community and for your own county.

Again, thank you for coming, and thank you for giving me the opportunity to come over here and meet with you. If, along the line anywhere you find that I can help you, let me know. I will be happy to do it. Thank you.

RESPONSIBILITY OF THE JUDICIARY

Address Delivered On Presenting Maurice Victor Barnhill As Chief Justice of the North Carolina Supreme Court
Raleigh
February 1, 1954

May It Please The Court:

Twenty-seven years ago a young solicitor of the Tenth Judicial District and a judge of the Superior Court, during the noon recess on the first day of a criminal term, were walking down the steps of the courthouse in Durham. The solicitor said to the judge, "I would like to know what your attitude will be towards accepting recommendations of the solicitor in the disposition of cases on the docket." The judge did not stop walking. His answer was, "That will depend in each case upon the recommendation." I was the solicitor, the man I am presenting as Chief Justice of the Supreme Court of North Carolina was the presiding judge. His answer to that question was typical of the man and his record as a jurist and, although he never failed to accept a recommendation made by me to him in the succeeding years during my term as solicitor, I always knew that he would not hesitate to do so if he did not, with confidence, feel that the recommendation was correct. I knew that day that I had met, and was dealing with, a man who understood the high responsibility of his office, and that he was willing to trust the discharge of his obligation to another only if consistent with his own ideas of justice and fairness.

A few years later, fate led me into other branches of public service but the judge stayed upon the bench, studying the law, increasing his knowledge of people and of the complex questions with which the courts had to deal. Specially difficult assignments were given him by succeeding governors until July 1, 1937, when he was appointed by a great governor as an associate justice of the Supreme Court of North Carolina in which capacity he has served with distinction. He has a fine legal mind which, incisively and quickly, cuts through the form and finds the substance. His opinions are clear— in simple language. He inspires confidence and respect. Although not robust in body, he has an indomitable will power. Soft-spoken and gentle, he is also firm and forcible. Patient and tolerant, yet he is always courageous. He is a churchman without hypocrisy, and a devoted student of the law, with a passion that the supremacy of the law shall be maintained and that the rights and individual liberties of men, under the law, shall be preserved without fear or favor.

In my inaugural address I stated, "The profound respect which the people have always had for our courts and judicial system has been a powerful factor for good in the life of our State." This has resulted largely from the character and the ability of those who have administered our laws. I have undertaken to remember the high and tremendous responsibility placed upon the Chief Executive of this State in the selection of our judicial officers. I had this in mind when I was faced with the duty of naming a new Chief Justice, rather than the matter of his seniority. He will, in my judgment, as a man and as the chief judicial officer of our State, measure up to the highest traditions of this great

Photo Courtesy Herald Sun

Adlai E. Stevenson visits Governor Umstead, March 23, 1954. *Left to right:* Governor Umstead; Edward L. Rankin, Jr., private secretary to Governor Umstead; and Governor Stevenson.

Court, and will leave for all time to come, in his acts and decisions, a worthwhile contribution to the people of our State.

The solicitor who asked the judge the question on the courthouse steps in Durham in July, 1927, now as the Governor of the State of North Carolina, has the honor and the personal pleasure of presenting the judge to whom the question was asked to this Court as its next Chief Justice of the Supreme Court of North Carolina, Honorable Maurice Victor Barnhill.

THE NEED FOR AIDING THE SICK, THE HUNGRY, AND THE DISTRESSED

ADDRESS DELIVERED AT THE ORGANIZATIONAL MEETING OF THE RED CROSS IN THE HALL OF THE HOUSE OF REPRESENTATIVES

RALEIGH

February 8, 1954

Ladies and Gentlemen:

Thank you for this opportunity to speak briefly to this gathering of public-spirited citizens who have assembled here today to complete plans for the 1954 Red Cross Campaign for members and funds. I regret that I shall not be able to attend your luncheon at 1:30 today at the Raleigh Woman's Club, but I do welcome this opportunity to bring you a personal word of greetings and best wishes. I once served as chairman of the Red Cross Chapter in Durham and I know from firsthand experience some of your accomplishments as well as some of your problems.

The ravages, bitterness, and cruelty of war never have been able to destroy the humane instincts of mankind, and the present tense, uncertain condition of world affairs has not diminished the need for aiding the sick, the hunger-stricken and the distressed. Many of the nations of the earth recognized long ago the necessity of having some international organization prompted solely by its desire to serve humanity, available in times of emergency and calamity. Therefore, the Treaty of the Red Cross was promulgated at Geneva in 1864 and ratified by the United States in 1882.

The Congress of the United States in 1905 granted to the American Red Cross the charter under which it now operates, defined its powers and provided for the permanent management of its affairs.

Its emblem which is a Greek Red Cross on a white ground, is known all over the world. Its cross of red carries a message which has soothed and eased the pain and suffering of mankind since the day the supreme sacrifice on the Cross on the Hill of Golgotha gave to the world the hope of earthly freedom and the immortality of the soul.

The main purposes of the Red Cross in time of war are to assist men and women in the services and their families; to furnish voluntary aid to the sick and wounded and to prisoners of war; and, above all, to keep alive in the minds and hearts of men the elements of service, love and mercy.

Its purposes in time of peace are to assist the widows and orphans of servicemen; assist veterans in their dealings with the government; work with the various veterans' organizations in our country; aid and assist in recreation, entertainment and rehabilitation of those in veterans' hospitals; develop through the Junior Red Cross the idea of community and humane service in the minds and hearts of the youth of our country; prepare for and continue to carry on the system of national and international relief in such emergencies as pestilence, famine, fire, flood, and other calamities.

The Red Cross is a non-profit, non-political, and non-sectarian organization, and depends upon public contributions for existence. Wherever the fortunes of war or peace carry men, the Red Cross is there. Wherever local, state or international calamities occur, the Red Cross is there. It renders a personal service. It serves all races and denominations. It knows no creed except the doctrine of mercy. On its far-flung fronts of activity, both at home and abroad, it seeks to comfort, assist and serve those in distress. It is one of the greatest human service organizations in existence.

North Carolina is proud of its participation in Red Cross activities and its many contributions to the growth of Red Cross. This great humanitarian organization is a reliable and hard-working agency through which the people of our State, our Nation, and the world can be served, whether they are across the street, across the State, or across the ocean. People have learned that through Red Cross the goodness and generosity of the individual gathers force and effectiveness.

This spirit of being a good neighbor to all people in distress or trouble has won for the Red Cross a place of respect and honor in the minds and hearts of the people of North Carolina. Citizens of this State contributed last year 82,000 pints of blood to the Red Cross blood program, one of the most vital responsibilites which the Red Cross has undertaken to accept. Although half of the blood contributed by North Carolinians last year was turned over to the use of the National Defense Department, some of this miraculous fluid was processed into gamma globulin which was used in last summer's epidemics in Caldwell, Catawba, and Avery counties. Meanwhile, Home Service workers in the 121 Red Cross Chapters in North Carolina carried on their work each day helping in problems and emergencies affecting the welfare of veterans, servicemen and their families. Working with Red Cross Field directors at military installations throughout the world, these chapters maintain a direct link with our young men and women in service and their folks back home. The Red Cross stands ready and prepared to deal with disasters wherever they occur.

I commend each and every one of you who have a part in the work of the Red Cross. No one can truly evaluate the blessings we all receive from its far-flung program. I know I speak for the people of North Carolina when I say that we are all grateful for the Red Cross, its officers, staff, field personnel, and its many generous volunteer workers. I wish for all of you and for the Red Cross every success during 1954 and the years ahead.

THE BIRTH OF THE NATION AND THE DEMOCRATIC PARTY

ADDRESS[1] DELIVERED IN INTRODUCING
GOVERNOR ADLAI E. STEVENSON
CHARLOTTE
April 2, 1954

Mr. Chairman, Governor Stevenson, Ladies and Gentlemen:

When Thomas Jefferson, the founder of the Democratic Party, wrote the Declaration of Independence, he expressed, in simple and beautiful language, the passion for individual liberty which had developed through the years in the minds and in the hearts of the men of that day. Upon the signing of the Declaration, a Nation was born. The Democratic Party was there at the time of its birth.

When the Constitution of the United States was being worked out, the influence and the principles of the Democratic Party were there. Upon its adoption, the Republic came into existence, guaranteeing individual liberty to all the citizens; guaranteeing the collective freedom of our citizens which is our national security, and preserving the rights of the states. Since that time the Democratic Party, in season and out of season, in victory and defeat, has guarded well the rights and the individual liberties, under the law, of the people of the United States.

In 1952 the Democratic Party nominated a great American to carry its banner. He ran that race like the thoroughbred which he was. (Applause) . He accepted his defeat like the fine sportsman that he is. Then, and since that time, when chaos and confusion reigns within the ranks of the party in control, he speaks with a clarity and a courage that is the principle of the Democratic Party, with a brilliance that has not been excelled, and seldom equalled. They, and all of us, are proud of him. We welcome him to North Carolina, and now I present to you, Governor Adlai Stevenson.

---

[1] This address was delivered at the State Democratic Rally held at the Armory Auditorium, Charlotte. Mr. James J. Harris was general chairman of the rally and presided at the meeting. Mr. Everett Jordan, Chairman, State Democratic Executive Committee, introduced Governor Umstead, who in turn introduced Governor Stevenson.

NORTH CAROLINA TESTS WEIGHTS AND MEASURES

ADDRESS DELIVERED AT THE DEDICATION OF A BUILDING HOUSING THE CALIBRATING APPARATUS AND LABORATORIES FOR TESTING WEIGHTS AND MEASURES

RALEIGH

April 8, 1954

The need for the erection of this building is expressed in the Uniform Weights and Measures Law of this State, which reads in part as follows: *G. S.,* Sec. 81-9. "The State Superintendent of Weights and Measures or his deputies or inspectors at his direction, shall, upon written request of any citizen, firm, or corporation, or educational institution in the State, test or calibrate weights, measures and weighing or measuring devices used as standards in the State." Therefore, due to a lack of facilities to carry out the mandates of the law, in the fall of 1951, the State Superintendent of Weights and Measures, with the Commissioner of Agriculture and a committee appointed by the Oil Jobbers Association presented the situation to the Assistant Director of the Budget and later to the Council of State. The Council of State unanimously approved of the building of a Calibrating Station and the Superintendent was instructed to proceed with plans accordingly.

It developed, however, before final plans were completed, that the Dawson Street Highway Project would make it necessary for the Gasoline and Oil Laboratories to vacate their quarters, and as a consequence, laboratory space was added to the Calibrating Station project. Thus, it is that the calibrating apparatus and the laboratories are housed in this one building.

I would now like to take a few minutes to enumerate quickly the facilities which are housed in this building and to say that we are proud of them. Here before you are automatic print-ticket gravimetric scales, and automatic print-ticket volumetric measuring devices (known as meters), with numerous attachments which remove, as much as possible, all human errors in the calibration of weights or measures. These scales are so arranged as to record the total weight of a vehicle, or to record the weight of each individual axle or a combination of axles. It is my understanding that no such installation has ever been made in the United States or in the world.

The main use for these scales will be to double check, by weight, the volumetric calibration of vehicle tanks, which means that if the meter reading should be in error, the scales will detect it, and vice versa. We have here liquid measures ranging from one-tenth of a grain to 1,000 pounds, (and incidentally there are 7,000 grains to a pound). We have scales ranging in capacity from 1 milligram to 170 tons, or 340,000 pounds, with a sensitivity of 1/2000th part of an ounce on the small scale and 2 pounds on the large one. We also have test weights equal to 60,000 pounds.

In the laboratory you will see equipment for testing electric meters, gasoline meters, and water meters, and provers for testing vapor meters. You will also see calorimeters for determining the B.T.U. content of fuels and apparatus for analyzing lubricating oils, and for determining the octane rating of gasoline, the antiknock rating of diesel fuel, and the testing of kerosene for adulteration and flash point, in addition to apparatus for making other tests dealing with motor fuels. Also we have in this "Calibrateum" equipment for testing accuracy of both liquid and vapor meters which will be used in the measuring of liquefied petroleum gas. We have means for determining the load-bearing strength of concrete block, the safety of tobacco curers, the calibration of surveyor's chains and steel tapes, and expect to have in the very near future, equipment for calibrating measuring devices and tanks used in the distribution of anhydrous ammonia and other liquid fertilizers. To sum up, we have, or expect to have everything needed to carry out the mandates of the law. We hope that before you leave, you will go through the laboratories and observe for yourself that we are adequately equipped to render the service which the law requires, and we want you to ask the personnel any questions which may be of special interest to you.

Now without further ado, I hereby declare this Calibrating Station to be formally open for the purpose of rendering service to the people of the great State of North Carolina.

NATURAL AND HUMAN RESOURCES

ADDRESS[1] DELIVERED BEFORE THE FIFTY-EIGHTH CONVENTION OF THE NORTH CAROLINA BANKERS' ASSOCIATION
PINEHURST
May 11, 1954

Mr. President, Mr. MacLean, Ladies and Gentlemen:

I am deeply indebted to my splendid friend for his kind and generous introduction. It might be of interest to you to relate one incident in connection with this young man and the bank he represents. In 1924 it was my privilege to manage the campaign of his illustrious father in my county when he was candidate for governor in the primary. Twenty years later Hector MacLean, son of a governor, managed my campaign in his county. I doubt if such a thing has happened many times in the history of North Carolina.

I am very happy to be here this morning, not only to pay personally and officially my respects to the great banking industry in North Carolina but also because one of my friends of many years, since 1912 at Chapel Hill, John P. Stedman, is your outgoing president; and also because your incoming president, Honorable Edwin Pate of Laurinburg, is not only a fine friend of mine but has made many great contributions to the development of our State. I am very happy to have had the privilege of listening to the very fine oration of the young lady from Mecklenburg; and, I can say to you gentlemen, and you can pass it on to your sons, that I am afraid I have witnessed this morning another field in which the women have attained supremacy, that of oratory. Having at times in my younger days been interested at frequent intervals in this business of oratory, and since listening to her this morning, I have just about concluded that the worst spot on a program in any convention would be to have to follow her.

I do not have a manuscript; I don't have any notes. I shall speak to you very briefly because I came down here primarily to see you, to talk with you, to shake hands with many of you again

[1] This address was delivered extemporaneously and the copy we have was taken from a stenographic record.

for the first time in about a year and a half or two years. I understand you are having a great convention and I am delighted. Now, with your permission let me talk about North Carolina just a few moments, as the young lady talked about Mecklenburg. When she talked about Mecklenburg she was talking about North Carolina, because it's a very important part of our State. Her description of "The Big Change" was a wonderful thing. I know that every one of you who heard her must have been tremendously impressed. Your Association through the leadership of John Stedman is to be congratulated for sponsoring this contest all over the State, letting people know how far we have come in the first half of this generation. But we can't stop there; we must consider how far we yet have to go.

Here in North Carolina we have two great resources—human resources and natural resources. We are undertaking to do much for our human resources, as we should, because our human resources are our greatest asset. We must have good schools, we must have hospitals; we must have mental institutions; we must have public health services; we must have welfare services; we must have the churches from which we obtain our spiritual inspiration. We must have everything, if you please, that goes into the making of the character and the life of a real man and woman. That is the development of our greatest resource. Now, to do that we must conserve, use and develop to the greatest extent our natural resources. That is what Miss Davis was telling you about this morning; she was relating to you the story of the simultaneous development of both.

Here in North Carolina we have a heritage equal to that of people anywhere. Since the War Between the States we have had a hard struggle, but now we have come a long way and we can see the milestones of progress which we have made. Now, all of these things that develop our human resources cost money. If we are to improve our school system, if we are to improve our mental health program, if we are to improve our over-all health program in North Carolina, and our public health program, the medical care program, if we are to improve our welfare program in the State, if we are to do all of those things which build the life of men and women, we must constantly have more money. Where is it coming from? It must come from our natural resources; it must come from the brains of our people applied to the use of what we have; it must come from a diversified and improved agriculture which today, perhaps, if I may be bold enough to say so in the face of the splendid report rendered by your agricultural committee, perhaps the greatest need in the field of agriculture—and not confined to that in North Carolina—is scientific research. We must improve our farm income; we must improve our per capita income throughout the structure of our State; we must have good roads; we must conserve, protect and free our water supply from as much pollution as possible. Sound agricultural practices and soil conservation not only prevent fertility from washing away from the hills of the farmer but it keeps the reservoirs which supply your towns and cities from filling up. Soil conservation, water conservation and water purification is the business of all the people of North Carolina and not just the farmer.

We must do all that we can to develop our ports and encourage more trade in and with the commerce of the world. We must develop our fishing industry, develop our tourist industry to a larger and more effective degree, both in the east and west, in the Piedmont and in these Sandhills. The State has been blessed with almost any kind of recreation or scenic beauty which could be desired by our tourists. We must develop our tremendous industrial opportunities. All of it involves our natural resources.

There was a time when North Carolina didn't have any money, when we had to rely upon outside funds for the development of our State. Those of you who are here this morning know that that day is past.

That brings me to one point I wish to emphasize: We are not only interested in these things about which I have been speaking, we are not only interested in obtaining new and diversified industry in North Carolina, but we are also interested in the development of local industries, of the expansion of industries we already have. In both of these two fields the services of the bankers of North Carolina are absolutely essential. It is just as necessary, if you will permit me to say so, for you to look with favor and undertake to help a wise, sound venture with the funds which belong to the depositors of your bank as it is for you to say "No" to an obviously unsound venture. You are not only the trustees of the funds placed in your care, but along with it, in my judgment and from my experience with banks, you have an additional responsibility—that is, in the use, protection and conservation of those funds, you have a duty to develop the community in which you live, and I know in my time the bankers of North Carolina have understood and performed this duty to a high degree.

Now then, during the past year and a half the number of speeches I could make have been greatly reduced and along with it—for which many people have no doubt given thanks—the length of my speeches has necessarily been reduced. I therefore, now, have about reached my ten minutes; but I wish to close by telling you this: We have everything in North Carolina to make the next fifty years as great as the last fifty years have been. We have a fine base upon which to build. Our people are patriotic, courageous, energetic, looking for adventure and opportunity, and that's what this land offers you. Let us try to keep here in the State more of our young men and women; let's give them an opportunity here to work out their great adventure of life, their opportunity, which to me is a much greater word than "security." There is no substitute for opportunity; no security is so great as opportunity. Let's see to it that young men and women in North Carolina have an opportunity here where they have lived and grown up and been educated, have that opportunity for that "adventure" in North Carolina. Co-operate with your respective communities all over this State, with the Chambers of Commerce and industrial groups, with agriculture, with everything that contributes to the over-all economic and spiritual and human welfare of North Carolina. It is all one state although we have a hundred counties. If you live in a town and you think you can get an industry and you try and you don't have something the industry wants, please let the Department of Conservation and Development in Raleigh or me know about it; let's help some place in North Carolina get it, if we can. Let's realize that what affects the development of Cherokee County also affects the development of Currituck County, that a three-cent sales tax collected in Brunswick County helps the public schools in Ashe County. Let us realize, all of us, that there is a oneness of purpose and a oneness in reality about this thing that we call "North Carolina" which we all love and which we want to see during the next fifty years outstrip the progress of "The Big Change."

You can help! I beg of you to do it. Thank you very much.

LIBRARIES ARE A PART OF OUR EDUCATIONAL SYSTEM

ADDRESS[1] DELIVERED AT THE DEDICATION OF THE PUBLIC LIBRARY
CANTON
June 21, 1954

Ladies and Gentlemen:

I am deeply grateful to my friend, Mr. Reuben B. Robertson, for his very generous and kind introduction, and I am very glad that I can be in Canton and in Haywood County today. It's a long way from here to Raleigh, but I think all of us down there should come up here occasionally and just see again what a fine part of North Carolina this section is. Furthermore, I think it would be good for those of you who live here likewise to visit the eastern part of North Carolina when you have an opportunity, because since I've been Governor, I've been trying to say that all parts of this State are great, that all parts of this State are important, and that when something is done that helps one section, it also helps all other sections. So I am delighted for that reason and many others to be here on this auspicious occasion.

I have no manuscript. I have no prepared speech. I came here to pay my respects to one of America's and North Carolina's greatest citizens, the gentleman who introduced me, Mr. Reuben B. Robertson. I came here to say to you who are his friends and neighbors that his contributions over the years to this State and this Nation, as well as to this community, have been great and continuous. I come to thank him personally for all that he has

---

[1] Brandon P. Hodges presided at this meeting and Reverend W. Harold Groce, pastor, Central Methodist Church, Canton, pronounced the invocation. Reuben B. Robertson introduced Governor Umstead.

meant to me since I became Governor—for his support, for his advice, for his willingness always to help my administration.

I would also like to pay my respects to Brandon P. Hodges, who, with the consent of the company for which he works, came to Raleigh last Fall and devoted seven weeks assisting in putting over the bond issue of this State for better mental hospitals and mental care and better school facilities. So I am indebted to the company which has made this occasion possible today.

I understand that the first public library was opened in Canton in 1937 in one room provided by the Freel Furniture Company for that purpose. And many citizens were interested in it, and that probably through the years the one organization that may have done more than any other is the Canton Women's Club.

A library is a great institution. You heard the bit of poetry that Mr. Robertson cited with reference to books. Truly all that he said is more than true. Books give us information as to what people in the past have done; books give us inspiration as to what we should try to do; books are the gateway to all the accumulated information of all the times since civilization began; books and the secrets they reveal become the working tools of the man who uses them for a better life, and for better living.

This great library that you are today dedicating is a tribute not only to Mr. Reuben B. Robertson, who gave the lot, but to his son and to those who operate the Champion Foundation, who gave this fine building for this library. It will stand here for many years as a tribute to the farsightedness and wisdom and devoted public service of every person who had a hand not only in this lot, but in developing a spirit in the town of Canton which has moved men and women to be willing to work and toil and sacrifice in order that you might have a library. Had it not been for all their work, I am quite sure that no one would have been willing to have built the library building, because a mere building would not have accomplished the purpose.

I suppose that for generations to come that your children and their children will come here to this building seeking information, seeking truth, seeking inspiration and seeking that which points to straight thinking and right living. After all, whatever we do that fails to point in those two directions perhaps fails basically. This library, the books that will be in it, point in both of those directions. They say to all of us that what our forefathers did, what men before them did, in creating principles of right living and straight thinking are still sound. The contents of these books say more than that to us, however; they say to us that any citizen who has enjoyed the fruits of their labor or those who have worked in the past have an obligation to those that come in the future.

Someone said once that civilization is a contract between the living and the dead. There is a lot in that; a contract though, which has to be mainly kept and carried out by the living; a responsibility to those that have gone before and a responsibility to those who shall come after. The philosophy finds itself working in every phase of human activity—in business, in religion, in education, in commerce, in all things that keep the tide of civilization moving onward and upward. And so, I am happy to be here today, to have a part in something which means so much to North Carolina, not only from the standpoint of the encouragement of cultural matters, but also in the very practical way libraries are a part of any real educational system. This will mean a great thing not only to Canton, but all of this county, because anything which builds and improves the cultural citizenship in one section, not only helps the county, but as I said in the beginning, helps the entire State of North Carolina.

Many of us believe that we have come a long way in this State and that we have a long way to go. We have to depend upon the fine type of citizens which we find all over this State to conserve and use not only our human resources, but to do likewise with our natural resources, to include everything we have so that they will mean more to the children who shall come after us. And so it is that this library is a part of that great scheme of building, a part of developing and improving. I congratulate the town of Canton. I congratulate the Champion Foundation. I congratulate every man and woman in this town who has put forth any effort in connection with this beautiful library and those years of toil which have led up to it today. And I congratulate again Mr. Reuben B. Robertson, already referred to as an industrial statesman, justly so, for his farsightedness in all matters pertaining to the welfare of his community, his State and Nation.

Now, ladies and gentlemen, I am glad to be back in Canton. I feel that this is one of the friendliest places I know. I came through here one afternoon on my way to Cherokee a few years ago and had left all the clothes I had down at my mother-in-law's in Rutherford County, except the pants I had on. I went to one of your shops up here on your Main Street, and I believe the name of the concern was Cole and Wykle—or Kykle, I've forgotten which—and I purchased there the suit of clothes which I have on now, and I can prove it to you by the label inside of the coat—and it's Wykle. I had it right the first time. They were so nice to me and helped me so much in my distress that I really felt like I ought to come back and buy a suit again from them, and I intend to do it someday.

Now then, this great community, this great industry which you have here, this great county with its diversification of agriculture and industry, all the fine things that are in this section of Western North Carolina, they impose upon you and upon me and upon every citizen of this great Western section a profound duty to use these resources to make North Carolina a better place in which to live, in which to work, in which to send your children to school, and in which to go to church. It is a happy occasion for me to be here. I congratulate all of you again and I shall look forward with real pleasure to the next opportunity which I shall have to visit you again. Thank you very much.

OUR HERITAGE GIVES US INSPIRATION, COURAGE, AND FAITH

ADDRESS [1] DELIVERED AT THE DEDICATION OF THE WACHOVIA MUSEUM AT OLD SALEM
WINSTON-SALEM
September 18, 1954

Mr. Chairman, Mr. Gray, Dr. Rondthaler, Mr. Morehead, the other distinguished gentlemen who attended school in this building, Mr. Mayor, Ladies and Gentlemen:

It is indeed a pleasure for me to have the opportunity of being here with you this morning for this auspicious occasion. I extend my congratulations, thanks, and compliments to all of those who

[1] This speech was transcribed from a tape recording made by Radio Station WSJS, Winston-Salem, North Carolina.

have contributed either money, talent, or time towards the restoration project we witness here today.

North Carolina is a mixture of the old and the new. It seems to me somehow that down through the years we have been able, with a pride of heritage, to keep our feet firmly planted upon the solid soil of the times that are past and at the same time our eyes upon the goal of the progress of civilization. It has been said that civilization itself is a covenant between the dead, the living, and the yet unborn. Here today we perhaps are in the middle of that covenant.

For some two hundred years the Moravians who settled in this area and their descendants have poured into the life stream of North Carolina, this Nation, and the world, something of strength, sturdiness, integrity, hope, faith, and courage, which have contributed mightily to the development of this Commonwealth and to this Republic.

This great institution, by its instruction to the womanhood of North Carolina, has also made a powerful contribution to the welfare of this State. We cannot live in the past but we glory in our heritage. And from the past and from that heritage we must always draw inspiration, courage, and faith, without which people perish and republics die; without which dictators control mankind and the thinking of men and women.

So we come today to dedicate—or rather to open—the first of the restored buildings in this marvelous project, which will mean when completed, not just a local matter but much to all of the State and to the people of this country. As we open this restored building today and as we think of its history, of the men who went to school here and their contribution towards making our lives richer and more meaningful, let us think of it as a source of endless inspiration, a source of faith, a source of renewed dedication to all of the things for which those who have used this building through the years have so firmly stood—in the building of character, in the building of lives of men and women, in the building of a state, and in the building of a republic. And let us hope that it stands here for generations to come to serve our children and their children and remind them that there is no substitute for truth, that there is no substitute for rugged honesty or honest toil, to remind them that it will require tomorrow the same elements of character to make a great world and keep it free that it required yesterday; and as we pass today, as those of you who have contributed to this great program are undertaking to keep the covenant between those who have gone and those who are to come, let all of us rededicate ourselves to those principles and let us more fully carry out our part of the contract.

Now, ladies and gentlemen, at the request of the committee, it is an honor for me and a pleasure, as Governor of North Carolina, to cut the ribbon which will officially open the first of the restored buildings in this marvelous project that you call "Old Salem."

PUBLIC SERVICE FOR MANKIND

ADDRESS[1] DELIVERED AT THE DEDICATION OF THE COOPER MEMORIAL HEALTH BUILDING RALEIGH

September 25, 1954

Dr. Dixon, Ladies and Gentlemen:

It is a pleasure and an honor for me as Governor of North Carolina to be permitted to have a part in this program this morning to do honor to a man who gave his life, literally, that others might live and live more abundantly, live longer and be more healthy.

It has been said that no man comes to true greatness who has not felt in some degree that his life belongs to his race, and that what God has given him, He has given him for all mankind. Dr. George M. Cooper's life, I think, was a fine illustration of just what those lines mean. He worked day and night, sometimes without many tools, often with but little encouragement, to help

[1] Dr. George Marion Cooper (April 24, 1876-December 18, 1950), was born in Sampson County. He graduated from the Medical College of Virginia in 1905 and practiced medicine in Clinton until 1911. During this period Dr. Cooper was interested in preventive medicine and served on a part-time basis as county physician for Sampson County. In 1913, he became Superintendent of Health on a full-time basis. Because of his work with that county, which was recognized throughout the State, he was called to the staff of the North Carolina State Board of Health as head of the Department of Rural Sanitation. He served the State Board of Health in various capacities during the remainder of his life, winning many honors and recognitions throughout the country for his devoted public service.

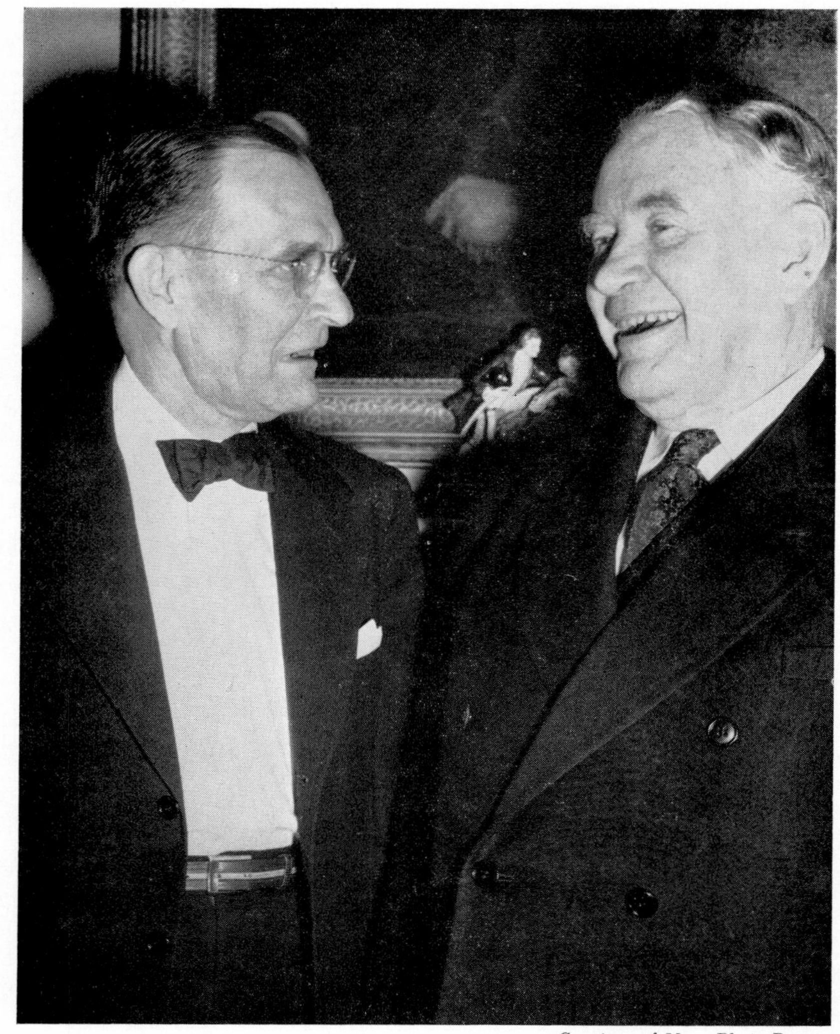

Courtesy of Muse Photo Bureau

Governor Umstead (*left*) and Senator Alben W. Barkley, Washington, D. C., April 26, 1954.

the people who could not help themselves. He gave completely of what God had given him to his race. This morning North Carolina can be proud that it has produced men like Dr. Cooper to develop one of the finest public health systems to be found in the country, to develop preventive medicine and the practice of those things which are conducive to the prevention of disease among our people.

This is neither the time nor the place, and I am not the person, to dwell long upon the efficiency and the accomplishments of the public health program in North Carolina over the years, but having been permitted once to serve for a few years as a member of a local health board, I think I know what it has meant to the people of this State. Here, then, this morning we accomplish two things: We pay honor to a person who gave his life to his people and to his State, and we open a great building equipped far beyond the dream, I suppose, of Dr. Cooper when he began public health work in North Carolina.

This new building, I am sure, will not only be a symbol of the confidence of the people of North Carolina in the public health system of the State, but I think it will be more than that. It will be a recognition of what men like Dr. Cooper accomplished, a recognition of what men like Dr. Norton and his associates are now doing, a recognition of the work of the members of the board of public health, and it will stand there through the years as a challenge to all who shall come after us, that they too shall make a contribution to the welfare of the people.

I suppose there is nothing truer than the statement that nothing is worth much to an individual without health and without faith. With health and faith, we can go a long way toward making North Carolina a more wholesome, a safer, a more healthy, a happier, and a more prosperous place in which to live. I, therefore, am glad to have the opportunity of paying my tribute, along with you, to Dr. Cooper, of paying my respects to those who now are charged with the responsibility of carrying out a program of public health and preventive medicine in North Carolina, and to express my thanks to the members of that board and all of those health officers and assistants all over the State who make a contribution to the effectiveness of our great program of public health. Thank you.

STATEMENTS AND ARTICLES FOR THE PRESS

GOVERNOR UMSTEAD AT WATTS HOSPITAL[1]

January 13, 1953

We visited Governor Umstead at Watts Hospital this afternoon and found him in good spirits and much improved. He assured us that he wants the business of the Legislature and the State to continue uninterrupted in any way by his illness. It is his intention for the report of the Advisory Budget Commission and the appropriation bills to be submitted to the General Assembly as soon at it is possible and practicable. He plans to submit his Budget Message to the General Assembly at a later date. He feels that he will be able to fulfill all the functions of his office that are necessary at this time.

THE INAUGURATION OF PRESIDENT EISENHOWER[2]

January 13, 1953

Governor Umstead today requested Lieutenant Governor Luther H. Hodges to act as his representative at the inauguration of President-elect Dwight D. Eisenhower. Governor Umstead is providing Mr. Hodges with the use of his personal car and a chauffeur to drive to Washington and represent the State at the inaugural ceremonies. Governor Umstead had planned to attend the inauguration prior to his illness.

He also announced the appointment of an Inauguration Committee from North Carolina consisting of B. Everett Jordan, State Chairman of the Democratic Executive Committee; J. M. Baley of Marshall, State Chairman of the Republican Committee, and Mr. George R. Ross, Director of the Department of Conservation and Development.

---

[1] John W. Umstead, Jr., a brother of Governor Umstead, and Edward L. Rankin, Jr., Private Secretary, visited the hospital and afterward issued from the Governor's office the statement above.

[2] The above statment was issued while Governor Umstead was a patient at Watts Hospital.

EDUCATIONAL RADIO AND TELEVISION COMMITTEE

January 16, 1953

Governor Umstead today announced the names of twelve members of the newly created State Educational Radio and Television Commission which was created by joint resolution of the Legislature on Wednesday, January 14. The Governor named Irving E. Carlyle, Winston-Salem, as Chairman. Other members are: Reuben B. Robertson, Canton; L. Y. Ballentine, Raleigh; John Harden, Greensboro; Dr. John R. Cunningham, Davidson; Mrs. J. W. Bunn, Raleigh; F. J. Blythe, Charlotte; C. McD. Davis, Wilmington; Dr. Charles F. Carroll, Raleigh; Knox Massey, Durham; James H. Clark, Elizabethtown; and William B. Rodman, Washington.

The Commission was created to study and report upon the possible uses of eight television channels which the Federal Communications Commission has allocated to North Carolina for educational purposes. Commission members are to receive no compensation except necessary expenses and are to make a report to the Governor at the earliest practical date.

In his Inaugural Address Governor Umstead said that sufficient time has not elapsed since the development of this modern method of communication to determine its probable effect in the field of individual, group or mass education. "Certainly its importance is sufficient to place upon the State, through its proper officials, the serious obligation of a thorough investigation, to the end that we may avoid, if possible, becoming involved in an unwise venture, if it is determined to be that; and, in order that we may take full advantage of an opportunity in the field of education, if it is determined to be wise and proper."

The State Educational Radio and Television Commission will hold its first organizational meeting in the Governor's office at 2 P.M. on Tuesday afternoon, February 12. Irving E. Carlyle of Winston-Salem, the Chairman and the other eleven members of the Commission will receive their formal commissions from the Governor at this time.

Following this ceremony in the Governor's office, the new Commission will begin its first public hearing in the Senate Chamber at 2:30 P.M. The hearing will cover the following considerations: (a) Existing proposals concerning the use of any or all of the eight channels allocated to North Carolina by the Federal Communications Commission until June 2, 1953. (b) The development of such plans and arrangements as may be found necessary for utilizing any or all of the channels, with particular reference to the operation and management of television facilities for educational purposes. (c) The devising of a plan for financing the arrangements set forth above.

Chairman Carlyle has written a letter to the mayors of the eight cities to which a station has been allocated and requested each of them to appoint from his community a committee on educational radio and television. These committee members have been urged to be present at the public hearing.

Representatives from education, commercial broadcasting, and from the public are invited to appear at this hearing.

Mr. Carlyle said that the Commission is making plans for a second meeting of the Commission in Raleigh about March 10 to bring the work of the Commissioner into closer focus.

APPOINTMENT OF FRANK T. ERWIN

January 28, 1953

Governor Umstead today appointed Frank T. Erwin of Durham as acting chairman of the Alcoholic Board of Control. Mr. Erwin succeeds Robert W. Winston, who has resigned.

Governor Umstead pointed out that Mr. Erwin is accepting this appointment purely as a temporary arrangement to assist the Governor in this matter at this time. It is the Governor's intention to relieve him of his duties in not more than three months.

Mr. Erwin is president and treasurer of the Erwin Oil Company of Durham. A graduate of Davidson College, he worked for Standard Oil Company for sixteen years before going into business for himself in 1945. He is a member of the Durham County Alcoholic Board of Control and formerly served on the Wildlife Resources Commission as chairman. He resigned from this Commission in 1950 to accept the ABC post in Durham.

Mr. Erwin served as Chairman of the Durham County Welfare Board for six years and was Chairman of the War Price and Rationing Board, Gas Division, in Durham during the war years. He is past president of the Kiwanis Club and past director of that organization. He is also a member of the Board of Deacons of the Watts Street Baptist Church.

The new acting chairman is married and has two sons, aged eleven and fifteen.

GOVERNOR UMSTEAD RETURNS TO THE MANSION

February 6, 1953

Governor Umstead left Watts Hospital this morning at 10:00 A.M. and came to Raleigh in his personal automobile. He was accompanied by Mrs. Umstead and his physician, Dr. R. G. Fleming of Durham.

He will continue his period of rest at the Executive Mansion under the supervision of Dr. Hubert B. Haywood of Raleigh. Dr. Fleming said that the Governor made the trip satisfactorily and that his condition is good.

Dr. Fleming plans to visit the Governor and confer with Dr. Haywood at regular intervals during his period of convalescence at the Mansion. Visitors will be restricted until further notice.

HEART FUND CAMPAIGN

February 13, 1953

It is my understanding that the annual Heart Fund Campaign in Raleigh is being launched tomorrow by the members of the Raleigh Pilot Club. I am happy to lend my support to this local effort on the part of the people of Raleigh to contribute to the constant and intensive battle which is being waged by medical science against heart disease. Statistics show that diseases of the heart are accountable for one half of all the deaths in our State. The Heart Association and its many volunteer workers are doing a great job of educating the public against the damages of heart disease and in promoting a sound program of research and community service.

LAFAYETTE MILLER CASE REVIEWED [1]

February 16, 1953

The Governor has carefully considered and reviewed the entire file in the case of Lafayette Miller and after discussing this matter fully with Mr. N. F. Ransdell, Commissioner of Paroles, he does not plan to intervene in any way with the execution of this sentence.

ENGINEERS' WEEK

February 20, 1953

It is my understanding that the week beginning February 22 and ending February 28 has been designated as Engineers' Week in North Carolina. I am happy to give my approval of this special designation honoring the great profession which has pioneered, developed, and brought to fruition many of the vast benefits of our economic, industrial and social well-being. Engineers create new industries and make new processes, products, and facilities available to business, agriculture, industry, and the public. The application of science, skill, training and experience in the hands of our professional engineers helps our modern civilization solve many of its most complex problems.

At the present time there is a national shortage of engineers and this Engineers' Week is one means of calling to the attention of all young men the many opportunities available for employment in the engineering profession. The need for engineers in industry and civilian life extends to almost every field, for

[1] Lafayette Miller, a Negro of Beaufort County, was accused of killing Harvey C. Boyd and of forcing Mrs. Boyd into the trunk of the Boyd's car and taking the car. He was tried, convicted, and sentenced to death by lethal gas. The case was appealed through the Supreme Court of North Carolina and the federal courts, and in each case the decision of the lower court was upheld. See 235 *North Carolina Reports,* p. 394.

engineering is everywhere—transportation, communications, food, clothing, and improvement of the health and environment of all mankind.

FOUR-H CLUB OPENS DOORS OF OPPORTUNITY [1]

February 26, 1953

The 4-H Club boys and girls in North Carolina will have the best wishes of all the people in our State when they mark the observance of National 4-H Club Week, March 7-15. From its first beginning here in North Carolina in 1909, the 4-H Club has grown into an organization of more than 2,000,000 farm boys and girls, which has reached into every state in this Nation and many foreign countries. It is significant that North Carolina leads all other states with more than 140,000 boys and girls enrolled in this splendid program. Many sectional and national honors have been won by North Carolina boys and girls. Still more important is the influence that 4-H work has had in the lives of our people.

In teaching better practices in agriculture and homemaking and in citizenship training and leadership development, 4-H has opened new doors of opportunities and widened the horizons of more than three million young people who have participated in the 4-H program since its beginning in North Carolina.

To these members, past and present, their parents, the local leaders, the county farm and home agents, and the leaders who have directed this program, I offer my sincere congratulations for past honors and achievements and my very best wishes for continued success and greater achievements in the future.

NATIONAL WILDLIFE WEEK

March 14, 1953

Governor William B. Umstead today announced that the week from March 15 through 21 has been designated "National Wild-

[1] This statement was issued just prior to the annual 4-H Club Week. The statement was addressed "To All North Carolina 4-H Club Members" and was sent to newspapers throughout the State.

life Week," and urged special observance of the event in North Carolina.

"In connection with placing emphasis on conserving our wildlife resources," Umstead said, "we should not overlook the importance of our other renewable natural resources, soils, forests, and waters, on which our valuable wildlife depends."

In announcing National Wildlife Week, Governor Umstead pointed out that in business value to North Carolina, nearly $100,000 is added to the State's total wealth each year. This is the amount spent annually by Tar Heel hunters and fishermen in pursuit of their favorite sport.

"In addition to the business value of wildlife," Umstead said, "there is an incalculable esthetic value. No one can place a price tag on the recreational value of our wildlife—a priceless heritage which we can cherish and utilize only as long as we give attention to conserving it and our other natural resources."

National Wildlife Week is sponsored by the National Wildlife Federation, Washington, D. C. and affiliated state organizations. It started in 1938 with a proclamation by President Roosevelt who called the attention of the public as well as conservation leaders to the need for protecting natural resources from further exploitation and loss.

The 1953 observance of National Wildlife Week is the second in a series dedicated to specific species of wildlife in danger of extinction. Last year's week was devoted to preservation of the Florida Key deer, a subspecies of miniature deer recently reduced by fires, hunters, and natural enemies to only thirty or forty animals. This year's keynote is the prairie chicken, a species of grouse once abundant in the great plains states but now reduced to a dangerously low population.

Rod Amundson, Chief of the North Carolina Wildlife Resources Commission's Education Division, and who is serving as State Chairman for Wildlife Week this year, stated that field employees of the commission will give special attention to encouraging special wildlife conservation programs in schools and among civic and rural organizations.

THE SHRINERS' SPRING CEREMONIAL

April 8, 1953

I welcome this opportunity to send my personal greetings and best wishes to the visiting Shriners attending the Oasis Temple's Spring Ceremonial in Greensboro on May 22-23. I know that you will enjoy your visit to Greensboro and that your program will prove to be most interesting.

North Carolina is proud of the charitable aims of Shrinedom and Masonry in general. Your constant efforts in behalf of our orphaned and crippled children are major contributions to the public welfare. I wish for you and your entire organization every success during the Spring Ceremonial and the coming year.

ISRAEL'S FIFTH ANNIVERSARY

April 19, 1953

I take pleasure in asking the people of North Carolina to join with their many Jewish friends throughout the State and country in the celebration and observance of the fifth anniversary of the establishment of the State of Israel.

Americans everywhere are proud of the progress this ancient but young democratic Nation has achieved. We join with the Jewish people everywhere in recognition of "Yom Atzmous," the Hebrew term for "Israel Independence Day" on Monday, April 20.

SOUTHERN REGIONAL CONFERENCE OF AGRICULTURAL EDUCATION [1]

April 24, 1953

In behalf of the people of North Carolina, I extend a hearty welcome to the members of the Southern Regional Conference of Agricultural Education and their guests. We are honored that

[1] This general letter of welcome was sent to members of the conference which was held in Asheville, April 27-May 1, 1953.

you selected a city in our State as the site for your 1953 conference and we want you to feel welcome while you are our guests.

Since the Southern States are primarily agricultural, our future prosperity will depend largely upon the leadership, training and achievements of our rural youth. I commend you for the excellent program of agricultural education which has become a vital part of our public school program. The outstanding achievements of the Future Farmers of America and the veterans who have enrolled in the Institutional On-Farm Training Program are indicative of the soundness of your program and the thoroughness with which it has been planned and conducted. The years ahead will present many new agricultural problems; but I am confident that our farmers, under the leadership of well-trained agricultural leaders, will be able to solve these problems and continue to improve their standard of living.

As Governor of a state where agriculture plays such an important part in its welfare, I am sincerely interested in your efforts and the contribution you are making toward a better Southland. I hope that your conference here in North Carolina will be a successful and pleasant experience and that the knowledge and inspiration acquired will result in great achievements in the years ahead.

LAFAYETTE MILLER CASE [1]

April 29, 1953

Governor Umstead held a conference today with Mr. Herman Taylor of Raleigh, attorney for Lafayette Miller, and Mr. N. F. Ransdell, Commissioner of Paroles, and reviewed fully the facts in connection with the death sentence imposed on Miller in the Superior Court of Beaufort County in January, 1952. From the review and after careful consideration, the Governor stated that he could find no just reason to intervene in the sentence imposed.

---

[1] See footnote on page 135.

COMMITTEE TO WELCOME KOREAN WAR VETERANS

April 30, 1953

Governor Umstead announced today that he has appointed a committee of three veterans to plan a welcome for any returning Korean war veterans from North Carolina who have been released from Communist prison camps. Ray Galloway of Raleigh, past State Commander of the American Legion, will serve as chairman of the committee. Other members will be General Pearson Menoher of Southern Pines, who recently retired from forty years active service with the Army, and Mr. Garland E. Bobbitt of Raleigh, a charter member of the American Legion in North Carolina and an outstanding leader in veteran activities.

"North Carolina is grateful to these returning prisoners of war for the sacrifices and hardships they have suffered for us and for our nation," the Governor said. "It is only appropriate that we extend them a welcome upon their return from prisoner of war camps. I know that all veterans and all veteran organizations will join with this committee of three to make every effort to express the gratitude of North Carolinians to these men and to all returned veterans of the Korean conflict."

Mr. Galloway is a veteran of World War I, a member of the North Carolina Veterans Commission, and has been active in veteran affairs for the past twenty-five years. General Menoher is a graduate of the United States Military Academy, class of 1915 with General Eisenhower, and holds decorations and battle stars from World War I, World War II and the Korean conflict. The General assumed command of the 24th Infantry Division in 1950 when General Dean was captured by the Communists. He was later hospitalized back to the United States and until a few months ago was Deputy Post Commander of Fort Bragg. Mr. Bobbitt served overseas in World War I, was Post Commander of American Legion, Post No. 1 in Raleigh and has been Chef de Gare of Voiture 620 of Raleigh.

MENTAL HEALTH WEEK

May 1, 1953

There is presently a great need in North Carolina as well as in the Nation for action for the prevention, treatment, and cure of mental illness. To this end the week of May 3-9, 1953, has been designated as "Mental Health Week."

The North Carolina Mental Hygiene Society, in co-operation with the National Association for Mental Health, local Mental Hygiene Societies and more than thirty state-wide agencies and organizations in North Carolina, is working diligently in the fight against mental illness.

Co-operating bodies include: Local Mental Hygiene Societies, State Hospitals Board of Control including Alcoholic Rehabilitation Unit, State Board of Public Welfare, State Board of Health, State Department of Public Instruction, State Commission for the Blind, Eugenics Board of North Carolina, North Carolina Congress of Parents and Teachers, Home Economics Extension Service of North Carolina State College, North Carolina Council of Churches, the Red Feather agencies, and others.

New and effective methods for the treatment of mental illness, research, preventive measures, child guidance and counseling are keeping many personal and family disorders from becoming critical. The welfare of our citizens is dependent upon the broadest possible application of the principles of mental health.

Therefore, as Governor of North Carolina, I am calling upon all people in our State to participate in the observance of "Mental Health Week" and to give its program their fullest support.

OUR OBLIGATION TO THE MENTALLY ILL

May 8, 1953

North Carolina is just completing its observance of "Mental Health Week" which has been so designated to emphasize the need for action in the prevention, treatment, and cure of mental illness. I would like to commend the North Carolina Mental Hygiene Society, in co-operation with the National Association for Mental Health, local Mental Hygiene Societies and more than thirty-four agencies and organizations in North Carolina, for their diligent efforts in the fight against mental illness.

One of our greatest obligations is to our mentally ill. During the last few years great progress has been made in their treatment and care. Much remains to be done, however, and continued emphasis should be placed upon the curing of our mentally ill.

New and effective methods for the treatment of mental illness, research, preventive measures, child guidance and counseling are proving effective. The welfare of all our citizens is dependent upon the broadest possible application of the principles of mental health.

APPOINTMENT OF THE HIGHWAY COMMISSION

May 11, 1953

Governor Umstead today announced his new Highway Commission and also released the report of the five-man committee, authorized by the General Assembly, which has been studying the reorganization of the State Highway Divisions. Governor Umstead has given his full approval to the report of the committee which divides North Carolina into fourteen highway divisions to replace the previous ten divisions. Complete details of the new division organization are contained in the attached copy of the committee's report.

A. H. Graham of Hillsboro was appointed Chairman of the State Highway and Public Works Commission. Mr. Graham is a former Speaker of the House, Lieutenant Governor and former Chairman of the State Highway and Public Works Commission.

The Governor announced his selection of the following Highway Commissioners:

Division 1.—J. Emmett Winslow, Hertford

Former Sheriff of Perquimans County, former State Senator, hardware merchant and oil distributor.

Division 2.—H. Maynard Hicks, Snow Hill

Prominent supply merchant and citizen of Greene County and former Chairman of the County Board of Elections.

Division 3.—C. Heide Trask, Wilmington

Prominent businessman and farmer of New Hanover County.

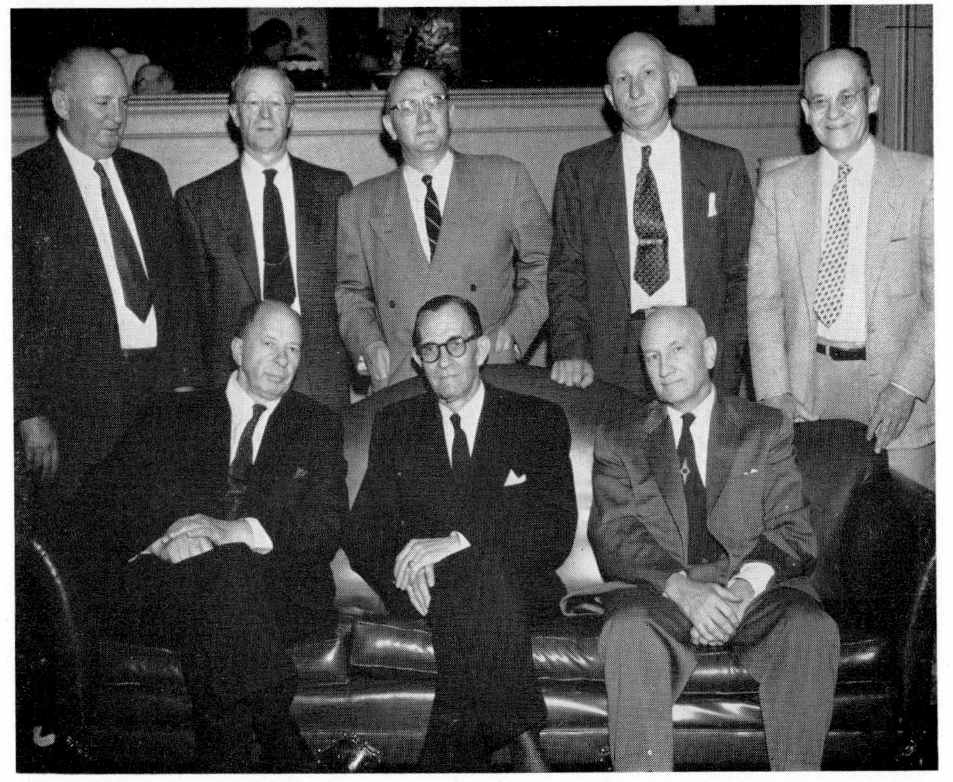

Some of the graduates of the University (class, 1916) attending the Civitan Club, Greensboro, May 7, 1954. *Seated left to right:* Robert B. House, Chapel Hill; Governor Umstead; and McDaniel Lewis, Greensboro. *Standing left to right:* S. H. Hobbs, Jr., Chapel Hill; Curtis A. Holland; Dr. Fred M. Patterson, Greensboro; Roger A. McDuffie, Greensboro; and Clyde A. Fore, Siler City.

Division 4.—M. E. Robinson, Goldsboro
Manufacturer and operator of extensive farming interests. Former Chairman of the Wayne County Board of County Commissioners.

Division 5.—Donnie A. Sorrell, Durham
Garage operator and a dealer in automobile parts. Former President of the Chamber of Commerce and active for many years in the civic and public affairs of Durham.

Division 6.—C. A. Hasty, Maxton
Businessman, farmer and Chairman of the Board of County Commissioners of Robeson County.

Division 7.—John (Jack) Van Lindley, Greensboro
Nurseryman, former member of the City Council of Greensboro, and member of the Executive Committee of the Jefferson Standard Life Insurance Company.

Division 8.—Forrest Lockey, Aberdeen
Railroad operator and Mayor of the town of Aberdeen.

Division 9.—James A. Gray, Jr., Winston-Salem
Official of the Piedmont Publishing Company, President of the Board of Trustees of Old Salem, Inc.

Division 10.—James A. Hardison, Wadesboro
Oil distributor and former member of the State Highway Commission.

Division 11.—W. Ralph Winkler, Boone
Prominent businessman and automobile dealer.

Division 12.—June F. Scarborough, Statesville
Oil distributor and active civic leader.

Division 13.—J. F. Snipes, Marion
President of the McDowell Building and Loan Association, former Chairman, City of Marion School Board and former Chairman of the Board of County Commissioners of McDowell County.

Division 14.—H. E. Buchanan, Hendersonville
Theater operator and for a number of years legislative representative of the theaters in North Carolina, from which position he has resigned.

The Governor has devoted a great deal of his time and conferred with delegations from a number of counties before selecting these fourteen men and the Chairman. He feels that he has a Highway Commission composed of men of character and business experience whose services will prove a credit to the State of North Carolina.

The Governor has felt that counties which have not had a Highway Commissioner during the past eighteen years should have consideration. The only exception which he has made to this policy is in the case of Mr. James A. Hardison who formerly served on the Highway Commission during the administration of Governor Ehringhaus. He is a classmate and a long time personal friend of Governor Umstead.

The Chairman and all members of the Commission will serve a four-year term, expiring May 1, 1957.

RESIGNATION OF BRANDON P. HODGES

May 20, 1953

I accept reluctantly and with profound regret the resignation of Brandon P. Hodges as State Treasurer. I commend him for the splendid services he has rendered as Treasurer of the State and also in the matter of obtaining new industry in North Carolina—an assignment which was done beyond the call of duty.

I am exceedingly sorry that I shall not have the benefit of his services and wise counsel during my administration. I wish him every possible success in his new work.

EXECUTIVE CLEMENCY FOR CLYDE BROWN DECLINED [1]

May 22, 1953

Hosea V. Price, attorney for Clyde Brown of Winston-Salem, North Carolina, conferred with the Governor at 10:00 A.M. on Friday, May 22, 1953, and urged Governor Umstead to commute

[1] Clyde Brown, a Negro of Winston-Salem, was accused of assaulting and ravishing Betty Jane Clifton in her father's radio shop, June 16, 1950. At the September, 1950, term of Superior Court, Brown was tried, convicted, and sentenced to suffer death by lethal gas on October 20, 1950. The case was appealed to Supreme Court and on February 2, 1951, this court upheld the lower court. The case was pursued in federal and state courts throughout 1951, and always the higher court upheld the lower courts.

the death sentence of Clyde Brown to life imprisonment. The Governor pointed out that prior to the trial of this case in the Superior Court of Forsyth County that the defendant had admitted his guilt and was convicted of assault and rape of a seventeen-year old girl on the 16th day of June, 1950.

The Governor further observed that this conviction had been reviewed and upheld by the North Carolina Supreme Court and that the United States Supreme Court had sustained this conviction on two different occasions; that on the record in this case there appears to be nothing which would justify executive clemency. Therefore, he declined to intervene in the death sentence to be executed on Friday, May 29, 1953.

RALEIGH SPELLER'S CASE [1]

May 25, 1953

Herman L. Taylor and Samuel S. Mitchell, attorneys for Raleigh Speller, conferred with the Governor on Friday, May 22, 1953, and urged Governor Umstead to commute the death sentence of Raleigh Speller to life imprisonment.

The Governor stated that this prisoner had been convicted on three separate trials in the Superior Court of Bertie County and that the case had been reviewed and considered by the North Carolina Supreme Court on three different occasions and that the matter had been presented to the United States Supreme Court and reviewed by this Court on two different occasions, and that on record in this case, there appears to be nothing which would justify executive clemency. Therefore, he declined to intervene in the execution of the death sentence to be executed on Friday, May 29, 1953.

[1] Raleigh Speller was accused of raping Mrs. Aubrey Davis of Bertie County. He was tried, convicted, and sentenced to death by lethal gas at the November term of Bertie County Superior Court. Speller appealed the conviction and was granted a new trial. He was again convicted and again granted a new trial. He was convicted a third time after which he appealed to U. S. District and Supreme courts, and in each the verdict of the lower courts was upheld.

SOUTH KOREAN STEERING COMMITTEE

June 8, 1953

A steering committee to assist in the campaign to raise funds for war-stricken civilians of South Korea was appointed today by Governor William B. Umstead.

The North Carolina campaign, now getting under way, is headed by George P. Geoghegan, Jr., Raleigh banker. It is part of a nation-wide drive to raise at least $5,000,000 to provide medicine, shelter, food and other necessities for 10,000,000 South Koreans now facing starvation and disease.

Contributions may be sent to: Aid to Korea, Raleigh, North Carolina. Because of the urgent need for quick emergency aid, Governor Umstead has requested North Carolinians to send in their contributions immediately. All contributions are tax deductible.

Appointed to the campaign steering committee were James H. Clark, Elizabethtown; R. S. Dickson, Charlotte; George Watts Hill, Durham; R. H. Livermore, Pembroke; R. Flake Shaw and Dr. John Wilson, Greensboro; William P. Saunders, Aberdeen; H. Patrick Taylor, Wadesboro; Warren R. Williams, Sanford; Gurney P. Hood of Raleigh, who is campaign treasurer; Hargrove Bellamy, Wilmington; Don S. Elias, Asheville; and Irving Carlyle, Winston-Salem.

The campaign has been strongly endorsed by President Eisenhower.

"Our own fighting men in Korea have been contributing to the cause of Korean assistance much more than we who have remained at home," said the President. "By contributing to this cause, we can support the personal efforts of our own troops."

American soldiers in Korea, struck with sympathy for the long-suffering South Korean civilians, have given over $13,000,000 from their own small pay to help ease the war victims' pitiful condition. Hospitals, homes, and orphanages are being maintained solely by funds donated by American fighting men.

Governor Umstead has emphasized that millions of sick and homeless persons in war-devastated South Korea need immediate help, and he has urged North Carolinians to give as quickly and as generously as possible.

FIFTIETH ANNIVERSARY OF POWERED FLIGHT

June 9, 1953

Governor Umstead today announced the membership of the commission authorized by the recent General Assembly which will co-ordinate North Carolina's efforts in the observance this year of the Fiftieth Anniversary of Powered Flight. This Commission will work with a national organization headed by General James Doolittle.

Governor Umstead appointed Mr. Carl Goerch of Raleigh as Chairman of the Commission. Mr. Goerch is a publisher, radio commentator, and aviation enthusiast. He is also president of an organization of private fliers in the State.

The Honorable Lindsay C. Warren of Washington, D. C., Comptroller of the United States, was named as Honorary Chairman of this Commission in recognition of his efforts in the founding of the Wright Brothers Memorial at Kitty Hawk and for his continuing interest and efforts in developing all phases of aviation in North Carolina.

Other members of the Commission are:

Mr. Tom Davis, Winston-Salem, President of Piedmont Airlines; Colonel Max Washburn, Shelby, a leader in Civil Air Patrol activities; Mr. Aycock Brown, Manteo, well-known coastal writer and photographer; Mr. Hugh Morton, Wilmington, developer of Grandfather Mountain as a major tourist attraction and active in many other state affairs; Mr. Henry Vann, Clinton, State Senator and private flier; The Honorable Herbert Bonner, Washington, D. C., Congressman from the First District; Mr. Frank Thompson, Raleigh, member of the Raleigh-Durham Airport Commission; and Dr. Christopher Crittenden, Raleigh, Director of Archives and History.

All of these terms will expire March 31, 1955.

INTEGRATION OF PUBLIC SCHOOLS[1]

June 9, 1953

Until I have an opportunity to study the statement made by the Supreme Court of the United States in announcing its deci-

[1] On May 17, 1953, the U. S. Supreme Court handed down its decision concerning the integration of public schools throughout the Nation.

sion to postpone action in the pending cases of segregation in public schools, I will have no statement to make with reference thereto.

Furthermore, I will have no statement to make with regard to the effect of the delay upon the school bond issue until I have had an opportunity to study the matter and confer with a number of other people.

THE DEATH OF WILLIS SMITH [1]

June 26, 1953

In the death of Senator Willis Smith North Carolina and the Nation have sustained a serious loss.

As Speaker of the North Carolina House of Representatives, as President of the American Bar Association, as an active practicing attorney, as a Senator of the United States from North Carolina and as a splendid Christian gentleman, he has rendered a great service to his State and to his Nation.

I was distressed to hear of his death, and extend my deepest sympathy to Mrs. Smith and the members of his family.

NORTH CAROLINA PERMANENT IMPROVEMENT BONDS

July 10, 1953

At a meeting of the Governor and Council of State this afternoon issuance of $14,250,000 State of North Carolina Permanent Improvement Bonds was authorized and it was decided that sealed bids for the bonds would be received by the State Treasurer at his office in Raleigh until eleven o'clock A.M., E.S.T., August 19, 1953, and delivery to the purchasers on or about September 9.

The bonds will be general obligations, dated July 1, 1953, and

---

[1] Willis Smith, son of Willis and Mary Shaw (Creecy) Smith, was born December 19, 1887, in Norfolk, Virginia; graduated from Atlantic Collegiate Institute, Elizabeth City; Trinity College (now Duke University), and received his law degree there in 1912. He represented Wake County in the House of Representatives in 1927, 1929, and 1931. He was elected to the United States Senate, November 7, 1950. See *North Carolina Manual,* 1953, p. 399.

will mature annually on July 1, without option or prior payment, $525,000, 1958; $550,000, 1959; $575,000, 1960 to 1966 inclusive; $600,000, 1967; $600,000, 1968; $625,000, 1969; $625,000, 1970; $2,200,000, 1971; $2,200,000, 1972; and $2,300,000, 1973.

More descriptive details and other pertinent information will be contained in a prospectus which will be available for circularization by July 24, 1953.

EVELYN ELIZABETH HENDRICKS PRESENTED THE GOVERNOR'S AWARD

July 20, 1953

Governor Umstead presented The Governor's Award to Miss Evelyn Elizabeth Hendricks of Nash County as the outstanding handicapped North Carolinian for 1953 at 12:30 today.

This was a very heart-warming experience for all those present. The narrative of Miss Hendricks, a victim of rheumatoid arthritis, reads like a fairy story. In spite of the handicap of being confined to a wheel chair she has always been interested and taken an active part in a variety of activities.

Evelyn's education did not end when she was forced to stop school. She had long been interested in the out of doors, and often a friend or neighborhood children would take her "rambling afield." This required a great deal of effort since she and the wheel chair had to be lifted over fences, ditches, and across streams. She was a keen observer, and kept notes. An early project was the making of a survey of the wild plant life of her county, and she identified more than 500 native species. These field trips inspired her to write a column for the local newspaper, entitled "Time to Ramble," which was published for a couple of years. This experience also created a desire to sketch and paint wild flowers, and since no teachers were available, she started to teach herself. Although both hands are crippled, the right one became worse, so she taught herself—a long slow process—to use her left hand. Later the North Carolina Division of Vocational Rehabilitation arranged for her to attend a term at the summer school of Duke University, where she made an "A" grade. Although her main interest and work was in herbarium, she had a few art lessons, and a painting of her magnolias was placed in Duke Hospital. She also drew many sketches of wildlife which she had hoped to get published in children's story books, but was not successful in getting these published.

Evelyn taught herself to use a typewriter, learning on her brother's old portable. She hit the keys with a rubber tipped pencil, which was very tiresome, since her hands were so severely deformed. A Rehabilitation Counselor visited her home and recognized the difficulty she was encountering with her typing. He decided to contact a typewriter manufacturer to see if an electric typewriter might be donated. Today she has an electric one presented by an anonymous company.

In 1947, as a guest observer, Evelyn attended the North Carolina School for Crippled Children, which was held in Chapel Hill, seat of the University of North Carolina. This opened up a whole new line of inquiry and activity, giving new impetus to her life. She attended lectures on anatomy and orthopedics, having recently acquired an interest in arthritis, the cause and cure of which is yet unknown. Reading articles on medical research, she learned to identify the type she has, rheumatoid, which is called "the great crippler" due to its destructive effects on the joints. Now, with a definite purpose in mind, she tried to learn everything she could about rheumatic diseases. Quickly she developed an intensive interest in research and a fervent wish to be able to make some contribution to this new field of inquiry.

She delved into anatomy, genetics, allergies, and psychology. Widening the scope of her interests, she wrote to eminent physicians, authors of textbooks, and medical foundations, asking if there were any way in which she could make a contribution to research, and offering to be of service in any way possible writing case histories, making pedigrees—even to being a "guinea pig" for research and experimentation. The various doctors, specialists, and authors answered her letters, giving helpful suggestions, comments, and offers of assistance. She was also furnished medical data from ten different hospitals, always with the written permission of the patients involved.

One thing in particular Evelyn wished to investigate—all her life she had heard it said that "rheumatism runs in the family."

She began going to libraries, reading scientific papers and reports, consulting medical journals, and borrowing textbooks on heredity and medical genetics, technical works that would be beyond the comprehension of most readers.

Her native Nash County is the main field of her activities, where she has traveled extensively, investigating interrelated families who have members suffering from arthritis. A genealogy of over 2,000 names of these families has been compiled. This information was submitted to various interested doctors, and in 1949, Dr. Robert M. Stecher, President-elect of the International Association Against Rheumatism, and former President of the American Rheumatism Association, went to Nash County to meet Evelyn and inspect her research project. He was so impressed with her pedigrees and medical reports that his comment was, "This is a gold mine." Later Dr. Stecher wrote "Your work in gathering data is absolutely invaluable. I am very happy to collaborate with you in any way; I shall be glad to help with the writing of an article on the hereditary aspects of arthritis, if you wish me to, whether I am co-author or not. You are welcome to all my clinical skill and arthritic reputation."

One of the most momentous events in her career came in the summer of 1950. Dr. Maurice Whittinghill, a young geneticist at the University of North Carolina's Department of Zoology, became interested in Evelyn and her work. Analyzing the material she had, he offered to collaborate with her in the publication of a scientific paper, and urged her to come for conferences as often as she could. The following spring a paper under their joint authorship, "Studies on the Inheritance of Rheumatoid Arthritis in a Nash County Pedigree," was presented at a meeting of the North Carolina Academy of Science at Duke University. Other papers dealing with hereditary diseases were also prepared and presented at various medical meetings as a result of data which she had collected.

How did this indefatigable wheel chair research worker get about to make these studies and attend the meetings? An attendant or nurse can easily pick up tiny Evelyn to carry her in and out of homes, libraries, and conference rooms. Such an attendant accompanied her constantly. Of course finances were bound to become a problem. In the beginning Evelyn's parents had financed the research, but after more than $400.00 had been spent, it was realized that this was entailing too much of a sacrifice on the part of a semi-invalid father and mother who were of modest means. Evelyn began looking for outside funds, as she understood that even though her important studies should be published, they would bring no monetary return. No payment is made for articles in those scholarly scientific journals. In September 1949, a civic club of Rocky Mount, North Carolina, gave a grant of $500.00 to cover expenses for two years. In September 1951, through the efforts of Dr. Whittinghill, the U. S. Public Health Service awarded a grant of $3,963,00 for a year's research. Dr. Whittinghill, Supervisor of the Project, appointed Evelyn as his research assistant. For the first time in her life, she was earning a salary! The grant also included funds for a maid-chauffeur, as well as mileage for the family car when she used it on the project. In September 1952, a second grant was awarded in the amount of $6,878,00.

Because she grappled with "the influence of heredity on arthritis," countless numbers of men, women, and children may be spared a life of affliction through findings of medical men based on her "pedigrees" and reports.

INDUSTRIAL DEVELOPMENT AND COMMUNITY RESPONSIBILITY [1]

July 20, 1953

The very fact that you are studying this guide to economic development in your community is an excellent indication of healthy thinking. As I pointed out plainly and emphatically when I became Governor—and as I strongly reiterate here—it is my firm belief that increased industrial development is now one of our State's most important goals.

Under the aggressive, business-like leadership of its Director, Ben E. Douglas, the Department of Conservation and Development is the spearhead for industrial development on a state-wide

[1] This statement appeared in *Community Guide to Economic Development in Friendly North Carolina* (Raleigh: Department of Conservation and Development), p. 2.

basis. It plays favorites to no area and no group—it is ready and anxious at all times to co-operate with every community that shows itself ready for planned action. Some excellent results have been obtained, with substantial and gratifying additions to our State's industries.

The Department, however, cannot do the whole job. A most important role must be played by each community, in its own interest and as its share of the entire State's progressive development. Many communities are already functioning enthusiastically along these lines, and each addition to this growing list of communities adds value to our efforts.

That is why I say "Congratulations" to you, and to everyone in your community who is interested in formulating plans, followed by spirited action, to achieve the goals you wish to obtain.

As your Governor, and as a fellow-citizen of our beloved North Carolina, I wish you the best of success!

SCHOOL AND HOSPITAL BOND ORGANIZATION

August 1, 1953

Brandon P. Hodges, consultant for Champion Paper and Fibre Company, and John Harden, Vice-President of Burlington Mills, will head up the organized effort in behalf of the $72,000,000 bond drive for North Carolina schools and mental hospitals, Governor William B. Umstead announced today.

Mr. Hodges and Mr. Harden will be co-chairmen of the campaign which will present the bond program to the voters of the State in advance of the October 3 bond election provided by the 1953 General Assembly.

A state-wide organization will be set up to promote a wide interest in the bonds and the co-chairmen will direct this activity in the interest of the proposed bond issues. The election will pass on $50,000,000 in public school bonds and $22,000,000 in bonds for mental hospitals.

The bond organization will open state headquarters in Raleigh late in August and Hodges and Harden will be in charge. Both are well known in North Carolina business and political circles and are veterans of several political campaigns and assignments.

Mr. Hodges lives in Asheville and has served in the State Senate, been a member of the Senate Appropriations Committee and on the Advisory Budget Commission, in addition to serving in several local elective and appointive offices and on state boards and commissions. Mr. Harden was a North Carolina newspaperman for years, served as secretary to Governor R. Gregg Cherry, was assistant manager of Governor Umstead's campaign when he ran for the United States Senate, and also has served on several state commissions and boards.

Mr. Hodges resigned as Treasurer sometime ago to join Champion Paper and Fibre Company. Mr. Harden has been a Vice-President of Burlington Mills for five years. Mr. Hodges will primarily handle organizational work in the bond campaign and Mr. Harden will handle the press and promotional work. Both men have been made available for this assignment by their respective companies.

Governor Umstead today paid tribute to Reuben B. Robertson, Chairman of the Board of Directors of Champion Paper and Fibre Company, and to J. Spencer Love, Chairman of the Board of Burlington, for their "patriotic interest in North Carolina and their co-operation in making available for this important assignment the services of Mr. Hodges and Mr. Harden."

"North Carolina's future, in the realm of public education and care of our mentally ill is at stake," Governor Umstead said, and "We are fortunate at this crossroads point to have two men who will contribute their time and their talents to this important task, and to have two progressive North Carolina companies that take this degree of interest in helping to shape the sort of North Carolina we will have tomorrow and the sort of job we will do with our young people and our unfortunates."

BUILDING WORLD PEACE [1]

August 5, 1953

The University of North Carolina at Chapel Hill through its Extension Division is sponsoring its Seventh Annual High School

[1] This statement was addressed to the high school principals and teachers of North Carolina in order to inform them of his support for this program among high school students of the State.

Award Peace Study and Speaking Program. The subject for discussion this year will be, "Building World Peace: How Can the United Nations Prevent Communist Aggression and Preparation for Aggression?"

The purpose of this annual program from the beginning has been to encourage high school students of the State to study and discuss ways and means of attaining and maintaining world peace. In my opinion, the 1953 subject is timely, important, and worthy of study by every high school student.

The United Nations and our great Nation are wrestling with this very problem of preventing Communist aggression. The success or failure of these efforts should concern every North Carolinian. It is appropriate that the issues involved be thoroughly studied and discussed in our public schools.

I am pleased to endorse this program and to commend to the high school students of North Carolina this opportunity to acquire a personal knowledge of this timely and important subject.

STATE EMPLOYEES SERVE THE PEOPLE OF NORTH CAROLINA [1]

August 12, 1953

It is a pleasure to bring you greetings upon the occasion of your annual convention here in Raleigh.

As state employees, we are all privileged to serve the people of North Carolina to the best of our ability. Regardless of what our job may be, we should be proud that we work for the State and should make every effort to be courteous and helpful not only to our fellow citizens but also to those who may come into or pass through our State from elsewhere.

As employees of the State, all of us must work together for more efficiency and for a better understanding of our common aims and problems. I am sure that as Governor of North Carolina I can count on your co-operation and assistance in providing the people of the State with an efficient and effective administration

[1] This message was addressed "To the Members of the North Carolina State Employees Association," on the occasion of their annual convention held in Raleigh.

of its affairs. To achieve this goal, I seek your sympathetic understanding of our problems and the wholehearted support of every state employee in making North Carolina a better place in which to live.

NEED FOR AGRICULTURAL DEVELOPMENT AND STOPPAGE OF SOIL EROSION [1]

August 14, 1953

Agriculture is still the pride of our State. More people work on farms in North Carolina than in any state in the Union—about one-third of our population. The cash income from farm crops is now about $900,000,000 per year, and is an important part of our State's economy.

The improvement in agriculture during the past fifteen years is obvious on every hand. We must continue this improvement and endeavor to raise the average per capita income of the people working on our farms in North Carolina. The large number of agricultural workers accounts in a large measure for our low per capita income. Contrary to the views of many people, the majority of those who make a living on the farm are not getting rich. The Federal Farm Program, the Extension Service, State College, the experiment stations, vocational agriculture teachers, teachers of home economics, the State Department of Agriculture, the Rural Electrification Authority, the Production Marketing Administration, the Forest Service, the Soil Conservation Service, the Farm Home Administration, the Farm Credit Administration, and other agricultural agencies make a mighty team for the advancement and improvement of agriculture in North Carolina. I commend the Farm Bureau and the Grange for their splendid efforts for agriculture. It shall be my purpose to work with all of these agencies, and I recommend and suggest the following:

We should have a co-operative movement on the part of the appropriate agencies, the farmers, cities and towns and all of our people, for a unified and effective effort to stop erosion of soil.

---

[1] This statement appeared in the *Scotland Neck Commonwealth*, August 14, 1953.

We need more improved pasture land, more dairy and beef cattle and more poultry.

There should be a greater utilization of our forest resources and a comprehensive and effective forestry program, including adequate fire protection, and a wider use of recommended forest improvement practices.

We need more effective methods of protecting and using our water resources and our wildlife.

We need additional processing plants for agricultural products, and we should develop better and expanding marketing facilities for our poultry, fruit, vegetables, and livestock. Every effort should be made to eliminate such inequalities in freight rates affecting agriculture in North Carolina as may now exist.

We should expand our program of agricultural research.

My belief in the value of agricultural research is of long standing, and I will support such a program. We have learned from industry that research is essential to progress. This is true of agriculture also. A greater effort should be made to carry to the farmers the splendid results of our research program. Every effort should be made by the State and every agency involved, and by all of our people, to conserve, enrich and use properly God's good earth, which with its water, trees and grasses, has supported all the generations before us, to the end that it will be able to continue to support, feed and clothe the generations yet to come.

DEATH OF CAMERON MORRISON [1]

August 20, 1953

I was distressed today to hear of the death of Honorable Cameron Morrison of Charlotte.

He served the State as Governor, and as a member of the Congress of the United States in both the House of Repre-

[1] Cameron Morrison was born October 5, 1869, at Rockingham, Richmond County. He was the son of Daniel M. and Martha (Cameron) Morrison. He attended schools in Richmond County, but did not have the opportunity to attend college. He studied law in the school operated by Judge Robert P. Dick in Greensboro, and was licensed to practice law in February, 1892. His father was a Republican, but on attaining his majority he announced he was a Democrat. He represented Richmond County in the state Senate in 1901, and served a term as mayor of the town of Rockingham. He was for many years, prior to his becoming Governor in 1921, active in the political campaigns of the State.

sentatives and the Senate. He was one of North Carolina's greatest citizens and made many contributions to the progress and development of the State. He possessed positive qualities of leadership and used them for the benefit of the people.

He will be greatly missed, and I extend to the members of his family my deepest sympathy.

PARENT-TEACHER MEMBERSHIP MONTH

September 15, 1953

It is a pleasure to call to the attention of all parents and teachers in North Carolina that the month of October will be observed as "Parent-Teacher Membership Month." During this month the North Carolina Congress of Parents and Teachers will make its annual campaign for membership. The PTA program concerns the welfare and education of our children and deserves the full co-operation of every parent and every teacher.

Membership in the PTA gives every parent and teacher a splendid opportunity to exert a constructive influence on all phases of community life that are related to the well-being and advancement of our children.

CITIZENSHIP DAY

September 16, 1953

It has been called to my attention that the Congress of the United States has designated the 17th of September of each year as "Citizenship Day" in commemoration of the signing of the Constitution in 1787 and in recognition of all who, coming of age or by naturalization, enjoy the privileges and bear the responsibilities of citizenship. The profound meaning of the Constitution has become more clear to all of us in this age of peril.

In view of this annual observance of Citizenship Day, I take pleasure in designating September 17 as Citizenship Day in North Carolina and call upon all our citizens to renew and reaffirm on Citizenship Day their allegiance to, and faith in, the prin-

Photo Courtesy of F. Clyde Wilkerson

Governor Umstead in Washington, D. C., July 16, 1954, visiting the North Carolina senators whom he appointed. *Left to right:* Alton A. Lennon of Wilmington; Governor Umstead; and Sam J. Ervin, Jr., of Morganton.

ciples and ideals to which our Constitution gives historic testimony.

North Carolina will be represented in Washington on September 17, as one of the thirteen original states, to participate in Citizenship Day ceremonies to be held at the Washington Monument. At that time the Honorable Edwin Gill, State Treasurer of North Carolina, acting in my behalf, will lay a wreath at the foot of the Washington Monument as a part of the ceremonies.

SAFETY AMONG OUR PEOPLE

September 22, 1953

I understand that each year approximately five million adults and children are killed or injured by accidents in the home. This is a terrible toll and results in family tragedies and hardships which often could be prevented. It has been called to my attention that the week of October 5-11 has been designated as "Emergencies Can't Wait Week" as a positive means of impressing the public with the importance of accident prevention in the home and the necessity of always being prepared at home to take care of emergency accidents.

I am happy to co-operate with any worthy effort to promote safety among our people, and I hope that the designation of this week in North Carolina will result in making our people more conscious of home accidents and thereby prevent the loss of life and injury to our fellow human beings.

HOME OWNERSHIP

September 24, 1953

It has just been called to my attention that this week is being observed across the Nation as "National Home Week" as a means of encouraging and promoting private home ownership.

Home ownership provides one of the strongest encouragements in good citizenship. Anything that can be done to increase home ownership in North Carolina contributes to continued progress and the common welfare. In recent years home builders of North Carolina have provided an unprecedented number of fine new homes for our citizens. New communities have been built—our cities have been improved, and the opportunity to own a home has been made available to more people than ever before.

In view of the many benefits to North Carolina resulting from the work of the home building industry, it is fitting that we take note of the many accomplishments of this industry and the substantial increase in home ownership among our citizens.

BOND ISSUES FOR PUBLIC SCHOOLS AND MENTAL HOSPITALS

September 30, 1953

I was pleased when the General Assembly of North Carolina voted to submit to the people on October 3 two bond issues to provide for vitally needed public school facilities, mental hospitals, and institutions for feeble-minded children. In my judgment these two bond issues deserve the active support of every North Carolinian interested in the welfare and progress of our State.

We have constructed in North Carolina many school buildings during the past few years. However, our school population is rapidly increasing and the need has not been met. The fact is that crowded schoolroom conditions must be relieved in North Carolina if we are to do in this generation what should be done for the education of our children and for the development of our State.

Our obligation to our mentally ill is universally recognized. During the past few years great progress has been made in their treatment and care. Much remains to be done and continued emphasis must be placed upon the curing of our mentally ill. There is not sufficient room in our institutions for the children or adults who need attention. The need is urgent, not only for proper training schools for the feeble-minded white and Negro children of the State, but also for the construction and equipment of sufficient facilities to meet the needs of adults now and for some years to come. We have worked at this problem in piece-meal fashion long enough. The mentally ill have no spokesman except those whose hearts have been touched by the need for better facilities, care and treatment.

The responsibility for the education of our children and the proper care of our mentally ill is the obligation of every citizen of North Carolina, and I urge every voter to support and vote for the two bond issues on October 3. It is a challenge which we must meet.

NEWSPAPER BOY DAY

October 1, 1953

It has been called to my attention that the annual observance of Newspaper Boy Day will be held in Raleigh on Friday, October 2, 1953. This will be the sixth annual luncheon and trip for representative newspaper boys across North Carolina. This recognition is sponsored each year by the newspapers of our State and I wish to commend them for a splendid program.

The free press of America and of North Carolina provides a vital service in bringing us the news of the day. However, despite the best efforts of our news-gathering organizations, our news editors and the latest printing devices, many readers would not receive their daily newspapers if it were not for the regular and dependable daily deliveries made by our newspaper boys. At the same time they gain valuable experience as young independent businessmen who are responsible for their own routes and their own collections.

I am pleased to call attention to the observance of annual Newspaper Boy Day in North Carolina. I hope that the visit of these young men to Raleigh this year will be highly successful and that they will learn a great deal from their visit to the state capital.

FIRE PREVENTION WEEK

October 2, 1953

Since the earliest recorded history, fire has been a hazard to human life and property. The ravages of fire down through the years have caused an untold amount of suffering and destruction.

In these modern times, fire prevention is still a matter of great importance and the losses through fires continue to remain a major threat to life and property. It has been called to my attention that the week beginning October 4, 1953, will be observed nationally as Fire Prevention Week; and it is a pleasure for me to designate this same week for special thought and effort in fire prevention in North Carolina.

I earnestly request the citizens of North Carolina during Fire Prevention Week to devote special thought and effort to the reduction of fire hazards and the consequent losses. The consideration of these problems should include industrial fires, forest fires, and any possible fire hazards affecting schools, churches, and homes in order to help prevent the needless loss of life and property.

NORTH CAROLINIANS URGED TO VOTE

October 2, 1953

On Saturday the people of North Carolina will go to the polls to vote on two bond issues which would provide badly needed public school and mental hospital facilities. I have great faith that the voters will give these bond issues their approval. I would like to urge, however, that every voter exercise his privilege of voting so that the outcome will be decisive.

The people of North Carolina do care for their children and mentally ill, and I am confident that they will respond to this challenge for a better tomorrow in North Carolina.

HONORARY TAR HEELS

October 5, 1953

Governor Umstead has issued Honorary Tar Heel Commissions to nine persons recently in recognition of outstanding service to the State in the field of public relations.

These are the first commissions the Governor has issued in the original, or "Down Home Chapter" of Honorary Tar Heels. Membership in the "Down Home Chapter" is limited to out-of-state residents nominated by the State Advertising Division of the Department of Conservation and Development who have performed conspicuous service to the State as editors, writers, photographers, entertainers, public speakers, or in other public relations capacities.

The original, or "Down Home Chapter" of Honorary Tar Heels, was formed in 1946 by Governor R. Gregg Cherry, Private Secretary John Harden and Bill Sharpe, then manager of the State News Bureau. Its purpose was to recognize outstanding service in publicizing North Carolina and to encourage continued interest in the State.

Membership is world-wide and constantly changing because one of the few rules of the informal organization is that if a member fails to attend three successive meetings, or cannot make a satisfactory excuse therefor, he is dropped from the roster.

The membership has included persons in the United States, Canada, Australia and the British Isles. The new members are:

S. L. A. Marshall, Associate Editor, *Detroit News,* Detroit, Michigan.

Don Short, Travel Editor, *Cosmopolitan Magazine,* New York, N. Y.

Sam P. Weems, Superintendent, Blue Ridge Parkway, Roanoke, Virginia.

Leonard R. Barnes, Associate Editor, *Motor News,* Detroit, Michigan.

Frank Scherschel, Assistant Picture Editor, *Life,* New York, N. Y.

Michael Frome, Travel Editor, American Automobile Association, Washington, D. C.

Bill Wolf, Outdoor Writer, *Saturday Evening Post,* and *Field and Stream,* Upper Darby, Pennsylvania.

William M. Perry, Superintendent, Senate Periodical Press Gallery, Washington, D. C.

Usually there are two or three meetings a year, two in North Carolina and one in New York. The New York meeting was held last February, and in May there was a get-together in Linville. An autumn meeting is scheduled at Nags Head for October 23-25.

The organization is unusual in that it has no formal constitution or by-laws. There are no dues. Members pay their own expenses to and from meeting places, but are entertained by local hosts, who are assisted by the Director, members of the Board of Conservation and Development and members of the State Advertising Division Staff. The Governor attends when possible, and when he is unable to do so, he designates his Private Secretary or other state officials to represent him.

The meetings are strictly stag, and no speeches over five minutes long are permitted—and few of them at any one meeting. One of the few rules of the organization prohibits the discussion of business in any form. Fishing and other sports, or just plain unmolested resting are the principal features of these gatherings of out-of-staters who have rendered conspicuous service to North Carolina and who wish to continue their contacts with their friends in the State.

AMERICAN EDUCATION WEEK

October 19, 1953

American Education Week will be observed during the week of November 8-14, and I would like to take this opportunity to give it my hearty endorsement. A sound program of public education is essential to successful self-government, and the establishment and maintenance of good schools in our State is a personal responsibility shared by every citizen. We, in North Carolina, are justly proud of the progress we have made in public education. The overwhelming majority in votes given the

$50,000,000 in school bonds at the October 3 election is a splendid indication of the support our people continue to give public education in North Carolina.

Intelligent support of a sound public school program can best be given by a people well informed about school programs and school needs. It is the purpose of the thirty-third annual observance of American Education Week to make a special effort to inform all citizens about the needs and the opportunities of our public school system. I urge all citizens to visit their schools during American Education Week, to learn more about school programs and school systems, and to assist in every way in developing and improving our public schools.

STATE PORTS OPEN NEW AVENUES OF COMMERCE[1]

October 19, 1953

North Carolina has now completed two excellent ports, one at Morehead City and one at Wilmington, which are operated by the North Carolina State Ports Authority. The construction of these ports was another step in the development of our State. However, the port facilities as such cannot, and will not, bring to us a substantial export and import trade. In view of the increasingly competitive nature of world-wide overseas shipping, this trade must be developed through a sound program, which will pay great dividends to the State of North Carolina. The successful operation of these ports will require skilled specialists and considerable time and planning. The General Assembly of 1953 reorganized the membership of the North Carolina State Ports Authority and, under the provisions of this statute, I have made my appointments. All members of the Ports Authority are capable businessmen with sound judgment and ability to direct the operation of these facilities.

Our ports at Morehead City and Wilmington are gateways to the seven seas and will serve as valuable avenues of commerce

[1] This message by Governor Umstead was included in the December issue of the magazine, *North Carolina Ports*, the official publication of the State Ports Authority. The magazine seeks to promote wider interest and use of all harbor and waterway assets the State possesses.

in promoting greater prosperity and growth for North Carolina. Their real contribution to the future development and advancement of North Carolina will depend upon how effectively we can make them serve the interest of our State. This is a big job and will require tireless energy and the best talent that can be found.

I am confident that our state ports will make a real contribution in attracting new industry for North Carolina. We know that many industrial leaders are looking to the South as the land of opportunity for expansion and future growth. These new ports must be considered as utilities designed for transportation, like our highways and our railroad lines, connecting our inland transportation system with water transportation to the world, and will open new avenues of commerce for industries in our State.

The ports will also serve agriculture and agricultural products. This should result in substantial savings to our farm people and to our State. We are first in the growth of flue-cured tobacco and the manufacture of tobacco products, so it is only natural to expect tobacco to be important in the export trade through our ports. However, textiles, cotton, furniture, peanuts, foodstuffs and grain will be among the other products that can be expected to be exported in bulk. Some of the imports probably will include certain types of tobacco, Egyptian cotton, mahogany logs from South America for furniture and veneers, bauxite for the manufacture of aluminum, steel, iron and other ores, fertilizers, and many other products.

I firmly believe that this state ports program is a sensible, progressive and far-reaching project for North Carolina. We have made great strides in many fields, such as education, highways, agriculture, business, industry, conservation and development, health and financial growth and stability. It is my sincere belief that the promotion of our state ports will contribute to the sound, yet dynamic, growth of North Carolina.

INVITATION TO ATTEND THE STATE FAIR [1]

October 20, 1953

It is my pleasure and privilege, personally and on behalf of the State of North Carolina, to invite you to participate in the 1953 State Fair. I commend it to you as a great exposition, worthy of your interest and attendance.

Celebrating this year its 100th birthday, the Fair offers opportunities for entertainment, relaxation, education and broadening of the cultural outlook. With the completion and full use this year of the new State Fair arena, the judging and exhibition facilities are unexcelled anywhere in the South.

The State Fair has proved its value during the past years. As many have discovered in the past, the Fair is more than a display of fruits and vegetables, livestock and machinery, manufactured goods and handicrafts. It is a unique educational and inspirational experience which leads to a greater appreciation of the vast and varied scope of North Carolina's agriculture, industry, and commerce, as well as our natural and human resources.

From the standpoint of attendance and the number of participants, the Fair is the biggest annual event held anywhere in North Carolina. We are looking forward this year to the most colorful, entertaining, educational, inspirational and useful Fair in history. You are invited to have a part in it.

EXECUTIVE CLEMENCY DECLINED IN THE DANIELS' CASE [2]

October 30, 1953

After a careful study and consideration of the cases of Bennie Daniels and Lloyd Ray Daniels, and after hearing those who have asked to be heard, including the attorneys for the prisoners,

---

[1] This invitation to the citizens of North Carolina to attend the 1953 State Fair appeared in the *Premium Book* of the State Fair.

[2] Bennie and Lloyd Ray Daniels of Greenville, North Carolina, at the May, 1949, term of Superior Court of Pitt County, were tried for the murder of William Benjamin O'Neal and were convicted without recommendation. Judge Clawson L. Williams sentenced both defendants to death. This case was appealed several times to the Supreme Court of North Carolina and to the Supreme Court of the United States. Each petition to these courts was denied. See *North Carolina Reports* 231, pp. 17, 341, 509 and 232, p. 196.

and after having sought counsel and advice of the Board of Paroles, I have concluded that there appears to be nothing involved in these cases which would justify the exercise of executive clemency and I have decided not to interfere with the judgment of the court in either case.

ALLOCATION OF MONEY FOR HAY PURPOSES[1]

November 3, 1953

The State of North Carolina (hereinafter called the "State") and the Secretary of Agriculture of the United States (hereinafter called the "Secretary") will co-operate, as in this agreement described, to make hay available to eligible farmers in the areas of the State heretofore or hereafter designated by the President or the Secretary of Agriculture of the United States as being within the major disaster area occasioned by drought under the authority of Public Law 875, Eighty-first Congress.

1. The Secretary hereby allocates to the State the sum of $69,000.00, for use by the Governor of the State, through such agencies and delegates as he may determine, subject to the conditions hereinafter described, in carrying out this agreement. Upon request of the Governor, advances will be made by the Secretary from time to time in such amounts aggregating not to exceed the allocation to the State, as are determined by him to be necessary for the performance of this agreement.

2. Farmers may participate in this program if they operate in any area designated as a disaster area for the purposes of furnishing feed for livestock under section 2 (d) of Public Law 115, Eighty-third Congress, and if they are certified as eligible by the County Drought Committee, established by the Secretary. The standards of eligibility to be followed shall be those determined by the Secretary and shall be the same as those in effect for farmers for participation in the Drought Emergency Program, 1953, and contained in *Production and Marketing Administration Instruction,* 1104 (53)-1, and amendments, except as provided in item 3 hereof.

---

[1] This statement was signed by Governor Umstead and Ezra T. Benson, Secretary of Agriculture of the United States.

3. The County Drought Committee shall certify the amount of hay which an eligible farmer may purchase at any one time not exceeding his necessary supply for a period of sixty days. Orders accompanied by such certificates may be placed with such person or agency as the State may determine.

4. The funds advanced hereunder shall be used to defray 50 per cent of the actual transportation cost of hay moved under published tariffs, or a comparable amount, as determined by the State, for hay moved by contract carrier, but in no event shall the amount exceed $10 per ton of hay delivered. The balance of the cost of the hay shall be paid by the farmer. The State shall obtain and hold available for a period of at least three years evidence of the payment of the transportation cost for hay under this program. Such evidence shall be made available for inspection by representatives of the Secretary upon request in order that it might be determined that the funds granted hereby are expended in accordance with the terms of this agreement.

5. None of the funds granted herein shall be used to pay the salaries or any other administrative expenses incurred or to be incurred by the State or any agency thereof in carrying out this program.

6. Any portion of the sums herein granted which are not used by the State in accordance with the provisions of this agreement shall be returned to the Secretary. The State shall furnish such reports of administration of this program as the Secretary may from time to time request.

7. No member of or delegate to Congress or resident commissioner shall be admitted to any part or share of this agreement, or to any benefit that may arise therefrom.

8. This agreement is entered into pursuant to and for the purposes of Public Law 875, Eighty-first Congress, as amended, this 3rd day of November, 1953. The provisions hereof shall not apply with respect to any hay delivered to farmers on or after the fifteenth day of April, 1954.

ANNIVERSARY OF THE UNITED STATES MARINE CORPS

November 10, 1953

Today, November 10, 1953, marks the 178th anniversary of the United States Marine Corps as a fighting force for liberty and justice. The men of the United States Marine Corps have served their country and their Corps well and faithfully throughout their long history from the American Revolution in 1775 to the battlefields in 1950.

We in North Carolina are proud that two of the largest Marine Corps bases in the Nation, the Marine Corps Air Station, Cherry Point, North Carolina, and the Marine Corps Base, Camp Lejeune, North Carolina, are located within our State. It is a pleasure to call attention to this 178th anniversary and ask that all our citizens call to mind the motto of the Corps, "Semper Fidelis," as we remember the Marine heroes of the past and present.

ANNUAL SALE OF CHRISTMAS SEALS

November 16, 1953

November 16 will be the opening day of the 47th annual Christmas Seal campaign conducted by the North Carolina Tuberculosis Association. This campaign will continue through Christmas Day, and during this period North Carolinians will have the opportunity to purchase Christmas Seals.

During 1952, five hundred and forty-three persons in North Carolina died as a result of Tuberculosis. There were 2,326 new cases reported in the State during the same year and there are an estimated 150,000 active cases in the United States. The program of the North Carolina Tuberculosis Association and its affiliates has contributed a great deal to the prevention of tuberculosis through health education, case finding, rehabilitation and research. The annual Christmas Seal sale has supported this splendid work since 1910 in North Carolina and I am confident it will receive again the wholehearted support of the people of North Carolina.

MAYFLOWER COMPACT

November 16, 1953

The 333rd anniversary of the signing of the Mayflower Compact will be observed on November 21, 1953. I am happy to call attention to the designation of November 21 as Mayflower Compact Day in North Carolina and suggest that appropriate observance of this anniversary be made by our schools, churches, civic and patriotic organizations and by the public generally.

The story of how the Pilgrim fathers contributed to the establishment of democratic self-government should be recognized and remembered by everyone. The forty-one men of the Pilgrim Company signed the Mayflower Compact and gave the first assurance that virtue, industry, and freedom were to find refuge here and thereby help establish the principle of constitutional self-government and individual liberty under the law.

WHITE CLOVER DAY

November 17, 1953

The American Veterans of World War II are planning to observe December 5, 1953 as White Clover Day in the State of North Carolina. On this day members of the AMVETS will sell White Clovers throughout North Carolina as a means of raising funds which will be used for welfare purposes by local posts of AMVETS.

I am pleased to note this designation of December 5 and call this worthy campaign to the attention of the people of North Carolina.

KOREAN CHILDREN'S DAY

November 19, 1953

I have been informed that a group of American women, headed by Mrs. Dwight D. Eisenhower as Honorary Chairman, have launched a nation-wide fund drive to provide CARE help for Korean children. Civilian casualties in Korea have resulted in 100,000 Korean infants and young children being orphaned and at least a million boys and girls are in dire need. The CARE for Korean Children Committee is asking that the day before Thanksgiving Day, Wednesday, November 25, be observed as Korean Children's Day, a day on which every citizen in North Carolina is requested to contribute toward a CARE package of food to be sent to children in Korea.

These Korean children deserve our assistance and I am glad to call attention to the designation of Wednesday, November 25, as Korean Children's Day. A generous response from North Carolinians to this campaign would be deeply appreciated.

GOLD STAR FAMILY WEEK

December 1, 1953

The week of December 7-13, 1953, is being observed throughout the Nation as Gold Star Family Week in acknowledgment of the sacrifices made by all those who lost loved ones in the service of our country. This week begins on the twelfth anniversary of the devastating attack on Pearl Harbor, and I consider it a suitable time to honor our Nation's war dead, to recall the sacrifices of our Gold Star Mothers, and to honor them by the proper observance of Gold Star Family Week.

YOUNG DEMOCRATIC CLUBS RESOLVE TO SUPPORT THE GOVERNOR

December 10, 1953

Whereas, the progress and development of the State of North Carolina since the turn of the century are a source of pride for every citizen of this State; and

Whereas, it is recognized that the advancement of our State is directly attributable to the safe and sane leadership which has guided the destiny of our state government; and

Whereas, the Honorable William B. Umstead has clearly demonstrated that it is his desire, intent and determination to continue the high principles, zeal and forthrightness which have been manifested in previous years;

Now, therefore, be it resolved by the Young Democrats of North Carolina in convention assembled in Raleigh, North Carolina, this date do pledge our earnest support to Governor Umstead and his administration, and express our appreciation for and confidence in his untiring efforts on behalf of all the people of North Carolina, and that a copy of this resolution be forwarded to the Governor as an indication of our esteem and confidence.

Whereas, the state administration of Governor William B. Umstead has sponsored the bond issues for the needs of our public schools and mental institutions, and the voters of the entire State have given overwhelming support to this program;

It is therefore resolved that the Young Democrats of North Carolina hereby commend the foresight of Governor Umstead and his state administration in promoting this bond program for the urgent needs of our schools and mental institutions and we recognize the lasting benefits which this step will play in the future growth of our State.

BILL OF RIGHTS DAY

December 15, 1953

It has been the custom of the Bill of Rights Commemorative Society of New York City to observe December 15 as Bill of Rights Day, as a means of commemorating the first meeting of Congress when this great document of human rights was adopted. I think it is most appropriate to remember the events which made it possible for our young Nation to draft and adopt the Bill of Rights—a cornerstone of our free and democratic form of government.

I commend these efforts to call attention to this important anniversary in our Nation's history. It is my hope that our people in this State will pause long enough today to express their thanks for the sound judgment and wisdom of our forefathers who drafted and adopted this priceless document.

DEATH OF JAMES YADKIN JOYNER [1]

January 25, 1954

I was distressed to learn of the death of Dr. J. Y. Joyner of La Grange. For well over a half century he has been one of North Carolina's most useful and outstanding citizens. His contribution to the welfare of the people of this State in practically every phase of its development and especially in the fields of education, agriculture and religious faith cannot yet be truly measured.

This generation and those yet unborn will owe him an everlasting debt of gratitude. His life was an inspiration to all who knew him, and his strength of character and lovable personality endeared him to the people of North Carolina. I had for him a deep personal affection and he will continue to live in the hearts and memories of all those who respect the fine qualities of mind and of heart which he possessed and so freely gave to his people and his State. I have lost a devoted friend and the State has lost one of its pillars of strength.

COMMITTEE TO CO-OPERATE WITH THE IZAAK WALTON LEAGUE

January 28, 1954

Governor William B. Umstead announced today that a committee he appointed recently to co-operate with the Izaak Walton League of America's plans for a national Young Outdoor Americans Conference in Chicago will meet in Raleigh on February 5. As a result of the meeting a North Carolina youth who has been active in the field of conservation will be awarded a free trip to Chicago in March.

[1] James Yadkin Joyner was born at Yadkin College, Davidson County, North Carolina, August 7, 1862, the youngest of a family of seven children. He graduated from the University of North Carolina in 1881. He married Effie E. Rouse of La Grange, December 14, 1887. In 1884 Joyner became superintendent of the schools in Winston, North Carolina, in 1889 he became superintendent of Goldsboro city schools, and in 1892 he became a professor of English literature and dean of the Normal School in Greensboro. Governor Charles B. Aycock appointed him Superintendent of Public Instruction in 1902, where he served until 1918 when he returned to his farm at La Grange and became active in the Carolina-Virginia Tobacco Growers Co-operative Association. When this organization was put into bankruptcy he returned to his farm, but was always interested in public affairs and particularly educational advancement in North Carolina.

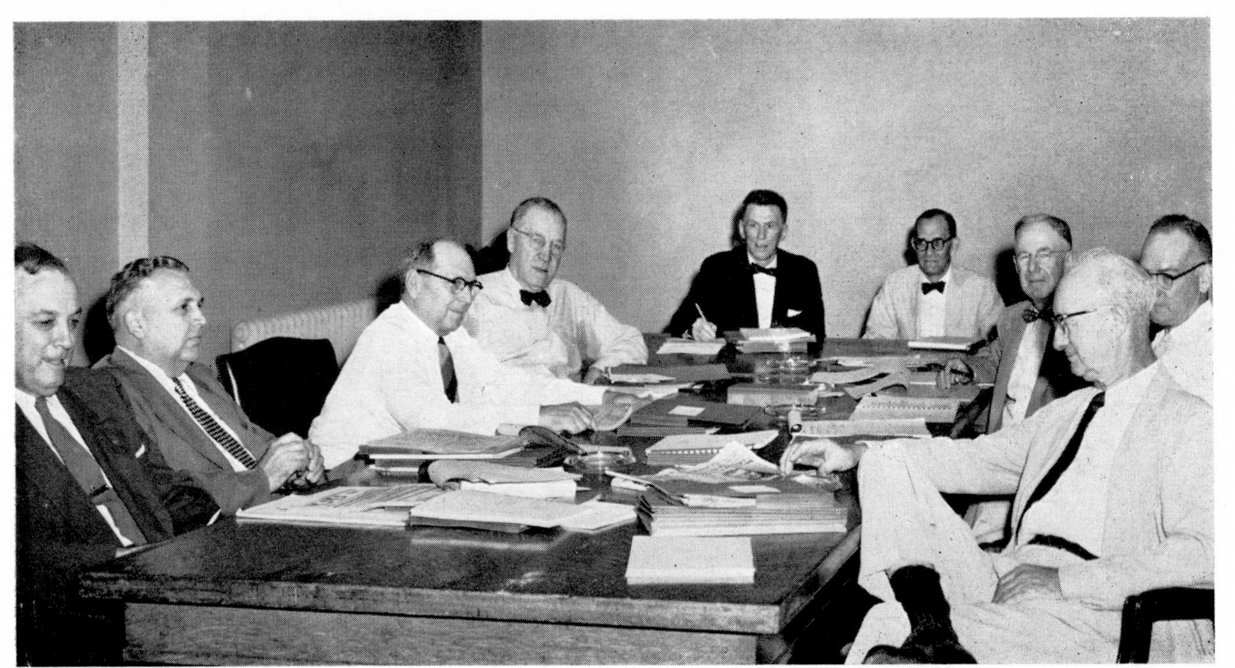

Advisory Budget Commission meeting in Raleigh, August 15, 1954. *Left to right:* Leroy Martin; Alonzo C. Edwards; W. B. Rodman, Jr.; J. Kemp Doughton; John D. Larkins, Jr.; Governor Umstead; D. S. Coltrane; L. D. Moore; and Claude Currie.

Serving on the committee are Clyde P. Patton, Executive Director of the Wildlife Resources Commission, Chairman; Forrest V. Dunstan, Commander, Elizabeth City Veterans of Foreign Wars; Roger W. Wolcott, President, North Carolina Forestry Association, Raleigh; W. L. McMillan, Commander, Rocky Mount American Legion, and E. B. Garrett, State Conservationist, U. S. Soil Conservation Service, Raleigh.

The committee will meet in the Wildlife Resources Commission's new offices at Glenwood Village, Raleigh, to discuss with youth group leaders and professional conservationists ways and means of increasing the interest of young people in conservation of natural resources, and rewarding those who are already doing outstanding work in this field.

Attending the meeting besides youth group and conservation leaders will be young people selected from Scouts, 4-H Clubs, FFA chapters, and other youth organizations, who have been doing outstanding work in natural resource conservation.

After hearing a discussion of problems of conservation in various fields such as forestry, soils, water and wildlife by group leaders and conservationists, and giving their own views on what ought to be done to make conservation work more effective, the young people will go into executive session to select from among themselves a delegate to the Young Outdoor Americans Conference in Chicago, March 10-12. The Izaak Walton League of America will pay the expenses of the chosen delegate, and will undertake to pay the expenses of one advisor-councilor from each of the youth group organizations represented at the Raleigh meeting.

APPOINTMENT OF WILLIAM H. BOBBITT

January 30, 1954

Governor Umstead announced today the appointment of Judge William H. Bobbitt of Charlotte as an Associate Justice of the Supreme Court of North Carolina to fill the vacancy created by the appointment of Associate Justice Barnhill as Chief Justice.

Judge William H. Bobbitt was born on October 18, 1900 in Raleigh. He has lived in Charlotte since 1913. He attended the

Charlotte schools and received his A.B. degree at the University of North Carolina in 1921. He also studied law at the University of North Carolina where he was a Phi Beta Kappa student and a member of the Golden Fleece. Davidson College conferred upon him an honorary degree, LL.D., in 1953.

He received his law license in 1921 at the age of twenty-one and began the practice of law in Charlotte as a member of the firm of Parker, Stewart, McRae and Bobbitt, and he practiced there until he became the resident judge of the 14th Judicial District on January 1, 1939, having been elected to that office in 1938. He has been the resident judge of the Judicial District since that time. He is now, and has been since its organization, a member of the State Judicial Council.

Judge Bobbitt married Miss Sarah Dunlap of Charlotte in 1924 and they have four children: Mrs. John W. Carter of Weldon; William H. Bobbitt, Jr., attorney at law of Charlotte; Miss Harriet Bobbitt, a student at Greensboro College; and, Mrs. Ekkehart Sachtler of New York City.

Judge Bobbitt is a member of the Dilworth Methodist Church in Charlotte where he teaches the Men's Bible Class and is a member of the Board of Stewards.

He is permanent president of the class of 1921 of the University of North Carolina.

Judge Bobbitt will take the oath as an associate justice of the Superior Court and is considered one of the outstanding jurists of the State.

Judge Bobbitt will take the oath as an associate justice of the Supreme Court of North Carolina at eleven o'clock, Monday morning, February 1, 1954.

APPOINTMENT OF FRANCIS O. CLARKSON

January 30, 1954

Governor Umstead announced today the appointment of Judge Francis O. Clarkson of Charlotte as the resident judge of the 14th Judicial District to fill the vacancy created by the appointment of Judge William H. Bobbitt as an Associate Justice of the Supreme Court of North Carolina.

Judge Clarkson was born in Charlotte on August 26, 1895, and attended the Charlotte schools. He received an A.B. degree from the University of North Carolina in 1916 and a LL.B. degree in 1917. He served in the Marine Corps during World War I and began the practice of law in Charlotte on January 1, 1919, as a member of the law firm of his father, the late Associate Justice Heriot Clarkson. He served an unexpired term as solicitor of the 14th Judicial District in 1922 and was appointed a special judge of the Superior Court on July 1, 1953.

Judge Clarkson married Miss Camma Burgess of Atlanta and they have four children: Mrs. Robert W. Stenglein of Saginaw, Michigan; Mrs. Robert E. Merritt of Mt. Airy; F. O. Clarkson, Jr., now in the military service; and, Miss Margaret Simmons Clarkson, a student at Hollins.

Judge Clarkson is a member of the Episcopal Church in which he has served in many capacities, including Chancellor of the Diocese of North Carolina. He has been active in civic and religious affairs of Mecklenburg County for many years.

Governor Umstead said that he has known Judge Clarkson intimately since 1912 when they entered the University of North Carolina at Chapel Hill. He considers him one of North Carolina's outstanding citizens and there has existed between them an intimate friendship for more than forty years.

Judge Clarkson will take the oath of office as resident judge of the 14th Judicial District in the Supreme Court in Raleigh, Monday morning, February 1, at eleven o'clock.

INDUSTRIAL DEVELOPMENT IN NORTH CAROLINA[1]

January 30, 1954

It is a pleasure to report to the many readers of *The News-Argus* that North Carolina is making progress in its efforts to increase industrial development in every section of the State.

Under the splendid leadership of its Director, Mr. Ben E. Douglas, the Department of Conservation and Development is working hard to stimulate interest and action in the field of

[1] This statement was prepared especially for *The Goldsboro News-Argus,* January 30, 1954.

industrial development on a state-wide basis. It does not play favorites in any area or to any group but it is ready and anxious at all times to co-operate with every community interested in planning some type of industrial development.

As I pointed out in my Inaugural Address, large segments of industry are moving south, and North Carolina should make every effort to get its share. We should also encourage expansion of the industry which we now have. New or expanded industry means employment for thousands of our people, increased per capita income and additional revenue for badly needed state services.

New industry means new job opportunities for thousands of young men and women, educated at the expense of the State, who leave our borders each year to find opportunity elsewhere.

It is gratifying to note that substantial progress is now being made in Eastern North Carolina in increasing the industrial development of this potentially great manufacturing section of our State. A recent survey made by the Wachovia Bank and Trust Company in co-operation with the Department of Conservation and Development revealed that "eastern North Carolina has gained more industries and has experienced greater expansion among its established manufacturing plants in the past ten years than has occurred there in the last century."

I commend *The News-Argus* for its continuing efforts and interest in the full development of our many resources and opportunities here in North Carolina.

NEED FOR EXPANDED FARM PROGRAM [1]

February 22, 1954

We have made great progress in agriculture in North Carolina, but much remains to be done.

According to published reports, the per capita income for North Carolina for 1952 was $1,049 and we ranked 45th among the states of the Union. In 1950 the population of North Carolina was a little more than 4,000,000. Of this number about 1,376,000 worked

[1] This statement appeared in *The News and Observer* (Raleigh), February 22, 1954.

on farms, a larger number than in any state in the Union. It is obvious, therefore, that the farm income largely affects our per capita income.

The total amount received for farm products, livestock and livestock products in 1952 amounted to more than $900,000,000, and in this respect we ranked thirteenth among the states. Approximately 70 per cent of our cash income is from tobacco, cotton, and peanuts. The livestock industry has made great gains in our State during the past few years, and since 1938 we have moved from thirtieth to twenty-third among the states in cash income from livestock. The number of our Grade A dairies has tremendously increased during the past six years and the production per cow has also substantially increased. The number of beef cattle has about doubled since 1949. We have also made substantial gains in the poultry industry. The number of laying hens is now about 35 per cent greater than in 1940 and the number of eggs produced has almost doubled. The gross income from the production of eggs is five times the amount received in 1940, and the number of broilers produced has doubled since 1948. In spite of this progress, livestock, livestock products, and poultry accounted for only about 22 per cent of our total cash farm income in 1952.

LIVESTOCK AND PASTURE

The farm people and farm leaders in North Carolina are to be commended for the progress made in the livestock and poultry industry. We will not have the agricultural per capita income or the total per capita income we should have until the livestock industry is developed to the point where it more fully utilizes the resources that are available in this State. We have had to reduce the acreage of our basic cash crops and, due to world conditions, more reductions may have to be made. This means that thousands of acres heretofore planted in basic crops should be used for improved pastures and for feed crops. Our climate is splendid for the production of livestock. Instead of ranking thirteenth among the states, it is entirely possible to rank among the upper five or six.

In this connection, markets, distribution and storage facilities are essential and need to be developed. The amount of livestock and livestock products now produced is far short of the needs of the people of our State. Certainly every effort should be made to supply our own demands.

Production of small grains and hay crops is not only profitable but aids in soil and water conservation and works well into a well-planned livestock program. I am informed that the grain and hay crops in this State could easily be increased around 25 per cent in the next five or ten years. This would call for adequate storage, both inland and at our ports.

Improved Practices

In addition to the above, every effort should be made to continue improved agricultural practices, rotation of crops, soil conservation and a proper forestry program, together with a planned system of handling our woodlands. Pulpwood can be made a source of annual income in many sections of the State without seriously depleting the supply. Careless handling of our woodlands and forests could result not only in a substantial loss of income but also in serious depletion of one of our great natural resources. Reforestation has an important part both in connection with the maintenance of our lumber and wood supply and also in any proper plan for the conservation of our soil and water resources.

All of the agencies of the state and federal governments dealing with the complex problems of agriculture have been teaching for years the necessity of diversified farming. Diversified farming calls for additional marketing skills, marketing and storage facilities, proper grading, transportation, improved methods of handling and a more effective use of information obtained by scientific research. The limitations upon the length of this article will not permit a detailed discussion of all of the things which I think necessary to raise the per capita income of the farmers of North Carolina to the point where it should be. I do wish to call attention to a part of the statement I made on agriculture in my Inaugural Address on January 8, 1953. I then stated as follows:

Must Stop Soil Erosion

"We should have a co-operative movement on the part of the appropriate agencies, the farmers, cities and towns, and all of our people, for a unified and effective effort to stop erosion of soil.

"We need more improved pasture land, more dairy and beef cattle, and more poultry.

"There should be a greater utilization of our forest resources and a comprehensive and effective forestry program, including adequate fire protection, and a wider use of recommended forest improvement practices.

"We need more effective methods of protecting and using our water resources and our wildlife.

"We need additional processing plants for agricultural products, and we should develop better and expanding marketing facilities for our poultry, fruit, vegetables, and livestock.

"Every effort should be made to eliminate such inequalities in freight rates affecting agriculture in North Carolina as may now exist.

"We should expand our program of agricultural research."

These needs still exist and deserve our best efforts.

EXPANDED RESEARCH

I believe that due to the work of the farm organizations, State College, the Extension Service, the State Department of Agriculture and other agencies that most people working on the farm now understand the value of reliable information with reference to soils, fertilizers, improved methods of farming, packaging, marketing, and other phases of agriculture. Therefore, it seems to me that perhaps the most important need of our State at this time in agriculture is an expansion of scientific research. Sympathetic General Assemblies, the federal government and the farmers themselves, through "Nickels for Know-How" have made possible an expanded program and yet it is my belief that it is still inadequate, although with the money we have and the facilities at hand, a splendid job is being done. We now know that scientific research for the farmer is just as essential as it is for industry and we must, I think, give it a place of high importance in any program designed to improve agriculture.

Along with our efforts in all other matters pertaining to the development of North Carolina, we must remember that agriculture is still a matter of prime importance to the State and we must continue to make every effort to increase the per capita income of the one-third of our population engaged in farming. This is essential for the over-all welfare of North Carolina.

NATIONAL FUTURE FARMERS OF AMERICA WEEK

February 23, 1954

It has been called to my attention that this week is being observed as National Future Farmers of America Week. The Future Farmers of America organization is composed of boys who are studying vocational agriculture in public schools in preparation for careers in farming. They strive to develop leadership, encourage co-operation, promote good citizenship, teach sound methods of farming and inspire patriotism among its members.

North Carolina now has 446 active chapters of the organization, with 21,916 active members at this time and more than 110,000 former members. The members of The Future Farmers of America perform valuable community services and provide important leadership in developing our agricultural economy and in building a better State.

As Governor of North Carolina, I urge all our citizens to take notice of the many contributions of The Future Farmers of America to our State and to encourage in every possible way the further growth of this splendid organization for our farm youth. The future prosperity and progress of North Carolina depends to a large degree upon the skills and efforts of these young men who will operate the many farms of our State.

GIRL SCOUT WEEK

March 3, 1954

The Girl Scouts of North Carolina and the Nation are observing Girl Scout Week this year on March 7-13. This week will mark the forty-second anniversary of the founding of this outstanding organization which began March 12, 1912 at Savannah, Georgia under the leadership of Mrs. Juliette Gordon Low.

Today there are over two million Girl Scouts in the United States who are participating in the celebration of Girl Scout

Week. The theme will be "Know Your Neighbors—Know Your Nation," and each day of the week will feature an activity typical of the Girl Scout program such as homemaking, arts and crafts, citizenship, health and safety, nature study and international friendship. I commend the Girl Scouts and their leaders for their sincere interest in learning more about their community and the State and Nation in which they live. We should all strive to be good neighbors wherever we live and have a better knowledge and understanding of those who live around us.

It is a pleasure to designate the week of March 7-13 as Girl Scout Week in North Carolina and to express the hope that Girl Scout work will continue to grow and flourish in our State. I extend to the Girl Scouts, their leaders, and their parents, my personal greetings and best wishes in the furtherance of the Girl Scout movement.

NORTH CAROLINA LEADS IN 4-H CLUB WORK [1]

March 4, 1954

National 4-H Club Week will be observed this year in North Carolina and throughout the Nation on March 6-14. This is an important time in the lives of thousands of young men and women in North Carolina who are enrolled and actively engaged in this splendid program. During this special week, I hope that more North Carolinians will become acquainted with 4-H Club Week and the healthy influence that this program has in the lives of our rural people.

North Carolina leads all other states in the Nation in the number of boys and girls enrolled as members in 4-H Clubs. There are over 140,000 young people in our State who are members of more than 2,000 clubs located in every one of our 100 counties. North Carolina is also a leader in 4-H Club work from a per capita and per family membership enrollment. In this connection, it should be remembered that North Carolina has more people working on farms than any other state in our Nation. I understand that our State's total 4-H Club membership is the equiva-

[1] This statement was issued just prior to the annual observance of 4-H Club Week. The statement was addressed "To All North Carolina 4-H Club Members" and was sent to newspapers throughout the State.

lent of one member for every two rural farm families, as compared with a national ratio of one for every three rural farm families.

In teaching better practices in agriculture, homemaking, citizenship training, and leadership development, our 4-H program has opened wide new doors of opportunities for more than three million young people who have participated in 4-H Club work since its beginning in North Carolina. I am extremely proud of the 4-H program, its leaders, its members and its many sponsors throughout the State.

I am pleased to designate the week of March 6-14 as National 4-H Club Week in North Carolina and wish for every 4-H Club member continued success and achievement during 1954 and the years ahead. I commend to the people of North Carolina, the pledge of the 4-H Clubs:

My Head to clearer thinking,
My Heart to greater loyalty,
My Hands to larger service, and
My Health to better living for
My club, my community and my country.

EFFORTS TO ATTRACT NEW INDUSTRY TO NORTH CAROLINA

March 8, 1954

Several native North Carolinians, who are now living and working in New York, want to help North Carolina in its campaign to attract more industries into the State, Governor Umstead said upon his return to his office today from a two-day stay in New York.

The Governor was accompanied by Director Ben E. Douglas of the Department of Conservation and Development, Eugene Simmons, who is a special aide to Director Douglas in the industry procurement campaign now in progress, and Edward L. Rankin, Jr., Private Secretary to the Governor.

Governor Umstead and his party met with a group of native North Carolinians and others at the Links Club last Friday afternoon and discussed plans to bring more industries into the State.

This meeting was arranged through the courtesy and assistance of General Kenneth Royall of Goldsboro, prominent New York attorney.

"We found the group enthusiastic and desirous of giving us all the help they can in helping us bring more industries into North Carolina," Douglas said.

The Governor, Douglas added, asked the group, all prominently identified in the business world, to help the State in its efforts to bring more industries into North Carolina by telling others of the advantages the Tar Heel State has to offer industrialists seeking Southern site locations. The Governor told the group they can help by furnishing prospects to the Department of Conservation and Development. He did not ask them to form any organized group for this purpose but to do what they can as individuals.

"These North Carolinians gave the impression of being highly honored by having the Governor of their native State come to New York and ask them to help in the efforts being made to increase per capita income in North Carolina," Douglas said. "Some of them told me they were not accustomed to having the Governor of their native State come to New York and ask their help."

The Conservation and Development Director said that he found the Tar Heel businessmen in New York generally feel the business outlook in 1954 will be good.

While in New York the Governor and his party were guests Friday night of the North Carolina Society there on the occasion of its 56th annual dinner and ball in the Hotel St. Regis.

Those meeting with Governor Umstead and his party last Friday were: Joseph McConnell, President, Colgate-Palmolive-Peet Company; Robert L. Huffines, Jr., President, Textron Corporation; Kenneth Towe, President, American Cyanamide Company; Vermont C. Royster, Associate Editor, *The Wall Street Journal;* Ben Few, President, Leggett and Meyers Tobacco Company; James L. Harrison, National City Bank; Arthur W. Page, a retired industrialist; Ben Page, American Tobacco Company; J. Dewey Dorsett, a top executive in a large insurance firm; Isaac B. Granger, Executive Vice-President, Chemical Bank and Trust Company; Herman High, Executive Vice-President, Vick Chemical Company; Harry Dalton, American Viscose Company; Robert

L. Hatcher, Chase National Bank; Earl Christian, General Royall, T. Palmer Jerman, and J. E. Bennett. Bennett will be the manager of the new plant of P. Lorillard and Company now being constructed at Greensboro.

THE POTENTIAL DANGER OF THE DRINKING DRIVER[1]

March 14, 1954

The sober driver on our highways who drives carefully, safely, and obeys the motor vehicles laws, has every right to expect to reach his destination without mishap. However, even with sober drivers at the wheel, there are far too many accidents on our State highways. So it is particularly appalling when our people are injured in automobile accidents caused by a drinking driver. A person who drinks intoxicants and then drives a motor vehicle on our streets and highways is a menace to law-abiding citizens wherever he drives.

While a solicitor, I witnessed the tragedy and heartache that is the inevitable result of mixing gasoline and whiskey. Safe driving on our state highways requires a sober, alert, and capable driver. The dulled reflexes of a drinking driver have no place on our public roads and streets. Yet, last year in North Carolina I understand that 7,899 of the drivers involved in all motor vehicle accidents had been drinking to some degree. In fatal accidents recorded, 385 drivers had been drinking. When you consider the potential danger of the drinking driver, it is good fortune that more fatalities did not occur last year.

We are now engaged in a determined program to make motor travel safer for all who use our highways—citizens and tourists alike. So far the results of our vigorous law enforcement program have been most encouraging. I hope that each North Carolinian will do his part to make this program successful.

I am grateful for this opportunity to call attention to the problem of the drinking driver. I commend the *Durham Morning Herald* for this material help in making our readers more conscious of the need for safe driving. The seriousness of the drinking driver menace should be evident to every thoughtful North Carolinian.

[1] This statement was prepared for the *Durham Morning Herald,* March 14, 1954.

SAFETY WEEK IN NORTH CAROLINA

April 12, 1954

The Twenty-Fourth Annual State-wide Safety Conference will be held in Raleigh on May 4-6 as a continuation of a valuable series of meetings which have made a substantial contribution to the cause of safety in North Carolina over the years. While this Conference is primarily concerned with industrial safety, its participants fully realize the over-all importance of safety activities in North Carolina, including highway safety, and safety in the home and on the farms.

Accident prevention is a positive activity worthy of the support and co-operation of every citizen. Modern industrial management in our State and Nation has made great strides in improving industrial safety through a sound and progressive program of a series of meetings which have made a substantial contribution to accident prevention. We are today in North Carolina applying some of the same principles of accident prevention in an intensive effort to prevent the toll of fatalities and injuries on our public highways and streets. Safety in industry, on the highways, in the home, and on the farm is our mutual problem.

As another means of calling attention to the value of accident prevention work, I hereby designate the week of May 3-8 as Safety Week in North Carolina.

GOVERNOR UMSTEAD SERVES AS CHAIRMAN OF DEFENSE FUND

April 14, 1954

Governor Umstead announced today that he has accepted President Dwight D. Eisenhower's invitation to serve as Honorary Chairman of the United Defense Fund in North Carolina. President Eisenhower, in his letter to Governor Umstead, said that he is serving as Honorary Chairman of the United Defense Fund throughout the country because of his "deep conviction that the defense of this country depends upon the voluntary activities of its citizens, as well as upon the authority of government."

The President has asked the governor of each state and territory to serve as Honorary Chairman of the United Defense Fund in his state or territory. General of the Army Omar N. Bradley, former Chairman of the Chiefs of Staff, is national campaign Chairman of UDF, succeeding Lieutenant General James H. Doolittle.

The United Defense Fund is a federation of national voluntary agencies providing help, welfare and recreational services for all of those engaged in the defense of this Nation. It is supported chiefly through Community Chest and United Fund campaigns. It includes United Service Organizations, United Community Defense Services, American Relief for Korea, American Social Hygiene Association, United Seamen's Service, and the National Recreation Association.

NATIONAL FESTIVAL OF SPORTS

April 14, 1954

It has always been true that healthy sports and recreation have been one of the best means of maintaining the health and physical welfare of our citizens. During this period of armed peace, our Nation needs to mobilize our human resources to the greatest extent possible.

I am pleased to co-operate with the National Festival of Sports in naming a state-wide committee to co-ordinate a state-wide Festival of Sports as a primary aid in the maintenance and conservation of the health of our citizens, as well as providing wholesome fun and recreation so essential to the general welfare.

Therefore, I hereby designate the period of April 19 through May 16 as National Sports Festival throughout the State of North Carolina and request the support and co-operation of everyone in the observance of this worthwhile program.

IMPROVED AGRICULTURAL PRACTICES

April 28, 1954

I appreciate this opportunity to express some views on the present and future farm outlook in North Carolina. I commend *The Daily Reflector* for its interest in agriculture through the issuance of an annual farm edition.

It seems to me that perhaps the most important need of our State at this time in agriculture is an expansion of scientific research. With the money we have and the facilities at hand, a splendid job in research is being accomplished. Sympathetic General Assemblies, the federal government, and the farmers themselves, through "Nickels for Know-How" have made possible an expanded program and have indicated the deep interest today in better scientific research.

In spite of all this, it is my belief that our research program in agriculture is still inadequate. We know that scientific research for the farmers is just as essential as it is for industry, and we must give it a place of high importance in any program designed to improve agriculture. The farm areas served by *The Daily Reflector* are vitally interested in tobacco. Our tobacco farmers know how agricultural research has enabled them to produce more and better tobacco per acre in spite of plant diseases and plant pests. With the current interest in tobacco having a low nicotine content, we again must look to our research facilities for the answer to another genuine threat to the markets for our tobacco products.

There is no doubt that we have made great progress in agriculture in North Carolina, but much remains to be done. According to published reports, the per capita income for North Carolina for 1952 was $1,049 and we ranked forty-fifth among the states of the Union. In 1950 the population of North Carolina was a little more than 4,000,000. Of this number about 1,376,000 worked on farms, a larger number than in any state in the Union. It is obvious, therefore, that the farm income largely affects our per capita income.

The total amount received for farm products, livestock and livestock products in 1952 amounted to more than $900,000,000 and in this respect we ranked thirteenth among the states. Approximately 70 per cent of our cash income is from tobacco, cotton, and peanuts. The livestock industry has made great gains in our State during the past few years, and since 1938 we have moved from thirtieth to twenty-third among the states in cash income from livestock. The number of our Grade A dairies has tremendously increased during the past two years and the production per cow has also substantially increased. The number of beef cattle has about doubled since 1949. We have also made substantial gains in the poultry industry. The number of laying hens is now about 35 per cent greater than in 1940 and the number of eggs produced has almost doubled. The gross income from the production of eggs is five times the amount received in 1940, and the number of broilers produced has doubled since 1948. In spite of this progress, livestock, livestock products, and poultry accounted for only about 22 per cent of our total cash farm income in 1952.

The farm people and farm leaders in North Carolina are to be commended for the progress made in the livestock and poultry industry. We will not have the agricultural per capita income or the total per capita income we should have until the livestock industry is developed to the point where it more fully utilizes the resources that are available in this State. We have had to reduce the acreage of our basic cash crops and, due to world conditions, more reductions may have to be made. This means that thousands of acres heretofore planted in basic crops should be used for improved pastures and for feed crops. Our climate is splendid for the production of livestock. Instead of ranking thirteenth among the states, it is entirely possible to rank among the upper five or six.

In this connection, markets, distribution, and storage facilities are essential and need to be developed. The amount of livestock and livestock products now produced is far short of the needs of the people of our State. Certainly every effort should be made to supply our own demands.

Production of small grains and hay crops is not only profitable but aids in soil and water conservation and works well into an effective livestock program.

I am informed that the grain and hay crops in this State could easily be increased around 25 per cent in the next five or ten years. This would call for adequate storage, both inland and at our ports.

In addition to the above, every effort should be made to continue improved agricultural practices, rotation of crops, soil conservation and a proper forestry program, together with a planned system of handling our woodlands. Pulpwood can be made a source of annual income in many sections of the State without seriously depleting the supply. Careless handling of our

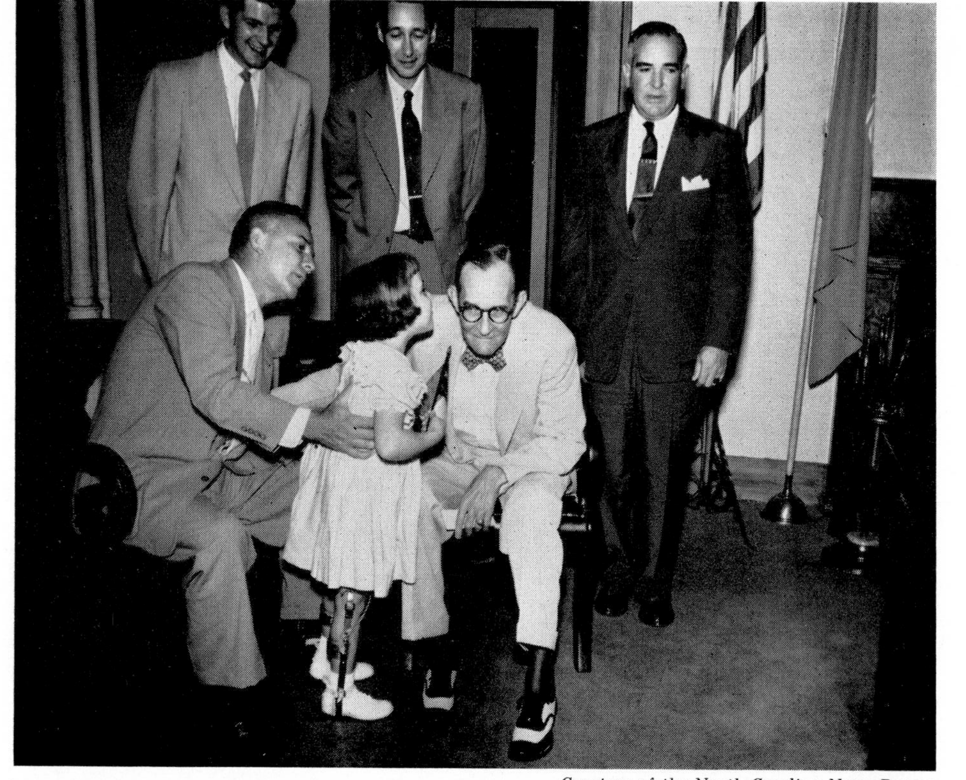

Courtesy of the North Carolina News Bureau

Governor Umstead, *(right seated)* on Oct. 1, 1954, buys from Ginger Massey of Durham the first ticket for the annual Carolina-Duke freshman football game scheduled to be played in Durham on Thanksgiving Day for the benefit of the Cerebral Palsy Foundation. Others are *(left to right)* Norman Massey *(seated)*; C. Wesley Gilbert; John F. Morrissey; and Horace Johnson.

woodlands and forests could result not only in a substantial loss of income but also in serious depletion of one of our great natural resources. Reforestation has an important part both in connection with the maintenance of our lumber and wood supply and also in any proper plan for the conservation of our soil and water resources.

I have always been deeply interested in agriculture. I was born on a tobacco farm in the northern part of Durham County and know from firsthand experience both the importance of the farmer's job and also the many difficulties with which he is beset in producing crops at a profit. In my Inaugural Address on January 8, 1953, I dealt with a number of the needs and problems of agriculture today. We should do more to stop erosion of our priceless soil. We need more and better pasture land and a greater utilization of our forest resources as well as more effective methods of protecting and using our water resources and our wildlife. North Carolina needs additional processing plants for agricultural products, and we should develop better and expanding marketing facilities for our poultry, fruit, vegetables, and livestock.

I am encouraged at the progress that has been made due to the willingness of our farm people to accept new and better ways of farming. The work of the farm organizations, State College, the Extension Service, the State Department of Agriculture, and other agencies, has contributed a great deal to the improvement of agriculture in North Carolina today. We must always remember that agriculture is still a matter of prime importance to our State, and we must continue to make every effort to increase the per capita income of the one-third of our people engaged in farming. This is a fundamental part of the over-all welfare of North Carolina.

MENTAL HEALTH WEEK

May 4, 1954

Each year the various states observe Mental Health Week for the purpose of making every American citizen aware of the increasing importance of mental health and also to help interested groups to work together in formulating better mental health programs in their own communities. In North Carolina the activities for this special week are co-ordinated by the North Carolina Mental Hygiene Society, Inc., through its local affiliates and the various state and community organizations. Nationally, it is directed and co-ordinated by the National Association of Mental Health in co-sponsorship with the National Institute of Mental Health of the federal government.

It is most commendable that some sixty county leaders in North Carolina are actively engaged in various programs promoting Mental Health Week. There is a new awareness about mental health in North Carolina as demonstrated by the appropriation of $22,000,000 since World War II in improvements to our state mental institutions, and more recently, in the overwhelming vote of approval given the mental hospital bond issue which provided another $22,000,000 for improving and enlarging our mental institutions, and for the construction of needed facilities for feeble-minded children. North Carolina is moving ahead to meet the challenging needs in the mental health field.

However, these needs are many. They include mental health clinics to serve as a first line of defense against emotional disturbances; more special teachers for mentally handicapped children; better facilities for training mentally defective children in institutions; and, additional provisions for the care of aged people. As of April 1, 1954, there were 9,844 people in our state mental hospitals alone. During the same month 1,843 children were in training schools for mental defectives.

I hereby designate May 2-9 as Mental Health Week in North Carolina and urge the co-operation of every citizen in learning more about the need for better mental health. An informed people will always respond to pressing needs in the mental health field.

COMMITTEE ON THE AMERICAN-KOREAN FOUNDATION [1]

May 5, 1954

At the request of the American-Korean Foundation, Governor Umstead announced today the appointment of a North Carolina Veterans Committee to serve as a part of the National Veterans Committee in connection with the American-Korean Foundation. The members of the Committee, suggested by the Foundation and named by Governor Umstead today, are as follows: W. L. McMillan of Rocky Mount, State Commander, American Legion, as Chairman; Forrest V. Dunstan of Elizabeth City, State Commander, Veterans of Foreign Wars; Thomas McCaffrey of Durham, Commander, North Carolina AMVETS; W. E. Whetstone of Charlotte, State Commander, D.A.V.; Mrs. A. Warren Neill of Charlotte, President, American Legion Auxiliary; Miss Ruby Reinhardt of Hickory, State President, Veterans of Foreign Wars Auxiliary.

THE DEATH OF CLYDE R. HOEY

May 13, 1954

I was deeply shocked to learn of the passing of Senator Clyde R. Hoey of Shelby yesterday. We in North Carolina have lost a great statesman, a splendid Christian gentleman, and a distinguished United States Senator. At the age of seventy-six Senator Hoey was serving ably and faithfully in the United States Senate, and through ten years of service in that great body, he had earned the respect, admiration and affection of his fellow Senators and government leaders everywhere. His career in public service has been an inspiration to all who admire and understand the value of leadership, integrity, ability, and morality in government.

Born in Shelby, North Carolina on December 11, 1877, Clyde

[1] This Committee was appointed by the Governor in support of the National Veterans Committee of the American-Korean Foundation. The North Carolina segment of the nation-wide drive was conducted by the leading veterans organizations in support of the campaign of the Foundation to raise $10,000,000 "to help the Korean people to help themselves."

Roark Hoey attended the public schools until twelve years of age, at which time he began working in a printing office where he stayed for four years, until he learned the printer's trade. At age sixteen he bought a country paper on credit and began editing and publishing this paper, which he continued for fourteen years. In the meantime, he studied law at home and attended summer law school at the University of North Carolina, after which he stood examination before the State Supreme Court in September, 1899, and was licensed to practice law.

While just twenty years of age, he was elected to the state House of Representatives and was re-elected to the House in 1900, and elected to the state Senate in 1902. He has served as Assistant United States Attorney for the Western District of North Carolina, as Congressman from the Ninth District, as Governor of North Carolina, as Democratic National Committeeman from North Carolina, and as United States Senator from North Carolina since 1944. He was re-elected to the Senate in 1950 for a term ending January 3, 1957.

Words can hardly describe the true character of Senator Hoey, whose gentle manner, keen mind, and sound thinking has meant so much to our State through his years of service. He was a statesman of the highest rank. He was intellectually honest and was able at all times to combine great kindness with great courage. He was probably known and loved by more people than any man in North Carolina. He was always fair and always fearless. My affection for him increased over the years, and I feel a deep personal loss, along with thousands of others throughout the State.

To his daughter, Mrs. Dan Paul of Pantego and Raleigh, and his two sons, Charles Hoey of Shelby, and Clyde R. Hoey, Jr., of Canton, and the other members of his family, I extend my heartfelt sympathy.

THE ACTIVITIES OF THE CORPS OF ENGINEERS, UNITED STATES ARMY IN NORTH CAROLINA[1]

May 14, 1954

As Governor of the State of North Carolina, I am particularly interested in conserving and improving the State's natural resources. One of our greatest resources is water. The North Carolina coastal waters, extending over 300 miles, have been actively navigated for nearly four centuries. The Outer Banks, a long chain of narrow barren islands paralleling the coast, inclose wide shallow sounds bordered by many harbors along the mainland shore. In these coastal waters, and in the rivers which penetrate the interior, the Corps of Engineers has improved 1,100 miles of navigable channels, of which forty-one miles are for deep-draft ocean vessels. On these federally-improved channels, commerce in shallow-draft vessels totals over 3,000,000 tons per annum and in deep-draft vessels over 5,000,000 tons per annum.

The Congress has authorized the Corps to investigate water resources developments for flood control, hydro-electric power and other purposes, in addition to navigation. Many projects have been recommended, and Congress has authorized some of them for construction. Several large river systems originate in the mountains of North Carolina or in the Piedmont plateau, and have considerable potential water power; however, Congress has not, to date, authorized any project which includes power development in North Carolina.

I understand that the Civil Works functions are contained in the present organization of the Corps of Engineers. They appear to be consonant with the policy of the Congress to promote economy and efficiency. I wish to quote:

> The Corps of Engineers, under the direction of the Secretary of the Army and in accordance with applicable statutes on assignments, will continuously and exclusively administer and discharge the civil works responsibilities of the Department of the Army pertaining to river and harbor and flood-control activities of the United States and will render to other agencies and departments of the federal government such engineering services as may be directed

---

[1] This statement was prepared by Governor Umstead and included in the mimeographed pamphlet entitled "Statement for Hearing, Task Force on Water Resources, Commission on Organization of the Executive Branch of the Government." (Raleigh, May 14, 1954), pp. 1-3.

or agreed upon by exercising the authority delegated in such matters by legislation, directive or order. These functions are performed in accordance with orders and regulations prescribed by the Chief of Engineers and through such field offices, laboratories, and experimental stations as he may designate or establish for the purpose. In war situations, or situations constituting a threat of war, military and civilian personnel engaged on civil works, and equipment utilized thereon, are transferred to defense activities, to the extent believed necessary.

It is well to note that the continuing Civil Works program of the Corps of Engineers has provided that agency with a base upon which to expand and to meet the requirements of military construction during periods of emergency. The impact upon the Corps of Engineers of military construction requirements in North Carolina during World War II and from the beginning of the Korean Emergency through the present time is reflected in this chart [1] (Exhibit A). It can be seen that a military construction load totalling more than $108,000,000 was carried during World War II. Ability of the Corps of Engineers to carry this load efficiently is attributed to the fact that the Corps of Engineers had a construction organization in being under the Civil Works program. A similar condition exists under the current situation, as shown by the chart,[1] for the fiscal years 1952 through 1956. In this instance, approximately $82,000,000 will be spent by the end of 1956 on military construction in North Carolina, and again we are fortunate in having the Civil Works nucleus of the Corps of Engineers. This nucleus has already expanded to handle the load and has already placed in actual work over $22,000,000 of the total of $82,000,000.

It has been my observation during my term as Governor of North Carolina, and while previously serving as United States Senator and as a member of the House of Representatives, that the Corps of Engineers performs its assignments efficiently.

Since 1828, the Corps of Engineers has been engaged in navigation improvement work in North Carolina, and this is still the principal civil function of the Corps in my State.

Public acceptance of the Civil Works program has weighed heavily in accomplishments of the Corps of Engineers. Of particular note are successive steps taken to improve water resources

[1] The charts are not included here, but are in the mimeographed pamphlet.

for navigation, so that these natural endowments may contribute their fair share toward the progress and security of the State and Nation. This past record, the Corps' present efficient and economic manner of handling its assignments, the pleasant and co-operative spirit exemplified in dealing with my State, and the great potential as a military construction agency, leave me with one conclusion—I strongly recommend that the Civil Works remain as a function of the Corps of Engineers.

RESOLUTION OF RESPECT IN HONOR OF CLYDE ROARK HOEY

May 14, 1954

Whereas, Clyde R. Hoey, on May 12, 1954, peacefully passed away while at his desk in the Senate Office Building in Washington, D. C., thus suddenly and unexpectedly ending his illustrious career as the senior Senator from North Carolina, and

Whereas, Clyde R. Hoey, as United States Senator, had, during his two terms of office, attained the loftiest heights of noble and patriotic statesmanship, fully justifying the confidence and esteem in which he was held by the people of this State and further enshrining him in the hearts and affections of the people of this State and making of him a national figure universally admired for the highest order of his service in the Senate, and

Whereas, Clyde R. Hoey served this State as Governor, after being elected by a great majority in 1936, and, as its Chief Executive, administered its business and affairs with a high degree of efficiency and in such a manner as to endear him to his associates in the state government, especially the members of the Council of State over which he presided, and to all of the people of the State regardless of party or other affiliations, and

Whereas, Clyde R. Hoey, while serving in the office of Governor and United States Senator, and in his entire career, was recognized as a Christian statesman with such qualities of character and great personal charm and oratorical ability that he was recognized as the silver-tongued spokesman for the educational, moral, religious, and political forces, which have contributed to the high accomplishments and destiny of this Commonwealth, and

Whereas, the imperishable record of service of Clyde R. Hoey, as Senator and Governor, as a lawyer, churchman, and citizen, will endure as an inspiration to this and succeeding generations, and

Whereas, the undersigned Governor and members of the Council of State join with thousands of their fellow citizens who mourn the passing of our beloved and admired Senator and desire to pay tribute to his memory and splendid record as a statesman, churchman, and citizen:

Now, therefore, be it resolved by the Governor and Council of State, acting together, that we do hereby declare our unlimited admiration and affection for our close personal friend, Clyde R. Hoey, who but yesterday was in our midst, brilliantly and devotedly performing his duties as senior Senator from North Carolina; and

That his passing is an irreparable loss to all of the people of his State and Nation and a real personal sorrow to each of us;

That a copy of this resolution shall be sent to Mr. and Mrs. Clyde R. Hoey, Jr., Mr. and Mrs. Charles Hoey, Mr. and Mrs. Dan Paul, as evidence of the sincere sympathy which we entertain for his entire family on account of the great sorrow which has come to them from so great a loss;

That a copy of this resolution shall be made available to the press and radio.

This 14th day of May, 1954.

William B. Umstead, *Governor,*
Thad Eure, *Secretary of State,*
Henry L. Bridges, *State Auditor,*
Edwin M. Gill, *State Treasurer,*
Charles F. Carroll, *Superintendent of Public Instruction,*
L. Y. Ballentine, *Commissioner of Agriculture,*
Forrest H. Shuford, *Commissioner of Labor.*

SUPREME COURT'S DECISION ON INTEGRATION

May 25, 1954

Governor Umstead held a conference this morning with the Attorney General and his staff; Dr. Charles F. Carroll, Superintendent of Public Instruction; and Mr. D. S. Coltrane, Assistant Director of the Budget, with reference to the recent decision of the Supreme Court regarding segregation in public schools. Chief Justice M. V. Barnhill attended the conference at the request of the Governor, not as a representative of the court, nor in his capacity as Chief Justice, but rather as a friend of the Governor.

Many of the complicated questions as to the effect of the decision of the Supreme Court upon the school situation in North Carolina were discussed. No decisions were reached and the Governor requested the Attorney General and his staff to continue to study the opinion as it relates to the Constitution and laws of the State. Other conferences will be held from time to time.

The Governor requested the Attorney General to accompany him to Richmond for the conference called by Governor Stanley [1] on Thursday, June 10, and Mr. McMullan readily agreed to go.

THE UNITED STATES SUPREME COURT REVERSES ITSELF ON PUBLIC SCHOOLS

May 27, 1954

When Governor Holden submitted the Fourteenth Amendment to the Legislature of this State for ratification he told the General Assembly that the amendment could not prevent the states from operating separate schools for the white and colored races. He recommended the ratification of the amendment, after having written several articles in his newspaper, *The Raleigh Sentinel*,[1] in which he assured the people of the State that the ratification would not in any way interfere with the separation of

---

[1] Thomas B. Stanley, Governor of Virginia.

[2] In the period from 1843 to 1868 W. W. Holden and associates issued the *Standard* under various titles—*North Carolina Standard, Semi-Weekly North Carolina Standard, Semi-Weekly Standard, Tri-Weekly Standard, Weekly Standard.* Mary Westcott and Allene Ramage (comps.), *A Checklist of United States Newspapers (and Weeklies Before 1900).* (Durham: Duke University, 1936), IV, 619-625.

the races in the public schools. At the same session of the General Assembly of 1868, when the Fourteenth Amendment was ratified, he recommended the enactment of legislation providing for separate schools for white and colored children of the State. In 1875, upon the return of the Democrats to power, a constitutional amendment was adopted providing for the separation of schools without discrimination against either race. In 1896, in Plessy *v.* Ferguson, the Supreme Court of the United States, with only one dissenting Justice, interpreted the Fourteenth Amendment as meaning that the states had a right to provide separate but equal facilities in the public schools. In other Supreme Court decisions since that time, the Court has unanimously recognized the principle of separate but equal facilities in public education.

Acting in accordance with the clear provisions of the North Carolina Constitution and in accordance with the decisions of the Supreme Court of the United States and every available historical precedent, this State and many others, since 1868, has provided separate schools for our white and colored children. Under this program the state, counties, and school districts, have invested millions and millions of dollars in providing facilities in a sincere effort to accommodate the tremendous demands of public education in our state system of public schools, based upon the heretofore recognized principle of separate but equal facilities. The recent expenditures for public school buildings have gone far to equalize substantially the school buildings available to both races.

Teachers' salaries have been fully equalized and great efforts have been made to comply with our constitutional requirements.

In view of this long-standing history and vast expenditure of funds, the decision of the Supreme Court of the United States on last Monday, reversing their own decisions which had stood for almost sixty years, has necessarily created a condition in this and the other states, which have constitutional and statutory provisions requiring the separation of the races in the public schools, which presents complications and difficulties of immeasurable extent. The Supreme Court of the United States itself, abruptly reversing its decision on this subject, has recognized the difficulties which it has created by ordering the five cases in which the decisions were rendered be restored to the docket for reargument sometime after October, 1954. In this very unusual course of action in a constitutional decision, this Court has stated that attorneys general of the seventeen states having constitutional and statutory provisions for separate schools would be permitted, upon application, to file briefs in answer to certain questions which the Court had heretofore submitted. These questions, submitted by the Court itself, suggest the many complications and difficulties which will be encountered in such a complete reversal of the systems of education heretofore in existence in these states. The questions indicate that the Court itself is unable to say how and when the principle which it has declared could be put into effect and what means could be employed by the several states to reverse the steps which they have heretofore taken in good faith in accordance with the former decisions of the Court. Overnight, this picture has been changed by the Supreme Court decision which has imposed upon this and other states a problem which demands the most careful thought of all of the people of this State.

However, the Supreme Court of the United States has spoken. It has reversed itself and has declared segregation in public schools unconstitutional. In my opinion its previous decisions of this question were correct. This reversal of its former decisions is, in my judgment, a clear and serious invasion of the rights of the sovereign states. Nevertheless, this is now the latest Supreme Court interpretation of the Fourteenth Amendment.

Overnight, this decision has brought to our State a complex problem—the wise solution of which will require the calm, careful, and thoughtful study of all of us. This is no time for rash statements or the proposal of impossible schemes. The problem is too big for any one person to decide. I shall seek the advice of the Attorney General, the Superintendent of Public Instruction, the State Board of Education, legislators and other citizens of this State as to the course we shall pursue and the character of the program we should follow in the light of the recent Supreme Court decision. In view of the fact that the Supreme Court has postponed the effective date of its decision until after the arguments at the fall term of court, no final conclusion as to our course and the program we shall follow is immediately necessary.

The problem we have in North Carolina, to some extent, is the same in other states similarly situated. Governor Stanley of Virginia, which state was involved in one of the cases decided by the Supreme Court, has called a conference to meet in Richmond, Virginia, on June 10. I have accepted an invitation to be present and have requested the Attorney General, Honorable Harry McMullan, to go with me. I realize that each state will have to work out its own problem, but I hope that the conference will be helpful in this grave and difficult situation.

APPOINTMENT OF FRANK CRANE

June 3, 1954

Governor Umstead announced today the appointment of Mr. Frank Crane as Commissioner of the North Carolina Department of Labor to fill the vacancy created by the death of the late Honorable Forrest H. Shuford. Mr. Crane will serve under this appointment until the next general election and the Governor stated that he would recommend to the State Democratic Executive Committee that it select Mr. Crane as the nominee of the Democratic Party in the general election to be held in November of this year.

Mr. Crane was born near Waxhaw in Union County in 1907. He graduated from Prospect High School in 1927, received an A.B. degree at the University of North Carolina in 1931, and was a graduate student at the University during the summers of 1931, 1932, 1933 and 1934. He was athletic director and economics instructor at Welcome High School in Davidson County, 1931-1934.

In August, 1934, he was appointed Safety Director of the North Carolina Industrial Commission and resigned in 1938 to become Administrative Assistant in the North Carolina Employment Service. He was a graduate in Personnel Management at North Carolina State College in 1939. He became Factory Inspector of the North Carolina Department of Labor in May 1939, and took a special course in wage and hour training in Washington, D. C., in 1939. He was appointed Director of Conciliation Service in the North Carolina Department of Labor in 1941 and has held that position until this date.

In 1938 he married the former Miss Edith Peacock of Raleigh and Elm City. He now resides at 802 Williamson Drive in Raleigh.

The Governor also stated that he had discussed the position of Commissioner of Labor with Mr. Lewis P. Sorrell, Deputy Commissioner of Labor, and was advised by Mr. Sorrell that he would prefer to retain his present position, and that he would co-operate to the fullest extent with Mr. Crane.

RESOLUTION OF RESPECT IN HONOR OF FORREST H. SHUFORD

June 3, 1954

Whereas, Forrest H. Shuford, Commissioner of Labor of North Carolina, was suddenly stricken and died in Washington, D. C., on the 19th day of May, 1954, while there attending to the duties imposed upon him by his office, and

Whereas, Forrest H. Shuford was appointed as Commissioner of Labor by Governor Clyde R. Hoey on September 12, 1938, and was thereafter elected in the general elections of 1938, 1940, 1944 and 1948 and 1952, to this very important position in the state government, and

Whereas, while serving as Commissioner of Labor, Forrest H. Shuford attracted national attention to the work being done by him and his office, as a result of which he was named to important positions and commissions serving on a national and international basis, and

Whereas, Forrest H. Shuford ably served as a member of the Council of State from the time that his office was made a constitutional one and, during this time, as a member of the Council of State, contributed his wise counsel and advice to deliberations and actions of this body, and

Whereas, Forrest H. Shuford, by his inborn courtesy and friendly manner, has endeared himself to the individual members of the Council of State with whom he has served, and

Whereas, all of the members of the Council of State entertain for him and the service which he rendered the State, the highest regard and appreciation, and

Whereas, in the death of Forrest H. Shuford, we have lost a close friend and associate in the state government, who will be long remembered and sadly missed from our company;

Now, therefore, be it resolved by the Governor and Council of State that, in the sudden and unexpected passing of Forrest H. Shuford, Commissioner of Labor, the Council of State has lost one of its most valuable members and his death has been a source of great sadness and keen regret on the part of his associates in state government.

Be it further resolved, that we extend to his dear wife and sons our deepest sympathy and regret, and that a copy of this resolution be sent to them, and copies made available to the press and radio.

This 3rd day of June, 1954.

William B. Umstead, *Governor,*
Thad Eure, *Secretary of State,*
Henry L. Bridges, *State Auditor,*
Edwin M. Gill, *State Treasurer,*
Charles F. Carroll, *Superintendent of Public Instruction,*
L. Y. Ballentine, *Commissioner of Agriculture,*
Charles F. Gold, *Commissioner of Insurance.*

APPOINTMENT OF SAM J. ERVIN, JR.

June 5, 1954

Governor Umstead announced today the appointment of Judge Sam J. Ervin, Jr., of Morganton, North Carolina, to the United States Senate to fill the vacancy created by the death of the late Senator Clyde R. Hoey. Judge Ervin will serve under this appointment until the general election of 1954, and the Governor announced that he would recommend to the State Democratic Executive Committee that Judge Ervin be selected by it as the Democratic nominee in the general election this fall for the remaining unexpired two years of Senator Hoey's term.

Judge Ervin is the son of Samuel James and Laura (Powe) Ervin, and was born at Morganton, September 27, 1896; graduated from the University of North Carolina with an A.B. Degree in 1917, and from Harvard Law School with an LL.B. Degree in 1922; served in France with the First Division for eighteen months in the First World War; was wounded in battle, twice cited for gallantry in action, and awarded the French Fourragere, the Purple Heart with one Oak Leaf Cluster, the Silver Star, and the Distinguished Service Cross; admitted to the North Carolina bar in 1919 and subsequently licensed to practice before various federal agencies and courts, including the Supreme Court of the United States; engaged in practice of law at Morganton since 1922 with exception of periods of service on the bench; has served in the following capacities, namely: Representative from Burke County in General Assemblies of 1923, 1925, and 1931; Chairman, Burke County Democratic Executive Committee, 1924; Trustee, Morganton Graded Schools, 1927-1930; member, State Democratic Executive Committee, 1930-1937; Trustee, University of North Carolina, 1932-1935, 1946-1949; Judge, Burke County Criminal Court, 1935-1937; Judge, North Carolina Superior Court, 1937-1943, resigning to resume practice of law; member, State Board of Law Examiners, 1944-1946; member, North Carolina Hospital and Medical Care Commission, 1944; Government Appeal Agent, Burke County Service Board No. 2, and Chairman, Burke County Labor Mobilization Board, Second World War; Representative from Tenth North Carolina District in 79th Congress, 1946-1947, declining to seek renomination to resume practice of law; Chairman, North Carolina Commission for Improvement of Administration of Justice, 1947-1949; Trustee, Davidson College, 1948-1950; Associate Justice, State Supreme Court, since February 3, 1948, having been originally appointed to such office by Governor Cherry[1] and having been subsequently elected thereto in November, 1948 and November, 1950. Received Honorary LL.D. degree at University of North Carolina, 1951. Member of the following organizations: North Carolina Bar Association, North Carolina State Bar, American Bar Association, Association of Interstate Commerce Practitioners, American Judicature So-

[1] R. Gregg Cherry, Governor, 1945-1949.

ciety, General Alumni Association of University of North Carolina, (President, 1947-1948), American Legion, Veterans of Foreign Wars, Disabled American Veterans, Society of the First Division, Army and Navy Legion of Valor, Morganton Kiwanis Club, Morganton Chamber of Commerce, State Literary and Historical Association, Southern Historical Association, American Historical Association, Junior Order, Knights of Pythias, Knights Templar, Scottish Rite Masons (32nd degree), Morganton Presbyterian Church (elder); married Margaret Bruce Bell of Concord, N. C., June 18, 1924; three children: Sam J. Ervin, 3rd, Margaret Leslie Ervin, and Laura Powe Ervin.

The Governor stated, "I believe the outstanding record, character and ability of Judge Ervin eminently qualifies him for the high office of United States Senator. As a student, as a soldier, as a lawyer, as a judge, and as a citizen, his record has been outstanding. He is widely known throughout the State and has the confidence and the respect of all those who know him. I believe he will make a distinguished United States Senator and will reflect honor and credit upon the State of North Carolina in keeping with the high standards established by the late Senator Clyde R. Hoey and other great men who have served this State in the United States Senate."

Judge Ervin will resign next week as a member of the Supreme Court of North Carolina, and sometime during the week will present his credentials to the Senate of the United States at which time he will take his oath of office.

APPOINTMENT OF CARLISLE W. HIGGINS

June 8, 1954

Governor Umstead announced today the appointment of Honorable Carlisle W. Higgins, formerly of Alleghany County, now of Winston-Salem, as Associate Justice of the Supreme Court of North Carolina to fill the vacancy created by the appointment of Judge Sam J. Ervin, Jr., as a member of the Senate of the United States.

Courtesy of Jack Williams

Mrs. William Bradley (Merle Davis) Umstead.

Mr. Higgins was born and reared in Alleghany County. He was graduated from the University of North Carolina in 1912, received his LL.B. degree from the same institution in 1914, and was admitted to the bar the same year. He served as a member of the House of Representatives in 1925 and as a member of the State Senate in 1929. For a number of years he was a law partner of the late, beloved Rufus L. Doughton, and was Solicitor of the 11th Judicial District of North Carolina. In 1934 he was appointed United States District Attorney for the Middle District of North Carolina and served in that capacity until 1946. Because of the fine record he made as District Attorney he was selected by the Department of Justice to prosecute, on behalf of the United States Government, Japanese war criminals, and remained in Japan on this assignment for more than a year. Upon the conclusion of this assignment in 1947, he began the practice of law in Winston-Salem, where he now lives. Mr. Higgins is now a member of the National Democratic Executive Committee from North Carolina.

Mr. Higgins is sixty-four years of age. In 1916 he married Miss Myrtle Bryant of Sparta and they have two children. At the University of North Carolina he was intercollegiate debater, and he served in the United States Army during World War I. He is a Mason, a member of the American Legion, and a member of the North Carolina and American Bar associations.

"Mr. Higgins is widely known and recognized in the State as an outstanding lawyer, a man of sterling character and splendid judgment, with a fine sense of fairness and justice," the Governor said, "and in my opinion he will make a splendid Supreme Court Judge and will measure up to the highest traditions of our Court of last resort."

The Governor stated that he would recommend to the State Democratic Executive Committee that it select Mr. Higgins as the nominee of the Democratic Party in the general election this fall. He further stated that it will probably be several weeks before Mr. Higgins will take the oath of office since the Supreme Court is now in recess and will not convene for the fall term until sometime in August.

ROBERT HAMER'S SENTENCE COMMUTED

June 9, 1954

Governor Umstead announced today that several weeks ago he read the entire record on file with the Board of Paroles in the case of Robert Hamer (colored), who was convicted of rape in the Superior Court of Duplin County in September 1953, and was sentenced to death.

After reading the record the Governor requested the State Board of Paroles to make a careful and thorough investigation of this case. The Board has done so and all of the members of the Board have recommended to the Governor that the sentence of Robert Hamer be commuted from death to life imprisonment.

Acting upon this recommendation, the Governor today commuted the sentence of Robert Hamer from death to life imprisonment.

GOVERNOR UMSTEAD ATTENDS THE CONFERENCE OF SOUTHERN GOVERNORS RICHMOND, VIRGINIA

June 10, 1954

I was glad to attend the Conference of Southern Governors in Richmond, Virginia, yesterday. Nine governors were present and representatives of six other governors, all at the invitation of Governor Stanley of Virginia.

In extending the invitation to the Conference, Governor Stanley stated that he thought the Conference would serve a useful purpose for the exchange of information and views without contemplating any organization or adoption of any group plan.

The Conference was helpful and instructive. Many of the problems arising from the recent decision of the Supreme Court with reference to segregation in the public schools were considered and discussed. No over-all program or plan was agreed upon, and it was apparent that the authorities in the various states, mostly affected by the decision, are studying all phases of the matter in an effort to determine what program or policy should be followed in each respective state.

Honorable Harry McMullan, Attorney General of North Carolina, and Dr. Charles F. Carroll, Superintendent of Public Instruction, attended the Conference with me; and they, too, thought the Conference was helpful and instructive.

BIRTHDAY OF THE SIGNING OF THE DECLARATION OF INDEPENDENCE

July 2, 1954

North Carolina will join the Nation this weekend in observing the 178th birthday of the signing of the Declaration of Independence. I believe it is appropriate at this time to make this observance more than a day for speeches, flag-waving, firework displays, and band concerts. It should be more than a mere pause in our busy and bustling daily life to pay homage to an ancient and venerable document.

July 4th is the official birthday of our Republic, and a day on which we should give serious and constructive thought to the past, present, and future of our great Nation. It is a day on which we should thoughtfully consider our heritage of freedom, justice and independence as conceived and set forth in the Articles of the Declaration of Independence and the Constitution. Most important of all, it is a day when we should reaffirm our faith and wholehearted belief in this heritage, which has been responsible for the remarkable growth and progress we enjoy today, and in spite of world-wide confusion and existing perils, we should determine to protect and preserve our heritage.

The concepts of the Declaration of Independence, which were considered so revolutionary in 1776, are just as vibrantly alive and vitally essential to our existence today as they were when the tones of the Liberty Bell were first heard here and throughout the world.

July 4th is also the 128th anniversary of the death of Thomas Jefferson, author of the Declaration of Independence, third President of the United States, and founder of the University of Virginia. He died in his home at Monticello, Virginia, in 1826. An articulate statesman, philosopher, and scientist, Jefferson was a man whose life's work was devoted to the expression and establishment of all the freedoms necessary to create and preserve our Republic. Throughout his life, Jefferson constantly reiterated the theme, "The will of the people is the only legitimate foundation of any government." Democracy was his passion and we can be thankful he spent his life nurturing its growth. We Americans who have been fortunate enough to inherit the fundamental principles set down more than a century ago by the great architect of our Republic, must maintain these principles at all costs.

Since this weekend is both a state and national holiday, I would like to call attention to the urgent need for safe and sane driving on our highways. The Motor Vehicles Department and the State Highway Patrol will make every effort to enforce the motor vehicle laws during this weekend and thereby protect the safety of our traveling public as much as possible. However, the primary responsibility for safety on our highways still remains with the individual drivers, and I urge everyone who travels on our highways to drive carefully, obey the cardinal laws of safe driving and thereby live to enjoy the blessings of this Republic. For after all, the preservation of our human resources is one of the greatest responsibilities of our citizenship.

VOLUNTEER MOTOR VEHICLE SAFETY CHECK

July 8, 1954

Motor Vehicles Commissioner Edward Scheidt has reported to me that approximately 100,000 automobiles and trucks have been inspected with regard to the safety of their operation since the Voluntary Vehicle Safety Check movement was launched by the Carolina Safety League less than two months ago. That is encouraging but the number of inspections and the number of approved green stickers appearing on the windshields throughout the State should be multiplied in the weeks and months ahead.

The mechanical safety of the automobiles North Carolinians drive is a very important part of the campaign we are waging against death and injury on our highways. And no man can know that the vehicle he drives is safe unless it has been inspected.

Now that such inspection is offered without cost, under the program of the Carolina Safety League, there is no good reason why all of us should not take the precaution of inspection.

I call upon the automobile owners of North Carolina to take advantage of the Voluntary Vehicle Safety Check and I suggest to the newspapers, radio stations and television stations of the State that they will perform a real service by keeping this campaign before the people.

A hundred thousand green stickers is encouraging but we should have a million as evidence of our effort to make North Carolina a safer state in which to drive, to live, and to raise one's children.

SENTENCE OF CHARLES GALES COMMUTED

July 21, 1954

Governor Umstead announced today his decision to commute the sentence of Charles Gales of Hoke County from death to life imprisonment. Gales was sentenced for first degree murder in the January, 1954, term of the Superior Court of Hoke Couty.

The Governor's decision concurred with the recommendation of the State Board of Paroles that this prisoner's sentence of death be commuted to life imprisonment.

ADVISORY COMMITTEE APPOINTED TO STUDY SEGREGATION

August 4, 1954

Governor Umstead announced today appointment of the Governor's Special Advisory Committee on Education to study the problems resulting from the decision of the Supreme Court of the United States with reference to segregation.

The Committee appointed by the Governor is as follows:

Dr. F. D. Bluford of Greensboro, President of the Agricultural and Technical College;

J. H. Clark of Elizabethtown, former member of the State

Senate and now Chairman of the North Carolina Medical Care Commission;

Miss Ruth Current of Raleigh, formerly of Rowan County, now State Home Demonstration Agent;

Dr. Gordon Gray of Chapel Hill, President of the University of North Carolina;

Fred B. Helms of Charlotte, a prominent attorney, former President of the North Carolina State Bar Association, and now a member of the State Judicial Council;

Dallas Herring of Rose Hill, Chairman of the Duplin County Board of Education;

R. O. Huffman of Morganton, a prominent businessman;

W. T. Joyner of Raleigh, an outstanding attorney;

Mrs. Helen S. Kafer of New Bern, Administrator of the Kafer Memorial Hospital, former President of the New Bern Parent-Teacher Council and now a member of the New Bern City School Board;

Holt McPherson of High Point, Editor of *The High Point Enterprise* and well-known newspaperman;

James C. Manning of Williamston, Superintendent of Schools in Martin County;

Mrs. Hazel Parker of Tarboro, Negro Home Demonstration Agent in Edgecombe County;

Honorable Thomas J. Pearsall of Rocky Mount, prominent farmer and businessman, and former Speaker of the House of Representatives in the Legislature;

Dr. Clarence Poe of Raleigh, Chairman of the Board of Editors of *The Progressive Farmer* and an outstanding leader in education and agriculture;

I. E. Ready of Roanoke Rapids, Superintendent of Roanoke Rapids City Schools;

Dr. Paul A. Reid of Cullowhee, President of Western Carolina College, and formerly connected with the State School Board;

Dr. J. W. Seabrook of Fayetteville Teachers' College;

Judge L. R. Varser of Lumberton, formerly an Associate Justice of the Supreme Court of North Carolina, and now Chairman of the State Board of Law Examiners;

Arthur D. Williams of Wilson, Chairman of the Wilson County

Board of County Commissioners, and a prominent farmer and businessman.

The Governor announced that he was greatly pleased that Honorable Thomas J. Pearsall has consented to serve as Chairman of the Committee, and the Governor has called a meeting of the Committee in his office in Raleigh at twelve o'clock noon on Wednesday, August 11.

The Governor further stated, "I consider the personnel of this Committee to be outstanding and I am deeply grateful for the willingness of these patriotic citizens to serve further the State of North Carolina."

RECOMMENDATIONS TO THE STATE DEMOCRATIC EXECUTIVE COMMITTEE

August 4, 1954

Governor Umstead announced today that when the State Democratic Executive Committee meets here in Raleigh on Thursday, August 12, he will recommend the election of Mr. B. Everett Jordan, present State Chairman, to be National Committeeman; Senator John D. Larkins, Jr., of Trenton, as State Chairman, and Mrs. Mary Laurens Richardson of Raleigh to be re-elected Vice-Chairman of the State Democratic Executive Committee.

The Governor further stated: "On account of the very fine record Mr. Everett Jordan has made as State Chairman during the past five years, I have been very anxious for him to remain in that office at least during the next two years. However, Mr. Jordan advised me a few days ago that owing to the heavy demands his personal business has been making on his time during the past four months, he is no longer in a position to devote the time necessary to meet the requirements of the chairmanship to which he has devoted so much time during the past five years. So, with reluctance, I agreed to his request to be relieved of the duties of chairmanship. I was very pleased, however, that he did agree to continue in his service to the Party as Democratic National Committeeman to succeed the Honorable Carlisle W. Higgins.

I am sure Mr. Jordan will continue to make a splendid record in his new position.

"I am recommending to the Committee the election of Senator John D. Larkins, Jr., of Trenton as the new State Chairman. Senator Larkins has been an active worker in the cause of democracy for many years. He was chairman of the Democratic Executive Committee of Jones County for ten years. He has headed up more Jackson Day dinners than any person in the State, having presided over ten of these annual fund-raising dinners. He has been a member of the State Senate for several sessions, where he served with distinction as chairman of important committees. He is now a member of the Advisory Budget Commission, of which he is Chairman.

"Also, I gladly recomend that Mrs. Mary Laurens Richardson of Raleigh be retained as Vice Chairman of the Executive Committee. She has been a splendid leader in the Democratic cause. I know she will continue to give the same unselfish service in behalf of the Party."

MARCH OF DIMES CAMPAIGN

August 6, 1954

I urge all North Carolinians to give generously to the March of Dimes Campaign, August 16-31. Because the usual January campaign of the National Foundation for Infantile Paralysis fell short of its goal by $20,000,000, I am informed that this second fund-raising effort is now necessary.

According to the National Foundation for Infantile Paralysis for the years 1949-1953 inclusive, there were only four states which had a smaller percentage of cases of polio than North Carolina. As of this date, we have had reported 62.5 per cent fewer cases of polio than we had during the same period last year, while in the Nation, as a whole, there have been only 5 per cent fewer cases than last year. In view of these significant facts, we should express our gratitude and thanks for our good fortune by supplying additional funds to carry on research toward improving prevention and rehabilitation of infantile paralysis victims. The

Foundation has been of inestimable help in providing research grants for studying the disease in all its aspects, for recruitment of professional personnel to care for the sick, for its "equipment bank" of respirators, rocking beds, hot pack machines, crutches, wheel chairs, and other special supplies.

The cost of care has risen higher than ever before. At this time when victory seems so much nearer through a vaccine that would provide more lasting immunity, we must give generously to develop more rapidly dependable control over this crippling and costly disease.

I not only urge our citizens to give to the March of Dimes as generously as they can, but I also hope that as many people as possible will work in this special campaign to obtain much needed funds.

THE NEED FOR A DIVERSIFIED FARM PROGRAM [1]

August 13, 1954

I would like to commend *The Goldsboro News-Argus* for its genuine interest in the improvement of agriculture in North Carolina. I also appreciate this opportunity to discuss some of our agricultural problems.

I have always been deeply interested in agriculture. I was born and reared on a tobacco farm in the northern part of Durham County and know from firsthand experience both the importance of the farmer's job and also the many difficulties with which he is beset in producing crops at a profit. In my Inaugural Address on January 8, 1953, I discussed a number of the needs and problems of agriculture of today and now call attention to these again. We should do more to stop erosion of our priceless soil. We need more and better pasture land and a greater utilization of our forest resources as well as more effective methods of protecting and using our water resources and our wildlife. North Carolina needs additional processing plants for agricultural products, and we should develop better and expanding marketing facilities for our poultry,

[1] This statement was prepared for *The Goldsboro News-Argus* (Farm Edition), August 13, 1954.

fruit, vegetables, and livestock. These objectives as outlined in my Inaugural Address will continue to have my interest and support.

It seems to me that perhaps the most important need for our State at this time in agriculture is an expansion of scientific research. With the money we have and the facilities at hand, a splendid job in research is being accomplished. Sympathetic General Assemblies, the federal government, and the farmers themselves, through "Nickels for Know-How" have made possible an expanded program and have indicated the deep interest today in better scientific research.

In spite of all this, it is my belief that our research program in agriculture is still inadequate. We know that scientific research for the farmers is just as essential as it is for industry, and we must give it a place of high importance in any program designed to improve agriculture. The farm areas served by *The Goldsboro News-Argus* are vitally interested in tobacco. Our tobacco farmers know how agricultural research has enabled them to produce more and better tobacco per acre in spite of plant diseases and plant pests.

There is no doubt that we have made great progress in agriculture in North Carolina, but much remains to be done. According to published reports, the per capita income for North Carolina for 1952 was $1,049, and we ranked forty-fifth among the states of the Union. In 1950 the population of North Carolina was a little more than 4,000,000. Of this number about 1,376,000 worked on farms, a larger number than in any state in the Union. It is obvious, therefore, that the farm income largely affects our per capita income.

The total amount received for farm products, livestock, and livestock products in 1952 amounted to more than $900,000,000; and in this respect, we ranked thirteenth among the states. A large part of our cash income is from tobacco, cotton, and peanuts. The livestock industry has made great gains in our State during the past few years, and since 1938 we have moved from thirtieth to twenty-third among the states in cash income from livestock. The number of our Grade A dairies has tremendously increased during the past two years, and the production per cow has also substantially increased. The number of beef cattle has about doubled since 1949.

We have also made substantial gains in the poultry industry. The number of laying hens is now about 35 per cent greater than in 1940 and the number of eggs produced has almost doubled. The gross income from the production of eggs is five times the amount received in 1940, and the number of broilers produced has doubled since 1948. In spite of this progress, livestock, livestock products, and poultry accounted for only about 22 per cent of our total cash farm income in 1952.

The farm people and farm leaders in North Carolina are to be commended for the progress made in the livestock and poultry industry.

We will not have the agricultural per capita income or the total per capita income we should have until the livestock industry is developed to the point where it more fully utilizes the resources that are available in this State. We have had to reduce the acreage of our basic cash crops and, due to world conditions, more reductions may have to be made. This means that thousands of acres heretofore planted in basic crops should be used for improved pastures and for feed crops. Our climate is splendid for the production of livestock. Instead of ranking thirteenth among the states, it is entirely possible to rank among the upper five or six.

In this connection, markets, distribution and storage facilities are essential and need to be developed. This amount of livestock and livestock products now produced is far short of the needs of the people of our State. Certainly every effort should be made to supply our own demands.

Production of small grains and hay crops is not only profitable but aids in soil and water conservation and works well into an effective livestock program. I am informed that the grain and hay crops in this State could easily be increased around 25 per cent in the next five or ten years. This would call for adequate storage, both inland and at our ports.

In addition to the above, every effort should be made to continue improved agricultural practices, rotation of crops, soil conservation and a proper forestry program, together with a planned system of handling our woodlands. Pulpwood can be made a source of annual income in many sections of the State without seriously depleting the supply. Careless handling of our woodlands and forests could result not only in a substantial loss of income but also in serious depletion of one of our great natural resources. Reforestation has an important part both in connection with the maintenance of our lumber and wood supply and also in any proper plan for the conservation of our soil and water resources.

I am encouraged at the progress that has been made in this State due to the willingness of our farm people to accept new and better ways of farming. The work of the farm organizations, State College, the Extension Service, the State Department of Agriculture and other agencies has contributed a great deal to the improvement of agriculture in North Carolina today. It has been my pleasure as Governor to work closely with these agencies in many matters relating to our agricultural economy.

We must always remember that agriculture is a major factor in the progress, growth and welfare of our State. To increase substantially the per capita income and to utilize properly and conserve our resources, we must make every effort to expand, improve and diversify agriculture, and take advantage of every opportunity within our ability and means to increase the income of those who are engaged in farming. This is fundamental to the over-all development and progress of North Carolina.

VETERANS' MONTH IN NORTH CAROLINA

August 18, 1954

I have been informed that the Veterans of Foreign Wars of North Carolina will observe the month of September as Veteran's Month as a means of calling attention to the contribution made by our veterans and also the problems which many of our veterans and their families face today.

I am happy to join with the VFW of North Carolina in paying tribute to all our citizens who are veterans of past wars. Our State and our Nation should never forget the services rendered by the brave men and women of North Carolina who served in the

Armed Forces during time of national peril. Many of our young men did not return from this service and many families in North Carolina have lost loved ones. Among the veterans who returned, there are many who have serious personal problems resulting from their service. This is especially true of the disabled veterans and their families.

I am pleased to designate the month of September as Veterans' Month in North Carolina and express the hope that our people will follow the leadership furnished by the Veterans of Foreign Wars in properly observing this special month.

LABOR DAY OBSERVANCE

September 4, 1954

Monday, September 6, will be observed in North Carolina and throughout the Nation as a public holiday in recognition of our working people. The first Labor Day was actually observed in New York City in 1882 and since that date the first Monday in September has generally been observed as a day of recognition for the contributions made by labor to the strength, prosperity and wealth of our country. In 1901 the General Assembly of North Carolina set aside that day each year as a public holiday for our citizens.

Labor is the human energy which spins the giant wheels of industry and converts the raw materials into the finished products which are necessary to our daily lives. Labor also performs with skill the innumerable services which are equally necessary to our living. Labor is both the brain and muscle of individual people who are striving, hoping, living, and working together in various industrial and business organizations. It is probably best described as our human resource. No matter how great our industrial plant and equipment, our machines and buildings represent only potential productivity until they are manned by the millions of skilled employees who make them produce.

In honoring labor, we do not minimize the other necessary elements in industry. Our industry is a highly integrated institution, composed of three elements—labor, management, and capital. All of these are equally indispensable to the functioning of modern industry. Actually, they are interdependent.

The people who manage our resources, the folks who work with them, and those who furnish the capital to make these jobs and equipment possible, must all co-operate to make any industrial enterprise successful. A tolerant and understanding attitude between labor and management and the mutual acceptance of responsibility in working out solutions to common problems are essential.

North Carolinians have demonstrated their ability to solve labor-management problems without resorting to widespread work stoppages. Relations between workers and managers are peaceful. We have had few strikes and lockouts and we have lost very little production on account of work stoppages.

During the fiscal year 1953-54, there were only fourteen strikes in North Carolina, involving 1,494 workers and resulting in 21,686 man-days lost. These are the lowest annual strike figures ever recorded by the State Labor Department's Conciliation Service since it began in 1941. They represent a tiny fraction of one per cent of the national total for the same period. This excellent record of co-operation between labor and management was achieved at a time when new industries were still being established and older industries were still being expanded in our State. During this period nearly a million North Carolinians were engaged in non-agricultural employment of all types and 450,000 were employed in our factories.

In recognition of the many contributions made by our working people, both union and non-union, I urge all of our citizens of North Carolina to observe properly Monday, September 6, as Labor Day in our State.

AMERICAN JEWISH TERCENTENARY MONTH

September 8, 1954

September, 1954, marks the three hundredth anniversary of the settlement of the Jews in what is now the United States of America. This event is significant not only because America is the "Mother of Exiles" for the oppressed of many lands, but because this settlement opened a new era in the history of human co-operation.

The American Jews have made many contributions to the social, cultural and economic life of our Nation. Their industry, initiative, imagination, and spiritual ideals have enabled them to accomplish great things. They have become part of the American family and we are proud of the contributions they have made.

The first settlement of the Jewish faith was made at New Amsterdam on September 12, 1654. Citizens of the Jewish faith first came to North Carolina from the West Indies at the end of the 17th century and they have played a notable part in the growth and progress of our Commonwealth. I think it is most appropriate to mark this anniversary with our reaffirmation of the purposes and ideals to which our great Republic is dedicated, as we work one with another toward the creation of a better world.

Therefore, I hereby designate the month September 12 to October 12, 1954 to be known as American Jewish Tercentenary Month in North Carolina and I request that the communities of this State join in proper recognition of this historic event.

CITIZENSHIP DAY

September 15, 1954

Governor Umstead announced today that he has designated the Honorable Henry L. Bridges, State Auditor of North Carolina, to be his official representative at the National Conference of Citizenship which will be held in Washington, D. C., September 15-17, 1954. Mr. Bridges will participate in the wreath laying ceremony at this ninth annual meeting of the Conference in which North Carolina participates as one of the thirteen original states.

Every September 17 is observed as "Citizenship Day" by a joint resolution of Congress and by proclamation of the President of the United States. It is a special day to commemorate the formation and signing of the Constitution in 1787 and to commemorate United States citizenship by honoring young people who have reached voting age as well as those who have been naturalized.

The North Carolina State Florist Association is furnishing an appropriate wreath decorated with the State flower which Mr. Bridges will use in the ceremony on September 17.

THE ANNUAL RURAL HEALTH CONFERENCE

September 21, 1954

For the past six years professional and lay leaders from all over North Carolina have met together for an annual Rural Health Conference to share experiences, needs, and interests in this important field of medical care. The Seventh Annual Rural Health Conference will be held in Raleigh on Wednesday, September 29, with the theme, "Community Action, the Key to Rural Health's Door."

We should all be proud of the many advances made in medical and public health services during recent years, and we should not lose sight of the fact that further advances are needed to meet our rapidly expanding population. A good rural health program is needed to arouse more interest in better sanitation, better nutrition, better housing and better health conditions generally. A good rural health program is one designed to teach rural people to help themselves attain better health.

I wish to commend the State Medical Society, the North Carolina Health Council, the North Carolina State Board of Health, the State Department of Agriculture, and all other agencies and organizations which assist in bringing about a better understanding of rural health problems and which work for the improvement of rural health in our State.

In recognition of the vital importance of rural health work, I am happy to designate the week of September 26, 1954, as Rural Health Week in North Carolina. This special week will be highlighted by the 1954 Rural Health Conference on Wednesday, September 29.

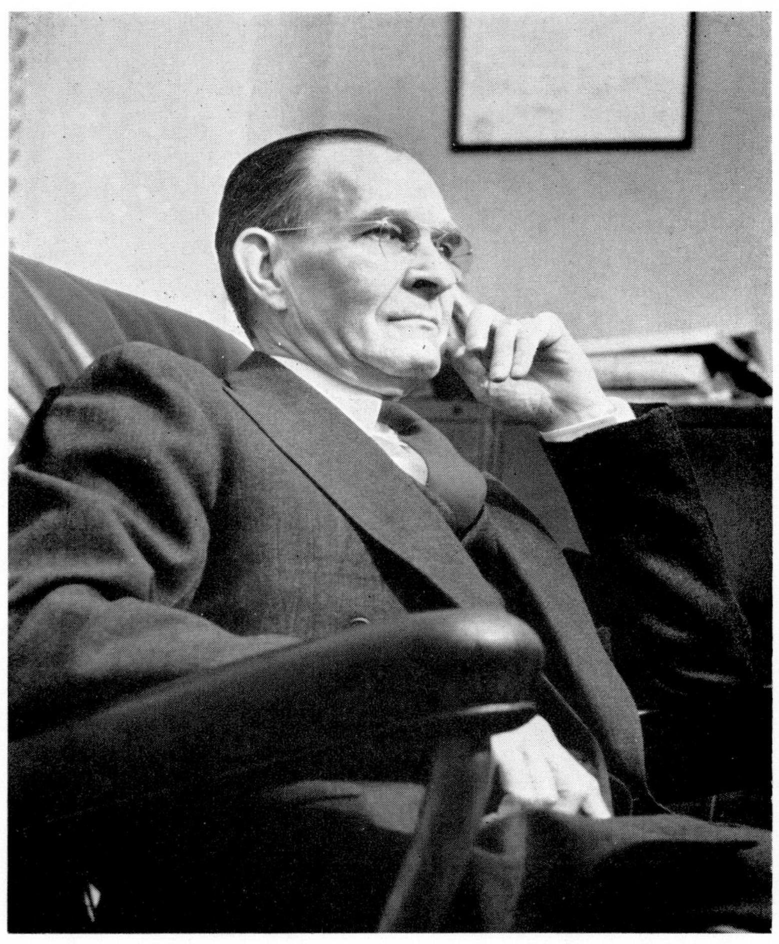

William B. Umstead in his office at Durham, North Carolina, November, 1953, prior to his inauguration.

THE DEMOCRATIC PARTY IN NORTH CAROLINA

September 27, 1954

We in North Carolina will have the opportunity on November 2 to exercise again our priceless right as citizens to vote for the candidates and the party of our choice. Under our system, the state and federal governments are operated and controlled by political parties so that every vote cast is a vote for a party as well as the man.

For more than fifty years, the Democratic Party has been in power in North Carolina. The Democrats have won and held the confidence of the majority of the voters in our State during these years because of the record which has been made. We have given our State sound, progressive government. We have done much with the means at our disposal. Nurtured by the stable atmosphere of our government, North Carolina has flourished as one of the outstanding Southern States and is rapidly taking its place as one of the truly great states of the Union. The Democratic Party is the party of progress and growth and we are committed to the continued development of our State for the welfare of all.

For the first time in many years, we face a November election with the Republican Party in control of the national administration. I believe, however, that we stand an excellent chance to regain control of the Congress. We must campaign vigorously to make this prediction a reality. We must remind the voters of the outstanding record of the Democratic Party in North Carolina. We must point out that the Democratic Party has the able and intelligent leadership necessary to meet pressing problems of our State, Nation and world today, and that our Party is worthy of the continued support of the people of North Carolina and of this Republic.

I call upon all Democrats to vote and work for the election of all candidates on the Democratic ticket in the coming election and thereby make a contribution to party stability and good government in North Carolina and the Nation.

DEATH OF ROBERT L. DOUGHTON

October 1, 1954

I was distressed this morning to hear of the death of Honorable Robert L. Doughton of Laurel Springs, who for forty-two years served as a member of Congress from North Carolina and was Chairman of the Ways and Means Committee of the House of Representatives longer than any man in the history of this Republic.

R. L. Doughton was born in Laurel Springs, North Carolina on November 7, 1863. He was educated in the public schools at Laurel Springs and Sparta. He was a farmer, stock raiser, and banker. He served as a member of the State Board of Agriculture in 1903 and as State Senator from the 35th District in 1908. He was director of the State prison system from 1909 to 1911. He was first elected to the 62nd Congress and continued to serve until he voluntarily retired on January 3, 1953.

He delivered the keynote address at the State Democratic Convention in Raleigh in the spring of 1946, and served as National Committeeman from North Carolina from 1952 until the spring of 1954. He married Miss Lillie S. Hix in 1898 who died about eight years ago.

It is difficult, in a short statement, to do justice to the character and life of R. L. Doughton. He was endowed with great physical strength and great moral courage. He believed in hard work and in rugged honesty. His practical approach to legislative matters and his ability to cut through to the core were recognized by all who knew him. During his long service in Congress he probably sponsored and influenced the passage of more good legislation and helped to kill more bad legislation than any man in the history of this Nation. For many years he was, for all practical purposes, a Congressman-at-Large from North Carolina. He loved and faithfully served the people of his District. He also loved and served all of the people of our State. He left many monuments in North Carolina. Buildings on the campus of Appalachian State Teachers' College; a system of lowered railroad tracks through the city of High Point; a public health building at Chapel Hill; federal courtroom facilities in Durham, and other similar projects throughout the State will stand for years to come as evidences of his many contributions to North Carolina. Children yet unborn will be benefitted by legislation sponsored by him, such as the Social Security Act and the Unemployment Compensation Act.

During the six years I served in the House of Representatives, from 1933 to 1939, he helped me in every way possible. He was the hardest worker in Congress and he worked intelligently and effectively. He had the respect and admiration of all members of the House and he held it during his long tenure of office. As Chairman of the Ways and Means Committee, he had the ability to cut through statistics, figures, statements by economists and financiers, and measure the testimony being presented in terms of common sense and understandable language. He was rugged and he was kind. His loyalty was unsurpassed and his devotion to his friends a passion of his life. He lived simply but greatly. He walked intimately with many Presidents, and he walked, as a friend, with the humblest citizens in his District. The bonds of friendship which existed between us were of long standing and unbreakable. I not only had profound respect for him but also a deep affection which had increased through the years.

Along with thousands of others, I am grateful for his long life of service, and feel a deep personal loss in his passing. To the members of his family I extend my heartfelt sympathy.

APPOINTMENT OF CARL GOERCH

October 5, 1954

Governor Umstead announced today the appointment of Mr. Carl Goerch of Raleigh, well-known private flyer, journalist, and radio commentator, as his official and personal representative in civil aviation matters. The appointment of an aviation representative was made at the request of Mr. Charles H. Gartrell, Commissioner of the Kentucky Department of Aeronautics, who is president of the National Association of State Aviation Officials.

Since North Carolina has no State Department of Aeronautics, Mr. Goerch will act as advisor and representative to the Governor in civil aviation matters, and will keep in touch with the exchange of information about private and commercial flying between the various states.

The Governor expressed his appreciation that Mr. Goerch has accepted this appointment with the understanding that he would serve at no cost to the State, and would be available on his own time to advise and assist in civil aviation matters which might arise.

HURRICANE HAZEL DISASTER COMMITTEE

October 19, 1954

There was a conference held this morning in the Governor's Office by members of the Hurricane Disaster Committee and others to review and discuss the latest findings of the damages suffered throughout Eastern North Carolina as a result of Hurricane Hazel. Present were: Brigadier General Edward Griffin, Chairman of the Disaster Committee and Director of Civil Defense for North Carolina; Major General John Hall Manning, Adjutant General for North Carolina; Mr. W. H. Rogers, Jr., State Highway Engineer; Honorable Henry L. Bridges, State Auditor; Mr. K. C. Lattimer, Director of Field Service for the American Red Cross; Mr. Clarence Moore and Mr. Dixon Smith of Richmond, Virginia, with the Small Business Administration; and Mr. E. L. Rankin, Jr., Private Secretary to Governor Umstead.

It was the recommendation of General Griffin and his Committee that Wrightsville Beach, Carolina Beach, and Kure Beach should qualify for emergency allocation of funds to assist them in renovating and repairing their municipal plants. It was the Committee's recommendation that these funds be restricted to water and sewer allocations and that Wrightsville Beach receive $200,000, Carolina Beach $200,000, and Kure Beach $20,000. General Griffin stated that these three beach communities obviously suffered the greatest damage and needed help as soon as possible to be able to furnish such services as water and sewerage. The battalion of Army Engineers from Fort Bragg will concentrate its efforts in clearing the streets and public areas of debris so that the public officials can begin to make the necessary repairs to the water and sewerage lines.

General Manning reported that there are now eleven National Guard units or components of units on active duty in the stricken areas. Washington and Warsaw are the two latest units to go on duty and are being used to guard against looting in the Pamlico River section. General Griffin emphasized that the Federal Civil Defense Administration under the provisions of Public Law 875 can render emergency temporary assistance to the State or political subdivisions only and that no allocations or services are made to businesses or private interests. Public Law 875 is primarily concerned with assisting municipalities in restoring essential services which will permit the life of that community to continue and this assistance is further restricted to temporary repairs and not permanent improvements.

Mr. Lattimer reported briefly on the activities of the American Red Cross in Eastern North Carolina. The Red Cross has been busy in Eastern North Carolina from the first warning on the path of the hurricane and all chapters in Eastern North Carolina were immediately alerted to the possible danger of a hurricane. Shelters were established and provided for evacuees during the storm and the full force of the field service has been busy since that time and meeting the needs of individuals and families during the immediate emergency. Need and not loss is the basis upon which assistance to disaster sufferers is given through the Red Cross. Mr. Lattimer pointed out that the Red Cross does not make loans to families or individuals having needs as a result of a disaster, but does give direct assistance to help families return to normal living by providing such things as repairing or rebuilding of homes, providing household furnishings and other rehabilitation essentials.

Mr. Moore, the Regional Director of the Small Business Administration, and Mr. Smith have just completed a tour of a large portion of the disaster area and plan to open temporary offices in the area by Friday of this week. Twenty-seven counties in Eastern North Carolina have been declared disaster areas under the provisions of the Small Business Act of 1953. Mr. Moore pointed out that commercial banking and loan establishments in

Eastern North Carolina will give all loan assistance possible within the limits of their resources and that his administration stands ready to supplement this effort by providing disaster loans on an individual basis for the purpose of rebuilding and replacing business or personal dwellings. The interest rate on industrial loans is 3 per cent for home construction or repair and 5 per cent for business loans. The maximum maturity date on disaster loans is twenty years on housing for personal occupancy and ten years for all others. Mr. Moore reported that he will open an office at 100-A Custom House in Wilmington by Friday and is now considering opening an office in the Headquarters of Civil Defense in Raleigh. The permanent state office is at the Independence Building in Charlotte.

Following the meeting, General Griffin, Mr. Rogers and General Manning flew to the Morehead City area to investigate storm damages there and to discuss the situation with municipal officials.

REPORT ON HURRICANE DAMAGES

October 20, 1954

Brigadier General Edward Griffin, Chairman of the Hurricane Disaster Committee and Director of Civil Defense for North Carolina, reported to Governor Umstead this morning by telephone concerning the result of his preliminary investigation of hurricane damages in the Coastal area. He had just returned from a visit to the Morehead City, Beaufort, and the Atlantic Beach areas and had talked there with municipal officials about the damages suffered.

As a result of this investigation, General Griffin and his Committee recommended to Governor Umstead an additional $235,000 to the sum of $420,000 requested yesterday in behalf of Wrightsville Beach, Carolina Beach and Kure Beach. The Committee recommended $100,000 for Atlantic Beach, $75,000 for Beaufort, and $60,000 for Morehead City. A conference was held with General Griffin, State Treasurer Edwin M. Gill, Assistant Director of the Budget D. S. Coltrane, and E. L. Rankin, Jr., Private Secretary to Governor Umstead. After a further discussion of the

Committee's recommendation, the Governor was contacted by telephone and he recommended that $100,000 be allocated from the Contingency and Emergency Fund for the use of the Civil Defense Organization in aiding these stricken communities in restoring essential and basic utilities. He also requested that a meeting of the Council of State be called to consider and take action upon his recommendation immediately.

At the request of Governor Umstead, Secretary of State Thad Eure presided over a meeting of the Council of State and the Governor's recommendation was presented by Mr. Rankin and a further report of the hurricane damages was made by General Griffin. Attorney General Harry McMullan has given Governor Umstead his opinion that such an allocation can be legally made from the Contingency and Emergency Fund under the provisions of Chapter 166 of the 1953 *Session Laws* which deals with Civil Defense. After considerable discussion, the Council of State voted unanimously to approve this allocation.

A telegram was sent to President Eisenhower from Governor Umstead requesting an allocation of $555,000 under authority of Public Law 875, 81st Congress to supplement state, local and private agencies in their efforts in this major disaster.

Governor Umstead has kept in constant touch with the developments following the hurricane and he has expressed his deep interest and concern in rendering all assistance possible to municipalities, counties, and individuals suffering from hurricane damages. He has requested General Griffin to act as his personal representative in visiting every county which has suffered from the hurricane and to evaluate the storm damages as quickly as possible.

The Governor also announced the appointment of the Honorable George Dill, Mayor of Morehead City, as a member of the Hurricane Disaster Committee which is headed by General Griffin.

APPOINTMENT OF COMMITTEE ON REFUGEES

November 2, 1954

Governor Umstead announced today that in keeping with a request from the President of the United States and the Department of State, he has named the following as members of the

Governor's Committee to Implement the Refugee Act of 1953:

Lloyd C. Amos, Chairman, County Commissioners of Guilford County, and immediate past President of the State Association of County Commissioners, Greensboro; L. Y. Ballentine, Commissioner of Agriculture, Raleigh; Father Michael J. Begley, Superintendent, Catholic Orphanage, Nazareth; Reverend Raymond M. Bost, Pastor, Holy Trinity Lutheran Church, 1417 Regent Place, Raleigh; Rabbi Harry N. Caplan, 620 Aycock Street, Raleigh; Dr. L. L. Carpenter, Editor, *Biblical Recorder,* Raleigh; Frank Crane, Commissioner of Labor, Raleigh; W. M. Ficklen, Secretary, Chamber of Commerce, Charlotte; and Colonel Henry E. Kendall, Employment Security Commission, Raleigh.

In view of the fact that the members of this Committee will receive no pay and no allowance for expenses, with one or two exceptions, most of them have been named in the area of the immediate vicinity of Raleigh.

The Governor also announced that he has requested Dr. Ellen Winston, Commissioner of Public Welfare in North Carolina, to serve as Chairman of this Committee.

DEATH OF W. C. HARRIS

November 2, 1954

I was distressed to hear this morning of the death of Judge W. C. Harris, who for many years has been an outstanding Superior Court Judge in this State.

His fairness, wisdom, understanding of human nature, friendliness and courtesy to all those who came into his court, coupled with a desire to do justice always to all men, will be remembered by lawyers and laymen alike for many years to come.

As Solicitor of the Tenth Judicial District, I had many opportunities to observe his fine qualities, and I developed for him a profound respect and a deep affection which have continued through the years. The State has lost a faithful and able public servant, and I have lost a fine friend.

I extend to the members of his family my deepest sympathy.

VETERANS' DAY IN NORTH CAROLINA

November 2, 1954

For many years, it has been the custom to commemorate November 11th, the anniversary of the ending of World War I, by paying tribute to the heroes of that struggle, and by rededicating ourselves to the cause of peace. In more recent years the United States has been involved in two other great military conflicts which have added millions of veterans living and dead, to the honor rolls of this Nation.

The Congress, by an act approved June 1, 1954, changed the name of Armistice Day to Veterans' Day as a means of paying appropriate homage to the veterans of all its wars who have contributed so much to the preservation of our Republic. I believe that this is a wise move on the part of the Congress, and I hereby designate Thursday, November 11, 1954, as Veterans' Day in North Carolina. On that day let all of us solemnly remember the sacrifices of all those who fought so valiantly to preserve our heritage of freedom, and let us turn with renewed efforts to the task of promoting an enduring peace so that their efforts shall not have been in vain.

In order to insure proper and widespread observance of this anniversary, all veterans, all veterans' organizations, and all of our people are asked to join in this observance.

ENFORCEMENT OFFICERS—FIRST LINE OF DEFENSE[1]

November, 1954

The invitation extended to me by *Law and Order* in behalf of 5,155 Chiefs of Police, to write a guest editorial is one which I am delighted to accept. As Governor of the State of North Carolina, I am indebted for this privilege and for an opportunity to say a word on behalf of the maintenance of law and order.

Our form of democratic government is based upon justice according to law and the preservation of public order. The security of life, liberty and property depends upon our success in our

[1] This guest editorial appeared in the November issue of *Law and Order,* and is herewith reproduced by special permission of the copyright owner.

efforts to prevent violations of our criminal laws and unlawful trespasses upon the rights of our citizens. The police officers who enforce our laws are just as essential in this endeavor as are our courts and solicitors. The law enforcement officer is our first line of defense against disorder and crime. And, just as a chain is no stronger than its weakest link, so our legal system is no stronger than the effectiveness and honesty of our law enforcement officers in the performance of their duties.

Law enforcement officers in the United States have a long and constantly growing tradition of straightforward and efficient administration of the law without fear or favor. Their work has given reality to the idea that the law should be no respecter of persons. In some countries the agencies of law enforcement have become instruments of oppression by means of which those who hold views at variance with the government may be persecuted. This was true under the Nazi regime in Germany and is now true under the Communist regime in Russia. How fortunate we are that our law enforcement officers in the aggregate compose a great instrument for protection of our human freedoms rather than an instrument of a dictator or tyrant in the ruthless destruction of the lives and liberties of our people. All of us consider our policemen as friends who may be called upon to render aid and assistance in the name of law and order, and the men who obey our laws have nothing to fear from them.

It is a task which staggers the imagination to protect more than one hundred and sixty million people in their daily activities, whether in the market place, in the school, or in the home. Our law enforcement officers have accepted this challenge and are daily performing this task. They are symbols as well as custodians of our liberities under law. The efficient and honest men of this group who have accepted this challenging work as their profession deserve every citizen's support and encouragement in the performance of their duties.

I congratulate the law enforcement officers of our country upon the fine service they have performed for the citizens of this country and I anticipate that every law enforcement officer will endeavor to increase the value and efficiency of his profession as has been done in the past.

The men who enforce the laws of our country possess one of the deepest trusts which it is within the power of our people to bestow. We have reason to know that that trust has not been misplaced for in the past you have fought the good fight, you have kept the faith. We are confident that your efforts in the future in behalf of law and order will not only reflect those high standards demonstrated in the past but will also become accelerated. This is a great challenge which I am sure you can meet and, indeed, you must meet it for, in you, American liberty under law lives and moves and has its being.

SAFETY PROGRAM [1]

As Governor of North Carolina I am keenly interested in highway safety. One of the greatest threats to North Carolinians today is the rising toll of highway accidents. The deaths, injuries and property damages resulting from these accidents should concern every person in our State.

It is my sincere wish that you operate your motor vehicle without mishap. Your chances of doing so will depend largely upon your own efforts. Know the fundamentals of safe driving and practice them constantly. Remain alert; drive within the speed limits set by law or dictated by road conditions; keep your car under control at all times; and maintain the mechanical fitness of your automobile or truck.

The decision of whether or not you will escape an accident remains largely with *you*. It will take the combined efforts of every individual motorist to make our highways and streets arteries of safe travel rather than avenues of death and destruction.

[1] This statement was printed and sent to individuals who had applied for and passed the examination for renewal of their state drivers' licenses, and was also issued with the 1954 auto license plates.

LETTERS AND TELEGRAMS

January 9, 1953

Mr. D. S. Coltrane,
Assistant Director of the Budget,
The Budget Bureau,
Raleigh, North Carolina.

Dear Dave:

In the month of June, 1952, by order of Governor Scott, you were relieved of the major duties and responsibilities of the office to which you were commissioned on July 1, 1949.

This is to advise you that I, as Governor, am hereby restoring to you all rights, privileges, and powers useful and necessary to the just and proper discharge of the duties of your appointment and those duties pertinent to the office of Assistant Director of the Budget of the State of North Carolina.

Very truly yours,
William B. Umstead, *Governor.*

February 12, 1953

Honorable E. T. Bost, Jr., *Speaker,*
House of Representatives,
North Carolina General Assembly,
Raleigh, North Carolina.

Honorable Luther H. Hodges,
Lieutenant Governor of North Carolina,
Raleigh, North Carolina.

Gentlemen:

I am informed that there has been considerable discussion as to whether or not a separate bill should be introduced authorizing immediate payment of the 10 per cent salary increase, retroactive to July 1, 1952, and the press has recently published an article to the effect that such bill was being contemplated and would probably be introduced within the next day or two.

In order that all state employees and members of the General

Assembly may fully understand the situation, I shall appreciate it if you will read this letter so that it may be fully publicized throughout the State.

There is in the Budget Appropriation Bill, which is now under consideration by the Appropriation Committee, provision for this 10 per cent retroactive increase and I feel confident that the bill will be enacted without this provision being changed. The amount of the increase for the current year is exactly in accordance with the recommendations I have made. However, Section 143-15 of the *General Statutes* (this being a part of the Executive Budget Act) reads as follows:

> The provisions of this article shall continue to be the legislative policy with reference to the making of appropriations and shall be treated as rules of both branches of the General Assembly until and unless the same may be changed by the General Assembly either by express enactment or by rule adopted by either branch of the General Assembly.
>
> The General Assembly may reduce or strike out such item in the Budget Appropriation Bill as it may deem to be in the interest of the public service, but neither House shall consider further or special appropriations until the Budget Appropriation Bill shall have been enacted in whole or in part or rejected, unless the Governor shall submit and recommend an emergency appropriation bill, or bills, when enacted, shall continue in force only until the Budget Appropriation Bill shall become effective, unless otherwise provided by the General Assembly.

This means, of course, that neither House of the General Assembly should consider any special appropriations until the Budget Appropriation Bill shall have been enacted in whole or in part or rejected, unless the Governor shall submit and recommend an emergency appropriation bill. A salary increase under the circumstances now existing cannot, in my opinion, be construed as an "emergency appropriation bill." While I would like to see this 10 per cent increase paid to all employees at the earliest possible date, I could not, of course, ask the Appropriation Committee to proceed in a manner contrary to law, and I feel that the employees who are to be the beneficiaries of this increase and the General Assembly will wholeheartedly agree with me in this respect.

Sincerely yours,

William B. Umstead, *Governor.*

February 16, 1953

The Honorable William B. Umstead,
Governor of North Carolina,
Raleigh, North Carolina.

Dear Governor Umstead:

This letter is to express my views on "Educational Television" which are based on expressions from the Alamance County Community Council of which I have served as president and school people with whom I am in daily contact. We consider the action of the Federal Communications Commission in holding TV channels open for education a most forward movement. We recognize the importance that television will play in the future of the thinking of the people of this country. Therefore, it is mandatory that, in order to lift the level of the thinking of our people, that some TV channels be operated by sources other than commercial interests.

It is our expressed opinion that the Legislature of North Carolina will support substantially educational television in North Carolina.

Yours very truly,
L. R. Wooten,
Director of Instruction,
Alamance County Public Schools.

March 27, 1953

Her Majesty Queen Elizabeth II,
London,
England.

Your Majesty:

As Governor of the State of North Carolina, may I express my pleasure at this opportunity to wish you a long and prosperous reign. North Carolina is happy to join with the other states of the Union in sending you its own state flower, the dogwood blossom. This beautiful flower covers many parts of our State, from the mountains to the sea, during the spring.

One of the thirteen original colonies, North Carolina has many historical connections with Great Britain. The first English colonies in America were planted in the 1580's on Roanoke Island, now part of the coast of North Carolina. The actual name of our State is derived from Latin "Carolus," in honor of King Charles I of England. A large number of our citizens are direct descendants of English, Scotch, and Irish peoples. Your great Nation has many friends here.

On behalf of the people of North Carolina, I extend to you and your people every good wish for a peaceful and prosperous reign.

With kindest regards and best wishes, I am

Sincerely yours,
William B. Umstead, *Governor.*

April 4, 1953

Mr. J. H. McKenzie, *General Chairman,*
Rowan County Bicentennial Committee,
Salisbury, North Carolina.

Dear Mr. McKenzie:

It is with a great deal of pleasure and satisfaction that I extend to you and the people of Rowan County my hearty congratulations and personal greetings on the two hundredth anniversary of your county. I know that you have awaited this historic event with great anticipation. It is with deep regret that I will not be able to attend and extend my best wishes in person to Rowan County.

Rowan County should be proud of its two hundred years. As the "mother" of many counties, Rowan has been an important link in the history of North Carolina. When Salisbury was established in 1755, it was an outpost of western civilization. It was from Rowan County that Daniel Boone set forth on his expedition to explore Kentucky and to establish the first settlement there.

Your county has always stood for political freedom. Rowan was among the first counties to take active leadership in working toward independence in the days prior to and leading up to the

Revolution. Many distinguished leaders in the economic, political, cultural, and social life of North Carolina have come from Rowan.

Speaking for all of the people of North Carolina, I wish you every success with your Bicentennial Celebration. North Carolina is proud of Rowan County, its fine people, and its many contributions to our history and the American way of life.

With kindest regards and best wishes, I am

Sincerely yours,
William B. Umstead, *Governor.*

April 6, 1953

Mr. President, Mr. Speaker And
Members Of The General Assembly:

The State Educational Radio and Television Commission which was appointed pursuant to Joint Resolution No. 10, adopted at the beginning of this session of the General Assembly, has filed with me a report of its activities and recommendations as provided for in Section 7 of said resolution. A copy of the report, embodying the recommendations of the Commission, is submitted to you for your consideration.

I recommend that necessary legislation be enacted to comply with the recommendations embodied in the Commission's report. A bill entitled an act "to continue the North Carolina Educational Radio and Television Commission created by Joint Resolution No. 10 of the 1953 General Assembly to authorize counties and municipalities to contribute funds to said Commission and to appropriate $12,000 to said Commission for the biennium 1953-1955;" and, a resolution "requesting the Federal Communications Commission to continue its reservation of educational television channels in this State and to allocate additional educational television channels beyond those presently located in North Carolina," have been prepared for introduction in the Senate to accomplish this purpose and are being offered for your consideration.

With kindest regards, I am

Sincerely yours,
William B. Umstead, *Governor.*

(TELEGRAM)

April 14, 1953

Mr. Eugene Thomas,
Tarboro,
North Carolina.

May I extend my heartiest congratulations to Miss Lurlyne Greer of Winston-Salem and Mr. Harvie Ward of Tarboro upon their selection as Teague Award Winners [1] for 1953. This is an outstanding achievement of which North Carolina is extremely proud. I deeply regret that I am unable to be present and extend my best wishes to Miss Greer and Mr. Ward in person.

With kindest personal regards.

William B. Umstead, *Governor.*

April 21, 1953

Most Reverend Vincent S. Waters, D.D.,
Residence of the Bishop,
15 North McDowell Street,
Raleigh, North Carolina.

Dear Bishop Waters:

It is a pleasure to offer my sincere wishes to the Seventh Annual State Convention of the North Carolina Catholic Laymen's Association, which will convene in the City of Goldsboro, North Carolina, on May 2 and 3, 1953. I extend a warm welcome to the visiting bishops, priests, sisters, and laymen who will be assembled for deliberation of the Convention theme—"Teaching Religion."

This is a most suitable and appropriate theme. I am confident that your decisions at the Convention will do much to foster the spirit of democracy in our great State, as our democratic way of life is based upon our religious convictions.

[1] The Teague Award, presented annually to the outstanding male and female amateur athletes of the Carolinas, was established in 1935 honoring Judge Lewis E. Teague of High Point, North Carolina. The nominees for the award are chosen by the newspapers and radio stations of the two Carolinas.

I am happy to extend my best wishes to you and to your Auxiliary Bishop, the Most Reverend James J. Navagh, D.D., for a most successful Convention. May it be productive of many ideas which will help all citizens of North Carolina and our country.

With kindest regards and best wishes, I am

Sincerely yours,
William B. Umstead, *Governor.*

April 22, 1953

Senator Clyde R. Hoey,
United States Senate,
Washington, D. C.

Dear Senator Hoey:

In April of 1952, after a three and one-half year freeze on television station construction, the Federal Communications Commission allocated 242 of the 2,053 television channels exclusively to education for a one-year period beginning on June 2, 1953. Since April, 1952, education throughout the Nation has been extremely active in working toward the activation of these channels.

Upon my suggestion the 1953 General Assembly of North Carolina authorized in January an Educational Radio and Television Commission. This Commission held its organizational meeting and a public hearing on February 12. It has conducted a preliminary engineering and program survey; has had appointed local educational television committees in each of the eight cities to which allocations were assigned; namely, Asheville, Chapel Hill, Charlotte, Durham, Greensboro, Raleigh, Wilmington and Winston-Salem; held as informational meeting for legislators on March 10; and has adopted the attached recommendations which I have approved and passed on to the General Assembly for consideration.

The educators, commercial broadcasters, and many citizens are interested in retaining these channels exclusively for education for at least two years longer in order to give education an opportunity to investigate thoroughly the possibilities and potentialities of their use for educational purposes.

I sincerely hope that you will acquaint the members of the Federal Communications Commission with North Carolina's interest in retaining the eight educational channels allocated to North Carolina on an exclusive basis for at least two years beyond the June 2 deadline.

With kindest regards, I am

Sincerely yours,
William B. Umstead, *Governor.*

April 22, 1953

The Honorable Clyde R. Hoey,
Senate Office Building,
Washington, D. C.

Dear Senator Hoey:

My attention has been called to the omission of the appropriation for the Blue Ridge Parkway from the Interior Department Appropriation Bill, which I understand is now under consideration in the Senate. I am taking this opportunity to express to you my deep interest in the further completion of this great highway. I will personally appreciate anything that you can do to insure that this appropriation, which I understand is for $6,000,000, be reinstated in this bill.

As you know, the tourist business is one of the greatest industries in our State and provides a great deal of revenue for many of our citizens who otherwise would have little. The popularity of the Blue Ridge Parkway is increasing tremendously each year and I am informed that in 1952 the Blue Ridge Parkway attracted 3,374,962 visitors. Obviously, the longer we can successfully entertain these visitors, the more money they will distribute among our citizens. Further construction of the Blue Ridge Parkway, in my opinion, will provide some of the facilities which we need so badly to hold these visitors within our borders. Therefore, with a full appreciation of the need for balancing the national budget, I think that the small amount requested for the Parkway should be considered an investment of the highest order, rather than an item that could readily be deleted from the budget.

With kindest regards, I am

Sincerely yours,
William B. Umstead, *Governor.*

April 29, 1953

Mr. Albert Zeno,
Ambassador's Dinner Headquarters,
Room 724, Charlotte Hotel,
Charlotte, North Carolina.

Dear Mr. Zeno:

The State of North Carolina joins the free world in reaffirming the independence of the State of Israel, which has inspired freedom-loving people everywhere with its devotion to the principles of human liberty. I believe that the friendship and mutual trust between America and Israel will endure and flourish, for our relationship is firmly rooted in a common devotion to democratic practices and ideals.

I take pleasure in asking the people of North Carolina to join with their many Jewish friends throughout the State and Nation in the celebration and observance of the fifth anniversary of the establishment of the State of Israel. May I also express my pleasure upon the occasion of the visit to North Carolina by His Excellency Abba Eban, Israeli Ambassador to the United States. We are proud to have the Ambassador of this ancient but young democratic Nation to visit in the City of Charlotte and join in a salute to the State of Israel through its Independence Bond Issue.

With kindest regards and best wishes, I am

Sincerely yours,
William B. Umstead, *Governor.*

April 1953

Honorable William B. Umstead,
Governor of North Carolina,
Raleigh, North Carolina.

Dear Governor Umstead:

In accordance with the provisions of Senate Bill No. 88, 1953 Session of the General Assembly, your Committee, appointed pursuant to said act, herewith files this report and recommendation.

Since its appointment, your Committee has made an extensive study of the boundaries of the highway divisions of the State as they are now constituted. This investigation has consisted of numerous consultations with you, with highway officials and engineers, and with many other citizens of the State who are interested in the development and maintenance of a state-wide highway system commensurate with the needs of the State as a whole. In our investigation, study, and recommendation, we have been particular not to sacrifice the general state-wide interest to local desires for the establishment of any division in any particular area.

We submit herewith as a part of this report, for your approval, a map upon which is designated and outlined a redivisioning of the State into fourteen divisions which we feel is in the public interest. In increasing the divisions to fourteen in number, your Committee has, in its best judgment, divided the State into divisions substantially of equal size on the joint basis of area, population and mileage. An examination of the map of the proposed revision which is attached hereto will disclose that the formula prescribed by the statute has been substantially followed.

FIRST DIVISION

Bertie
Camden
Chowan
Currituck
Dare
Gates
Hertford
Hyde
Martin
Northampton
Pasquotank
Perquimans
Tyrrell
Washington

SECOND DIVISION

Beaufort
Carteret
Craven
Greene

Jones
Lenoir
Pamlico
Pitt

THIRD DIVISION

Brunswick
Duplin
New Hanover
Onslow
Pender
Sampson

FOURTH DIVISION

Edgecombe
Halifax
Johnston
Nash
Wayne
Wilson

FIFTH DIVISION

Durham
Franklin
Granville
Person
Vance
Wake
Warren

SIXTH DIVISION

Bladen
Columbus
Cumberland
Harnett
Robeson

SEVENTH DIVISION

Alamance
Caswell
Guilford
Orange
Rockingham

EIGHTH DIVISION

Chatham
Hoke
Lee
Montgomery
Moore
Randolph
Richmond
Scotland

NINTH DIVISION

Davidson
Davie
Forsyth
Rowan
Stokes

TENTH DIVISION

Anson
Cabarrus
Mecklenburg
Stanly
Union

ELEVENTH DIVISION

Alleghany
Ashe
Avery
Caldwell
Surry
Watauga
Wilkes
Yadkin

TWELFTH DIVISION

Catawba
Alexander
Cleveland
Gaston
Iredell
Lincoln

THIRTEENTH DIVISION

Buncombe
Burke
Madison
McDowell
Mitchell
Rutherford
Yancey

FOURTEENTH DIVISION

Cherokee
Clay
Graham
Haywood
Henderson
Jackson
Macon
Polk
Swain
Transylvania

Having heretofore sought your advice and counsel in performing the task before us, we herewith submit, for your approval, this report, and recommend to you that the State be divided into fourteen divisions as indicated above.

Respectfully submitted,
Walter H. Woodson, Sr., *Chairman*
W. P. Saunders
Reuben B. Robertson, Sr.
T. Boddie Ward
J. Hampton Price

After careful consideration of the needs of the State, I have determined that it is in the public interest that the number of highway divisions be increased from ten to fourteen, and I hereby approve the foregoing report of the committee appointed by me pursuant to the act of the General Assembly referred to in this report.

This the 11th day of May, 1953,

William B. Umstead, *Governor.*

May 26,1953

Honorable William B. Umstead,
Governor of North Carolina,
Raleigh, North Carolina.

Dear Governor Umstead:

Congratulations on what I understand is a complete recovery. We were all concerned when you got sick and are pleased that it was not more serious.

Recently you asked me to take a matter up with the Federal Communications Commission concerning our North Carolina plans for the use of television for educational purposes. You were under the impression that the channels reserved for use in North Carolina will expire June 2 and were disturbed over that probability.

I did as you requested and have received a reply from the Commission indicating that your fears were unfounded. I am enclosing a copy of the letter from the Commission on the subject. Attached to the copy of that letter is a copy of a public notice which will interest you if you have not already seen it.

It was a pleasure to be of some service to you. Please call on me again if you have anything you wish me to do.

With best regards always, I am

Sincerely yours,
Charles Raper Jonas, *Representative,*
U. S. Congress.

(TELEGRAM)

Chicago, Illinois.
May 29, 1953

Honorable William B. Umstead,
Governor,
Raleigh, North Carolina.

Your State voted award for Outstanding Achievement in Driver Licensing in 1952 National Traffic Safety Contest. Our heartiest congratulations to you and your citizens. We will be glad to assist in suitable presentation ceremony if desired. Confirming letter follows.

Ned H. Dearborn, *President,*
National Safety Council.

June 4, 1953

Mr. Irving E. Carlyle,
Attorney at Law,
Winston-Salem, North Carolina.

Dear Irving:

I have been advised by the Attorney General's office that the members of the Television Study Commission which I appointed several months ago do not have to be reappointed under the act passed by the General Assembly continuing the Commission. Therefore, I want you to continue to serve as Chairman, and I will appreciate it if you will advise the members of the Commission that they do not have to be reappointed and that they are still members of this Commission.

I am grateful for the work which you have done already and I know that the members of the Commission will continue to do a splendid job for the State. I enclose a pamphlet which might be of interest to you.

With kindest regards, I am

Sincerely yours,
William B. Umstead, *Governor.*

June 1953

The Editor,
The Inner World,[1]
Raleigh, North Carolina.

Dear Sir:

I am happy to send a word of greeting to the staff of *The Inner World* upon the occasion of the first anniversary of this publication. It is my hope that you have found your newspaper useful and informative. May you and your thousands of readers gain something worthwhile from each issue during the coming year.

I am sure that the first anniversary of *The Inner World* means a great deal to the editorial staff and you should look upon it as a challenge to do better in the coming year. I hope that all of the inmates of the state prison system will look ahead to a better day when they will be able to rejoin the outer world as useful and law-abiding citizens. With faith and confidence in the ability of

[1] *The Inner World* is edited, printed, all on their leisure time, and paid for by the prisoners. This paper goes to all the camps and institutions keeping them informed of what is happening throughout the system. It is a medium by which the prisoners can express themselves to each other and to those outside of prison who are interested in those inside the prison. The paper is not censored except by its editorial staff.

any man to reform, our parole system will do the best it can to speed this process. The eventual success of the paroles system, of course, depends upon the performance of the men who are released to return home to their families.

With best wishes, I am

Sincerely yours,
William B. Umstead, *Governor.*

Sanford,
North Carolina.
July 10, 1953

His Excellency William B. Umstead,
Governor of North Carolina,
Raleigh, North Carolina.

Dear Governor Umstead:

Pursuant to authority granted by you to the undersigned committee to make a study and recommendation for the establishment of one or more nursing training courses at state-supported institutions, under Senate Bill 439, 1953 General Assembly, we beg to report:

On the 29th of June your Committee met with authorities and others interested in the establishment of a Nursing School at Winston-Salem Teachers' College; and on the same day consulted with authorities and those interested in the establishment of a school at Agricultural and Technical College in Greensboro; and on the 1st day of July we met with the authorities and those interested in the establishment of a Nursing Training School at the North Carolina College located in Durham.

We believe that these three state-supported institutions are eminently qualified to handle the establishment of a Negro Collegiate School of Nursing.

Your Committee is of the opinion that two schools ought to be established, but that the same ought not to be open until a minimum of twenty students are enrolled the first year and until the college authorities obtain the service of a competent and qualified director. This statement is made by reason of the fact that your Committee is intensely interested in the success of these schools and feels that they should be a necessary requirement.

We recommend that one school be established in Greensboro, North Carolina, in conjunction with the Agricultural and Technical College. A statement as presented to the committee by the authorities of Agricultural and Technical College is hereto attached, which gives the proposed curriculum of the three-year course and also what was considered by the authorities to be an adequate budget for the biennium.

We further recommend that a training school be established in Winston-Salem, North Carolina, in conjunction with the Winston-Salem Teachers' College. We believe that the attention of the ensuing General Assembly ought to be called to the fact that possibly a third school should be established at Durham, in connection with the North Carolina College in Durham. The Committee does not pass upon the budgets for each of these schools and suggests that the actual amount of expenditures for such purpose be left to the discretion of the Assistant Director of the Budget, Mr. Dave S. Coltrane.

We further desire to state that in our deliberations we had the advice and counsel of Dr. Elizabeth Kemble, who is head of the School of Nursing at Chapel Hill, and also Dr. William Richardson, School of Public Health in Chapel Hill, and feel greatly indebted to these people for their information and advice.

Dr. Williams, President of the Elizabeth City State Teachers' College, advised the Committee that the Trustees desired a hearing as to establishing a Negro Nursing School at this college, and the Chairman talked to Dr. Williams over the telephone and explained that the Elizabeth City State Teachers' College did not have access to a Negro hospital and thought there would be some complications in this respect. However, Dr. Williams insisted upon a hearing and had a committee appointed from his board to meet with your Committee in Raleigh on the 10th day of July, at 10:00 o'clock in the forenoon. Your Committee met in Raleigh today to hear the plea of Dr. Williams, but we are now advised that Dr. Williams stated that the committee appointed from his Board of Trustees felt that it would be impracticable for Elizabeth City State Teachers' College to press further its claim for a nurses training course at the present time.

We are happy to have had an opportunity to serve in the capacity for which we were appointed and remain with much respect,

Very sincerely,
Warren R. Williams, *Chairman*
Ruth Council
Reid Holmes

July 21, 1953

Mr. Walter Spivey,
Tabor City,
North Carolina.

Dear Mr. Spivey:

I appreciate your telephone call to my secretary with reference to the public schools.

During the last General Assembly I did all I could do for the schools. I recommended, and the General Assembly approved, a 10 per cent retroactive increase for school teachers to July 1, 1952. It also provided for a 10 per cent increase during the next two years. There were a number of other items which I recommended and which were approved.

The question of teachers is serious and I am sure the State Board of Education is doing the best it can in this connection.

With kindest regards and best wishes, I am

Sincerely yours,
William B. Umstead, *Governor.*

July 31, 1953

To The Officers And Men Of The Fayetteville Independent Light Infantry:[1]

Gentlemen:

It is a pleasure to have this opportunity to congratulate you on the 160th anniversary of the Fayetteville Independent Light Infantry and to welcome the units of Centennial Legion of Historic Military Commands participating in your anniversary celebration.

The Fayetteville Independent Light Infantry has a special record of continuous service since August, 1793. It was founded because the people of Fayetteville were alarmed about the threat of war and the hostile attitude of Spain toward the United States.

[1] This congratulatory message from Governor Umstead was prepared for inclusion in a souvenir program.

In the firm and positive action to be expected of your people, the Fayetteville Independent Light Infantry was immediately organized to be of any assistance needed. In the War of 1812, the F.I.L.I. participated and during the Civil War this company furnished many officers for the Confederate service.

Your devotion to duty and your readiness to stand for what is right are worthy of the highest commendation. May you continue to render this splendid service in the years ahead.

With kindest regards and best wishes, I am

Sincerely yours,
William B. Umstead, *Governor.*

August 11, 1953

Honorable R. L. Doughton,
Laurel Springs,
North Carolina.

Dear Mr. Doughton:

Thanks for your letter of August 7 with which you enclosed a copy of your letter of August 5 to Mr. Stephen A. Mitchell submitting your resignation as National Committeeman for North Carolina.

I, of course, regret that you felt it necessary to resign and I want to thank you again for the splendid service you have rendered the party since you were named National Committeeman.

I do not feel that it is necessary to have a meeting of the Executive Committee until sometime this fall to select your successor.

I was glad to see Horton for a few minutes last week and I shall look forward to the pleasure of seeing you whenever you are in Raleigh.

With kindest regards and best wishes always, I am

Sincerely yours,
William B. Umstead, *Governor.*

August 14, 1953

Honorable William B. Umstead,
Raleigh,
North Carolina.

Dear Governor Umstead:

The Prison Advisory Council is much concerned and perturbed, as we know you are, over the prison system of North Carolina and its many critical problems. Since the appointment of a Director of Prisons and recommendations concerning his duties and authority come from you, we are sending to you our consensus of opinion concerning the present critical aspects of the administration of the prison system. Members of the Council have conferred at length both with the Honorable A. H. Graham, Chairman of the State Highway and Public Works Commission, and Mr. Walter F. Anderson,[1] Director of Prisons, in an effort to have all the facts. This letter, however, reflects only the careful and considerate judgment of the Council. May we urge you to consider our advice under the two following phases.

1. It is our mature and unanimous judgment that effective prison administration both from a humane and practical standpoint is impossible under the present subordination of the Prison Department to the State Highway and Public Works Commission. This is because human values and normal problems of welfare and security are made secondary to fiscal matters, to the building of roads and to outmoded processes of penology. North Carolina has not placed fiscal considerations first in her support of social security, social welfare, public health, public education, and public mental institutions. The Prison Advisory Council is well aware of the need for and desires a prison administration that is economically sound. The Council, however, does not see how the State of North Carolina can demand that the Prison Department, alone of all its social agencies, be run on the basis of paying its own way by the work of its inmates. We have been leaders in North Carolina in many social advances yet we are the only state

[1] Walter F. Anderson was not retained as Director of Prisons. Governor Umstead appointed Mr. William F. Bailey to this position, and Mr. Bailey was given broader powers in the administration of the Prison Department.

in the Union that has its penal program subordinated to a division of highways and public works which makes its major decisions in handling human penology only in terms of their costs.

Our first urgent recommendation, therefore, is also a continued one. We repeat again that we believe the only possible approach to a solution of the many problems in prison administration is the separation of the Prison Department from the Department of Highways and Public Works.[1] We urge that this be done as soon as it is possible within the framework of legislative action. We believe there is already adequate information supporting our recommendations that the Prison Department be made administratively distinct from the Department of Highways and Public Works. If further study is considered necessary, we urge that you appoint, as soon as possible, a commission to make this investigation. We further recommend that we, along with experts in the fields of finance, personnel administration, penology, law, public welfare, and education be given adequate representation on this commission.

2. While we are convinced that no enduring and satisfactory plan of prison administration is possible under the existing subordination of the Prison Department to the Department of Highways and Public Works, we recommend the following as the best possible interim action:

(1) We urge that you reappoint Mr. Walter F. Anderson as Director of Prisons. It is our mature judgment that it will be difficult, if not impossible, to find in North Carolina anyone who can fulfill the duties of this position as well as Mr. Anderson. Mr. Anderson has demonstrated his devotion to the horrendous task of prison administration. His experience in these problems is of untold value to the State. His honesty and sincerity of purpose as well as his administrative ability cannot be replaced easily. The transition from a purely custodial system to a system looking toward prisoner rehabilitation possibly has been attendant with problems of morale and dissatisfaction on the part of some. Any change is difficult to assimilate. We, in recommending Mr. Anderson's reappointment, are standing firm in the efforts of this Coun-

[1] The Prison Department was not separated from the Department of Highways and Public Works until General Assembly of 1957, effective July 1, 1957.

cil to advance prison administration in North Carolina, to conserve the gains which have been made, and to pave the way for a more effective prison system.

(2) We recommend that the rules and recommendations for governing the prison system, submitted to the Highway and Public Works Commission, be adopted without further delay. It is assumed that, in adopting these rules, definite status will be given to the Director of Prisons and that procedures for employment and discharge of prison personnel will be so set up that the Director of Prisons can give them direction and consistency. It is assumed further that with the adoption of these regulations, the superintendent of women's prison would ordinarily be a woman with experience, maturity, and training in penology or related fields. The reasons for this assumption are self-evident in the nature of the problems involved in the supervision of women prisoners.

(3) Provisions for closer liaison and consultation between the Highway and Public Works Commission and the Prison Advisory Council and the Director of Prisons are a first essential. This consultation will involve all phases of the prison system including fiscal, personnel, and administrative aspects, and problems. Only through closer consultation can the Council perform its statutory functions. Nothing is to be gained by a failure to take advantage of close co-operation between two groups officially charged with prison affairs.

The Prison Advisory Council repeats that the recommendations under Paragraph 2 of this memorandum are simply stop-gap measures until the prison system is set up administratively independent of the Highway and Public Works Commission. Unless these recommendations are adopted, it is unfair, both to you, as Governor of North Carolina, and to us, the members of the Prison Advisory Council, for us to remain as members of the Prison Advisory Council. We believe it would be much better for us to resign so that we can freely devote our efforts to a greatly augmented campaign to pull North Carolina out of the present untenable position it is in as regards effective prison administration. We are confident that if present trends continue the prison situation in North Carolina will be little less than disgraceful.

We respectively urge you, therefore, to give your prompt and careful consideration to our recommendations,

Respectfully yours,
William McGehee, *Chairman,*
W. W. Andrews,
Mrs. J. Melville Broughton,
Mrs. Kate Burr Johnson,
Howard W. Odum.

CC: The Honorable A. H. Graham,
Walter F. Anderson,
Members, Prison Advisory Council.

August 22, 1953

Mr. William McGehee, *Chairman,*
Prison Advisory Council,
Marshall Fields Company,
Leaksville, North Carolina.

Dear Mr. McGehee:

I acknowledge with thanks the receipt of your letter of August 14 to which I have given careful consideration.

With regard to the first phase of your letter, I wish to advise that it is my present intention to recommend to the next General Assembly that the Prison Department be separated from the State Highway and Public Works Commission and as to the desirability of such separation, I do not believe that further study is necessary. However, with reference to the administrative and financial problems involved, it is my belief that careful study of a suitable plan is necessary since the administration of the prison system involves the welfare of thousands of prisoners and the expenditure of over nine million dollars. In my Inaugural Address I recommended that such a plan be duly considered by the Commission for Reorganization of State Government. I intend to have a plan of operation worked out prior to the meeting of the next General Assembly.

The second phase of your letter was divided into three parts. The first was a recommendation for the reappointment of Mr.

Walter F. Anderson as Director of Prisons. I am glad to have your recommendation and it has had my serious consideration.

Second: You recommend that the rules and regulations governing the prison system submitted to the State Highway and Public Works Commission be adopted without further delay. I have not seen a copy of the proposed rules and regulations. It is my understanding that in conference on Wednesday of this week satisfactory agreements were reached with reference to the rules and regulations for presentation to the State Highway and Public Works Commission at the next meeting.

Third: You suggested closer liaison and consultation between the State Highway and Public Works Commission, the Prison Advisory Council, and the Director of Prisons. It seems to me that this is a good suggestion and that it should be arranged.

In the last paragraph of your letter you stated that unless all three recommendations under the second phase of your letter are complied with that it would be best for the Prison Advisory Council to resign. I regret that you included this statement because I do not like threats. I welcome recommendations as to appointments and as to any other phase of the operation of the state government, but I cannot concede that any person, group of persons or any advisory council has the right to tell the Governor of North Carolina that he should appoint any particular person to any particular position, nor do I concede the right of any person, group of persons or advisory council to say that the Governor of North Carolina must comply with any recommendations with reference to the prison system or any other department of the state government.

I am deeply interested in the rehabilitation of prisoners. I know that this is essential. It is my purpose to see that a sound program of rehabilitation is continued to the end that every effort may be made to save from a life of crime offenders sentenced to prison. At the same time, I firmly believe that discipline and order in a prison system are essential. I do not know what actual experience you have had with criminals or with prisons. I served ten years as prosecuting officer in criminal courts, and had actual experience with both criminals and prisons. During these ten years my experience taught me the need of both rehabilitation and discipline.

Section 148-88 of the *General Statutes of North Carolina* provides as follows:

"It is the duty of the Council to advise with the prison director on all matters pertaining to prison administration, the employment, training, custody, and discipline of prisoners and all other phases of prison management. The Council shall study thoroughly the State prison system and shall from time to time make recommendations for the improvement thereof to the State Highway and Public Works Commission."

Under the provisions of the above quoted section, I see it to be the duty of your Council to advise the Prison Director and make recommendations to the State Highway and Public Works Commission, and while I deeply appreciate the work of your Council, I do not deem it to be your function to operate the prison system.

On July 22, 1952 you wrote me and suggested that the Prison Advisory Council would appreciate an opportunity to confer with me with reference to the operation of the State Prison Department. On August 1, I wrote you that I would be delighted to talk with the Prison Advisory Council and suggested that the conference be deferred until after the general election the first week in November. I stated, however, that if you and your Council preferred to see me before that time, I would be glad to arrange it. You wrote me on August 5 that it would be satisfactory with you to have the conference after the general election and that if you found that the Council desired an earlier conference, you would write me. According to my files, I have received no further communication from you until your letter of August 14, 1953, and my secretary has advised me that you have made no request for a conference. I shall be glad to confer with the Prison Advisory Council at any time.

I am sending a copy of this letter to each member of your Council.

With kindest regards and best wishes, I am

Sincerely yours,

William B. Umstead, *Governor.*

CC: Mr. Wiley W. Andrews,
Mrs. Kate Burr Johnson,
Mrs. J. Melville Broughton,
Dr. Howard W. Odum.

(TELEGRAM)

The White House
Washington, D. C.
August 31, 1953

Honorable William B. Umstead,
Governor of North Carolina,
Raleigh, North Carolina.

In absence of the President, your telegram requesting federal assistance for the areas in North Carolina affected by the drought has been referred to the Federal Civil Defense Administrator who is authorized by executive order to make the necessary investigation and report. The Administrator is requesting further information from the Department of Agriculture. As soon as report is received the President will decide on whatever action is appropriate under Public Law 875—Eighty-Second Congress.

Bernard M. Shanley,
Special Counsel to the President.

(TELEGRAM)

August 31, 1953

The Honorable Dwight D. Eisenhower,
President of the United States,
The White House,
Washington, D. C.

Exhaustive survey by State Agricultural Mobilization Committee, of which the Director of the Production and Marketing Administration is the Chairman, has reported to me that the counties of Alamance, Alexander, Caswell, Davie, Durham, Franklin, Granville, Guilford, Harnett, Orange, Person, Rockingham, Vance, Wake and Warren in North Carolina come within the disaster conditions resulting from the drought which would entitle them to be declared by you as disaster areas under Public Law 875.

The Mobilization Committee has made a careful and exhaustive study of conditions in the counties named and I urge you immediately to declare them disaster areas in order that they may take advantage of the provisions of Public Law 115. The drought in these areas has not only been severe, produced disastrous results, but the drought continues.

It is our belief that additional counties in the State, after the investigation has been completed, should be declared disaster areas because of the continuation of the severe drought. I will notify you as to any further counties as rapidly as I receive the information. Your prompt and favorable action upon this request will be greatly appreciated. Kindest regards.

William B. Umstead,
Governor of North Carolina.

(TELEGRAM)

Governor's Office.
September 8, 1953

The Honorable Dwight D. Eisenhower,
President of the United States,
The White House,
Washington, D. C.

The State Agricultural Mobilization Committee has after further study reported to me that the counties of Chatham, Halifax, Hoke, Iredell, Lee, Mecklenburg, Moore, Randolph and Surry, in North Carolina, come within the disaster conditions resulting from the drought, which would entitle them to be declared by you as disaster areas under Public Law 875. These counties are in addition to the ones about which I wired you on August 31.

I urge you immediately to declare them disaster areas in order that they may take advantage of provisions of Public Law 115. The drought in these areas has been severe and has produced disastrous results.

Your prompt and favorable action upon this request will be greatly appreciated.

William B. Umstead, *Governor.*

(TELEGRAM)

Lowry Air Force Base, Colorado.
September 16, 1953

Honorable William B. Umstead,
Governor of North Carolina,
Raleigh, North Carolina.

Existing situations in the drought affected portions of your State have been examined by the Department of Agriculture and have been favorably reported to me by the Federal Civil Defense Adminstration. I have today declared that part of the State of North Carolina which has been adversely affected by the drought as a "major disaster" area eligible for federal assistance under authority of Public Law 875, Eighty-First Congress as amended. Such assistance will be made available by the Secretary of Agriculture under the provisions of the above stated law and in accordance with authority vested in him by Public Law 115, Eighty-Third Congress, in specific areas determined eligible by him.

Dwight D. Eisenhower.

(TELEGRAM)

The White House,
Washington, D. C.
September 22, 1953

Honorable William B. Umstead,
Governor of North Carolina,
Raleigh, North Carolina.

I have your telegram of today and regret exceedingly that the drought situation in North Carolina continues to be so critical. Have referred your request to the Secretary of Agriculture who will give it most careful consideration.

Dwight D. Eisenhower.

(TELEGRAM)

September 22, 1953

Honorable Dwight D. Eisenhower,
President of the United States,
Washington, D. C.

Accept appreciation for approval of sixteen counties for feeds for drought relief. Drought continues critical. Ground too dry to plant winter grazing crops. Hay and roughage production throughout dry area estimated at one-third of normal. Hay production below normal throughout North Carolina and adjoining areas. Much of crop has already been fed and no reserve available. Beef and dairy cattle in this State get 70 to 90 per cent of total nutrients from roughages. Need for hay is critical for both beef and dairy animals. Agricultural adjustments for more efficient resource use have increased improved pasture acreage 500 per cent in last ten years. July, August, and September to date have been by far driest on record in many counties. Long-time program and dispersal of foundation herds are being seriously threatened. Every effort is being made to alleviate problem locally but substantial amount of additional roughage is needed. Urgently request that hay be made available through emergency measures.

William B. Umstead,
Governor of North Carolina.

(TELEGRAM)

September 23, 1953

The Honorable Dwight D. Eisenhower,
President of the United States,
White House,
Washington, D. C.

On August 31 and September 8 I wired you that the State Agricultural Mobilization Committee had reported to me that twenty-four counties in North Carolina should be declared disaster areas. Of the twenty-four counties you have declared sixteen to be disaster areas. Your declaration did not include the counties of Davie, Iredell, Mecklenburg, Randolph, Chatham, Moore, Hoke, Harnett. I urge you to reconsider these counties because it is my information that each of these counties should be declared disaster areas. The drought in our State continues to be severe and your immediate attention will be deeply appreciated. With regards.

William B. Umstead,
Governor of North Carolina.

September 29, 1953

Mr. D. LeRoy West, *Deputy Clerk,*
Register of Deeds Office,
Clinton, North Carolina.

Dear Mr. West:

Thank you very much for your kind letter of September 25. I am very much interested in "Employ the Physically Handicapped Week" and I am, also, interested in the work of the commission which I have recently appointed. I hope very much that the commission will be able to assist the handicapped throughout the State.

I deeply appreciate your letter and, also, the newspaper article which you sent me, and I extend to you my best wishes.

With kindest regards, I am

Sincerely yours,
William B. Umstead, *Governor.*

(TELEGRAM)

October 1, 1953

Mr. E. J. James, *President,*
Southeastern Association of State Highway Officials,
George Vanderbilt Hotel,
Asheville, North Carolina.

I extend my greetings and best wishes to you and to each member of your organization meeting in convention at Asheville. North Carolina is honored and pleased to have the Southeastern Association of State Highway Officials conduct its 12th Annual Convention in our State.

We in North Carolina are doing everything possible to meet the growing needs for more and better public roads. Close co-operation between the states in highway matters is essential if we are going to give our people the best primary highways possible with available funds. The sharing of mutual experience and knowledge in dealing with pressing highway problems means a great deal to each state participating in your Association.

I am confident that under your able direction the 12th Annual Convention will prove a great success. I deeply regret that I cannot attend your Convention because of other engagements.

With kindest regards and best wishes.

William B. Umstead,
Governor of North Carolina.

October 2, 1953

Mr. E. F. Windsor,
3811 Cameron Avenue,
Greensboro, North Carolina.

Dear Mr. Windsor:

I acknowledge the receipt of your recent letter in which you asked certain questions which I shall undertake to answer. I am informed that the $200,000,000 road bonds have been reduced about $17,600,000 and that the interest on said bonds since they were issued has amounted to something over $11,000,000. I am also informed that the 1 per cent gasoline tax levied at the time the road bonds were issued has been more than sufficient to pay the principal and interest on these bonds. The $25,000,000 from the school bonds has been spent in the construction of schools throughout the State, as it was intended. You will have to find out locally the disposition of your special school tax and fees from the courts.

I am advised that the interest on the $25,000,000 school bonds has amounted, up until this time, to about $811,000.

No part of the $50,000,000 proposed on the bond issues to be voted on this Saturday will be used on building at any college in the State. The money will be used for the construction of public school buildings and the $22,000,000 for mental institutions will be used for mental hospitals and training schools for feeble-minded children.

I hope this information answers the inquiries contained in your letter.

With kindest regards, I am

Sincerely yours,
William B. Umstead, *Governor.*

(TELEGRAM)

High Point, North Carolina,
October 7, 1953

Honorable William B. Umstead,
Governor of North Carolina,
Raleigh, North Carolina.

We consider hepatitis epidemic has reached serious stages.[1]

---

[1] There was a hepatitis epidemic in Jamestown, Guilford County, North Carolina, and some of the citizens felt that the local health officers were against mass inoculation. The above telegram was sent to Governor Umstead soliciting his efforts in behalf of controlling the disease by inoculation or other means. There was a disagreement among the health officials as to the necessity for, and the results of, mass inoculation of gamma globulin for this epidemic.

Strongly urge you to release immediately gamma globulin for mass inoculation of Jamestown Township, Guilford Couty.

T. C. Ragsdale, *Mayor,*
Town of Jamestown.

(TELEGRAM)

Raleigh, North Carolina.
October 8, 1953

The Honorable T. C. Ragsdale,
Mayor of Jamestown,
Jamestown, North Carolina.

Have contacted Dr. J. W. R. Norton, State Health Officer, this morning and requested him to call you immediately and do anything he can with reference to the hepatitis epidemic in Jamestown Township.

William B. Umstead, *Governor.*

October 16, 1953

Mr. R. Flake Shaw, *Executive Vice-President,*
North Carolina Farm Bureau Federation, Inc.,
P. O. Box W-4,
Greensboro, North Carolina.

Dear Flake:

Thanks very much for the letter from you and C. Gordon Maddrey with reference to the proclamation I issued regarding "Farm Bureau Week."

I assure you that it is always a pleasure for me to do anything I can for the Farm Bureau in North Carolina. It has rendered, and is rendering, a splendid service not only to the farmers of our State, but to the State as a whole.

With kindest regards and best wishes, I am

Sincerely yours,
William B. Umstead, *Governor.*

October 23, 1953

Honorable Sinclair Weeks, *Secretary,*
U. S. Department of Commerce,
Washington, D. C.

Dear Mr. Weeks:

I understand that the Raleigh-Durham Airport Authority has requested a hearing on the matter of closing the U. S. Weather Bureau at the Raleigh-Durham Airport.

I will appreciate it if you will favorably consider this request for a hearing in order that the facts in connection with this matter may be presented to you.

With kindest regards, I am

Sincerely yours,
William B. Umstead, *Governor.*

October 29, 1953

Mr. Jesse Cole,
1941 Perry Street,
West Durham, North Carolina.

Dear Mr. Cole:

The Cerebral Palsy Hospital in Durham has, in my opinion, rendered an outstanding service since it was established a few years ago. It had then, and has now, my hearty support.

The Durham Cerebral Palsy Foundation was created to aid and assist the hospital in every way and to furnish recreational facilities and extra entertainment for the children being treated in the hospital. It was organized by a large number of outstanding citizens in the City of Durham.

I am pleased that there is to be an Annual Cerebral Palsy Football Classic, the proceeds from which will be used by the Foundation to carry on its splendid work. I hope very much that the Football Classic will be a tremendous success and that it will produce a substantial fund for the use of the Foundation.

With kindest regards and best wishes, I am

Sincerely yours,
William B. Umstead, *Governor.*

January 11, 1954

Mr. H. B. Miller, *Director,*
White House Conference on Highway Safety,[1]
General Service Building,
Washington 25, D. C.

Dear Mr. Miller:

I enclose herewith a list of those I have named as members of North Carolina's delegation to the White House Conference on Highway Safety, and I will appreciate your extending to each of them a formal invitation.

I do not know how many of them will be able to attend the meeting but I hope that most of them can go.

With kindest regards and best wishes, I am

Sincerely yours,
William B. Umstead, *Governor.*

Mrs. Bessie B. Ballentine,
Executive Secretary,
North Carolina Automobile Dealer's association,
Raleigh, N. C.

H. Galt Braxton,
Kinston, N. C.

Mrs. Harry B. Caldwell,
Greensboro, N. C.

Charles F. Carroll, State Superintendent of Public Instruction,
Raleigh, N. C.

R. Lawrence Cooper,
410 East Main Street,
Clayton, N. C.

Champion McDowell Davis,
President, Atlantic Coastline Railroad,
Wilmington, N. C.

Tom W. Davis, Chief of Police,
Raleigh, N. C.

W. E. Debnam, News Commentator,
Radio Station WPTF,
Raleigh, N. C.

H. R. Dowd,
Charlotte, N. C.

Mrs. Lucy Rhodes Duncan, President,*
Business and Professional Women's Clubs,
Smithfield, N. C.

Forrest V. Dunstan, Commander,
Veterans of Foreign Wars,
Elizabeth City, N. C.

R. T. Ellett,
Charlotte, N. C.

C. A. Fink, AF of L,
Salisbury, N. C.

[1] This letter was in response to President Eisenhower's call for a White House Conference on Highway Safety. The purpose of the Conference was to develop nation-wide public support at the community level for proven methods of improving street and highway safety.

* Persons designated by an asterisk did not attend the Conference. See mimeographed report entitled, "Delegates Attending White House Conference on Highway Safety," (Washington, D. C., February 17-19, 1954), William B. Umstead Papers, State Department of Archives and History, Raleigh.

A. H. Graham, Chairman,
State Highway Commission,
Raleigh, N. C.

Thompson Greenwood, Executive Secretary,*
North Carolina Merchants' Association,
Raleigh, N. C.

Cecil B. Haskins,
140 Henry Avenue,
Asheville, N. C.

Captain J. Herbert Hayes,
305 Duncan Street,
Raleigh, N. C.

Robert D. Holleman,
Depositors National Bank,
Durham, N. C.

Carl B. Hyatt, Jr.,
City Hall,
Asheville, N. C.

Walter P. Johnson,
Sparta, N. C.

Paul A. Jones,
Winston-Salem Automobile Club,
Winston-Salem, N. C.

Weimar Jones, President,
North Carolina Press Association,
Chapel Hill, N. C.

Mrs. Grady E. Kirkman, President,
North Carolina Federation of Women's Clubs,
Greensboro, N. C.

J. D. Klutz,
2426 Hutchinson Avenue,
Charlotte, N. C.

Reverend Morton R. Kurtz,
Executive Secretary, North Carolina Council of Churches,
Duke Station,
Durham, N. C.

H. D. Lisk, CIO, *
110 West Sixth Street,
Charlotte, N. C.

Thomas O. McCaffrey, Comd.,*
AMVETS of North Carolina,
Durham, N. C.

F. L. McGuire,
Camp Lejeune, N. C.

William L. McMillan, Commander,
American Legion,
Rocky Mount, N. C.

Gene Ochsenreiter, President, *
North Carolina Junior Chamber of Commerce,
Asheville, N. C.

J. T. Outlaw, Executive Vice-President, North Carolina Motor Carriers' Association,
Raleigh, N. C.

I. Mayon Parker,
Ahoskie, N. C.

William T. Ritter,
Winston-Salem, N. C.

Finley K. Rogers,
Clarkton, N. C.

Sheldon M. Roper,
Roper Building,
Lincolnton, N. C.

Leroy W. Sams,
Winston-Salem, N. C.

Edward Scheidt, Commissioner,
Department of Motor Vehicles,
Raleigh, N. C.

R. Flake Shaw, Executive Director,
North Carolina Farm Bureau,
Greensboro, N. C.

J. B. Smith, Jr.,
Box 13,
Greenville, N. C.

Miss Lane Soutar, Director,
Becon Safety Council, Incorporated,
Hickory, N. C.

S. G. Sparger, Executive Secretary,
North Carolina Petroleum Industries Committee,
Raleigh, N. C.

Major Charles A. Speed, Director,
Safety Division, State Highway Patrol,
Raleigh, N. C.

Mrs. Davetta L. Steed, Executive
Secretary, North Carolina League
of Municipalities,
Raleigh, N. C.

Mrs. Eugenia P. Vann Landingham,
Box 729,
Tarboro, N. C.

James I. Waller,
Winston-Salem, N. C.

Mrs. J. Vivian Whitfield, President,
Farm Bureau Women,
Burgaw, N. C.

Jack S. Younts, Secretary-Treasurer,
North Carolina Association of
Broadcasters, Incorporated,
Southern Pines, N. C.

January 19, 1954

To The Officers And Men Of Headquarters,
552d AAA Gun Battalion:

At the request of your Commanding Officer, Lieutenant Colonel Zebulon L. Strickland, Jr., I am happy to present to your Battalion a North Carolina flag which has flown over our State Capitol here in Raleigh. I understand that this state flag will occupy a position of honor in your consolidated mess hall.

North Carolina is proud of its young men who are now serving in the Armed Forces of the United States. Our people realize the value of loyal service necessary to protect the welfare and safety of our Nation. Our State has always contributed its share of volunteers for service in all branches of the Army, Navy, Marine Corps, and Coast Guard.

As Governor of North Carolina, I send you my congratulations and best wishes during your tour of duty in Germany. As Americans serving overseas, you represent the best and the finest traditions of our country. I am confident that you are fully aware of your responsibilities, and I know that we have every reason to be proud of you. While the threat of World War III has diminished somewhat, we must keep our guard up and maintain basic defense forces against possible aggression. Your part in this over-all defense of Europe is important.

With kindest regards and best wishes, I am

Sincerely yours,
William B. Umstead, *Governor.*

March 2, 1954

Miss Susan Ruby King,
710 Walker Avenue,
Greensboro, North Carolina.

Dear Miss King:

I acknowledge the receipt of your letter of February 13.

For a number of years, I know that the Lions Club in North Carolina have been very much interested in assisting the blind and, as I understand it, this is one of the main projects of the Lions Clubs International. I know that they have done much good in this State. I repeat, as I wrote you on February 12, that I do not know how many of the members of the Blind Commission are members of Lions Clubs. If you desire this information, I suggest that you write to each member of the board and ask him. I assume that you have a list of the board, and if you do not, I shall be glad to furnish it to you. I could not very well write to all of the boards in the State to find out if they belong to some organization upon being requested to do so by some individual in the State, and if I do it in one case, I would be setting a precedent which would apply to all other cases of a similar kind.

I assure you of my interest in seeing that all of our citizens receive justice and fair play insofar as I have the authority. I have been interested for years in the program for the blind in this State and still am.

I appreciate the last paragraph of your letter and I am glad to say that I am improving and am slowly regaining my strength.

With kindest regards and best wishes, I am

Sincerely yours,
William B. Umstead, *Governor.*

March 3, 1954

Mr. George P. Geoghegan, Jr., *Chairman,*
North Carolina Committee for the American-Korean Foundation,[1]
Raleigh, North Carolina.

Dear George:

I acknowledge with thanks your kind letter of March 2 with reference to the expiration of the license of the North Carolina Committee for the American-Korean Foundation on May 1, 1954.

I agree with you that perhaps there is no further necessity to continue this Committee and any future contributions can be sent direct to the American-Korean Foundation in New York. I think it would be proper for you to advise Dr. Winston that your Committee has been discontinued, and if there is any need for any further statement from me, I shall be glad to comply.

I wish once again to thank you and the members of your Committee for the splendid work which you did and for the very substantial contributions which you raised and sent to the Korean Foundation. I will appreciate it if you will express my thanks to each member of your Committee.

With kindest regards and best wishes, I am

Sincerely yours,
William B. Umstead, *Governor.*

The White House,
Washington, D. C.
May 19, 1954

The Honorable William B. Umstead,
Governor of North Carolina,
Raleigh, North Carolina.

Dear Governor Umstead:

I want once again to thank you for the fine reception accorded me yesterday by you personally and by the people of North

[1] The American-Korean Foundation was conducting a nation-wide campaign "to help the Korean people to help themselves." The campaign was conducted by mail solicitation on a membership basis to support activities in such fields as health and social welfare, education and cultural relationships.

Carolina. I enjoyed every minute of my stay with you, and I am most appreciative of the many courtesies you extended to me.

With my hope that you did not find the day too tiring, and with warm regard,

Sincerely,
Dwight D. Eisenhower, *President.*

May 26, 1954

The Honorable Dwight D. Eisenhower,
The White House,
Washington, D. C.

Dear Mr. President:

I wish to thank you very much for your kind and thoughtful letter of May 19.

It was a pleasure for me to see you in Charlotte. We were delighted to have you visit our State and I think the people assembled there greatly manifested their friendly spirit and cordial welcome.

With kindest regards and best wishes, I am

Sincerely yours,
William B. Umstead, *Governor.*

June 1, 1954

The Ogden Junior Chamber of Commerce,
Ogden,
Utah.

Gentlemen:

Thank you for this opportunity to send my greetings and best wishes to the Ogden Junior Chamber of Commerce and the National Junior Chamber of Commerce Convention through the facilities of the famous Pony Express. North Carolina is proud of the young men who constitute the membership of the Junior Chamber of Commerce in this State, and I understand that the

North Carolina Jaycees will be well represented at the National Convention at Colorado Springs.

As the Governor of what was one of the original thirteen colonies, I extend my best wishes to the State of Colorado. I also wish the Ogden Jaycees every success with their attempt to recreate the famous Pony Express ride of 1860-1861. I am pleased to know that this letter will be among the mail to be carried on this famous ride.

With kindest regards and best wishes, I am

Sincerely yours,
William B. Umstead, *Governor.*

June 24, 1954

Mr. W. E. Pace, *Secretary,*
Colonial Bath, Incorporated,
Bath, North Carolina.

Dear Mr. Pace:

I acknowledge with thanks the receipt of your kind letter of June 14 asking me to serve as an Honorary Trustee of your Corporation. This I shall be glad to do.

I also wish to express my deep interest in the restoration of the Town of Bath. I think it will mean much to our State, and I am grateful to you and your associates for what you are doing about the matter.

With kindest regards, I am

Sincerely yours,
William B. Umstead, *Governor.*

July 9, 1954

To The Young Democrats Of North Carolina:

It is always a pleasure to send my greetings and best wishes to the Young Democrats of North Carolina. I am grateful for what you have done in the past for the Democratic Party in our State, and I am confident that you will continue to give our Party your active and loyal support in the months ahead.

I, of course, believe that we will win an overwhelming victory on November 2, but we must campaign vigorously throughout the State to make this prediction a reality. I urge the Young Democrats to contact the young men and women in our State who have become twenty-one years of age since the last election, get them registered, and get them to vote the straight Democratic ticket. We need and must have vigorous young people who believe in the great principles of the Democratic Party and who are willing to work for these principles.

The Democratic Party in North Carolina has provided our State with efficient, effective and progressive government in the past half century. I urge all Young Democrats to reaffirm their faith and belief in the Democratic Party. I am sure that you will make a powerful contribution to the success of our Party in the November election and in the years ahead.

With kindest regards and best wishes, I am

Sincerely yours,
William B. Umstead, *Governor.*

July 28, 1954

To The Members Of The Elizabeth City High School Band:

I have just been informed that you will make an appearance at the Veterans of Foreign Wars National Encampment at Philadelphia the first week of August. This is indeed a tribute to each of you, your director and many sponsors and friends.

In view of the outstanding record and reputation of your band, I take pleasure in appointing your organization as Official Ambassador of North Carolina representing our State at this great national meeting of the Veterans of Foreign Wars. I am confident that you will represent our State in a splendid manner.

With kindest regards and best wishes, I am

Sincerely yours,
William B. Umstead, *Governor.*

July 30, 1954

The Honorable George A. Smock, II,
Mayor of Asbury Park,
Asbury Park, New Jersey.

Dear Mayor Smock:

I am glad to learn that the official flag of the State of North Carolina will again participate in the mile-long patriotic pageant to be held in Asbury Park on July 31 as part of the Seventh Annual "Salute to the States."

I understand that you have selected Pvt. Robert Moose of Dallas, North Carolina, who is now serving with the United States Army at Fort Monmouth, New Jersey, to raise the state flag as part of this ceremony.

North Carolina is proud to take its place with the other states of the Nation during this outstanding event. Our State and its people have always rendered the highest patriotic service to our Nation.

I wish for you, the citizens of Asbury Park, Fort Monmouth and the United States Signal Corps every success in this Seventh Annual pageant.

With kindest regards and best wishes, I am

Sincerely yours,
William B. Umstead, *Governor.*

July 30, 1954

Dr. Franklin B. Wilkins,
337 North Greenleaf Avenue,
Whittier, California.

Dear Dr. Wilkins:

Thank you for informing me that the annual picnic of North Carolinians in the Los Angeles area was held on Sunday, July 18. I am pleased to know that so many citizens of "The Old North State" maintain their interest in North Carolina by an annual picnic day each year.

As Governor of North Carolina, I would like to extend to each member of the North Carolina State Society my kindest regards and best wishes. Our State is proud of all its citizens, including those who make their lives and careers in other states.

North Carolina continues to grow at a rapid pace and is doing its very best to meet the many challenges of today. It is my hope that you will maintain a warm interest in North Carolina and will be able to visit the State as often as you can.

With kindest regards and best wishes, I am

Sincerely yours,
William B. Umstead, *Governor.*

(TELEGRAM)

August 3, 1954

Mr. William Campbell,
Post Regional Chairman,
Care of Boy Scouts of America,
Raleigh, North Carolina.

Let me extend my warmest regards and appreciation to you and your entire organization throughout North Carolina as you plan to raise funds to carry on the Boy Scout program during 1955. This worthy organization should have the support of every person in the State who loves America and wants to keep it strong.

William B. Umstead, *Governor.*

August 4, 1954

Mr. Chester A. Brown,
Jewish American Times Outlook,
Southeastern Building,
Greensboro, North Carolina.

Dear Mr. Brown:

Thank you for this opportunity for me to send you my greetings and very best wishes to Jewish people everywhere on the occasion of the Jewish New Year. I wish for you during the coming year good health, happiness, and prosperity.

We are well aware of the many contributions made to the life of North Carolina and to the Nation by the members of the Jewish race. Your skill, talents, and industry are well recognized in the business world, professional fields, the arts and elsewhere.

With kindest regards and best wishes, I am

Sincerely yours,
William B. Umstead, *Governor.*

August 5, 1954

The Honorable Herbert Hoover,
Care of The Governors' Conference,
1313 East Sixtieth Street,
Chicago 37, Illinois.

Dear Mr. Hoover:

I would like to take this opportunity to extend to you my very best wishes upon the occasion of your eightieth birthday on August 10. As the oldest living ex-President of the United States, you have reached a position of esteem and affection in the hearts of millions of Americans.

We in North Carolina join with Americans everywhere in wishing you good health and happiness on your eightieth birthday.

With kindest regards and best wishes, I am

Sincerely yours,
William B. Umstead, *Governor.*

August 25, 1954

The Honorable Dwight D. Eisenhower,
President of the United States,
The White House,
Washington, D. C.

Dear Mr. President:

The North Carolina USDA Drought Committee has made an exhaustive survey of conditions resulting from drought in several sections of North Carolina and has reported to me that the counties of Burke, Caswell, Catawba, Cleveland, Gaston, Hoke, Lincoln, Polk, and Rutherford come within the disaster conditions which would entitle them to be declared by you as Drought Disaster Areas under Public Law 875.

It is the opinion of the Committee that additional counties in the State, after the investigation has been completed, should also be declared Drought Disaster Areas.

I am enclosing herewith a copy of a memorandum from the Secretary of the North Carolina USDA Drought Committee containing factual information which reveals the true condition in the counties named, and I urge you to declare immediately these counties as disaster areas in order that they may take advantage of Public Law 115. According to this Committee report, the serious lack of rainfall in the last few months has caused severe deterioration of hay and row crops as well as pastures. Drought conditions started approximately four years ago with dry weather being experienced during the fall sowing of grain crops and has continued each year thereafter. The supply of feed and hay crops has been decreasing each year. This survey also reveals that conditions are so severe in these counties that major liquidation of basic foundation herds of cattle and sheep will be made unless immediate assistance is received.

With kindest regards and best wishes, I am

Sincerely yours,
William B. Umstead, *Governor.*

August 27, 1954

The Honorable William B. Umstead,
Governor of North Carolina,
Raleigh, North Carolina.

Your request of August twenty-fifth for a "Disaster Area" declaration by the President under Public Law 875 has been noted sympathetically. In the absence of the President, the matter is being referred at once to the Administrator of the Federal Civil Defense Administration who is authorized to make the necessary investigation. The Administrator is requesting further information from the Department of Agriculture. His report will be expedited as much as possible and just as soon as it is received the President will take whatever action is appropriate under Public Law 875.

Sherman Adams, *Assistant to the President.*
September 2, 1954

Honorable Dwight D. Eisenhower,
President of the United States,
White House,
Washington, D. C.

Dear Mr. President:

On August 25 I wrote you concerning drought conditions in several sections of North Carolina and requested that nine counties be declared as drought disaster areas under Public Law 875. The North Carolina USDA Drought Committee has now furnished me with additional information concerning drought conditions in four other counties: Alexander, Anson, Caldwell, and Iredell. The Committee has found that conditions existing in these counties should entitle them also to be declared as drought disaster areas.

I am enclosing herewith copy of a memorandum from the Secretary of the North Carolina USDA Drought Committee containing factual information about the condition of pastures and the supply of hay, corn and feed on hand. In view of the continued dry weather in these drought sections of our State, I urge you to declare these four counties, as well as the nine counties requested earlier, drought disaster areas in order that they may take advantage of Public Law 115.

It is the opinion of the North Carolina USDA Drought Committee that additional counties in the State, after an investigation has been completed, should be declared drought disaster areas because of the serious lack of rainfall.

With kindest regards, I am

Sincerely yours,
William B. Umstead, *Governor.*

September 16, 1954

The Honorable Dwight D. Eisenhower,
President of the United States,
The White House,
Washington, D. C.

Dear Mr. President:

On August 25, upon the recommendation of the North Carolina USDA Drought Committee, I requested that the counties of Burke, Caswell, Catawba, Cleveland, Gaston, Hoke, Lincoln, Polk, and Rutherford be declared Drought Disaster Areas.

On September 2, upon the recommendation of the North Carolina USDA Drought Committee, I recommended that the counties of Alexander, Anson, Caldwell, and Iredell be declared by you as drought disaster areas.

On September 1, I received acknowledgment of my letter of August 25; and on September 11, I received an acknowledgment of my letter of September 2. Since the receipt of these letters, I have read in the papers that my request had been denied upon the recommendation of the United States Department of Agriculture. I have received no notice of such denial either from you or from the Department of Agriculture.

I do not know what type of investigation has been conducted by the United States Department of Agriculture with reference to the drought situation in the above-mentioned counties. I do know that the Committee in North Carolina made a careful and thorough investigation, and I respectfully ask that my previous request be further considered and more carefully investigated. In addition to the counties above named, there are other sections in the State such as Alleghany County where the drought situation is exceedingly serious.

I would greatly appreciate it if you will let me hear further about this matter at the earliest convenience, because it is of tremendous importance to the people of our State.

With kindest regards and best wishes, I am

Sincerely yours,
William B. Umstead, *Governor.*

(TELEGRAM)

Governor's Office.
September 24, 1954

Mr. Otis Banks, *Executive Secretary,*
North Carolina Highway Employees' Association,
Hotel Robert E. Lee,
Winston-Salem, North Carolina.

I extend to you and the North Carolina State Highway employees my warmest greetings and best wishes upon the occasion of your Ninth Annual Convention which is now being held in Winston-Salem. I am sorry it will not be possible for me to attend, but I do want to wish for you a successful and profitable Convention. I am proud of our State Highway employees and the splendid work which they are doing.

With kindest regards, I am

William B. Umstead, *Governor.*

October 1, 1954

To The People Of North Carolina:

December 3, 1954 will be observed throughout North Carolina as "Sir Walter Raleigh Day." This is in keeping with legislation enacted by the General Assemblies of 1947 and 1953 which authorized this celebration and empowered the State Superintendent of Public Instruction "to permit voluntary donations to be made by the school children of the State for the erection of a memorial in the City of Raleigh in honor of Sir Walter Raleigh."

As we make plans for the observance of "Sir Walter Raleigh Day," it is appropriate that we recall the long and glorious history of our State and resolve that our future shall always reflect credit upon our noble heritage. It is with a spirit of reverence, devotion and dedication that we commemorate the day set aside to honor the 400th anniversary of the man whose illustrious name is borne by our Capital City.

This observance should quicken our interest in the history, growth and progress of North Carolina. I hope that from this celebration our people will receive renewed inspiration to make North Carolina an even greater state—one worthy of the vision of Sir Walter Raleigh.

With kindest regards and best wishes, I am

Sincerely yours,
William B. Umstead, *Governor.*

October 14, 1954

Mr. Horace Johnson, *Chairman,*
Second Annual Cerebral Palsy Football Classic,
Durham, North Carolina.

Dear Mr. Johnson:

I am pleased to give my hearty support to the Second Annual Cerebral Palsy Football Classic, which will be played on Thanksgiving Day for the benefit of the Durham Cerebral Palsy Foundation. The efforts in behalf of this Football Classic and the Foundation deserve commendation.

I am familiar with the splendid work of the Durham Cerebral Palsy Foundation and its worthwhile program to aid and assist the Cerebral Palsy Hospital in Durham in every way possible. It is my hope that the Second Annual Football Classic will be a tremendous success and that it will produce a substantial fund for the use of the Foundation.

With kindest regards and best wishes, I am

Sincerely yours,
William B. Umstead, *Governor.*

(TELEGRAM)

October 15, 1954

The Honorable Dwight D. Eisenhower,
President of the United States,
The White House,
Washington, D. C.

I should like to add my endorsement to those you have already received in behalf of the appointment of Judge John J. Parker of Charlotte, North Carolina, as a member of the Supreme Court of the United States.

I have known Judge Parker for more than thirty years. He was a brilliant student at the University of North Carolina, and for many years has been the senior judge on the Circuit Court of Appeals of the Fourth Judicial Court. His ability, fairness and judicial temperament are widely known. I consider him one of the ablest jurists in this country. I urge you to consider carefully his long record of distinguished service and I hope very much that you will see fit to elevate him to the Supreme Court.

With kindest regards.

William B. Umstead,
Governor of North Carolina.

The White House,
Washington, D. C.
October 22, 1954

The Honorable William B. Umstead,
Governor of North Carolina,
Raleigh, North Carolina.

In reply to your telegram of October 20 and in further connection with my recent designation of a major disaster area in North Carolina because of Hurricane Hazel, I have today approved the formal recommendation for allocation of funds submitted by the Administrator of Federal Civil Defense and based upon a survey of the disaster damage. Federal Civil Defense Administration representatives will be in touch with you regarding funds available and necessary procedures to effect such assistance. I trust that this action will be of effective assistance in alleviating suffering and hardship.

Dwight D. Eisenhower.

Dear Friend:

It is a pleasure to greet you through the courtesy of the Welcome Wagon service.[1]

North Carolina is proud of its reputation as a friendly state, and we are glad that you have selected it as your new home. I trust that you are enjoying your community life and are finding happiness in your new surroundings.

North Carolina is a state of great diversification—in scenery, in agriculture, in industry, and in recreation. I hope you will be able to visit all parts of our State and find out more about it and its people. North Carolina is a good place to live, a good place to work, a good place to play, a good place to worship, and a good place to send your children to school.

We are constantly striving to make our State more prosperous and a better place in which to live. I know that you will be glad to help us.

As Governor of North Carolina I am happy to welcome you to this State, and wish for you and your family good health, happiness, and prosperity in the months and years to come.

With kindest regards and best wishes, I am

Sincerely yours,
William B. Umstead, *Governor*.

---

[1] The Welcome Wagon is a civic service extending a welcome to newcomers in various North Carolina communities. It wished to include among other greetings a letter from the Governor. This procedure was soon abandoned, however, because of the time required and the cost of labor and materials.

APPOINTMENTS

Name of Appointee	Address	Date Appointed	Date of Expiration
STATE BOARD OF CERTIFIED PUBLIC ACCOUNTANT EXAMINERS [1]			
Martin L. Black, Jr. [2]	Durham	6-10-53	5-1-56
Ernest W. Smith [3]	Lenoir	6-10-53	5-1-56
ADVISORY BUDGET COMMISSION (ALSO BOARD OF AWARDS) [4]			
Alonzo C. Edwards †	Hookerton	6-5-53	At pleasure of Governor
Leroy Martin [5]	Raleigh	6-5-53	At pleasure of Governor
STATE BOARD OF AGRICULTURE [6]			
Hoyle C. Griffin †	Monroe	5-13-53	5-4-59
George Kittrell [7]	Corapeake	5-13-53	5-4-59
Charles F. Phillips †	Thomasville	5-13-53	5-4-59

† Persons who served on the several boards during the previous administration and who were reappointed by Governor Umstead have a *dagger* by their names.

* Persons reappointed on the several boards during Governor Umstead's administration have an *asterisk* by their names.

[1] The Board consists of four members appointed by the Governor for a term of three years and until their successors are appointed. *The General Statutes of North Carolina,* Sec. 93-12. Hereafter the *General Statutes of North Carolina* will be cited as *G. S.*

[2] Succeeded G. C. Lundin.

[3] Succeeded Allen E. Strand.

[4] The Board is composed of two members appointed by the Governor to serve at his pleasure and the Chairmen of the Appropriation and Finance Committee of the House and Senate. The Governor is ex officio director. *G. S.,* Sec. 143-4.

[5] Succeeded Harry B. Caldwell.

[6] The Board is composed of the Commissioner of Agriculture (L. Y. Ballentine), who is ex officio chairman, and ten members serving six-year terms, appointed by the Governor with the confirmation of the Senate. *G. S.,* Sec. 106-2.

[7] Succeeded R. V. Knight.

Name of Appointee	Address	Date Appointed	Date of Expiration
COMMISSION TO PROMOTE, CONDUCT AND PARTICIPATE IN THE CELEBRATION OF THE FIFTIETH ANNIVERSARY OF POWERED FLIGHT [8]			
Herbert Bonner	Washington	6-9-53	3-31-55
Aycock Brown	Manteo	6-9-53	3-31-55
Dr. Christopher Crittenden	Raleigh	6-9-53	3-31-55
Tom Davis	Winston-Salem	6-9-53	3-31-55
Carl Goerch, *Chairman* [9]	Raleigh	6-9-53	3-31-55
Hugh M. Morton	Wilmington	6-9-53	3-31-55
Frank Thompson	Raleigh	6-9-53	3-31-55
Henry Vann	Clinton	6-9-53	3-31-55
Colonel George D. Washburn	Shelby	6-9-53	3-31-55
George P. Geoghegan, Jr. [10]	Raleigh	5-19-54	3-31-55
STATE BOARD OF ALCOHOLIC CONTROL [11]			
Frank T. Erwin, *Chairman* [12]	Durham	1-30-53	4-23-55
Thomas W. Allen, Sr., *Chairman* [13]	Creedmoor	8-3-53	4-23-55
Samuel B. Etheridge †	Washington	7-8-54	4-23-56
Frank T. Erwin [14]	Durham	8-3-54	4-23-56
Chief of the Malt Beverage Division [15]			
Leonard Kyle Mathews	Lillington	9-1-54	9-30-55

Appalachian State Teachers' College[16]

Boone

B. C. Brock †	Mocksville	5-8-53	5-1-57
Mrs. Harry B. Caldwell †	Greensboro	5-8-53	5-1-57
William J. Conrad, Jr. †	Winston-Salem	5-8-53	5-1-57
Fred N. Colvard †	Jefferson	5-8-53	5-1-57
J. R. Hix[17]	North Wilkesboro	5-8-53	5-1-57
Sam Jones †	Statesville	5-8-53	5-1-57
W. W. Mast †	Boone	5-8-53	5-1-57
Mrs. Eunice Moose[18]	Taylorsville	5-8-53	5-1-57
L. A. Dysart[19]	Lenoir	5-8-53	5-1-57

[8] The Commission is composed of a chairman and nine members appointed by the Governor. It co-ordinated North Carolina's efforts in the observance of the Fiftieth Anniversary of Powered Flight. This Commission worked with a national organization headed by General James Doolittle. The Commission ceased to exist after March 31, 1955. *State of North Carolina: 1953 Session Laws and Resolutions,* Ch. 351. Hereafter the *Session Laws and Resolutions* of the several years will be cited as *S. L.* and followed by the year, as *S. L., 1953.*

[9] Lindsay C. Warren of Washington, D. C., Comptroller of the United States, was named honorary chairman.

[10] Succeeded Frank Thompson, deceased.

[11] The Board consists of a chairman and two associate members, all appointed by the Governor for three-year terms. *G. S.,* Sec. 18-37, 38.

[12] Appointed acting chairman, succeeding Robert W. Winston, resigned.

[13] Succeeded Frank T. Erwin.

[14] Succeeded Sumpter C. Brawley.

[15] This appointment was made to insure the strict enforcement of the regulations of the Board. The appointee will be in charge of the administration of the division and shall be paid whatever the Board with the approval of the Governor shall fix. This official's term was not specified by law. *S. L., 1949,* Ch. 974, Sec. 11.

[16] The Board consists of nine members appointed by the Governor, with the consent of the Senate, for four-year terms. *G. S.,* Sec. 116-66, 67.

[17] Succeeded C. C. Faw, Sr.

[18] Succeeded Mrs. J. M. Lackey.

[19] Succeeded D. W. M. Roberts.

Name of Appointee	*Address*	*Date Appointed*	*Date of Expiration*
STATE BOARD OF ARCHITECTURAL EXAMINATION AND REGISTRATION [20]			
W. A. Bowles [21]	Charlotte	5-7-53	4-8-57
Henry Irven Gaines †	Asheville	5-7-53	4-8-58
John E. Ramsay [22]	Salisbury	6-18-54	4-8-59
STATE DEPARTMENT OF ARCHIVES AND HISTORY EXECUTIVE BOARD [23]			
Miss Gertrude S. Carraway †	New Bern	5-8-53	3-31-59
McDaniel Lewis †	Greensboro	5-8-53	3-31-59
Dr. W. T. Laprade †	Durham	5-8-53	3-31-59
Josh L. Horne [24]	Rocky Mount	8-11-54	3-31-55
STATE ART COMMISSION [25]			
Mrs. Katherine P. Arrington †	Warrenton	8-10-53	8-1-55
Edwin M. Gill †	Chapel Hill	8-10-53	8-1-55
Dr. Clarence Poe †	Raleigh	8-10-53	8-1-55
Robert Lee Humber †	Greenville	8-10-53	8-1-55
NORTH CAROLINA ART SOCIETY, INCORPORATED [26]			
Dr. C. Sylvester Green †	Durham	5-8-53	5-1-57
Mrs. Charles A. Cannon [27]	Concord	5-8-53	5-1-57
TOWN OF ATLANTIC BEACH [28]			
A. B. Cooper, *Mayor* † [29]	Morehead City	4-28-53	5-1-57
H. W. Anderson	Wilson	4-28-53	5-1-57

J. C. Lanier	Greenville	4-28-53	5-1-57
L. T. White	Raleigh	4-28-53	5-1-57
W. C. Whitehurst	Bethel	4-28-53	5-1-57

ATLANTIC STATES MARINE FISHERIES COMMISSION[30]

Russell A. Swindell	Swan Quarter	11-18-53	11-18-56

---

[20] The Board is composed of five members appointed by the Governor for five-year terms. *G. S.*, Sec. 83-2, 10.

[21] Succeeded Walter W. Hook.

[22] Succeeded J. Burton Wilder.

[23] The Board consists of seven members appointed by the Governor for six-year terms. *G. S.*, Sec. 121-1.

[24] Succeeded Dr. B. F. Brown, resigned.

[25] The Board is composed of five members appointed by the Governor. The terms are for two years, after the initial appointments, which are for one- and two-year terms. *G. S.*, Sec. 140-5.6.

[26] The Board is composed of sixteen members, four of whom are appointed by the Governor for a term of four years, eight of whom are chosen by the members of the North Carolina State Art Society, Incorporated, and four of whom are ex officio members, as follows: the Governor, the Superintendent of Public Instruction (Charles F. Carroll), the Attorney General (Harry McMullan), and the chairman of the Art Committee of the North Carolina Federation of Woman's Clubs. *G. S.*, Sec. 140-1.

[27] Succeeded Mrs. Charles M. Griffin.

[28] As recommended by the ballots of property owners, the mayor and four aldermen are appointed by the Governor for a term of four years each. Any vacancies are filled by the remaining aldermen and mayor, or aldermen. *Public Local Laws of North Carolina, 1937,* Ch. 433. Hereafter the *Public Local Laws of North Carolina* will be cited as *P. L. L.*

[29] Succeeded Newman Willis, mayor.

[30] Each state-which is represented on this Commission shall appoint three members. Of the members from this State, two serve ex officio, one of whom is designated by the Board of the North Carolina Department of Conservation and Development, from either the director of the Department, the chairman of the Committee on Commercial Fisheries, or the commissioner of Commercial Fisheries, and the other is designated by the Commission on Interstate Co-operation of the State, from a member of the North Carolina Legislature who is a member of the Commission on Interstate Commerce, ex officio. Terms of ex officio members expire at the time they cease to hold office. The third commissioner is a citizen of the State with a knowledge of and an interest in marine fisheries. He is appointed by the Governor with the consent of the Senate, for a three-year term. *G. S.*, Sec. 113-377.1, 377.3; *S. L., 1949,* Ch. 1086, Sec. 3.

Name of Appointee	*Address*	*Date Appointed*	*Date of Expiration*
BANKING DEPARTMENT, STATE BANKING COMMISSION[31]			
A. K. Barrus	Kinston	5-14-53	4-1-57
W. P. Saunders	Southern Pines	5-14-53	4-1-57
Oscar J. Mooneyham †	Forest City	5-14-53	4-1-57
Reuben B. Robertson, Sr.[32]	Canton	5-14-53	4-1-57
John W. Spears[33]	Lillington	5-14-53	4-1-57
Don S. Elias[34]	Asheville	3-17-54	4-1-57
STATE BOARD OF BARBER EXAMINERS[35]			
J. Marvin Cheek †	High Point	7-1-53	7-1-59
STATE COMMISSION FOR THE BLIND[36]			
Dr. Howard E. Jensen †	Durham	6-12-53	5-21-58
Joe W. Hood[37]	Wilmington	6-12-53	5-21-58
NORTH CAROLINA SCHOOL FOR THE BLIND AND DEAF[38] Raleigh			
A. B. Currin †	Dunn	6-2-53	5-1-57
D'Arcy Bradsher[39]	Roxboro	6-2-53	5-1-57
Mrs. Julian B. Hutaff[40]	Fayetteville	6-2-53	5-1-57
Mrs. B. C. Mangum[41]	Henderson	6-2-53	5-1-57
Tom L. Pendergrass †	Durham	6-2-53	5-1-57
James L. Penland	Asheville	6-2-53	5-1-57
Ben R. Roberts †	Durham	6-2-53	5-1-57

Fulton A. Huntley [42]	Wadesboro	6-2-53	5-1-57
J. B. Spilman, Jr. [43]	Greenville	6-2-53	5-1-57
Carroll W. Weathers [44]	Wake Forest	6-2-53	5-1-57
S. Linton Smith †	Raleigh	6-2-53	5-1-57

---

[31] The General Assembly of 1953 added two appointive members to the Commission, bringing the total membership to nine, including two ex officio members, who are: the State Treasurer (Brandon P. Hodges, resigned effective July 20, 1953, and after that date, Edwin M. Gill), who is Chairman, and the Attorney General (Harry McMullan). Terms of members appointed by the Governor are for four years, and the terms of the two new members expire April 1, 1957, with reappointment for four years. Five members of the Commission are to be practical bankers, the remainder are to be selected to represent fairly the industrial, manufacturing, business, and farming interests of the State. Any vacancies are filled by the Governor for unexpired terms. *G. S.*, Sec. 53-92; *S. L., 1949*, Ch. 372; *S. L., 1953*, Ch. 1209.

[32] Succeeded Reade R. Pickler.

[33] Succeeded R. Emmet Kerr.

[34] Succeeded Reuben B. Robertson, Sr., deceased.

[35] The Board consists of three members to be appointed by the Governor. Each member must be an experienced barber. The members of the Board are appointed for six-year terms. *G. S.*, Sec. 86-6.

[36] The Board is composed of eleven members, of whom six are appointed by the Governor to serve terms of five years. The Superintendent of the State School for the Blind and Deaf (E. N. Peeler), the State Supervisor of Vocational Rehabilitation (Charles H. Warren), the Secretary of the State Board of Health (Dr. J. W. R. Norton), the Director of the North Carolina Employment Service (Ernest C. McCracken), and the Commissioner of Public Welfare (Dr. Ellen Winston), are ex officio members. *G. S.*, Sec. 111-1, 2, 3.

[37] Succeeded Thomas S. Payne.

[38] The board of directors is composed of a membership of eleven appointed by the Governor and confirmed by the Senate for four-year terms. *G. S.*, 116-106.

[39] Succeeded T. F. Nance.

[40] Succeeded Mrs. T. C. Ringgold.

[41] Succeeded Mrs. Charles G. Doak.

[42] Succeeded D. T. Redfearn.

[43] Succeeded R. H. McLawhorn, Sr.

[44] Succeeded George D. Richardson.

Name of Appointee	*Address*	*Date Appointed*	*Date of Expiration*
NORTH CAROLINA BOARD OF BOILER RULES[45]			
Wilkes C. Price	Asheville	6-17-53	6-18-58
W. E. Shuping, Jr. †	Charlotte	6-17-53	6-18-58
William W. Lloyd †	Greensboro	8-20-54	6-18-59
ASSISTANT DIRECTOR OF THE BUDGET[46]			
D. S. Coltrane †	Raleigh	6-23-53	6-30-57
JOHN H. KERR RESERVOIR DEVELOPMENT COMMISSION[47]			
J. C. Bolton[48]	Rich Square	8-14-53	7-26-59
A. Leonidas Hux[49]	Roanoke Rapids	8-14-53	7-26-59
BUILDING CODE COUNCIL[50]			
Eccles D. Everhart[51]	High Point	3-13-53	4-19-55
Bernard Crocker, Jr., *Chairman* †	Raleigh	5-8-53	4-19-58
BURIAL ASSOCIATION[52]			
Don Gilliam, Jr.[53]	Tarboro	7-3-53	6-30-57
THE NORTH CAROLINA CAPE HATTERAS SEASHORE COMMISSION[54]			
P. Bruce Bateman[55]	Plymouth	2-24-54	1-12-58
Aycock Brown[56]	Manteo	2-24-54	1-12-58
Miles Clark †	Elizabeth City	2-24-54	1-12-58
S. Bunn Frink[57]	Southport	2-24-54	1-12-58
Don E. Scott †	Graham and Nags Head	2-24-54	1-12-58

[45] The Board is composed of six members, of whom five are appointed by the Governor for terms ranging from one to five years. Successors to these members are appointed for terms of five years each. The sixth member is the Commissioner of Labor (Forrest H. Shuford, and after June 3, 1954, Frank Crane), who serves ex officio and is Chairman of the Board. Of the five appointive members, one is a representative of the owners and users of steam boilers within the State, one a representative of the boiler manufacturers or boiler-makers within the State, one a representative of a boiler inspection and insurance company licensed to do business in North Carolina, one a representative of the operating steam engineers in North Carolina, and one a licensed heating contractor. The membership was amended in 1953, when an additional member was added, to represent heating contractors and length of future terms was increased from four to five years. Any vacancy is filled with a representative of the same class. *G. S.*, Sec. 95-54; *S. L., 1953*. Ch. 569.

[46] The Assistant Director of the Budget is appointed by the Governor for a term of four years. The Director of the Budget, who is the Governor, makes recommendations to the General Assembly as to the changes in organization, management, and general conduct of the various departments. *G. S.*, Sec. 143-2.

[47] The Commission is composed of ten members appointed by the Governor. Three ex officio members, including representatives from the North Carolina Recreation Commission (Henry M. Milgrom), the Wildlife Resources Commission (Ernest Beal), and the Board of Conservation and Development (Charles H. Jenkins), serve as members of this Commission only during their terms of office. Of the other seven members appointed, two serve for two years, two serve for four years, and three serve for six years. Reappointments are made for terms of six years. *G. S.*, Sec. 143-284.

[48] Succeeded L. R. Taylor.

[49] Succeeded Frank C. Williams, Jr., who entered military service.

[50] The Board is composed of five members who are appointed or removed by the Governor. Terms of appointments are for five years. The members are representative of the following fields: general contracting, architecture, structural engineering, plumbing and heating contracting, and a representative of organized labor. Vacancies are filled by appointments of the Governor for the duration of unexpired terms. *G. S.*, Sec. 143-139.

[51] Succeeded Albert L. Haskins, Jr., resigned March 4, 1953.

[52] The Commissioner is appointed by the Governor for a term of four years. His salary is fixed by the Governor. *G. S.*, Sec. 58-224.

[53] Succeeded Thomas Creekmore.

[54] This Commission consists of five members appointed by the Governor for four-year terms, and four ex officio members consisting of the Director of the Department of Conservation and Development (Ben E. Douglas), as Chairman, and three members of the Board of Conservation and Development (Amos Kearns, High Point; Cecil Morris, Atlantic; and Henry Rankin, Fayetteville), to serve at the Governor's pleasure. The Commission files annual reports with the Governor. *Public Laws of North Carolina, 1939*, Ch. 257. Hereafter the *Public Laws of North Carolina* will be cited as *P. L.*

[55] Succeeded Carleton Kelly.

[56] Succeeded Morris Burrus.

[57] Succeeded Woodrow Price.

Name of Appointee	*Address*	*Date Appointed*	*Date of Expiration*
BOARD OF DIRECTORS FOR THE NORTH CAROLINA HOSPITAL FOR CEREBRAL PALSY [58]			
George Hughes †	Pollocksville	7-1-53	7-10-59
Thomas O'Berry, *Chairman* †	Goldsboro	7-1-53	7-10-59
Dr. W. M. Roberts †	Gastonia	7-1-53	7-10-59
STATE BOARD OF CHIROPRATIC EXAMINERS [59]			
Dr. P. M. Starnes [60]	Hickory	6-2-53	5-5-56
Dr. C. H. Peters †	Rocky Mount	6-30-54	5-5-57
NORTH CAROLINA STATE CIVIL AIR PATROL AGENCY [61]			
Roy Rowe	Burgaw	9-2-53	9-1-55
Clyde Shreve	Summerfield	9-2-53	9-1-55
Henry H. Wilson	Monroe	9-2-53	9-1-55
NORTH CAROLINA STATE CIVIL DEFENSE AGENCY [62]			
William Flemming Bailey, *Director* [63]	High Point	1-23-53	At pleasure of Governor
Edward Foster Griffin, *Director* [64]	Louisburg	2-23-54	At pleasure of Governor
MOSES H. CONE MEMORIAL HOSPITAL BOARD [65] Greensboro			
Roger McDuffie [66]	Greensboro	5-7-53	May 1957
L. P. McLendon †	Greensboro	5-7-53	May 1957
General James R. Townsend †	Greensboro	5-7-53	May 1957

CONFEDERATE WOMAN'S HOME [67]

Fayetteville

A. E. Cook †	Fayetteville	5-23-53	5-9-55
Mrs. Robert Bruce Cook †	Durham	5-23-53	5-9-55
Mrs. J. Y. Gatewood †	Yanceyville	5-23-53	5-9-55
Mrs. Robert Grady Johnson [68]	Burgaw	5-23-53	5-9-55
E. Bruce McFayden †	Fayetteville	5-23-53	5-9-55

---

[58] The Board is composed of nine members serving two-, four-, and six-year terms. Reappointments are for six years. The 1945 General Assembly authorized name changed, and the 1953 General Assembly further amended the name to "The North Carolina Cerebral Palsy Hospital." *G. S.*, Sec. 131-127, 128; *S. L., 1945*, Ch. 504; *S. L., 1953*, Ch. 893.

[59] The Board consists of three members appointed by the Governor for three-year terms. Members must be practicing chiropractors of integrity and ability and residents of the State. No more than two members shall be graduates of the same school or college of chiropractic. *G. S.*, Sec. 90-140, 141.

[60] Succeeded Dr. Lee E. Kiser.

[61] This agency is composed of three members appointed by the Governor, and six ex officio members specified by the Legislature: the Adjutant General of the State of North Carolina (John H. Manning), and the deputy Wing Commander, the Executive Officer, the Adjutant, the Communication Officer, and the Co-ordinator of the Civil Defense of the North Carolina Wing of the Civil Air Patrol. The Chairman (Lt. Col. Robert E. Ridenhour, Jr., Commanding Officer of the North Carolina Wing of the Civil Air Patrol), serves ex officio. Members serve a term of two years, and vacancies in the appointive membership are filled by the Governor, who may also remove any member appointed by him. The Agency was created by a law enacted in 1953. *G. S.*, Sec. 167-1; *S. L., 1953*, Ch. 1231.

[62] The membership of this Agency consists of one member appointed by the Governor to serve at his will, and six ex officio members, including: as Chairman, the Governor; as executive vice-chairman, the Commissioner of Motor Vehicles (Edward Scheidt); the Executive Secretary of the State Board of Health (Dr. J. W. R. Norton); the Chancellor of the North Carolina State College (Col. J. W. Harrelson, resigned September 1, 1953, and after that date, Carey H. Bostian); the Director of the State Bureau of Investigation (James W. Powell); and the general counsel for the North Carolina League of Municipalities (George F. Franklin). *G. S.*, Sec. 166-3, 4.

[63] Succeeded E. Z. Jones.

[64] Succeeded William F. Bailey. Mr. Bailey resigned August 31, 1953, after being appointed Director of Prisons.

[65] The Board is composed of fifteen members, three of whom are appointed by the Governor for four-year terms. *P. L., 1913*, Ch. 400.

[66] Succeeded Paul Schenck, Jr.

[67] The Board is composed of seven members appointed by the Governor for two-year terms. The State Treasurer (Brandon P. Hodges and after June 20, 1953 Edwin M. Gill), is treasurer of the Board. *G. S.*, Sec. 112-2.

[68] Succeeded Mrs. A. L. Thompson.

Name of Appointee	*Address*	*Date Appointed*	*Date of Expiration*
Mrs. E. R. McKeithan, *Chairman* †	Fayetteville	5-23-53	5-9-55
Mrs. H. L. Stevens, Jr.[69]	Warsaw	5-23-53	5-9-55
U. S. Senators from North Carolina[70]			
Alton A. Lennon[71]	Wilmington	3-18-53	1-3-55
Samuel J. Ervin, Jr.[72]	Morganton	6-5-54	1-3-57
Board of Conservation and Development[73]			
Ben E. Douglas, *Director*	Charlotte	7-10-53	At pleasure of Governor
Members			
Charles S. Allen †	Durham	7-10-53	7-1-55
Robert M. Hanes	Winston-Salem	7-10-53	7-1-55
Leo Harvey	Kinston	7-10-53	7-1-55
Amos Kearns	High Point	7-10-53	7-1-55
W. J. Damtoft †	Asheville	7-10-53	7-1-57
Scroop W. Enloe, Jr. †	Spruce Pine	7-10-53	7-1-57
Charles H. Jenkins †	Aulander	7-10-53	7-1-57
Miles J. Smith †	Salisbury	7-10-53	7-1-57
W. B. Austin †	Jefferson	7-10-53	7-1-59
H. Carl Buchan, Jr.	North Wilkesboro	7-10-53	7-1-59
Hugh M. Morton †	Linville and Wilmington	7-10-53	7-1-59
Cecil Morris	Atlantic	7-10-53	7-1-59
T. Max Watson	Forest City	7-10-53	7-1-59
Eric W. Rodgers[74]	Scotland Neck	7-23-53	7-1-55

Henry Rankin	Fayetteville	7-24-53	7-1-55
W. Eugene Simmons[75]	Tarboro	7-17-54	7-1-57

SPECIAL PEACE OFFICERS, DIVISION OF PARKS, FOR DEPARTMENT OF CONSERVATION AND DEVELOPMENT[76]

	On duty at		
Milton F. Perry[77]	Fort Macon	3-18-53	At pleasure of Governor
Cedric P. Squires[78]	Crabtree Creek	4-22-53	At pleasure of Governor
Arthur T. Pierce	Fort Macon	5-26-53	At pleasure of Governor
Bruce Price	Cliffs of the Neuse	5-26-53	At pleasure of Governor
Hal F. Haire	White Lake	7-8-53	At pleasure of Governor
J. Knox Harrington *	Lake Waccamaw	7-8-53-54	At pleasure of Governor
Elbert N. Herring	White Lake and Lake Waccamaw	7-8-53	At pleasure of Governor

[69] Succeeded Mrs. C. D. Baucom.

[70] When a vacancy occurs in the office of United States Senator from this State, other than by expiration of a term, the Governor appoints a citizen to fill the vacancy until there is an election. If a vacancy occurs in this State's Representatives to Congress, the Governor issues a writ of election and by proclamation requires the voters to vote for a Representative to Congress to fill the vacancy. *G. S.*, Sec. 163-101, 105.

[71] Succeeded Senator Willis Smith, deceased June 25, 1953, to serve the remainder of his unexpired term.

[72] Succeeded Senator Clyde R. Hoey, deceased May 12, 1954, for the remainder of Senator Hoey's term. Elected to the Senate at the general election on November 2, 1954.

[73] The Board consists of a director and fifteen members appointed by the Governor for two-, four-, and six-year terms; reappointments are for six-year terms. The Director is appointed for a term designated by the Governor, but not to exceed the term of office of the Governor making the appointment. *G. S.*, Sec. 113-4, 5, 9; *S. L. 1953*, Ch. 81.

[74] Resigned to become assistant director of the Department of Conservation and Development.

[75] Succeeded Eric W. Rodgers.

[76] These special officers consist of employees designated by the Director of the Department of Conservation and Development, and commissioned by the Governor to serve at his pleasure. *S. L., 1947*, Ch. 577.

[77] Resigned May 16, 1953.

[78] Crabtree Creek State Park is now The William B. Umstead Memorial State Park.

Name of Appointee	*Address*	*Date Appointed*	*Date of Expiration*
Willard M. Wooten [79]		7-8-53	At pleasure of Governor
Howard R. Sargent	Town Creek Indian Mound	7-9-53	At pleasure of Governor
Daniel W. Jones	Fort Macon	8-21-53	At pleasure of Governor
Dewitt Powell	Jones Lake	5-26-54	At pleasure of Governor
Wayland H. Horton, Jr.	Reedy Creek	5-26-54	At pleasure of Governor
Joseph W. Best	White Lake	5-31-54	At pleasure of Governor
John A. Hemingway	White Lake and Lake Waccamaw	5-31-54	At pleasure of Governor
Paul E. Bannerman	Pettigrew State Park	6-17-54	At pleasure of Governor
William W. Wood, Jr.	Town Creek Indian Mound	6-17-54	At pleasure of Governor
Vance G. Smith	Fort Macon	9-16-54	At pleasure of Governor

STATE LICENSING BOARD FOR GENERAL CONTRACTORS [80]

V. B. Higgins †	Greensboro	5-14-53	12-31-56
N. K. Dickerson, Jr. †	Monroe	5-14-53	12-31-57
Roy L. Goode †	Charlotte	6-29-54	12-31-58

BOARD OF EXAMINERS OF ELECTRICAL CONTRACTORS [81]

W. A. Darden † [82]	Greenville	6-12-53	4-15-55
Elwood C. Peale † [83]	Burlington	6-12-53	4-15-57
R. S. Fouraker † [84]	Raleigh	6-30-54	4-15-57

BOARD OF EXAMINERS FOR LICENSING TILE CONTRACTORS [85]

F. R. Smith [86]	Winston-Salem	6-17-53	4-12-58
O. A. Ritch [87]	Charlotte	7-1-53	4-12-55
David G. Allen †	Raleigh	7-2-54	4-12-59

STATE BOARD OF CORRECTION AND TRAINING [88]

Name	Residence	Appointed	Term Expires
Clyde A. Dillon, *Chairman* †	Raleigh	7-2-53	7-1-59
W. N. Harrell †	Wilson	7-2-53	7-1-59
Dr. W. A. Stanbury †	Asheboro	7-2-53	7-1-59
Paul B. Bissette [89]	Wilson	9-29-53	7-1-59
M. S. Hayworth [90]	Rocky Mount	7-2-54	7-1-59

BOARD OF COSMETIC ART EXAMINERS [91]

Name	Residence	Appointed	Term Expires
Mrs. R. J. Hinshaw †	North Wilkesboro	8-26-53	7-1-56
Mrs. Ann Jenkins †	Edenton	8-26-53	7-1-56
Mrs. Ralph E. Hanna [92]	Dunn	8-26-53	7-1-56

---

[79] On duty as a temporary park ranger.

[80] The Board is composed of five members appointed by the Governor for five-year terms. Vacancies are filled by appointment of the Governor. *G. S.*, Sec. 87-2, 4.

[81] The Board consists of three members appointed by the Governor for three-year terms, and two ex officio members as follows: the State Electrical Engineer (N. E. Cannady), who is also the Chairman, and the secretary of the Association of Electrical Contractors of North Carolina (Mrs. J. H. Anderson). *G. S.*, Sec. 87-39.

[82] Representing municipal electric inspectors.

[83] Representing electrical contractors' business.

[84] Representing the Engineering School of the University of North Carolina.

[85] The Board members consist of five persons appointed by the Governor for five-year terms. *G. S.*, Sec. 87-30, 31.

[86] Succeeded J. K. Davis.

[87] Succeeded J. R. Renfrow, Jr.

[88] The nine Board members are appointed by the Governor for two-, four-, and six-year terms, with subsequent appointments for six-year terms. The Commissioner of Public Welfare (Dr. Ellen Winston), is an ex officio member. If he deems it in the public interest, the Governor may remove any member of the Board. *G. S.*, Sec. 134-90; *S. L., 1947*, Ch. 226.

[89] Succeeded W. N. Harrell, deceased.

[90] Succeeded Dr. W. A. Stanbury, deceased.

[91] The Board consists of three members appointed by the Governor for three-year terms. *G. S.*, Sec. 88-13.

[92] Succeeded Mrs. Iris H. Lawrence.

Name of Appointee	Address	Date Appointed	Date of Expiration
NORTH CAROLINA SCHOOL FOR THE DEAF[93]			
Reverend James R. Fortune †	Durham	5-13-53	4-1-57
W. S. McCord †	Charlotte	5-13-53	4-1-57
Howard Moose †	Newton	5-13-53	4-1-57
R. J. Morris[94]	Marion	5-13-53	4-1-57
O. H. Pons †	Valdese	5-13-53	4-1-57
Dr. Howard E. Rondthaler †	Winston-Salem	5-13-53	4-1-57
Harry Wilson, Sr.[95]	Morganton	5-13-53	4-1-57
STATE BOARD OF DENTAL EXAMINERS[96]			
Dr. A. T. Jennette †	Washington	7-1-53	6-30-56
Dr. E. M. Medlin †	Aberdeen	7-1-53	6-30-56
Dr. William M. Matheson †[97]	Boone	8-11-54	7-31-57
Dr. Cleon W. Sanders †	Benson	8-11-54	7-31-57
NORTH CAROLINA COLLEGE[98] Durham			
Bascom Baynes †	Durham	6-18-53	5-1-57
Dr. J. W. Black †	Rocky Mount	6-18-53	5-1-57
C. A. Dandelake[99]	Tarboro	6-18-53	5-1-57
T. W. Ellis, Jr.[100]	Henderson	6-18-53	5-1-57
R. M. Gantt †	Durham	6-18-53	5-1-57
Dr. J. M. Hubbard †	Durham	6-18-53	5-1-57
Ernest B. Johnson[101]	Winston-Salem	6-18-53	5-1-57

Walter Jones, Jr. †	Rockingham	6-18-53	5-1-57
B. I. Satterfield †	Timberlake	6-18-53	5-1-57
Banks Wilkins [102]	Sanford	6-18-53	5-1-57
Senator Nelson Woodson [103]	Salisbury	6-18-53	5-1-57
Frank Banzet [104]	Warrenton	8-2-54	5-1-57

EAST CAROLINA COLLEGE [105]
Greenville

Edwin E. Rawls, Sr. [106]	Greenville	5-14-53	6-30-57
Frederick Willetts, Sr. [107]	Wilmington	5-14-53	6-30-55
I. H. O'Hanlon [108]	Fayetteville	8-5-53	6-30-59

[93] The Board is composed of seven members appointed by the Governor and confirmed by the Senate for four-year terms. *G. S.*, Sec. 116-121.

[94] Succeeded W. P. Elliott.

[95] Succeeded Mrs. Frank P. Tate.

[96] The Board consists of six members of the North Carolina Dental Society, elected by the Society at its annual meeting and commissioned by the Governor for three-year terms of office. *G. S.*, Sec. 90-22.

[97] The Dental Society requested expiration dates to be on July 31 hereafter.

[98] The Board is composed of twelve members appointed by the Governor and confirmed by the Senate for four-year terms. There is one ex officio member, the Superintendent of Public Instruction (Charles F. Carroll). The name was changed in 1947 to its present form. *G. S.*, Sec. 116-99; *S. L., 1947*, Ch. 189.

[99] Succeeded Fred A. Smith.

[100] Succeeded Dr. Robert M. Hendrick.

[101] Succeeded A. H. Bryant.

[102] Succeeded Malcolm McLeod.

[103] Succeeded Spencer Murphy.

[104] Succeeded Mrs. Lillie Braxton Dean.

[105] The Board is composed of twelve members appointed by the Governor and confirmed by the Senate for terms of six years. The Superintendent of Public Instruction (Charles F. Carroll), is ex officio chairman. *G. S.*, Sec. 116-59.

[106] Succeeded Miles L. Clark.

[107] Succeeded Charles F. Carroll.

[108] Succeeded John P. Stedman, resigned.

Name of Appointee	*Address*	*Date Appointed*	*Date of Expiration*
Dr. Lewis H. Swindell †	Washington	8-5-53	6-30-59
Arthur L. Tyler †	Rocky Mount	8-5-53	6-30-59
Merrill Evans [109]	Ahoskie	8-5-53	6-30-59
EAST CAROLINA INDIAN TRAINING SCHOOL [110] HERRING'S TOWNSHIP, SAMPSON COUNTY			
Levander Emanuel †	Godwin	3-20-53	10-28-57
Percy Simmons †	Clinton	3-20-53	10-28-57
J. T. Denning [111]	Clinton	7-20-53	10-28-53
STATE BOARD OF EDUCATION [112]			
Dr. B. B. Dougherty † [113]	Boone	4-1-53	4-1-61
Archibald McLean Graham † [114]	Clinton	4-1-53	4-1-61
Gerald Cowan [115]	Asheville	4-1-53	4-1-61
A. S. Brower † [116]	Durham	4-24-53	4-1-59
Oscar L. Richardson [117]	Monroe	4-24-53	4-1-59
COMMISSION ON HIGHER EDUCATION [118]			
Dr. F. L. Atkins	Winston-Salem	10-1-53	To report to next General Assembly
Dudley Bagley	Moyock	10-1-53	To report to next General Assembly
Victor S. Bryant	Durham	10-1-53	To report to next General Assembly
E. Y. Floyd	Raleigh	10-1-53	To report to next General Assembly
L. C. Gifford	Hickory	10-1-53	To report to next General Assembly
Mrs. Grace T. Rodenbough	Walnut Cove	10-1-53	To report to next General Assembly
Fred S. Royster	Henderson	10-1-53	To report to next General Assembly

STATE BOARD OF ELECTIONS [119]

J. Hampton Price, *Chairman, Democrat*	Leaksville	5-14-53	5-1-57
John G. Dawson, *Democrat*	Kinston	5-14-53	5-1-57
H. A. Mattox, *Democrat*	Murphy	5-14-53	5-1-57
J. E. Holhouser, *Republican*	Boone	5-14-53	5-1-57
J. E. Hill, *Republican*	Denton	5-14-53	5-1-57

[109] Succeeded Uran Cox.

[110] The Board is composed of six trustees appointed by the Governor for six-year terms. The Superintendent of Public Instruction (Charles F. Carroll), is an ex officio member and Chairman of the Board. *G. S.*, Sec. 116-89.

[111] Succeeded D. V. Carter, resigned.

[112] This Board succeeds that of 1943 and consists of thirteen members, one represents each of the eight educational districts, two serve at large, and three members serve ex officio, who are: the Lieutenant Governor (Luther H. Hodges), the State Treasurer (Brandon P. Hodges and after July 20, 1953 Edwin M. Gill), and the Superintendent of Public Instruction (Charles F. Carroll). Appointments are made by the Governor and confirmed by the General Assembly in Joint Session. The term of office upon appointments and reappointment is for eight years. The Constitution of North Carolina, Article 9, Section 8; *P. L., 1941,* Ch. 151; *S. L., 1943,* Ch.468.

[113] Actually appointed April 24, 1953.

[114] Actually appointed April 24, 1953.

[115] Succeeds D. Hiden Ramsey, declined.

[116] A. S. Brower's first term expired April 1, 1951. Governor Scott appointed Dr. Roma S. Cheek April 12, 1951, to succeed Brower, but the General Assembly failed to confirm the appointment; therefore, he continued to serve, and on April 24, 1953, Governor Umstead appointed him for a six-year term.

[117] Richardson succeeded J. H. Lineberger, whose term expired April 1, 1951. Governor Scott, on April 12, 1952, appointed Miss Margery Alexander to succeed Lineberger. The General Assembly failed to confirm Miss Alexander's appointment and Lineberger continued to serve until replaced by Oscar L. Richardson.

[118] This Commission is composed of seven members appointed by the Governor. A full report of the Commission's activities and recommendations is to be given the 1955 General Assembly. *S. L., 1953,* Res. 44.

[119] This Board is composed of five members appointed by the Governor, of which not more than three may be of the same political party. Members serve a term of four years. *G. S.*, Sec. 163-8.

Name of Appointee	*Address*	*Date Appointed*	*Date of Expiration*
ELIZABETH CITY STATE TEACHERS' COLLEGE [120]			
Lucius Blanchard [121]	Ahoskie	5-18-53	5-1-57
W. C. Chappell †	Belvedere	5-18-53	5-1-57
T. S. Cooper [122]	Sunbury	5-18-53	5-1-57
J. W. Davis †	Edenton	5-18-53	5-1-57
G. H. Ferguson †	Raleigh	5-18-53	5-1-57
Dr. E. L. Hoffler †	Elizabeth City	5-18-53	5-1-57
E. P. Leary [123]	Old Trap	5-18-53	5-1-57
G. R. Little, *Chairman* †	Elizabeth City	5-18-53	5-1-57
Mrs. T. C. Sawyer, Sr. †	Belcross	5-18-53	5-1-57
Dudley Bagley [124]	Moyock	7-9-53	5-1-57
EMPLOYMENT SECURITY COMMISSION [125]			
Henry E. Kendall, *Chairman* †	Raleigh	7-9-53	7-1-57
Crayon C. Efird [126]	Albemarle	7-9-53	7-1-57
Mrs. Quentin Gregory †	Halifax	7-9-53	7-1-57
Dr. Harry D. Wolf †	Chapel Hill	7-9-53	7-1-57
Advisory Council			
J. A. Bridger, [127] *Chairman, Representing Public*	Bladenboro	10-28-53	At pleasure of Governor
J. H. Gray, [128] *Chairman, Representing Public*	Robersonville	10-28-53	At pleasure of Governor
W. B. Horton, † *Representing Public*	Yanceyville	10-28-53	At pleasure of Governor
Mrs. R. C. Lewellyn, *Representing Public*	Dobson	10-28-53	At pleasure of Governor
Dr. J. W. Seabrook, *Representing Public*	Fayetteville	10-28-53	At pleasure of Governor

W. A. Egerton, *Representing Employers*	Enka	10-28-53	At pleasure of Governor
A. L. Tait, *Representing Employers*	Lincolnton	10-28-53	At pleasure of Governor
Melvin Ward, *Representing Employees*	Spencer	10-28-53	At pleasure of Governor
H. D. Lisk, *Representing Employees*	Charlotte	10-28-53	At pleasure of Governor

State Board of Registration for Engineers and Land Surveyors [129]

Robert B. Rice †	Raleigh	8-2-54	12-31-57
Grady S. Harrell †	Shannon	8-2-54	12-31-57
Walter J. Seeley [130]	Durham	8-2-54	12-31-57
William G. Brown, Jr. [131]	Concord	8-2-54	12-31-57
Arvin Page [132]	Winston-Salem	8-2-54	12-31-57

---

[120] The Board consists of nine members appointed by the Governor and confirmed by the Senate for four-year terms. *G. S.*, Sec. 116-103.

[121] Succeeded O. Ray Symonds.

[122] Succeeded H. L. Mitchell.

[123] Succeeded Harry Ferebee.

[124] Succeeded Lucius Blanchard, resigned.

[125] The Board is composed of seven members appointed by the Governor, one of which the Governor designates as chairman. Members serve a term of four years. *G. S.*, Sec. 96-3.

[126] Succeeded Bruce E. Davis.

[127] **This Council is appointed by the Governor to serve at his pleasure**, and is composed of an equal number of employer and employee representatives, who may fairly be regarded as representative because of their vocation, employment, or affiliations, and has members representing the general public as the Governor may designate. *G. S.*, Sec. 96-4 (e).

[128] Resigned.

[129] The Board consists of five members appointed by the Governor for terms of four years, with at least two members being appointed from the faculty of North Carolina State College, and no more than three members from the same branch of engineering. *G. S.*, Sec. 89-3.

[130] Succeeded H. D. Jones.

[131] Succeeded A. C. Lee.

[132] Succeeded C. L. Mann.

Name of Appointee	*Address*	*Date Appointed*	*Date of Expiration*
FAYETTEVILLE STATE TEACHERS' COLLEGE [133] Fayetteville			
John H. Cook †	Fayetteville	10-27-53	10-1-57
Victor Dawson	Fayetteville	10-27-53	10-1-57
Dr. W. P. DeVane	Fayetteville	10-27-53	10-1-57
Gurney E. Edgerton	Fayetteville	10-27-53	10-1-57
Dr. C. W. Furlong	Smithfield	10-27-53	10-1-57
R. J. Hester	Elizabethtown	10-27-53	10-1-57
W. E. Horner	Sanford	10-27-53	10-1-57
Emil Rosenthal [134]	Goldsboro	10-27-53	10-1-57
Stewart B. Warren	Clinton	10-27-53	10-1-57
FLUE-CURED TOBACCO CO-OPERATIVE STABILIZATION CORPORATION [135]			
E. Y. Floyd †	Raleigh	8-2-54	7-1-57
GASOLINE AND OIL INSPECTION BOARD [136]			
Garland E. Bobbitt †	Raleigh	10-23-53	At pleasure of Governor
G. Allen Ives [137]	New Bern	10-23-53	At pleasure of Governor
E. W. McDaniel [138]	Elkin	10-23-53	At pleasure of Governor
GENERAL STATUTES COMMISSION [139]			
J. Spencer Bell †	Charlotte	5-28-53	6-1-55
William Joslin †	Raleigh	5-28-53	6-1-55
Buxton Midyette [140]	Jackson	8-6-53	6-1-55

COMMISSION ON REORGANIZATION OF STATE GOVERNMENT [141]

Name	Residence	Date	Term
William B. Rodman, Jr.	Washington	10-1-53	To report to Governor
Thomas Turner	Greensboro	10-1-53	To report to Governor
Miss Harriet Herring †	Chapel Hill	10-1-53	To report to Governor
David Clark †	Lincolnton	10-1-53	To report to Governor
John D. Larkins, Jr.	Trenton	10-1-53	To report to Governor
William F. Marshall	Walnut Cove	10-1-53	To report to Governor
C. W. Tilson	Durham	10-1-53	To report to Governor
R. Grady Rankin	Gastonia	10-1-53	To report to Governor
W. Frank Taylor †	Goldsboro	10-1-53	To report to Governor

[133] The Board is composed of nine members appointed by the Governor and confirmed by the Senate for four-year terms. *G. S.*, Sec. 116-103.

[134] Succeeded Dr. M. E. Bizzell, declined.

[135] One Board member is appointed by the Director of Agricultural Extension or any public official or commission, in this case the Governor. *G. S.*, Sec. 54-146 (b).

[136] The Board is composed of five members, three appointed by the Governor to serve at his pleasure, and two ex officio members: the Commissioner of Agriculture (L. Y. Ballentine), and the Director of the Gasoline and Oil Inspection Division (C. D. Baucom). The 1949 amendment substituted the Commissioner of Agriculture for the Commissioner of Revenue as one of the two ex officio members. *G. S.*, Sec. 119-26; *S. L., 1949*, Ch. 1167.

[137] Succeeded Roby E. Taylor, declined.

[138] Succeeded C. A. Horne.

[139] The Commission consists of nine members, each of whom are appointed as follows for a two-year term: One each by the President of the North Carolina State Bar and North Carolina Bar Association, one each by the Deans of the Law Schools of Duke, Wake Forest, and the University of North Carolina, one each by the President of the Senate and the Speaker of the House of Representatives of the General Assembly, and two by the Governor. *G. S.*, Sec. 164-14 (a).

[140] Succeeded J. Spencer Bell, declined.

[141] This Commission is composed of nine members appointed by the Governor to study and make recommendations to him on or

Name of Appointee	*Address*	*Date Appointed*	*Date of Expiration*
THE GREENSBORO MUNICIPAL-COUNTY COURT [142]			
James B. Wolfe, Jr., *Judge*, Criminal Division [143]	Greensboro	12-15-53	1-1-56
STATE BOARD OF HEALTH [144]			
Dr. A. C. Current †	Gastonia	5-25-53	5-1-57
Dr. Hubert B. Haywood †	Raleigh	5-25-53	5-1-57
Mrs. J. E. Latta [145]	Hillsboro	5-25-53	5-1-57
Dr. John P. Henderson, Jr. [146]	Sneads Ferry	8-3-54	5-1-55
STATE HIGHWAY AND PUBLIC WORKS COMMISSION [147]			
A. H. Graham, *Chairman* [148]	Hillsboro	5-11-53	5-1-57
J. Emmett Winslow, *1st District* [149]	Hertford	5-11-53	5-1-57
H. Maynard Hicks, *2nd District* [150]	Snow Hill	5-11-53	5-1-57
C. Heide Trask, *3rd District* [151]	Wilmington	5-11-53	5-1-57
M. E. Robinson, *4th District* [152]	Goldsboro	5-11-53	5-1-57
Donnie A. Sorrell, *5th District* [153]	Durham	5-11-53	5-1-57
C. A. Hasty, *6th District* [154]	Maxton	5-11-53	5-1-57
John Van Lindley, *7th District* [155]	Greensboro	5-11-53	5-1-57
Forrest Lockey, *8th District* [156]	Aberdeen	5-11-53	5-1-57
James A. Gray, Jr., *9th District* [157]	Winston-Salem	5-11-53	5-1-57
James A. Hardison, *10th District* [158]	Wadesboro	5-11-53	5-1-57
W. Ralph Winkler, *11th District*	Boone	5-11-53	5-1-57
June F. Scarborough, *12th District*	Statesville	5-11-53	5-1-57
J. F. Snipes, *13th District*	Marion	5-11-53	5-1-57
H. E. Buchanan, *14th District*	Hendersonville	5-11-53	5-1-57

Committee to Consider Increasing the Number of Highway Divisions or Changing the Boundaries of Existing Districts[159]

T. Boddie Ward	Wilson	3-16-53	11-1-53
W. P. Saunders	Aberdeen	3-16-53	11-1-53
J. Hampton Price	Leaksville	3-16-53	11-1-53
W. H. Woodson, Sr., *Chairman*	Salisbury	3-16-53	11-1-53
Reuben B. Robertson, Sr.	**Canton**	3-16-53	11-1-53

---

before November 15, 1954. *S. L., 1953,* Res. 21.

[142] The Court is composed of three members appointed by the Governor for four-year terms. The members are the judge of the civil division, and the judge and prosecuting attorney of the criminal division of the municipal court of the City of Greensboro. *Private Laws of North Carolina, 1933,* Ch. 84, (hereafter cited as *Priv. L.*) *P. L., 1909,* Ch. 651; *P. L., 1939,* Ch. 300.

[143] Succeeding Judge E. Earle Rives, deceased.

[144] The Board is composed of nine members serving terms of four years, five of whom are appointed by the Governor and four of whom are elected by the North Carolina Medical Society. *G. S.,* Sec. 130-1, 7.

[145] Succeeded Mrs. James L. Hunt, resigned.

[146] Succeeded Dr. H. Lee Large, deceased January 29, 1954.

[147] The Commission is composed of a chairman and fourteen commissioners appointed by the Governor, each of whom serves a four-year term. *G. S.,* Sec. 136-1; *S. L., 1953,* Ch. 115.

[148] Succeeded Dr. Henry W. Jordan.

[149] Succeeded Henry Gray Shelton.

[150] Succeeded Guy Hargett.

[151] Succeeded Wilbur Clark.

[152] Succeeded Dr. R. E. Earp.

[153] Succeeded James A. Barnwell.

[154] Succeeded George Coble.

[155] Succeeded Otis Poole.

[156] Succeeded Paul Taylor.

[157] Succeeded Joseph Graham.

[158] Succeeded Dale Thrash.

[159] This Commitee is composed of five members appointed by the Governor and is report to him by November 1, 1953. *G. S.,* Sec. 136-1; *S. L., 1953,* Ch. 115.

Name of Appointee	Address	Date Appointed	Date of Expiration
THE HISTORIC SITES COMMISSION [160]			
Dr. Paul A. Reid *	Cullowhee	8-26-53-54	8-26-54-59
Mrs. Ernest Ives	Southern Pines	8-26-53	8-26-55
J. A. Stenhouse	Charlotte	8-26-53	8-26-56
William T. Polk	Greensboro	8-26-53	8-26-57
Dr. Hugh T. Lefler	Chapel Hill	8-26-53	8-26-58
SPECIAL OFFICERS, HIGHWAY AND PRISON DEPARTMENT [161]			
E. J. Harrington †	Lakeview	3-5-53	At pleasure of Governor
Calvin L. Miller †	Rockwell	3-5-53	At pleasure of Governor
J. D. Wilson †	Raleigh	3-5-53	At pleasure of Governor
Robert A. Stafford	Oak Ridge	8-28-53	At pleasure of Governor
Evan Grey Howe [162]	Raleigh	10-20-53	At pleasure of Governor
Claude Richard Cook [163]	Raleigh	2-16-54	At pleasure of Governor
Earl Bush [164]	Chapel Hill	3-16-54	At pleasure of Governor
A. F. Wadford [165]	Neuse	7-16-54	At pleasure of Governor
Robert E. Jones	Butner Youth Center	9-30-54	At pleasure of Governor
NORTH CAROLINA HOSPITALS BOARD OF CONTROL [166]			
David W. Royster [167]	Shelby	2-26-53	4-1-53
Wayland Spruill * [168]	Windsor	6-5-53-54	4-1-54-58
J. Melville Broughton, Jr. [169]	Raleigh	6-5-53	4-1-55
Mrs. Reba Gavin †	Kenansville	6-5-53	4-1-57
H. W. Kendall †	Greensboro	6-5-53	4-1-57

Warren R. Williams[170]	Sanford	6-5-53	4-1-57
Dr. Yates Palmer †	Valdese	6-5-53	4-1-57
David W. Royster †	Shelby	6-5-53	4-1-57
John T. Rodgers[171]	Asheville	6-5-53	4-1-57
Frank M. Kilpatrick †	Ayden	7-8-54	4-1-58
Thomas O'Berry †	Goldsboro	7-8-54	4-1-58
Advisory Committee			
Dr. Clifton West[172]	Kinston	6-10-53	4-1-57
Dr. J. M. Lynch †	Asheville	6-10-53	4-1-57
Dr. W. H. C. White[173]	Elizabeth City	6-10-53	4-1-57

[160] This Commission has a membership of six, of whom five are appointed by the Governor. The Director of the State Department of Archives and History (Dr. Christopher Crittenden), is the ex officio member and serves as secretary. Terms are for one, two, three, four, and five years, with reappointments for five years. *S. L., 1953,* Ch. 1197.

[161] The Governor is authorized to appoint officers for the purpose of transferring prisoners from place to place in the State, said officers to be commissioned specifically or generally to return escaped prisoners or other fugitives from outside the State. *G. S.,* Sec. 148-4.

[162] Succeeded Munsey S. Hodges.

[163] Succeeded Robert A. Stafford.

[164] Succeeded Evan Grey Howe, resigned for promotion.

[165] Succeeded Earl Bush.

[166] The Board consists of fifteen members appointed by the Governor. There must be one member from each of the twelve Congressional districts and three at large. The terms are for four years, and the Governor makes appointments to fill unexpired terms when vacancies occur. The institutions combined under this Board are: The State Hospital, Raleigh; The State Hospital, Morganton; The State Hospital, Goldsboro; The State Hospital, Butner; and The Caswell Training School, Kinston. *G. S.,* Sec. 122-7; *S. L., 1943,* Ch. 136; *S. L., 1945,* Ch. 925; *S. L., 1947,* Ch. 537.

[167] Succeeded Francis A. Whiteside, resigned.

[168] Succeeded W. G. Clark, Sr.

[169] Succeeded J. Dwight Barbour, resigned.

[170] Succeeded Dr. W. H. Kibler.

[171] Succeeded Kelly E. Bennett.

[172] Succeeded Dr. C. G. Parker.

[173] Succeeded Dr. J. A. Gill.

Name of Appointee	Address	Date Appointed	Date of Expiration
Dr. W. T. Ralph †	Belhaven	6-10-53	4-1-57
Dr. David J. Rose †	Goldsboro	6-10-53	4-1-57
Dr. John Bender †	Winston-Salem	6-10-53	4-1-57
Dr. M. C. Maddrey †	Roanoke Rapids	6-10-53	4-1-57
Dr. Thomas B. Suiter [174]	Rocky Mount	6-10-53	4-1-57
Dr. W. C. Mebane †	Wilmington	6-10-53	4-1-57
Dr. George L. Carrington †	Burlington	6-10-53	4-1-57
Dr. W. O. Duck †	Mars Hill	6-10-53	4-1-57
Dr. Glenn L. Hooper †	Dunn	6-10-53	4-1-57
Dr. George C. Ham †	Chapel Hill	6-10-53	4-1-57
Dr. Charles F. Strosnider †	Goldsboro	6-10-53	4-1-57
Dr. Lois F. Stanford †	Durham	6-10-53	4-1-57
Dr. James W. Vernon †	Morganton	6-10-53	4-1-57
Dr. Amos Johnson †	Garland	6-10-53	4-1-57
Dr. H. S. Willis †	McCain	6-10-53	4-1-57
Dr. V. K. Hart †	Charlotte	6-10-53	4-1-57
Dr. Munro McIntosh †	Marion	6-10-53	4-1-57
Dr. W. R. Berryhill †	Chapel Hill	6-10-53	4-1-57
Dr. Hubert B. Haywood †	Raleigh	6-10-53	4-1-57
Dr. W. T. Shaver [175]	Albemarle	6-10-53	4-1-57
Dr. W. C. Davison †	Durham	6-10-53	4-1-57
Dr. Lloyd J. Thompson †	Winston-Salem	6-10-53	4-1-57
Dr. Walter Spaeth [176]	Elizabeth City	7-3-53	4-1-57

NORTH CAROLINA INDUSTRIAL COMMISSION [177]

J. Frank Huskins, *Chairman*	Raleigh	5-28-53	5-1-59
Frank H. Gibbs [178]	Warrenton	9-13-54	5-1-55

COMMISSIONER OF INSURANCE [179]

Charles F. Gold [180]	Rutherfordton	10-26-53	Next general election

INSURANCE ADVISORY BOARD [181]

W. H. Andrews, Jr. †	Greensboro	1-14-54	9-1-57
Jack C. Koonce [182]	Jacksonville	1-14-54	9-1-57
L. M. Buchanan [183]	Greenville	1-14-54	9-1-57
D. M. Woodward, Jr. [184]	Conway	1-14-54	9-1-57

[174] Succeeded Dr. M. L. Stone.

[175] Succeeded Dr. Leslie B. Hohman.

[176] Succeeded Dr. W. H. C. White, deceased.

[177] The Board is composed of three members appointed by the Governor, one of which he appoints chairman. Members serve a term of six years. *G. S., Sec.* **97-77.**

[178] Succeeded Robert L. Scott, resigned.

[179] The Commissioner of Insurance is an elective official, but appointed by the Governor when there is a vacancy during the term, as in this instance. *G. S.*, Sec. 58-5.

[180] Succeeded Waldo C. Cheek, resigned.

[181] The Board is composed of seven members, six of whom are appointed by the Governor and one of whom, the Commissioner of Insurance (Charles F. Gold appointed October 26, 1953 to fill unexpired term of Waldo Cheek), is an ex officio member and Chairman. Appointments and reappointments are for four-year terms. The Governor appoints members to fill any unexpired term of office, and may remove members when he feels the public interest requires such action. *G. S.*, Sec. 58-27.1.

[182] Succeeded George A. Iseley.

[183] Succeeded Harry G. Latimer.

[184] Succeeded Fred Cochrane.

Name of Appointee	*Address*	*Date Appointed*	*Date of Expiration*
NORTH CAROLINA COMMISSION ON INTERSTATE CO-OPERATION [185]			
D. S. Coltrane	Raleigh	4-30-53	Next general election
Harry McMullan	Raleigh	4-30-53	Next general election
Forrest H. Shuford [186]	Raleigh	4-30-53	Next general election
Charles F. Carroll [187]	Raleigh	4-30-53	At pleasure of Governor
Dr. J. W. R. Norton [188]	Raleigh	4-30-53	At pleasure of Governor
Charles H. Jenkins, *Chairman* †	Raleigh	4-30-53	At pleasure of Governor
GOVERNOR'S COMMITTEE ON INTERSTATE CO-OPERATION [189]			
Charles F. Carroll [190]	Raleigh	4-30-53	At pleasure of Governor
Dr. J. W. R. Norton [191]	Raleigh	4-30-53	At pleasure of Governor
Charles H. Jenkins, *Chairman* †	Aulander	4-30-53	At pleasure of Governor
JUDGES OF THE SUPERIOR COURT OF NORTH CAROLINA [192]			
Clifton L. Moore [193]	Burgaw	12-29-53	12-31-58
Francis Osborne Clarkson [194]	Charlotte	2-1-54	12-31-62
Walter E. Johnston, Jr. [195]	Winston-Salem	6-1-54	12-31-58
SPECIAL JUDGES, SUPERIOR COURT [196]			
Francis Osborne Clarkson	Charlotte	6-29-53	6-30-55
Howard H. Hubbard	Clinton	6-29-53	6-30-55
Grover A. Martin	Smithfield	6-29-53	6-30-55
George B. Patton †	Franklin	6-29-53	6-30-55
Malcolm C. Paul	Washington	6-29-53	6-30-55

Susie Sharp †	Reidsville	6-29-53	6-30-55
R. Lee Whitmire	Hendersonville	6-29-53	6-30-55
Clarence W. Hall	Durham	6-29-53	6-30-55
Peyton McSwain	Shelby	6-29-53	6-30-55

[185] **This Commission is composed of sixteen members, fifteen** regular members, five of whom are members of the Governor's Committee on Interstate Co-operation. The Governor, at his own discretion, appointed one additional member to his Committee on Interstate Co-operation, thus bringing to six the number of representatives from the Governor's Committee. The other members are: five members named by the President of the Senate, and five members of the House designated by the Speaker. The Governor, the President of the Senate, and the Speaker of the House of Representatives are ex officio honorary non-voting members. The act is indefinite as to the term served by the members. *G. S.*, Sec. 143-181.

[186] **Succeeded Charles J. Parker.**

[187] Succeeded L. C. Rosser.

[188] Succeeded Thad Eure.

[189] **This Committee is composed of five members, two of whom a**re appointed from among state officials by the Governor for terms which expire at his pleasure, and it constitutes a part of the North Carolina Commission on Interstate Co-operation. The Governor, at his own discretion, may appoint one non-administrative official as an additional member, who also serves at his pleasure. Ex officio members are: the Budget Director or corresponding official (D. S. Coltrane, Assistant Director of the Budget, is named here, as the Budget Director is the Governor), the Attorney General (Harry McMullan), and the chief of staff of the State Planning Board or corresponding official (in this case, the Commissioner of Labor, Forrest H. Shuford, deceased May 19, 1954, succeeded by Frank Crane). In addition to the regular members, the Governor is an ex officio honorary non-voting member. *G. S.*, Sec. 143-180; *S. L., 1949*, Ch. 1065.

[190] Succeeded L. C. Rosser.

[191] Succeeded Thad Eure.

[192] There are twenty-one judges serving for terms of eight years. Terms begin in January following the election. Vacancies are filled by appointment of the Governor, to serve until the next general election. The Constitution of North Carolina, Article 4, Sections 21 and 25; *P. L., 1868-1869*, Ch. 270, Sec. 27-3.

[193] Succeeded John J. Burney, resigned December 29, 1953. Judge Moore served the remainder of Burney's term and was re-elected in the 1954 general election.

[194] Succeeded William H. Bobbitt, resigned February 1, 1954, to become Associate Justice. Judge Clarkson served until the 1954 general election, at which time he was re-elected.

[195] Succeeded John H. Clement, resigned March 10, 1954. He completed the unexpired term and was re-elected in the 1954 general election.

[196] The law provides for four special judges, two from the western judicial division and two from the eastern judicial division. The Governor is further authorized and empowered, if in his judgment the necessity exists, to appoint four additional judges, two from each judicial division. *G. S.*, Sec. 7-54, 56; *S. L., 1945*, Ch. 153; *S. L., 1947*, Ch. 24.

Name of Appointee	*Address*	*Date Appointed*	*Date of Expiration*
George M. Fountain	Tarboro	10-31-53	6-30-55
W. A. Leland McKeithan [197]	Pinehurst	2-9-54	6-30-55
EMERGENCY JUDGES, SUPERIOR COURT [198]			
W. H. S. Burgwyn	Woodland	7-1-53	
William A. Devin	Oxford	2-1-54	
John H. Clement	Walkertown	3-15-54	
W. C. Harris	Raleigh	10-1-54	
JUDGES OF THE SUPREME COURT OF NORTH CAROLINA [199]			
Maurice V. Barnhill, *Chief Justice* [200]	Raleigh	2-1-54	Next general election
William H. Bobbitt [201]	Charlotte	2-1-54	Next general election
Carlisle W. Higgins [202]	Winston-Salem	6-8-54	Next general election
THE COMMISSION ON JUVENILE COURTS AND CORRECTIONAL INSTITUTIONS [203]			
Mrs. Walter J. Carpenter	Lenoir	8-14-53	
Nat S. Crews	Winston-Salem	8-14-53	
Lee J. Greer	Whiteville	8-14-53	
William B. Harrison	Rocky Mount	8-14-53	
Terry Sanford	Fayetteville	8-14-53	

JUDICIAL COUNCIL [204]

E. T. Bost, Jr. [205]	Concord	6-12-53	6-2-55
John C. Rodman, Jr. [206]	Washington	6-12-53	6-2-55

COMMISSIONER OF LABOR [207]

Frank Crane [208]	Raleigh	6-3-54	Next general election

[197] Succeeded Francis O. Clarkson, resigned to become resident Superior Court judge.

[198] Justices of the Supreme Court, judges of the Superior Court, and regular or special judges who are retired, are subject to assignment as emergency judges by the Chief Justice of the Supreme Court of North Carolina (W. A. Devin, resigned January 1, 1954, and was succeeded on February 2, 1954, by Maurice V. Barnhill), when the assigned judge is unable to attend and hold court. This excepts judges retired because of accident or disease, who have not been restored to duty for limited service. A 1951 amendment substituted the Chief Justice of the Supreme Court for the Governor, as the official commissioning the emergency judges to hold court. *G. S.*, Sec. 7-50, 71; *S. L., 1951,* Ch. 491.

[199] The Supreme Court is composed of seven judges who serve terms of eight years each. The Constitution of North Carolina, Article 4, Section 21 and 25; *P. L., 1901,* Ch. 89, Sec 4; *P. L., 1937,* Ch. 16.

[200] Succeeded William A. Devin, resigned January 1, 1954.

[201] Succeeded Maurice V. Barnhill, appointed Chief Justice.

[202] Succeeded Samuel J. Ervin, Jr., appointed to the United States Senate, June 5, 1954.

[203] The Commission, composed of five members appointed by the Governor, is to report its findings to the Governor and the 1955 Session of the General Assembly. *S. L., 1953,* Ch. 1117.

[204] This Council consists of twelve members, two of which are appointed by the Governor. There are four members appointed by the Council of the North Carolina State Bar, one appointed by the Speaker of the House, and one by the President of the Senate. Ex officio members are: the Chief Justice (William A. Devin and after Feb. 2, 1954 M. V. Barnhill), or some other member of the Supreme Court, who serves as chairman; two judges of the Supreme Court who are designated by the Chief Justice, and the Attorney General (Harry McMullan). The term of the Chief Justice extends through his term of office if he designates no other member of the Supreme Court, the Attorney General serves during his term of office, and all other members serve for terms of two years. *G. S.*, Sec. 7-448, 449, 451.

[205] Succeeded M. T. Leatherman.

[206] Succeeded Jesse Jones.

[207] The Commissioner of Labor is an elective official, but whenever a vacancy occurs, the Governor appoints a citizen to serve until the next election. *G. S.*, Sec. 95-2.

[208] Succeeded Forrest H. Shuford, deceased May 19, 1954.

Name of Appointee	*Address*	*Date Appointed*	*Date of Expiration*
LEE COUNTY BOARD OF VETERANS' AFFAIRS [209]			
F. B. Brinn †	Sanford	7-29-53	7-1-56
W. H. Ray [210]	Sanford	7-29-53	7-1-56
James P. Seymore [211]	Sanford	7-29-53	7-1-56
NORTH CAROLINA LIBRARY COMMISSION [212]			
Reverend George F. Hill	Elizabeth City	8-20-53	7-1-57
NORTH CAROLINA MARKETING COMMISSION [213]			
Fred Colvard	Jefferson	11-19-53	
Boyd Campbell	Taylorsville	11-19-53	
J. E. Paschall	Wilson	11-19-53	
Dr. C. Brice Ratchford	Raleigh	11-19-53	
Grady Stevens	Shiloh	11-19-53	
Senator J. Vivian Whitfield	Burgaw	11-19-53	
John A. Winfield	Raleigh	11-19-53	
NORTH CAROLINA MEDICAL CARE COMMISSION [214]			
E. C. Daniel * [215]	Zebulon	7-3-53-54	7-1-54-58
Sample B. Forbus †	Durham	7-2-53	7-1-56
Dr. Clarence Poe, *Vice-Chairman* †	Raleigh	7-2-53	7-1-56
Ralph Ramsey [216]	Brevard	7-2-53	7-1-56
Dr. William R. Stanford †	Durham	7-2-53	7-1-56
Dr. J. Street Brewer †	Roseboro	7-2-53	7-1-57
James H. Clark, *Chairman* †	Elizabethtown	7-2-53	7-1-57

Dr. Walter L. Jackson †	High Point	7-2-53	7-1-57
Marshall I. Pickens [217]	Charlotte	7-2-53	7-1-57
Dr. W. M. Rich †	Durham	7-2-53	7-1-57
Dr. Paul F. Whitaker [218]	Kinston	7-2-53	7-1-57
Lloyd D. Hardy †	Raleigh	7-8-54	7-1-58
Dr. Harry L. Johnson †	Elkin	7-8-54	7-1-58
Miss Flora Wakefield †	Raleigh	7-8-54	7-1-58

[209] This Board is composed of six members, five of whom are appointed by the Governor, and one of whom, the chairman of the Board of County Commissioners, is a member ex officio. Members serve four-year terms. *S. L., 1945,* Ch. 599.

[210] Succeeded Edwin A. Dalrymple.

[211] Succeeded H. F. Oehler.

[212] This Commission, after July 1, 1953, is to be composed of eight members, the membership having been increased from five by the 1953 General Assembly. The Governor now appoints two members: one to serve a four-year term beginning July 1, 1953, and one for a four-year term beginning July 1, 1955. Their successors are also appointed for four-year terms. The North Carolina Library Commission now appoints four members, three for terms of four, three, and two years each, beginning July 1, 1953, and one appointed for a four-year term beginning July 1, 1954. Successors to members appointed by the Library Commission are to be appointed for four-year terms, and members are appointed to fill vacancies for the remainder of unexpired terms. The ex officio members include: the Superintendent of Public Instruction (Charles F. Carroll), and the State Librarian (Miss Carrie L. Broughton). *G. S.,* Sec. 125-18; *S. L., 1953,* Ch. 1102.

[213] This Commission is composed of seven members appointed by the Governor, and is to make recommendations to the 1955 General Assembly. *S. L., 1953,* Res. 32.

[214] The Commission consists of twenty members, of whom ten are appointed by the Governor, and eight are nominated by the various medical associations for appointment by the Governor. Of these, three are nominated by the North Carolina Medical Society, one by the North Carolina Hospital Association, one by the North Carolina Dental Society, one by the North Carolina Nurses Association, one by the North Carolina Pharmaceutical Association, and one by the Duke Foundation. Two members serve ex officio: the Secretary of the State Board of Health (Dr. J. W. R. Norton), and the Commissioner of Public Welfare (Dr. Ellen Winston). Terms vary from one to four years, with reappointments for four years. *G. S.,* Sec. 131-117.

[215] Succeeded Paul B. Bissette, resigned.

[216] Succeeded L. B. Prince, declined reappointment.

[217] Succeeded W. S. Rankin, resigned.

[218] Succeeded Dr. Zeno Edwards, resigned January 30, 1952.

Name of Appointee	*Address*	*Date Appointed*	*Date of Expiration*
STATE ADVISORY COUNCIL [219]			
Claude F. Gaddy †	Raleigh	7-9-53	7-1-57
Dr. Fred Hubbard [220]	North Wilkesboro	7-9-53	7-1-57
James P. Richardson †	Charlotte	7-9-53	7-1-57
James G. Stikeleather [221]	Asheville	7-9-53	7-1-57
Dr. David A. Young †	Raleigh	7-9-53	7-1-57
MERIT SYSTEM COUNCIL [222] (For Certain North Carolina Departments and Agencies)			
R. B. Justice [223]	Enka	5-14-53	4-8-59
Reverend J. B. Willis [224]	Hamlet	5-14-53	4-8-59
NORTH CAROLINA MILK COMMISSION [225]			
J. E. Wilson *	Albemarle	8-6-53-54	8-6-54-58
W. W. Fitzpatrick	Rougemont	8-6-53	8-6-55
H. G. Strom	Asheville	8-6-53	8-6-56
John Burn	Shelby	8-6-53	8-6-57
Thomas J. Pearsall	Rocky Mount	8-6-53	8-6-57
Oliver A. Swaringen	Concord	8-6-53	8-6-57
Fred M. Eagles [226]	Wilson	4-21-54	8-6-57
COMMISSIONER OF MOTOR VEHICLES [227]			
Edward Scheidt [228]	Raleigh	5-21-53	At pleasure of Governor
MUNICIPAL RECORDER'S COURT OF THE TOWN OF SILER CITY [229]			
J. Speight Wrenn, *Judge*	Siler City	12-10-53	1-1-58
T. F. Baldwin, *Solicitor*	Siler City	12-10-53	1-1-58

Board of Commissioners of Navigation and Pilotage for the Cape Fear River [230]

R. W. Cantwell †	Wilmington	5-14-53	4-15-57
Louis A. Hanson, *Chairman* †	Wilmington	5-14-53	4-15-57
H. S. McGirt †	Wilmington	5-14-53	4-15-57
M. R. Sanders †	Southport	5-14-53	4-15-57
R. M. Williams [231]	Wilmington	5-14-53	4-15-57

[219] The Council is established by the Governor. It consists of five members appointed for four-year terms. The Governor fills any vacancies for unexpired terms. *G. S.*, Sec. 131-120; *S. L., 1945*, Ch. 1096.

[220] Succeeded Dr. R. E. Earp.

[221] Succeeded George Watts Hill.

[222] The Council is composed of five members appointed by the Governor for six-year terms. No members shall have held political office or have been an officer in a political organization during the year preceding his appointment, nor shall he hold such office during his term. *G. S.*, Sec. 126-1.

[223] Succeeded Elbert E. Foster.

[224] Succeeded Jasper L. Memory, Jr.

[225] The Commission consists of seven members, six of whom are appointed by the Governor. The members represent: a producer, a producer-distributor, two distributors, a representative of public interests, a retailer, and the seventh member is the Commissioner of Agriculture (L. Y. Ballentine), serving ex officio. Terms of the Commission first appointed are: one for a term of one year, one for two years, one for three years, and three for a term of four years; thereafter appointments are made for four-year terms. *G. S.*, Sec. 106-266.7.

[226] Succeeded Thomas J. Pearsall, resigned.

[227] The Commissioner is appointed by, responsible to, and serves at the will of the Governor. *G. S.*, Sec. 20-2.

[228] Succeeded L. R. Fisher.

[229] The recorder who is designated as the judge of the court, is appointed by the Governor for a term of four years. Any vacancy is filled by the Governor for the unexpired term. The prosecuting attorney is also appointed by the Governor for a term of four years. *S. L., 1953*, Ch. 607.

[230] This Board consists of five commissioners appointed by the Governor. Terms are for four years and until their successors are appointed and qualified. *G. S.*, Sec. 76-1.

[231] Succeeded John M. Walker.

Name of Appointee	*Address*	*Date Appointed*	*Date of Expiration*
BOARD OF NURSE REGISTRATION AND NURSING EDUCATION [232]			
Mrs. W. D. James, Sr.	Hamlet	12-31-53	1-1-55
Dr. Moir S. Martin	Mount Airy	12-31-53	1-1-55
Miss J. Elizabeth White	Charlotte	12-31-53	1-1-55
R. M. Gantt, Jr.	Albemarle	12-31-53	1-1-56
Miss Willie Louise Harkey	Concord	12-31-53	1-1-56
Dr. Louten R. Hedgepeth	Lumberton	12-31-53	1-1-57
Miss Joyce Warren	Winston-Salem	12-31-53	1-1-57
Mrs. Priscilla Davis Ballance	Wilson	12-31-53	1-1-58
Mrs. Laura Davis	Waynesville	12-31-53	1-1-58
Mrs. Allie Christine Hill	Goldsboro	12-31-53	1-1-58
J. Lyman Melvin	Rocky Mount	12-31-53	1-1-58
Mrs. Dorothy Woods	Durham	12-31-53	1-1-58
COMMITTEE TO STUDY THE FEASIBILITY OF ESTABLISHING A PROGRAM OF NURSE TRAINING [233]			
Miss Ruth Council	Raleigh	6-11-53	7-1-53
Reid Holmes	Winston-Salem	6-11-53	7-1-53
Warren R. Williams, *Chairman*	Sanford	6-11-53	7-1-53
NORTH CAROLINA STATE BOARD OF OPTICIANS [234]			
H. R. Tolar [235]	Goldsboro	9-8-53	7-1-58
Robert L. Albertson [236]	Durham	11-3-54	7-1-59
STATE BOARD OF EXAMINERS IN OPTOMETRY [237]			
Dr. Kenneth W. Ramsey [238]	Marion	12-2-53	5-1-58
Dr. John D. Costabile [239]	Wilson	6-30-54	5-1-59

NORTH CAROLINA ORTHOPEDIC HOSPITAL [240]

Gastonia

Mrs. D. Kay Dixon †	Gastonia	8-4-53	4-4-59
Willis Frank Dowd †	Charlotte	8-4-53	4-4-59
Paul C. Whitlock †	Charlotte	8-4-53	4-4-59
J. Harold Lineberger [241]	Belmont	10-16-53	4-4-55

STATE BOARD OF OSTEOPATHIC EXAMINATION AND REGISTRATION [242]

Dr. Frank R. Heine †	Greensboro	5-29-53	5-1-58
Dr. Talmage T. Spence †	Raleigh	6-18-54	5-1-59

---

[232] The Board consists of twelve members. Five members are to be registered nurses, two are to be physicians, and two are to be representatives of hospitals operating nursing schools, who are not physicians, all nine of whom are appointed and commissioned by the Governor. Three members are appointed for one year, two for two years, two for three years, and two for four-year terms. All succeeding appointments are for terms of four years. Vacancies are filled for the remainder of unexpired terms by the Governor from a list of two nominees filed by the organization which previously nominated the member creating the vacancy, or by appointment of the Governor if such member was not a nominee of any organization. *G. S.*, Sec. 90-158; *S. L., 1953*, Ch. 1199.

[233] The Committee is composed of three members appointed by the Governor. It is to investigate the possibilities of establishing a nurses training program in state-supported educational institutions, and report to the Governor its findings and recommendations not later than July 1, 1953. *S. L., 1953*, Ch. 1208.

[234] The Board consists of five members appointed by the Governor from a list of names submitted by the North Carolina Opticians Association. Terms of the five members vary from one to five years, and subsequent appointments are for five years. The Governor appoints members to fill unexpired terms. *G. S.*, Sec. 90-238; *S. L., 1951*, Ch. 1089.

[235] Succeeded Edward W. Dula.

[236] Succeeded J. M. Barnette.

[237] The Board is composed of five members elected by the North Carolina State Optometric Society and commissioned by the Governor for five-year terms. Vacancies are filled by the Governor for unexpired terms. *G. S.*, Sec. 90-116.

[238] Succeeded Dr. E. Alan Bisanar.

[239] Succeeded Dr. Henry B. Day.

[240] The Board consists of nine members appointed by the Governor for six-year terms. *G. S.*, Sec. 131-1.

[241] Succeeded Mrs. E. F. McCulloch, resigned.

[242] The Board is composed of five members appointed by the Governor for terms of five years. The membership is selected from a number of not less than five practitioners of osteopathy recommended by the State Osteopathic Society. The Governor fills vacancies for unexpired terms in the same manner and may request an increase in the number recommended by the Society. *G. S.*, Sec. 90-130.

Name of Appointee	*Address*	*Date Appointed*	*Date of Expiration*
OXFORD ORPHANAGE [243]			
Benjamin Cone †	Greensboro	5-14-53	4-15-57
J. E. Rooker, Jr. †	Warrenton	5-14-53	4-15-57
Thomas L. Simmons †	Rocky Mount	5-14-53	4-15-57
COLORED ORPHANAGE OF NORTH CAROLINA [244] Oxford			
M. S. Currin †	Oxford	5-18-53	5-9-57
Ben K. Lassiter †	Oxford	5-18-53	5-9-57
Dr. Roy L. Noblin †	Oxford	5-18-53	5-9-57
N. W. Weldon †	Stovall	5-18-53	5-9-57
W. T. Yancey †	Oxford	5-18-53	5-9-57
NORTH CAROLINA NATIONAL PARK, PARKWAY, AND FOREST DEVELOPMENT COMMISSION [245]			
Kelly E. Bennett †	Bryson City	6-24-53	7-1-59
Francis J. Heazel †	Asheville	6-24-53	7-1-59
Reaves Noland [246]	Waynesville	6-24-53	7-1-59
William Medford [247]	Waynesville	7-9-53	7-1-59
Robert I. Presley [248]	Asheville	7-30-53	7-1-59
BOARD OF PAROLES [249]			
Judge W. A. Brame	Wendell	7-9-53	At pleasure of Governor
Johnson Matthews	Durham	7-9-53	At pleasure of Governor
Dr. Clarence H. Patrick, *Chairman*	Wake Forest	7-9-53	At pleasure of Governor

PEMBROKE STATE COLLEGE FOR INDIANS [250]

Name	Residence	Date Appointed	Term Expires
J. Oliver Brooks †	Fairmont	5-14-53	4-1-57
Lester Bullard †	Maxton	5-14-53	4-1-57
John L. Carter †	Pembroke	5-14-53	4-1-57
Zeb. A. Lowry	Pembroke	5-14-53	4-1-57
Steve Hammond	Lumberton	5-14-53	4-1-57
Lacy Cummins	Rowland	5-14-53	4-1-57
A. G. Lowry †	Rowland	5-14-53	4-1-57
Carl L. Maynor †	Pembroke	5-14-53	4-1-57
James A. Sampson †	Pembroke	5-14-53	4-1-57

[243] The Board is composed of nine members, three of whom are appointed by the Governor for four-year terms. *Priv. L., 1923,* Ch. 119; *S. L., 1953,* Ch. 60, Sec. 10.

[244] The Board consists of thirteen members, eight of whom are appointed by the General Assembly, and five white persons from Granville County appointed by the Governor for four-year terms. *G. S.,* Sec. 116-139, 140.

[245] The Commission is composed of seven members appointed by the Governor for terms of six years. In addition there are two ex officio members as follows: the Chairman of the State Highway and Public Works Commission (Dr. Henry W. Jordan, succeeded by Alexander H. Graham on May 11, 1953), and the Director of the Department of Conservation and Development (George R. Ross, succeeded by Ben E. Douglas on July 10, 1953). The Governor appoints members to fill unexpired terms. *G. S.,* Sec. 143-255, 256.

[246] Succeeded Charles Ray.

[247] Succeeded Reaves Noland, who was unable to serve.

[248] Succeeded Francis J. Heazel, resigned June 30, 1953.

[249] This Board was created by the 1953 General Assembly to succeed the Commissioner of Paroles, and the three members are appointed by the Governor to serve at his pleasure, one of whom he appoints chairman. At the end of each fiscal year the Board submits a report to the Governor. *G. S.,* Sec. 148-51.1, 52; *S. L., 1953,* Ch. 17.

[250] The Board is composed of eleven members appointed by the Governor and confirmed by the Senate for four-year terms. *G. S.,* Sec. 116-81.

Name of Appointee	Address	Date Appointed	Date of Expiration
STATE PERSONNEL COUNCIL[251]			
Fred S. Royster, *Private Industry Rep.*	Henderson	6-19-53	7-1-55
Wade Barber, *Member at Large*	Pittsboro	6-19-53	7-1-56
John Harden, *Member at Large*	Greensboro	6-19-53	7-1-57
Earl Crump, *State Employees' Rep.*	Wilson	6-19-53	7-1-57
Macon Miller, *Personnel Administration Rep.*	Spray	6-19-53	7-1-57
STATE BOARD OF PHARMACY[252]			
Roger A. McDuffie †	Greensboro	5-13-53	4-28-58
Harmon C. McAllister †	Chapel Hill	6-30-54	4-28-59
STATE EXAMINING COMMITTEE OF PHYSICAL THERAPISTS[253]			
Miss Celeste Hayden †	Raleigh	5-18-53	1-1-56
Miss Margaret Moore †	Chapel Hill	1-14-54	1-1-57
Dr. George Miller †	Gastonia	1-14-54	1-1-57
NORTH CAROLINA COMMISSION ON EMPLOY THE PHYSICALLY HANDICAPPED[254]			
Dr. Lennox Baker	Durham	8-26-53	At pleasure of Governor
Al Bechtold	Charlotte	8-26-53	At pleasure of Governor
Gary Davis	High Point	8-26-53	At pleasure of Governor
Lloyd Hardy	Raleigh	8-26-53	At pleasure of Governor
W. L. McMillan	Rocky Mount	8-26-53	At pleasure of Governor
Mrs. Marie B. Noell	Raleigh	8-26-53	At pleasure of Governor
June H. Rose, *Chairman*	Greenville	8-26-53	At pleasure of Governor

STATE BOARD OF EXAMINERS OF PLUMBING AND HEATING CONTRACTORS [255]

Ralph H. Haley †	Charlotte	5-18-53	4-25-59
L. L. Vaughan †	Raleigh	5-18-53	4-25-60
Robert Owen McGary [256]	Charlotte	3-2-54	4-25-58
W. H. Sullivan, *Chairman* †	Greensboro	6-30-54	4-25-61

POET LAUREATE [257]

James Larkin Pearson [258]	Guilford College	8-2-53	Remainder of administration

[251] The Council consists of five members appointed by the Governor, as the membership was reduced from seven to five by the 1953 General Assembly. At least one member is to be chosen from the field of personnel administration who is not an employee of the State, at least one member is to be engaged in the management of private business or industry, and not more than one member is to be chosen from the employees of the State. One member is appointed to serve a term of two years, one to serve a term of three years, and three members to serve terms of four years each. Succeeding appointments are made for four-year terms. *G. S.*, Sec. 143-35 (2); *S. L., 1953*, Ch. 1085.

[252] The Board is composed of five members appointed for five-year terms. They are elected by the North Carolina Pharmaceutical Association and commissioned by the Governor. *G. S.*, Sec. 90-55.

[253] The Board created in 1951, consists of five members, including at least one doctor and four physical therapists, appointed by the Governor from a list submitted to him by the North Carolina Physical Therapy Association, Inc. One member is to serve a one-year term, two serve two-year terms, and two serve three-year terms, or until their successor is appointed. After January 1, 1953, members are to be appointed triennially for three-year terms. The Governor appoints persons to fill unexpired terms and no member is allowed by law to serve more than two successive three-year terms. *G. S.*, Sec. 90-257.

[254] This Commission was established by the General Assembly of 1953 and is composed of ten members: three of whom, the Director of Rehabilitation (Charles H. Warren), the Director of the Employment Security Commission (Henry E. Kendall), and the Commissioner of Labor (Forrest H. Shuford and after June 3, 1954 Frank Crane), serve ex officio; and seven appointed by the Governor to serve at his will. The Governor designates one member as chairman. *S. L., 1953*, Ch. 1224.

[255] The Board is composed of seven members, each appointed by the Governor for a seven-year term with the term of one member expiring each year. Among those appointed there must be one member from the Engineering School and one member from the Division of Public Health of the Greater University of North Carolina, one from the State Board of Health, one plumbing inspector from some city of the State, one licensed master plumber, one heating contractor, and one licensed air conditioning contractor. Vacancies are filled by appointment of the Governor for the remainder of the unexpired term. *G. S.*, Sec. 87-16.

[256] Succeeded R. V. Sisk, resigned.

[257] *Public Laws of North Carolina, 1935,* Resolution No. 60.

[258] Succeeded Dr. Arthur Talmage Abernathy.

Name of Appointee	Address	Date Appointed	Date of Expiration
	NORTH CAROLINA PORTS AUTHORITY[259]		
Raymond Bryan	Goldsboro	6-21-53	6-1-57
Harold E. Coffey	Lenoir	6-21-53	6-1-57
Harvey W. Moore	Charlotte	6-21-53	6-1-57
A. G. Myers †	Gastonia	6-21-53	6-1-57
Edwin Pate	Laurinburg	6-21-53	6-1-57
W. Avery Thompson †	Hallsboro	6-21-53	6-1-57
J. H. White †	Winston-Salem	6-21-53	6-1-57
Henry A. Lineberger[260]	Belmont	11-4-54	6-1-57
	STATE PROBATION COMMISSION[261]		
Judge Wilson Warlick †	Newton	5-29-53	5-28-58
Major L. P. McLendon †	Greensboro	7-2-54	5-28-59
	PRISON ADVISORY COUNCIL[262]		
Mrs. J. Wilbur Bunn[263]	Raleigh	12-23-53	11-18-59
Wiley W. Andrews †	Goldsboro	12-23-53	11-18-59
	DIVISION OF PURCHASE AND CONTRACT[264]		
David Q. Holton[265]	Edenton	9-17-53	At pleasure of Governor
	NORTH CAROLINA RAILROAD[266]		
Directors			
Thomas W. Bird	Charlotte	7-8-53	7-8-54
W. E. King *	Rocky Mount	7-8-53-54	7-8-54-55

Harry L. Nettles † *	Asheville	7-8-53-54	7-8-54-55
Charles I. Rouzer *	Salisbury	7-8-53-54	7-8-54-55
Watson Brame *	North Wilkesboro	7-8-53-54	7-8-54-55
E. W. McDaniel *	Elkin	7-8-53-54	7-8-54-55
D. N. Stewart *	Raleigh	7-8-53-54	7-8-54-55
Harry Miller	Stony Point	7-8-53-54	7-8-54-55
J. Bobo Langston	Charlotte	7-8-54	7-8-55
Officers			
Thomas W. Bird, *President*	Charlotte	7-8-53	7-8-54
Kidd Brewer, *Secretary-Treasurer*	Raleigh	7-8-53	7-8-54
W. H. Hofler, *Attorney*	Durham	7-8-53	7-8-54
Brack Creel, *Expert*	Chapel Hill	7-8-53	7-8-54

[259] This board is composed of seven members appointed by the Governor from the State at large. Members are appointed for four-year terms with reappointment also for four years. Vacancies occurring in the membership are filled by the Governor for the remainder of unexpired terms. In 1953 the General Assembly amended the statute, reducing the membership of this board from nine to seven members, and the ex officio member, the director of the Department of Conservation and Development, was dropped. *G. S.*, Sec. 143-216; *S. L., 1953*, Ch. 191.

[260] Succeeded A. G. Myers, resigned.

[261] The Commission is composed of five members appointed by the Governor to serve for five years, one member's term expiring each year. Reappointments are for five-year terms, and the Governor fills vacancies occurring in the membership for the remainder of unexpired terms. *G. S.*, Sec. 15-201.

[262] This Council is composed of seven members, five of whom are appointed by the Governor and one of whom he designates as chairman. Initial appointments are for the following terms: one member for six years, two members for four years, and two members for two years with reappointments being for six-year terms. The Attorney General (Harry McMullan), and the Commissioner of Public Welfare (Dr. Ellen Winston), serve ex officio. *G. S.*, Sec. 148-86.

[263] Succeeded Mrs. Kate Burr Johnson.

[264] The Director of Purchase and Contract is appointed by the Governor and serves at his pleasure. *G. S.*, Sec. 143-63.

[265] Succeeded Charles M. Williams.

[266] The Board of directors consists of twelve members, eight of whom are appointed annually by the Governor with the advice and consent of the Council of State. See the bylaws of the North Carolina Railroad Company, and charter and amendments thereto. *P. L., 1854-1855*, Ch. 32; *P. L., 1873-1874*, Chs. 33, 54; *P. L., 1879*, Ch. 138; *P. L., 1891*, Ch. 392; *P. L., 1925*, Ch. 157.

Name of Appointee	Address	Date Appointed	Date of Expiration
J. Bobo Langston, *President*	Charlotte	7-8-54	7-8-55
Heman R. Clark, *Secretary-Treasurer*	Fayetteville	7-8-54	7-8-55
Eddy S. Merritt, *Attorney*	Hickory	7-8-54	7-8-55
Fred Hoover, *Expert*	Lenoir	7-8-54	7-8-55
Finance Committee			
Charlie A. Church *	Winston-Salem	7-8-53-54	7-8-54-55
R. Flake Shaw *	Greensboro	7-8-53-54	7-8-54-55
H. W. Calloway, Jr. *	Concord	7-8-53-54	7-8-54-55
Proxy			
James B. Wolfe	Greensboro	7-8-53	7-8-54
T. C. Hoyle, Jr.	Greensboro	7-8-54	7-8-55

ATLANTIC AND NORTH CAROLINA RAILROAD [267]

Name of Appointee	Address	Date Appointed	Date of Expiration
Directors			
Judson H. Blount † *	Greenville	8-5-53-54	8-5-54-55
M. G. Mann † *	Raleigh	8-5-53-54	8-5-54-55
Irvin W. Davis *	Beaufort	8-5-53-54	8-5-54-55
L. B. Jenkins *	Kinston	8-5-53-54	8-5-54-55
Harold Maxwell *	New Bern	8-5-53-54	8-5-54-55
W. R. Taylor *	Goldsboro	8-5-53-54	8-5-54-55
Kenneth R. Smith *	Raleigh	8-5-53-54	8-5-54-55
William W. Dowdy, Sr. *	New Bern	8-5-53-54	8-5-54-55
Officers			
Judson H. Blount, *Chairman* † *	Greenville	8-5-53-54	8-5-54-55
M. G. Mann, *President* † *	Raleigh	8-5-53-54	8-5-54-55

G. Paul LaRoque, *Secretary-Treasurer* *	Kinston	8-5-53-54	8-5-54-55
Frank Gibbs, *Attorney*	Warrenton	8-5-53	8-5-54
J. Melville Broughton, Jr., *Attorney*	Raleigh	8-6-54	8-6-55
Finance Committee			
Harvey Hamilton *	Morehead City	8-5-53-54	8-5-54-55
John F. Rhodes *	New Bern	8-5-53-54	8-5-54-55
Norris C. Reed, Jr. *	New Bern	8-5-53-54	8-5-54-55
Inspector			
Albert R. Bell *	New Bern	8-5-53-54	8-5-54-55
Proxy			
Garland E. Bobbitt † *	Raleigh	8-5-53-54	8-5-54-55

NORTH CAROLINA RECREATION COMMISSION [268]

Charles McCullers †	Kinston	7-23-54	7-1-57
Max A. Parrish †	Gastonia	7-23-54	7-1-58
R. W. Watkins †	Boone	7-23-54	7-1-58

NORTH CAROLINA RECREATION ADVISORY COMMITTEE [269]

Russell M. Grumman, *Chairman* †	Chapel Hill	7-23-54	7-1-55
Miss Augusta Barnett †	Asheville	7-23-54	7-1-55

[267] The Board is composed of twelve directors, eight of whom the Governor appoints annually. *P. L., 1852,* Ch. 136; *P. L., 1858-1859,* Resolution (p. 99); *P. L., 1891,* Ch. 483; *P. L., 1925,* Ch. 157.

[268] The Commission is composed of eleven members, seven of whom are appointed by the Governor, and four of whom are ex officio members as follows: the Governor, the Superintendent of Public Instruction (Charles F. Carroll), the Commissioner of Public Welfare (Dr. Ellen Winston), and the Director of the Department of Conservation and Development (Ben E. Douglas). Initial terms of appointive members vary from one to six years: five members serve terms of one to five years, and two serve terms of six years, with reappointment for terms of four years. Vacancies are filled by the Governor for the duration of unexpired terms. *G. S.,* Sec. 143-207.

[269] The Advisory Committee is composed of thirty members who are appointed for two-year terms. The Governor appoints one member as chairman and fills vacancies for the remainder of unexpired terms. *G. S.,* Sec. 143-210.

Name of Appointee	*Address*	*Date Appointed*	*Date of Expiration*
William J. Heard	Kinston	7-23-54	7-1-55
Mrs. Miles A. Hughey	Raleigh	7-23-54	7-1-55
B. G. Brooks †	Raleigh	7-23-54	7-1-55
Fred Grigg	Butner	7-23-54	7-1-55
Miss Ruth Current †	Raleigh	7-23-54	7-1-55
Q. A. Fetch †	Fontana Village	7-23-54	7-1-55
C. N. Carroll †	Raleigh	7-23-54	7-1-55
Lloyd B. Hathaway †	Winston-Salem	7-23-54	7-1-55
Reverend Harold J. Dudley †	Raleigh	7-23-54	7-1-55
Fred Fletcher †	Raleigh	7-23-54	7-1-55
Mrs. Maurice Honigman †	Gastonia	7-23-54	7-1-55
C. Walton Johnson †	Weaverville	7-23-54	7-1-55
Irvin Holmes	Durham	7-23-54	7-1-55
Wally Mars †	Monroe	7-23-54	7-1-55
Mrs. Chester A. Marsh †	West Jefferson	7-23-54	7-1-55
Ralph Johnson	Gastonia	7-23-54	7-1-55
E. Frank Ruble	Washington	7-23-54	7-1-55
Miss Dorothy Davis	Greensboro	7-23-54	7-1-55
Holt McPherson	High Point	7-23-54	7-1-55
I. E. Ready †	Roanoke Rapids	7-23-54	7-1-55
Bob Wright	Charlotte	7-23-54	7-1-55
Samuel Selden †	Chapel Hill	7-23-54	7-1-55
Miss Alice Suiter	Greensboro	7-23-54	7-1-55
L. J. Perry	Chapel Hill	7-23-54	7-1-55
Quillen Ward †	Rocky Mount	7-23-54	7-1-55

H. C. Hawn	Winston-Salem	7-23-54	7-1-55
Mrs. Joy Kirschner	Boone	7-23-54	7-1-55
William Stronach	High Point	7-23-54	7-1-55

BOARD OF CONTROL FOR SOUTHERN REGIONAL EDUCATION [270]

Charles F. Carroll †	Raleigh	7-28-53	6-30-57

NORTH CAROLINA LOCAL GOVERNMENTAL EMPLOYEES' RETIREMENT SYSTEM [271]

Sam J. Burrow, Jr. [272]	Asheboro	4-29-53	4-5-56
Clyde Gordon [273]	Burlington	4-29-53	4-5-57

---

[270] The Board consists of three members, one of whom is to be chosen from the field of education. Members are to be citizens of this State and are appointed by the Governor who serves ex officio, and continues as a member during his tenure of office. In the initial appointment of members, one member serves for two years, one for three years, and one serves the full term of four years, with succeeding appointments to be made for four years. Vacancies are filled for unexpired terms by appointment of the Governor. *S. L., 1949,* Resolution 26.

[271] The ten members on the board of trustees of the Local Governmental Employees' Retirement System consist of the board of trustees of the Teachers' and State Employees' Retirement System, and two other persons appointed by the Governor. Of the eight members on the board of trustees of the Teachers' and State Employees' Retirement System, six are appointed by the Governor, with the consent of the Senate, for four-year terms, and two serve ex officio as follows: the Superintendent of Public Instruction (Charles F. Carroll), and the State Treasurer (Brandon P. Hodges and after July 20, 1953 Edwin M. Gill). Of the two other persons appointed by the Governor, one must be a full-time executive officer of a city or town participating in the Retirement System, and one must be a full-time officer of the governing body of a county participating in the Retirement System, these to be appointed for a term of two-years each. At the expiration of these terms of office, the appointments are to be for four-year terms. *G. S.,* Sec. 128-28 (2).

[272] Succeeded Arnold Davis.

[273] Succeeded J. M. Byrd.

Name of Appointee	Address	Date Appointed	Date of Expiration
BOARD OF COMMISSIONERS OF THE LAW ENFORCEMENT OFFICERS' BENEFIT AND RETIREMENT FUND [274]			
B. E. Jordan †	Saxapahaw	5-18-53	At pleasure of Governor
W. B. Lentz †	Raleigh	5-18-53	At pleasure of Governor
Robert J. Pleasants †	Raleigh	5-18-53	At pleasure of Governor
C. C. Stoker †	High Point	5-18-53	At pleasure of Governor
BOARD OF TRUSTEES, TEACHERS' AND STATE EMPLOYEES' RETIREMENT SYSTEM [275]			
Sam J. Burrow, Jr. [276]	Asheboro	4-29-53	4-5-56
Clyde Gordon [277]	Burlington	4-29-53	4-5-57
COMMISSIONER OF REVENUE [278]			
Eugene G. Shaw †	Greensboro	6-29-53	1-1-57
RICHMOND COUNTY SPECIAL COURT [279]			
Walter M. Lampley, *Judge*	Rockingham	9-15-54	12-1-54
NORTH CAROLINA RURAL ELECTRIFICATION AUTHORITY [280]			
Cutlar Ballance †	Saint Pauls	6-24-53	6-5-57
George R. Hughes [281]	Pollocksville	6-24-53	6-5-57
Glenn Palmer †	Clyde	6-24-53	6-5-57
Gwyn B. Price, *Chairman* †	Raleigh	6-24-53	6-5-57
NORTH CAROLINA RURAL REHABILITATION CORPORATION [282]			
I. O. Schaub	Raleigh	11-19-53	11-19-54
Fred E. Harris	Bailey	11-19-53	11-19-55
Gaston Small	Elizabeth City	11-19-53	11-19-55

J. J. Hamlin, Jr.	Rutherfordton	11-19-53	11-19-56
Arthur D. Williams	Wilson	11-19-53	11-19-56

Commission on the Revision of the Public School Laws[283]

Fred Folger	Mount Airy	10-29-53
R. L. Harris	Roxboro	10-29-53

---

[274] The Board of Commissioners is composed of seven members, three of whom are ex officio members as follows: the State Auditor (Henry L. Bridges), who is ex officio Chairman, the State Treasurer (Brandon P. Hodges and after July 20, 1953 Edwin M. Gill), and the State Insurance Commissioner (Waldo C. Cheek and after June 6, 1954 Charles F. Gold). The other four members are appointed by the Governor to serve at his pleasure, one of whom shall be a sheriff, one a police officer, one from law enforcement officers employed by the State, and one representing the public at large. *G. S.*, Sec. 143-166.

[275] The Board is composed of eight members, six of whom are appointed by the Governor with the consent of the Senate for four-year terms, and two of whom are ex officio as follows: the Superintendent of Public Instruction (Charles F. Carroll), and the State Treasurer (Brandon P. Hodges after July 20, 1953 Edwin M. Gill), who is ex officio Chairman. One appointee of the Governor must be a member of the teaching profession, one must be an employee of the State Highway and Public Works Commission, and one a State employee. The remaining members must not be of the teaching profession or state employees. Reappointments are made for four-year terms. *G. S.*, Sec. 135-6; *S. L., 1947,* Ch. 259.

[276] Succeeded Arnold Davis, resigned.

[277] Succeeded J. M. Byrd.

[278] The law provides for a Commissioner of Revenue to be appointed by the Governor for a four-year term and until his successor is appointed and qualified. *G. S.*, Sec. 147-87.

[279] The judge of this special court is elected by vote of the people in the same general election as the officers of Richmond County. Any vacancies are filled by appointment of the Governor for the remainder of the unexpired term. In the original 1939 law the Governor appointed the judge for a two-year term. *G. S.*, Sec. 7-407; *P. L., 1941,* Ch. 60; *S. L., 1943,* Ch. 254.

[280] The Board is composed of six members appointed by the Governor for four-year terms. *G. S.*, Sec. 117-1.

[281] Succeeded Mrs. Hubert Boney.

[282] The General Assembly of 1953 changed the membership of the governing board from three to nine. Of these nine members five are appointees of the Governor, and from the five directors first named by the Governor, one is to serve a one-year term, two are to serve two-year terms, and two are to serve three-year terms each. After the initial appointments, terms are for three years each. The remaining four members serve ex officio and are: the Commissioner of Agriculture (L. Y. Ballentine), the Director of the Co-operative Agricultural Extension Service of North Carolina State College (David S. Weaver), the Director of the Division of Vocational Education, State Department of Public Instruction (J. Warren Smith), and the North Carolina State Director, Farmers Home Administration, U. S. Department of Agriculture (Horace J. Isenhour). *G. S.*, Sec. 137-31.3; *S. L., 1953,* Ch. 724.

[283] The Commission is composed of seven members appointed by the Governor, and it is to make recommendations to the next General Assembly. *S. L., 1953,* Res. 42.

Name of Appointee	*Address*	*Date Appointed*	*Date of Expiration*
Fred C. Hobson	Yadkinville	10-29-53	
Charles McCrary	Asheboro	10-29-53	
C. Reid Ross	Fayetteville	10-29-53	
H. J. Truett	Bryson City	10-29-53	
Stacy Weaver	Durham	10-29-53	
NORTH CAROLINA SANATORIUMS FOR THE TREATMENT OF TUBERCULOSIS [284] Sanatorium, Black Mountain, Wilson			
Charles A. Cannon †	Concord	4-29-53	4-29-59
Carl C. Council, *Chairman* †	Durham	4-29-53	4-29-59
Dr. M. A. Pittman [285]	Wilson	4-29-53	4-29-59
E. A. Rasberry †	Snow Hill	4-29-53	4-29-59
SOLICITORS, SUPERIOR COURTS [286]			
Elbert S. Peel [287]	Williamston	10-31-53	11-8-55
John J. Burney, Jr. [288]	Wilmington	12-29-53	11-8-55
Harvey A. Lupton [289]	Winston-Salem	6-1-54	11-8-55
STATE STREAM SANITATION COMMITTEE [290]			
Mrs. Karl Bishopric [291]	Leaksville	10-12-53	7-11-59
J. N. Vann [292]	Ahoskie	10-12-53	7-11-59
TOWN OF SURF CITY [293]			
R. L. Church, Jr., *Mayor*	Surf City and Hampstead	6-23-53	6-30-55
D. N. Lucas †	Surf City and Hampstead	6-23-53	6-30-55
G. C. Mercer †	Surf City and Hampstead	6-23-53	6-30-55

NORTH CAROLINA SYMPHONY SOCIETY, INCORPORATED [294]

J. Spencer Love †	Greensboro	5-8-53	3-10-57
Mrs. J. M. Broughton †	Raleigh	5-8-53	3-10-57

DEPARTMENT OF TAX RESEARCH [295]

James Sloan Currie, *Director* †	Raleigh	5-21-53	At pleasure of Governor

[284] The board of directors is composed of twelve members appointed by the Governor and confirmed by the Senate for terms of six years. The Secretary of the North Carolina State Board of Health (Dr. J. W. R. Norton), is an ex officio member. Vacancies are filled by appointment of the Governor and confirmed by the next succeeding session of the Senate. *G. S.*, Sec. 131-62, 63, 64.

[285] Succeeded L. Lee Gravely.

[286] Solicitors are elected by the qualified voters of the State for a four-year term and hold office until their successors are qualified. Vacancies are filled by appointment of the Governor until the next general election. The Constitution of North Carolina, Article 4, Section 23 and 25; *P. L., 1868-1869*, Ch. 270, Sec. 27-3.

[287] Succeeded George M. Fountain, resigned to become special judge of Superior Court.

[288] Succeeded Clifton L. Moore, resigned to become Superior Court judge.

[289] Succeeded Walter E. Johnston, Jr., who was appointed as resident judge.

[290] In 1951 the General Assembly created this permanent Committee within the State Board of Health, which is composed of eight members, six of whom are appointed by the Governor, and two of whom serve ex officio: the Chief Engineer of the State Board of Health (J. M. Jarrett), and the Chief Engineer of the Water Resources and Engineering Division of the Department of Conservation and Development (W. H. Riley). Of the members initially appointed by the Governor, two serve for two years each, two serve for four years each, and two serve for six years each, with subsequent appointments for six-year terms. The Governor appoints to fill vacancies, such being subject to Senate confirmation. *G. S.*, Sec. 143-213; *S. L., 1945*, Ch. 1010.

[291] Succeeded Mrs. Giles W. Cover.

[292] Succeeded W. P. Saunders, resigned.

[293] In the second week of June 1953, and at that time every two years, a mayor who also serves as a commissioner, and two other commissioners are appointed by the Governor from persons recommended to him as having had the highest number of votes in the general election. Vacancies are filled by appointment of the remaining commissioners for the duration of unexpired terms. *S. L., 1949*, Ch. 512, Sec. 12.

[294] The board of trustees consists of not less than sixteen members, of whom four are named by the Governor for four-year terms, ten are chosen by the North Carolina Symphony Society, and two serve ex officio as follows: the Governor, and the Superintendent of Public Instruction (Charles F. Carroll). Reappointments are for four-year terms. *G. S.*, Sec. 140-6; *S. L., 1943*, Ch. 755; *S. L., 1947*, Ch. 1049.

[295] The law provides that this officer be appointed by, responsible to, and shall serve at the pleasure of the Governor. *G. S.*, Sec. 105-451.

Name of Appointee	Address	Date Appointed	Date of Expiration
STATE EDUCATIONAL RADIO AND TELEVISION COMMISSION [296]			
Irving E. Carlyle, *Chairman*	Winston-Salem	1-22-53	
F. J. Blythe	Charlotte	1-22-53	
Mrs. J. W. Bunn	Raleigh	1-22-53	
L. Y. Ballentine	Raleigh	1-22-53	
Charles F. Carroll	Raleigh	1-22-53	
James H. Clark	Elizabethtown	1-22-53	
Dr. John R. Cunningham	Davidson	1-22-53	
C. McDowell Davis	Wilmington	1-22-53	
John Harden	Greensboro	1-22-53	
Knox Massey	Durham	1-22-53	
Reuben B. Robertson, Sr.	Canton	1-22-53	
William B. Rodman, Jr.	Washington	1-22-53	
NORTH CAROLINA TEXTBOOK COMMISSION [297]			
High School			
Dr. I. E. Ready	Roanoke Rapids	12-16-53	4-1-57
Mrs. Mary P. Brantley	Raleigh	12-16-53	4-1-57
Miss Bertha Cooper †	Elizabeth City	12-16-53	4-1-57
Miss Phebe Emmons †	Washington	12-16-53	4-1-57
C. B. Martin	Robertsonville	12-16-53	4-1-57
O. L. Norment	Asheville	12-16-53	4-1-57
Elementary			
Mrs. Carrie Abbot	Bryson City	12-16-53	4-1-57
Miss Mary Greenlee	Mooresville	12-16-53	4-1-57

Miss Marie Haigwood	Shelby	12-16-53	4-1-57
Miss Cornelia McLauchlin	Lillington	12-16-53	4-1-57
Luther Medlin	Greensboro	12-16-53	4-1-57
Miss Helen D. Wolff	Greenville	12-16-53	4-1-57

THOMASVILLE RECORDER'S COURT [298]

Thomasville

L. R. Hughes, *Judge* [299]	Thomasville	4-1-53	4-1-55
Charles F. Lambeth, Jr., *Solicitor* [300]	Thomasville	4-1-53	4-1-55

NORTH CAROLINA TOBACCO ADVISORY COUNCIL [301]

B. B. Suggs, Jr.	Greenville	12-14-53	6-1-56

---

[296] This Commission was created by the 1953 General Assembly to make recommendations concerning the uses proposed for television facilities for educational and cultural purposes. It consists of twelve members appointed by the Governor who are to report their activities and recommendations to him as soon as practicable. The Governor designates a chairman, and in choosing the total membership endeavors to appoint persons representative of education, industry, agriculture, and the public at large. *S. L., 1953*, Res. 10 and Ch. 1204.

[297] The Commission is composed of twelve members selected by the Governor and the Superintendent of Public Instruction (Charles F. Carroll), for a term of four years, with reappointments for four-year terms. Seven members must be teachers or principals from the elementary grades, and five must be from high schools. The Commission selects a chairman subject to the approval of the Governor and Superintendent. The Governor fills vacancies by appointment for the duration of unexpired terms. *S. L., 1945*, Ch. 707.

[298] The judge and solicitor are appointed by the Governor for two-year terms upon the recommendation of the City of Thomasville. *P. L. L., 1933*, Ch. 245.

[299] Succeeded W. H. Steed.

[300] Succeeded L. R. Hughes.

[301] This Council, promoting the sale and production of tobacco in this State, was recommended by the Department of Agriculture to be set up within its Division of Markets. A bill to authorize this Council was introduced to the 1947 General Assembly, but failed passage; however, the Board of Agriculture continued to sponsor this group as important to agriculture, industry, and economy of the State. Of the nineteen members appointed by the Governor, there are representatives from: the Plant Food Institute, North Carolina and Virginia; the tobacco belt warehouse associations and Burley markets; processing associations; manufacturers; allied tobacco industries; merchant and banker associations; and five members representing the tobacco growers at large. The fourteen ex officio members include: eight representatives from certain agricultural agencies, five from farm organizations in the State, and one from tobacco research, Duke University. The Council selects a chairman, and elects an executive committee of ten from the ex officio members. Appointive members serve two-year terms after the first day of June, following their appointment or until their successors are appointed and qualified, and vacancies are filled by appointment of the Governor as they occur. Ex officio members serve for the duration of the term of their respective offices.

Name of Appointee	*Address*	*Date Appointed*	*Date of Expiration*
	STATE TREASURER [302]		
Edwin M. Gill [303]	Raleigh	7-20-53	Next general election
	NORTH CAROLINA TURNPIKE AUTHORITY [304]		
James A. Hardison	Wadesboro	6-29-53	5-1-57
Forrest Lockey	Aberdeen	6-29-53	5-1-57
M. E. Robinson	Goldsboro	6-29-53	5-1-57
June F. Scarborough	Statesville	6-29-53	5-1-57
J. F. Snipes	Marion	6-29-53	5-1-57
Nello L. Teer, Sr. †	Durham	6-29-53	7-1-57
Edwin L. Jones †	Charlotte	8-20-54	7-1-58
	CAROLINA-VIRGINIA TURNPIKE AUTHORITY [305]		
Wayland Sermons *	Washington and Roper	11-30-53-54	7-1-54-58
Guy H. Lennon	Manteo	11-30-53	7-1-55
John G. Clark	Greenville	11-30-53	7-1-56
	TRYON'S PALACE COMMISSION [306]		
Mrs. O. Max Gardner [307]	Shelby	7-19-54	
	UTILITIES COMMISSION [308]		
Edward H. McMahan †	Brevard	5-14-53	2-1-57
Samuel O. Worthington [309]	Greenville	5-14-53	2-1-57
Stanley Winborne, *Chairman* †	Raleigh	5-14-53	2-1-59

North Carolina Veterans' Commission [310]

S. Amos Maynard †	Greensboro	5-14-53	5-16-58
Staton P. Williams †	Albemarle	8-20-54	5-16-59

---

[302] The office of State Treasurer is elective, but vacancies are filled by appointment of the Governor to serve until the next general election. The Constitution of North Carolina, Article 3, Section 13.

[303] Succeeded Brandon P. Hodges, resigned effective July 20, 1953.

[304] This group consists of ten members, including the Chairman of the State Highway and Public Works Commission (Alexander H. Graham), who serves as an ex officio member, and four members who serve initial terms of from one to four years inclusive, together with five members of the State Highway and Public Works Commission designated and appointed by the Governor, whose terms expire with their respective terms as members of the North Carolina State Highway and Public Works Commission. Reappointments of members are for four years, and vacancies are filled only for unexpired terms. *G. S.*, Sec. 136-89.14; *S. L., 1953*, Ch. 1116.

[305] This group is composed of four members, including the Chairman of the State Highway and Public Works Commission (Alexander H. Graham), who serves ex officio, and three members appointed by the Governor who serve initial terms of one, two, and three years respectively. Reappointments are made for four-year terms, and vacancies are filled by appointment of the Governor for the remainder of unexpired terms. *G. S.*, Sec. 136-89.3; *S. L., 1953*, Ch. 1159.

[306] The Commission consists of twenty-five members appointed by the Governor, and six ex officio members as follows: the Governor, the Attorney General (Harry McMullan), the Director of the Department of Conservation and Development (Ben E. Douglas), the Director of the Department of Archives and History (Dr. Christopher Crittenden), the Mayor of New Bern (Mack L. Lupton), and the Chairman of the Craven County Board of County Commissioners (George W. Ipock). The law does not specify the terms of the appointees. *S. L., 1945*, Ch. 791.

[307] Succeeded Clyde R. Hoey, deceased May 5, 1954.

[308] Five commissioners are appointed by the Governor, with the consent of the Senate, three serving six-year terms and two serving four-year terms. The General Assembly of 1949 increased the membership from three to five commissioners. The two additional commissioners were appointed for terms expiring February 1, 1953, after which time their successors serve terms of four years; successors to the original three members serve six-year terms. The Governor designates one member of the Commission as chairman. *G. S.*, Sec. 62-1, 4.

[309] Succeeded Joshua S. James.

[310] The Commission consists of five members appointed by the Governor, all of whom are veterans, whose terms vary from one to five years. Subsequent appointments are for five years, and vacancies are filled by the Governor for the duration of unexpired terms. *G. S.*, Sec. 165-5; *S. L., 1945*, Ch. 723.

Name of Appointee	*Address*	*Date Appointed*	*Date of Expiration*
NORTH CAROLINA BOARD OF VETERINARY MEDICAL EXAMINERS [311]			
Dr. C. E. Nicks †	Elkin	6-29-53	7-1-58
Dr. C. B. Randall [312]	Kinston	8-20-54	7-1-59
NORTH CAROLINA VOCATIONAL TEXTILE SCHOOL [313] Belmont			
R. S. Dickson [314]	Charlotte	8-7-53	7-1-56
John F. Matheson †	Mooresville	8-7-53	7-1-56
Ben R. Rudisill [315]	Cherryville	8-7-53	7-1-57
R. Grady Rankin [316]	Gastonia	8-7-53	7-1-57
STATE BOARD OF PUBLIC WELFARE [317]			
Irving E. Carlyle †	Winston-Salem	5-5-53	4-1-59
Frank A. Daniels, *Chairman* †	Raleigh	5-5-53	4-1-59
WESTERN CAROLINA COLLEGE [318] Cullowhee			
Allen J. Bell	Hayesville	5-26-53	5-2-55
James J. Harris	Charlotte	5-26-53	5-2-55
W. H. McDonald	Tryon	5-26-53	5-2-55
J. Ramsey Buchanan	Sylva	5-26-53	5-6-57
Hieronymous Bueck	Murphy	5-26-53	5-6-57
Mrs. F. S. Griffin	Robbinsville	5-26-53	5-6-57
Mrs. Robert Russell	Asheville	5-26-53	5-4-59
Frank H. Watson	Spruce Pine	5-26-53	5-4-59

E. J. Whitmire †	Franklin	5-26-53	5-4-59
Charles F. Gold	Rutherfordton	5-26-53	5-1-61
H. A. Helder	Canton	5-26-53	5-1-61
Philip Woollcott	Asheville	5-26-53	5-1-61

NORTH CAROLINA WILDLIFE RESOURCES COMMISSION [319]

James A. Connelly	Morganton	6-12-53	1-27-59
R. Floyd Crouse	Sparta	6-12-53	1-27-59
Charles T. Wilson [320]	Biltmore	6-12-53	1-27-59

[311] The Board is composed of five members of the North Carolina Veterinary Medical Association appointed by the Governor annually for five-year terms and until their successors are appointed and qualified. *G. S.*, Sec. 90-180.

[312] Succeeded Dr. Bruce H. Staton.

[313] The Board of Trustees is composed of six members appointed by the Governor, who serve four-year terms. An ex officio member is the Director of Vocational Education (J. Warren Smith). Reappointments are made for four-year terms, and vacancies are filled by appointment of the Governor for the remainder of unexpired terms. *G. S.*, Sec. 115-255.1; *S. L., 1945,* Ch. 806.

[314] Succeeded C. A. Cannon.

[315] Succeeded J. Chester Johnson.

[316] Succeeded William P. Elliott, Sr.

[317] The Board is composed of seven members appointed by the Governor, one of whom he designates chairman, and at least one member must be a woman. The members serve terms of six years, and any vacancy is filled by appointment of the Governor for the remainder of the unexpired term. *G. S.*, Sec. 108-1; *S. L., 1945,* Ch. 43.

[318] The board of trustees consists of twelve members, after the first Monday in May 1953, who are appointed by the Governor with the consent of the Senate. The General Assembly of 1951 increased the membership from nine to twelve. Terms of the board members are divided as follows: three serve for two years, three serve four years, three serve six years, and three serve for eight years; thereafter appointments are for eight-year terms, and the Governor fills any vacancies on the board for the remainder of the unexpired term. The General Assembly of 1953 amended the law to the effect that the name "Western Carolina Teachers' College" be changed to the present form. *G. S.*, Sec. 116-45, 46; *S. L.*, 1951, Ch. 1167; *S. L., 1953,* Ch. 1282.

[319] This Commission is composed of nine citizens informed on wildlife conservation and restoration problems and appointed by the Governor for terms of six years. Vacancies are filled by appointment of the Governor for the duration of unexpired terms. *G. S.*, Sec. 143-241; *S. L., 1947,* Ch. 263.

[320] Succeeded J. Walter Moore.

Name of Appointee	*Address*	*Date Appointed*	*Date of Expiration*
WINSTON-SALEM TEACHERS' COLLEGE [321]			
Winfield Blackwell, *Chairman* †	Winston-Salem	6-23-53	6-5-57
Rufus S. Hairston †	Winston-Salem	6-23-53	6-5-57
Harmon Linville †	Kernersville	6-23-53	6-5-57
Mrs. Birdie Robinson [322]	Winston-Salem	6-23-53	6-5-57
L. D. Long [323]	Winston-Salem	6-23-53	6-5-57
Clarence Pemberton [324]	Yanceyville	6-23-53	6-5-57
Julian Robertson [325]	Salisbury	6-23-53	6-5-57
John C. Whitaker [326]	Winston-Salem	6-23-53	6-5-57
W. F. Womble [327]	Winston-Salem	6-23-53	6-5-57
WRECK COMMISSIONERS [328]			
A. W. Drinkwater, † *Dist. 1 & 2,* Dare Co.	Manteo	5-24-54	2-21-56
Roy Eubanks, † *Dist. 2,* Carteret Co.	Beaufort	8-13-54	9-1-56
TOWN OF WRIGHTSVILLE BEACH [329]			
Michael C. Brown, *Mayor* [330]	Wrightsville Beach	6-15-53	7-5-55
R. A. Dunlea [331]	Wrightsville Beach	6-15-53	7-5-55
Murdock M. Dunn †	Wrightsville Beach	6-15-53	7-5-55
Richard F. Meier [332]	Wrightsville Beach	6-15-53	7-5-55
E. F. Peschau [333]	Wrightsville Beach	6-15-53	7-5-55
TOWN OF WHITE LAKE [334]			
W. M. Corbett, Jr., *Mayor*	White Lake	6-12-53	7-5-55
Hiram A. Melvin	Charlotte	6-12-53	7-5-55

James R. Nance	Fayetteville	6-12-53	7-5-55
Harry Womble	White Lake	6-12-53	7-5-55
Joe Woodlief	White Lake	6-12-53	7-5-55

---

321 The Board of Trustees is composed of nine members appointed by the Governor and confirmed by the Senate for four-year terms **G. S. Sec. 116-103.**

322 Succeeded Burke Wilson.

323 Succeeded Curtis Todd.

324 Succeeded T. E. Story.

325 Succeeded Clark Brown.

326 Succeeded G. G. Tucker.

327 Succeeded O. Arthur Kirkman.

328 Whenever necessary the Governor appoints wreck commissioners for the various districts in the State's coastal counties, who serve for two-year terms. Each commissioner is to live in the district for which he is appointed. *G. S.*, Sec. 82-2.

329 A mayor and four aldermen are appointed by the Governor from a list of the five candidates with the highest number of votes after the election every two years. The candidate with the highest number of votes is recommended as mayor and the four next highest as aldermen. At the occurrence of a vacancy in the office of mayor or alderman, the remaining aldermen recommend an appointee to the Governor. *S. L., 1951*, Ch. 637.

330 Succeeded Julien K. Taylor.

331 Succeeded Michael C. Brown.

332 Succeeded J. Holmes Davis.

333 Succeeded Dan D. Cameron.

334 The mayor and four commissioners are appointed by the Governor from a list of the five persons who received the highest number of votes in the biennial election. The law recommends that the person with the highest number of votes be appointed mayor and the other four be appointed commissioners. Any vacancies are filled by appointment of the Governor upon the recommendation of the remaining commissioners. *S. L., 1951,* Ch. 511.

Name of Appointee	*Address*	*Date Appointed*	*Date of Expiration*
ZEBULON BAIRD VANCE MEMORIAL COMMISSION [335]			
Dr. Leon H. Feldman	Asheville	10-28-53	10-29-55
Mrs. Lloyd M. Jarrett	Asheville	10-28-53	10-29-55
Hugh G. Mitchell	Statesville	10-28-53	10-29-55
Mrs. William F. Dickens	Enfield	10-28-53	10-29-57
Dr. Frontis W. Johnston	Davidson	10-28-53	10-29-57
Kenneth Tanner	Rutherfordton	10-28-53	10-29-57
Mrs. O. Max Gardner	Shelby	10-28-53	10-29-59
George W. McCoy	Asheville	10-28-53	10-29-59
George M. Stephens	Asheville	10-28-53	10-29-59

[335] This Commission was authorized by the 1953 General Assembly to establish a perpetual memorial at the birthplace and home of Zebulon Baird Vance. It is composed of nineteen members nine of whom are appointed by the Governor, three of whom are appointed by the Board of County Commissioners of Buncombe County, and three appointed by the City Council of Asheville. The remaining four members serve ex officio and are: the Director of the State Department of Archives and History (Dr. Christopher Crittenden), the Superintendent of Public Instruction (Charles F. Carroll), the Director of the Department of Conservation and Development (Ben E. Douglas), and the State Treasurer (Edwin M. Gill). Of the Governor's appointees, three serve six-year terms, three serve four-year terms, and three serve two-year terms; reappointments are made for six-year terms. Vacancies are filled by appointment of the board or authority that made the original appointment, and appointments to fill vacancies are made only for unexpired terms. *S. L., 1953,* Ch. 1234.

APPENDIX I

WILLIAM BRADLEY UMSTEAD
A PERSONAL TRIBUTE

Funeral of Governor Umstead held at Trinity Methodist Church, Durham, November 9, 1954

WILLIAM BRADLEY UMSTEAD

A PERSONAL TRIBUTE[1]

The history books of some future day will record the remarkable story of William Bradley Umstead from Mangum Township in Durham County, North Carolina, who felt the call to the service of his fellow citizens early in his life, and who made great sacrifices to equip himself for the responsibilities which the people of his State would place upon him. It will be a story of matchless dedication, devotion and service.

Beginning back in a home which was founded upon the principles of Christian charity and concern, he came to the altar of Mount Tabor Methodist Church at a very early age and gave his life to Christ. In his own words, this was the greatest single act of his life, and that altar where it happened was the most sacred spot in the world. When he was making his decision to offer himself to the people of North Carolina as their Chief Executive, we went to Mount Tabor. He said to me, "If I can render my finest Christian service to my people in this way, I want to do so. If I cannot, I do not want to run for this office." We knelt together at that sacred altar. It was always to this altar that his mind turned when he had to make decisions of importance.

His great life of unselfish service as teacher, lawyer, statesman, churchman, North Carolina's Chief Executive, devoted husband and loving father can be explained and understood only in the light of what happened a long time ago at Mount Tabor Church, when he met the Master Craftsman of personal service and gave himself to be fashioned by that Master.

William Bradley Umstead was one of North Carolina's greatest statesmen in the noblest tradition. He refused to stoop to win or to get ahead. He put principle above party or personal profit. He would not countenance any compromise of the right, adhering to principle in private and public life which could have hindered his political gains. Asking always first, "what is the right thing to do," then, when he had found what to him was right, he

[1] This tribute by his one-time pastor was delivered at the memorial service held in Trinity Methodist Church, Durham, N. C., on November 9, 1954.

pressed his frail body to the point beyond his limited physical strength to achieve it. He was a timid man by nature, but he always took his stand bravely against friend or foe in defense of fairness and justice and right. He was conscientious in all things, disciplined to attend to every detail, always serious where duty was involved. He would not delegate his duties; they were to him a sacred trust which demanded his personal prayers and attention.

I knew him most intimately in the relationship of minister and parishioner. In the seven years I was his minister, I found him faithful to the best at all times. If he was in the city on Sunday, he was in his church at the time of worship. He planned time in his busy life as a public servant to serve on the boards and committees of his church. He was a teacher of the Julian S. Carr Class. His church honored him by placing him in the most responsible positions. His minister always had access to his wise counsel and friendly encouragement, and found him eager to listen and advise in all matters. To have him as a devout member was a continuing joy. To have him as a warm personal friend was priceless.

A Christian gentleman. North Carolina's first citizen and patriot. A devout churchman. Statesman of the most notable tradition. Devoted husband and loving father. A friend to all.

Though we shall all miss him personally, and those who have the responsibility of guiding the affairs of State will miss his sound judgment and counsel, it is no time to mourn. For one with such high commitment and noble purpose, who faces the greatest odds of life and comes away victorious, whose indomitable spirit persists in expressing itself even in physical weakness, and comes to the end and to the limits of human endurance standing tiptoe in eagerness to carry on, cannot be stopped by the experience called death!

It is our solid faith that not only will his devotion to the right and his fixed purpose to achieve it be an inspiration to all who learn about it, but that this great spirit will go marching on triumphantly down through the centuries.

For us who knew you, dread of death is past! You took life, tiptoe, to the very last; It never lost for you its lovely look; You kept your interest in its thrilling book; To you, Death came, no conqueror, in the end—You merely smiled to greet another friend!

APPENDIX II

EDITORIALS FROM THE PRESS

WILLIAM BRADLEY UMSTEAD [1]

Greater love hath no man than this, that a man lay down his life for his friends.[2]

The flag is at half-staff before the Executive Mansion in Raleigh.

William Bradley Umstead, Governor of North Carolina, reluctantly has laid down his great responsibilities. His people have cause to mourn. He was a dedicated man.

Conscientious, self-exacting, he was the insatiable perfectionist. Chosen by his fellow citizens to direct their government, he accepted his selection as more than a privilege and a challenge. To him it was a sacred public charge and trust.

From boyhood, he exhibited the intense drive that burned him out before, it seems, his time. Not content with the horizons of the tobacco farm in the northern reaches of Durham County which gave him shelter at birth and molded his childhood, he harnessed his beloved horse, "Robbie," and sold sand and gravel to secure his education.

Schoolteacher, soldier, lawyer, solicitor, Congressman, Senator; an outward calm and an innate reserve cloaked, except from those close to him, the glowing inner fires which elevated him gradually above his more complacent fellows. He obeyed a personal passion to serve well wherever assigned, to fulfill the utmost potential of any opportunity presented to him, to prove a credit to his family, his community, his State, his country, and his friends.

As a Congressman for a relatively brief period, he impressed and won the high regard and admiration of his colleagues by his diligence, his insight and his thoroughness. He carried that same questing and determined spirit into the Governor's office.

His firmness of conviction and his high objectives led him, perhaps, to take too much upon himself. In his anxiety for care-

[1] *The Durham Sun,* November 8, 1954.

[2] John 15: 13.

ful attention to detail he found it difficult to delegate authority. If that was a fault, it may be ascribed to his scrupulous sense, in his natural humility, of duty.

Governor Umstead took office in a trying time in North Carolina's history. He carried with him a fervor for a sound, stable and prosperous Commonwealth. Stricken at the very inception of his crusade, he was impatient of the interruption, resolute in his determination to carry on at any cost—and at any cost it was.

Thus is his State reminded of the personal sacrifice which is the price of true public service; of the obligation the citizenry owes to those who are willing to devote their energies, their abilities and their very lives to the interests of society. North Carolina grieves today aware of its debt to his service and his memory.

THE STATE LOSES A FIRST CITIZEN [1]

The death of Governor William B. Umstead is an unfortunate climax to the personal tragedy of a dedicated man.

He loved his State and cherished what he looked upon as his official obligation, counting duty more sacred than life itself. In a sense then, death relieves Bill Umstead of a burden he would not have cast aside of his own choice. But death robs North Carolina of a consecrated servant and citizen.

When Governor Umstead was seized by a serious heart ailment shortly after his inauguration, many of his friends urged him to delegate most of the normal duties of the Chief Executive to other and stronger hands. It seemed a natural safeguard, essential to the preservation of life. A man less imbued with devotion to mission would have followed the advice with no twinge of conscience or any likely damage to his public esteem.

But Bill Umstead was not a man to abdicate or even to delegate. The destiny of the State became his own personal concern and he guided it from a hospital bed or from the Governor's Mansion with a careful, considered touch.

---

[1] *The Charlotte Observer,* November 8, 1954.

Portrait of Governor William B. Umstead. A gift of the Class of 1916 of the University of North Carolina presented to the State, February 19, 1957. Ceremonies were held in the House of Representatives; the presentation address was by Judge Francis O. Clarkson and acceptance by Governor Luther H. Hodges.

It would be inaccurate to reserve Mr. Umstead a place as the greatest governor of all time or even as one of the greatest that North Carolina has produced. He lacked the flair and projective personality of a public idol or the boldness and daring of a colorful leader. He walked in humility with a certain quiet reserve that was often mistaken for coldness; his concern for minor details sometimes seemed to obscure his broader vision.

Nonetheless, the two years of Bill Umstead's tenure have been years of progress in North Carolina—hesitant progress in some areas; cautious progress in many respects; but sound progress toward a better economy and a balanced program of agriculture and industry, commerce and conservation.

Bill Umstead lived for North Carolina. His death is tragic testimony to his dedication.

WILLIAM BRADLEY UMSTEAD [1]

With the death of William Bradley Umstead in Watts Hospital at Durham Sunday, North Carolina saw the passing of a governor who gave his life in the "line of duty" while serving the people just as well as any Tar Heel soldier who has died amidst the muck and flame of some far-flung battlefield.

There is no attempt here to evaluate the success of the administration of Governor Umstead, the merits of any state-wide programs that he might have had in mind or to declare that he was one of the best or worst governors ever to serve on Capitol Hill. Unfortunately and tragically the Umstead program—his ambitions for a better state—would have been launched in full at the approaching session of the state Legislature. What this program was and what grandiose plans this man with such a burning desire to serve had for his people now will never be known. And the State will be the loser in that much that William Umstead had in mind for the welfare and good of his people passed with his mortality at Durham Sunday.

---

[1] *The Raleigh Times,* November 8, 1954.

Almost from the very moment of his inauguration ill health and disappointment had plagued William Umstead, preventing the realization of his ambitions as Governor of North Carolina. He was a sick man when he stood on Fayetteville Street with the retiring Governor W. Kerr Scott and bravely waved his silk hat to the military parade that was marching in honor of his ascension to the State's highest post. Throughout his term of office he remained a sick man. For a good part of the time he guided the destinies of the State as best he could from a sick bed. But Umstead was a gallant and brave man. He would not give up. Had he resigned or taken things easier he might be alive today. It is probably unfortunate but certainly commendable that this was not the stuff of which Governor Umstead was made. He was elected Governor by the people of the State and he intended to serve in that capacity as long as he had breath. Mr. Umstead felt that the responsibility of administration and statesmanship was his. Delegating authority to lesser lights was certainly not one of his weaknesses.

In World War I Bill Umstead was a machine gunner and he served his Nation faithfully and at the risk of his life. His service as Governor was just as faithful and gallant and his determination to serve and do his duty this time cost him his life.

Flags will now fly at half-staff on state buildings and all citizens, humble and great alike, will salute the memory of this man whose failing health in his greatest hour of triumph and opportunity brought only futility and finally death.

Governors will come and governors will go but North Carolina will never have another man with a greater desire to serve his homeland than this former soldier, Senator, and lawyer from Durham County who was stricken down by fate at the greatest hour of his triumph.

North Carolina will do well to remember and repeat long and often the name of William Bradley Umstead. Honest public service, personal gallantry in the face of adversity and consideration for the common man are commodities that are becoming rarer and rarer with the passing of the years.

WILLIAM B. UMSTEAD[1]

Death came to William B. Umstead, North Carolina's Governor, Sunday morning after the ailing executive had put up a gallant fight. His passing came as a shock to all Tar Heels, even though word from his bedside had indicated that his condition was grave. He had won an enviable and unique spot in the hearts of his fellow citizens through his many years of devoted public service.

Governor Umstead, who was born in Durham County, took to politics early and worked his way up from prosecuting attorney in the Durham Recorder's Court to the United States Congress within a few years. He later served as U. S. Senator and in 1952 won the nomination of his party and election as Governor of North Carolina—truly in the American tradition.

In making this climb, he made many friends and in contrast to some, he created, relatively speaking, few enemies. His ability to shun personalities while fighting for principles dear to his heart won him a host of followers without alienating those who disagreed with him.

Although his health has been poor since he assumed office early in 1953, he stubbornly and determinedly drove himself on in an effort to keep faith with those who elected him to the highest office in the State. He died fighting on the front line for North Carolina, and deserves the recognition due a hero. He realized many vital problems coming before the General Assembly, and while the Constitution permitted him a way out—he could have stepped down and temporarily turned the reins of government over to Luther H. Hodges, Lieutenant Governor—he rejected the thought. He was the man chosen by his fellow Tar Heels to do the job, and to relinquish the post while there was breath in his body was as unthinkable as it would be for a soldier at the front to quit under fire until relieved. While some may question his judgment in this respect, none can doubt his sincerity and devotion.

The Governor was well known and loved in this community. His top project for the State—more industries and better schools—

[1] *Hickory Daily Record,* November 8, 1954.

were those dear to our citizens. They and the Governor talked and thought along the same lines. Governor Umstead was determined that North Carolina was to get new industries, and when the history of today is written, his role in putting the State further in the vanguard of progress will be recognized.

His ability to pick able men has been demonstrated several times during his brief tenancy in the Executive Mansion as death has struck hard among the top officials of his administration. He named two Senators, Alton B. Lennon and Sam J. Ervin, Jr., members to the State Supreme Court, and to top administrative posts in the state government.

The State is fortunate in having Luther H. Hodges as Lieutenant Governor. He, probably, is as well known in the State today as any state official, and his intimate acquaintance with members of the General Assembly will serve North Carolina well during the next two years. Our attitude toward Mr. Hodges has shifted during the past several years from one of skepticism when he first revealed his retirement from business life and determination to enter public service by way of the ballot. He surprised us by his overwhelming victory in the 1952 campaign for the Lieutenant Governorship, and his conduct since then has impressed us most favorably.

The death of Governor William B. Umstead is a loss to the State. The death of "Bill" Umstead is a blow to all his friends—and they are legion.

A DEVOTED PUBLIC SERVANT [1]

For the first time in sixty years the State of North Carolina today mourns a Chief Executive who died in office. The passing Sunday of Governor William B. Umstead at a hospital in his home City of Durham came as a surprise and shock to the whole State, although the seriousness of an illness which had twice hospitalized him in a single month was known to many close friends and associates and feared by the people generally.

[1] *The Dispatch* (Henderson), November 8, 1954.

Governor Umstead was deeply and sincerely grateful for the confidence of the citizens who entrusted him with the heavy responsibilities of high office, and his devotion and fidelity to that trust contributed much to the breakdown of his health and incapacitated him to the point of complete exhaustion. Having been discharged from the hospital only two weeks ago, he returned to Raleigh and undertook again to pick up the burdens which previously had proved too much for him to carry. Last Thursday he was taken back to the hospital and lived only three days.

The Governor belonged to that select company of North Carolinians who carried the rare distinction of having served as a legislator, a member of the national House of Representatives, as a United States Senator and then as Governor. Very few citizens have been so singularly honored in their careers across the years. Except for his appointment to the United States Senate, Mr. Umstead had been elected to all these offices.

He was a hard worker at every task to which he set his hands. To each he gave every ounce of energy he possessed, and in all instances rendered efficient service to his State. In his younger years he was solicitor of his judicial district, giving that up to run for Congress. In private life he was one of the outstanding attorneys of North Carolina and member of a leading Durham law firm.

North Carolina respected William B. Umstead for the high type of citizen that he was. He loved his State and its people and literally gave himself in their service. He burned out the last flicker of strength he possessed in an effort to discharge faithfully to the end of his days the heavy responsibilities of the governorship. It is safe to assume that no one regretted more than he his inability to accept the role of leadership which normally would have been his during the first legislature of his term as Governor and in months that followed. His concern over state finances at this time and problems that will confront the 1955 General Assembly weighed heavily upon him in recent days as he taxed his strength in sitting with the Budget Commission in devising a fiscal program for the coming biennium.

The Governor never completely overcame the frailties that resulted from the heart attack he suffered two days after his inauguration in January of last year. Even that was brought on in part by his studious attentiveness to his duties as a public servant.

A State which mourns its Chief Executive today will remember him for his ability, his extreme loyalty and fidelity and his intensive devotion to the welfare of the people he tried to serve to the utmost of his capacity. He will take rank as a statesman who possessed full knowledge of the requirements of high office and who sought, despite the limitations of his health, to meet all demands it imposed.

WILLIAM B. UMSTEAD [1]

With the death of Governor William Bradley Umstead, the State of North Carolina loses a man of the finest character and ability. He was an excellent lawyer, a politician in the best sense of the word, a patriot, an indefatigable worker, and a statesman. But all his accomplishments were solidly based on that strength of character out of which came his goodness, justice and wisdom.

He was a man whom conservatives looked on as a liberal and whom liberals looked on as a conservative; in truth those who knew him at all knew that he would invariably give careful consideration to any problem and then do exactly what he believed was right.

He was unusually reticent, and even shy for a man of his experience in public life, but those who knew him intimately found in him a warmth of friendship and a keenness of humor that always lay beneath the surface. His family and most of his friends called him "William"; a few intimates called him "Bill."

Former Governor R. Gregg Cherry, one of those who knew him best, wrote of him in the *State* magazine shortly after his election:

> In my mind the things that characterize William Umstead are the following descriptive words: Honest, sincere, capable, earnest, conscientious, modest, hard-working, fair, clean, serious, energetic—and above all other things a man of impeccable character.
>
> To merit such adjectives a man would have to be a man among men. Our next governor is just that. Throughout the recent campaign he demonstrated to his closest advisors that he was a great deal more interested in fighting fair than in winning. Suggestions from some quarters that he "rough it up"

[1] *Greensboro Daily News*, November 8, 1954.

were met with the firm answer that he had rather not be Governor of North Carolina than to gain votes in any manner that might be described as ungentlemanly.

Born on his father's farm in Durham Couty in 1895, William Umstead went to the University of North Carolina where he became an outstanding debater, speaker and student leader. His career has no blemish on it. On graduating he taught school in Kinston for a year, and then entered the U. S. Army in 1917 from an officers training camp, serving as first lieutenant in a machine gun company on the Western Front. Returning home after the war he studied law at Duke University, and then entered on a political career which took him from the post of solicitor in Superior Court to that of Representative in Congress where he earned an enviable reputation for ability and fairness. Resigning, he practiced law in Durham for five years and then re-entered politics, on his appointment by Governor Cherry to the United States Senate to succeed the late Senator J. William Bailey. Running for re-election he sustained his first and only defeat for public office, at the hands of former Governor J. Melville Broughton. In 1952 he was elected Governor of North Carolina and served with great ability, courage, discretion, and devotion to his high office beyond the call of duty until his untimely death. His conscientiousness and high conception of patriotism would not allow him to spare himself. He died in the service of his State to which he had given so much of his life, thought, and work.

Our sympathy goes out to his family and to those who knew him intimately. The State and people of North Carolina have suffered a heavy loss; nevertheless his example will not be lost but will elevate the life of his State for many years to come.

WILLIAM B. UMSTEAD [1]

William B. Umstead literally gave his life in the service of the people of North Carolina. Stricken by a heart attack just two days after his inauguration, he could have stepped down from the office he had just assumed. Some of his friends and advisers gave

[1] *Winston-Salem Journal,* November 8, 1954.

him that counsel. But he stuck it out to the end that came yesterday morning.

Governor Umstead served the State well, both before and after he became its Chief Executive. Although he was handicapped by poor health throughout his months in office as Governor, the accomplishments of his administration stand up well by comparison with those of his predecessors. In fact, he bore unusually heavy responsibilities and discharged them well.

In addition to the customary duties of administration and legislative leadership, Governor Umstead was called upon to fill a large number of high offices, vacated by death or resignation. Included in the list are two United States senators, a State Treasurer, a State Commissioner of Labor, a Chief Justice and two Associate Justices of the State Supreme Court.

In his Inaugural Address Governor Umstead set out his plans and hopes for a "better tomorrow" for North Carolina. Toward that end he recommended large bond issues for school construction and mental hospitals. These bond issues won the approval of the General Assembly and of the voters of the State. He urged a program to attract new industry to North Carolina; under the leadership of Robert M. Hanes of Winston-Salem, the Department of Conservation and Development has made important strides in that direction. He advocated reorganization of a number of state commissions and agencies, and the Legislature gave him the authority he sought.

The Supreme Court handed down its opinion in the public school segregation cases during Governor Umstead's administration. Under his wise guidance, North Carolina has followed a course which has attracted national attention and praise.

Some of the goals which the Governor had set for himself he had been unable to achieve so early in his term. He had proposed reorganization of the parole system, and just last week the people of the State approved a constitutional amendment to make this reform possible. He favored separation of the prison system from the Highway Commission. And he saw the necessity of giving North Carolina a modern highway system. These were some of the problems which Governor Umstead hoped to work out with the 1955 General Assembly.

The forthcoming session of the Legislature promises to be one of the most critical of recent years. The most serious problem with which it must deal is finances. State revenues are contracting, while the needs of state agencies are, if anything, expanding. The Governor had been greatly concerned about this dilemma and had been working closely with his Advisory Budget Commission on it. The next Legislature, too, may have to deal with the school segregation problem.

Such were the problems weighing on the Governor's mind and conscience at the time of his death. Who can say that they did not prove too great a strain for a man in his frail health and thus brought about, or hastened, his death? The Governor was aware of the hazard he faced, but he remained a steadfast servant of the people of his State to the very end.

WILLIAM UMSTEAD, AN ABLE GOVERNOR[1]

North Carolina lost an able, dedicated and valuable statesman and this southeastern section of the State lost a great friend and champion in the death yesterday of Governor William B. Umstead.

Mr. Umstead, who had carried out many of his progressive programs despite the hardships of a prolonged illness after he suffered a heart attack a few days following his inauguration in January, 1953, died suddenly in a Durham hospital. Even in his final battle, the Governor displayed his determination and great personal will by rallying enough to talk to members of his family only a few minutes before he died.

His death adds yet another Tar Heel statesman to the honor roll of those who died in the service of their State in recent years. The Governor, who had served in the Senate after the death of Senator Josiah W. Bailey, had appointed two senators, Alton A. Lennon and Sam J. Ervin, to complete the unexpired terms of men who died in office, Willis Smith and Clyde R. Hoey.

The accomplishments of Governor Umstead should long be remembered, not only for their benefits to the State and its citi-

[1] *The Wilmington News,* November 8, 1954.

zens, but for the personal sacrifices of the State's Chief Executive to carry on even a reduced work schedule after being weakened by a serious heart ailment.

Mr. Umstead truthfully died in the service of North Carolina. His condition became serious while attending a meeting of the Advisory Budget Commission last Thursday and he entered the hospital the same day. But when he contracted bronchial pneumonia, it was too much even for such a man as the fifty-nine year old Governor.

His twenty-two month term in office was marked by a quiet, determined approach to vital problems. He had more than the normal number of problems and even with the limitations imposed by his failing health he sought the reasonable and correct answers to such far-reaching items as the Supreme Court's anti-segregation ruling, declining state revenue which threatened to alter the entire program of state service, and two of the worst disasters ever to strike the State, last summer's drought and the devastation of Hurricane Hazel.

Governor Umstead's interest in the progress and expansion of North Carolina was evident in his decision to serve as the chairman of the Conservation and Development Board. In his plan to bolster the state economy, Mr. Umstead looked on the Coastal section as a region with vast undeveloped potentials. He was vitally interested in the advancement of such things as maritime economy and was seriously concerned with the need to use, and to protect, water resources.

The Governor all Tar Heels are mourning today did a lot for his State; he would have done even more if his activities had not been limited by his health. He could have resigned due to his heart condition, but the man who had served his State so long and well as Congressman, Senator and finally Governor, was a man who placed a lot of importance on duty and convictions.

He was working on numerous proposals to be submitted to the next General Assembly to answer current problems and to prevent future ones. By giving these ideas the consideration they deserve, the new Governor, former Lieutenant Governor Luther H. Hodges, and the Legislature will be honoring a great Tar Heel.

GOVERNOR UMSTEAD[1]

William Bradley Umstead, the first Governor of North Carolina to die in office in sixty-three years, found a frail body unable to meet the demands of an inexorable conscience. For him all decisions were difficult and the delegation of authority almost impossible.

Most governors have found their tenure in the State's highest office a period of climax and fruition. William Umstead experienced little but frustration as Governor. His natural tendency to worry was augmented by bad health and a series of problems which would have taxed a healthy and carefree governor. For Governor Umstead those problems meant loss of sleep and an almost total absence of relaxation and recreation.

William Umstead was not always a frustrated man or a sick one. He had a personality which attracted people and a capacity for leadership which brought him early recognition as a public official. He enjoyed public service in his county, district and State, and above all, in Congress. Indeed, although he subsequently held two higher offices, Mr. Umstead's three terms in Congress constituted the high point of his career, both in public service and personal gratification.

Few members of Congress have ever attained as high standing in Congress in so short a time. When he retired from Congress voluntarily in 1938 for the private practice of law, it was inevitable that he should return to politics both because of his own inclinations and the demands of his friends. After service as campaign manager for Governor Cherry in the primary and as Democratic State Chairman in the campaign of 1944, he resigned as Chairman planning to run for Governor himself four years later.

Instead when Governor Cherry offered him the Senate vacancy created by the death of Josiah W. Bailey, he accepted that post. However, he did not remain in the Senate long enough to rise to a position comparable to that he had held in the House and, from the day he took office, he had to divide his time between his duties and his candidacy to succeed himself.

---

[1] *The News and Observer* (Raleigh), November 8, 1954.

The first great frustration in William Umstead's life came in his defeat for the Senate in 1948 by the late J. Melville Broughton. It was the first and last defeat William Umstead ever experienced as a candidate and he never fully recovered from his disappointment.

Senator Broughton died a few months after his election and Umstead was again advised both to run for the Senate and to wait two years and run for Governor. With a serious throat ailment playing an important part in the decision, Mr. Umstead decided to take the latter course.

He was nominated for Governor only after a more hotly contested campaign than had been anticipated generally and entered office in a weakened physical condition. The day after he became Governor he sustained a heart attack.

Although forced to spend much of the 1953 legislative session in a hospital and the rest in semi-seclusion at the Governor's Mansion, Governor Umstead got the bulk of his legislative program, including bond issues for roads and mental institutions, through the General Assembly.

His worries increased instead of decreasing after the General Assembly adjourned. His legislative program included reorganization of many state agencies and he had more appointments to make than any other governor. He spent much time and thought in filling all of them, especially the two appointments he made to the United States Senate.

The prospects for the 1955 General Assembly were even more fearsome. When Umstead died he had not yet determined fully what new taxes he would recommend to meet declining revenues and increased demands of a larger school population. He was also looking forward anxiously to problems created by the decision of the Supreme Court of the United States to outlaw segregation in the public schools. His task as Governor was unfulfilled.

During his twenty-two months as Governor and the long years in other offices, William B. Umstead served his State conscientiously and ably, never counting the cost of that service in terms of personal convenience or comfort. The State could ask no more of any man. Governor Umstead gave such service to his last breath.

THE GOVERNOR[1]

William B. Umstead served his State intelligently and vigorously. He served it wisely—but too well.

Within three days after taking the oath of office of governor in 1953, Bill Umstead had become to all intents a crippled man. He never really overcame the wrenching post-inauguration heart attack that might better have slowed him down or, better still for his life's sake, caused him to resign after a suitable interval.

But Governor Umstead would not shirk his duty or alter his personal conception of it. He was resolved to serve as Governor —to serve fully. For this was the climax to a splendid career in the House, the Senate, and the most responsible councils of his State. And it killed him.

Only last Thursday he was asked, after a short but strenuous and nagging session of the Advisory Budget Commission over tax matters, "whether you plan to stick with the high legislative problems ahead?" The Governor snapped his lips. "Yes, sir," he said emphatically.

The Umstead administration cannot be assayed in the short term because of the closeness of tragedy. In the long term it will need comparative analysis: when we may say what is to happen, for instance, with the rest of the Umstead program.

Mr. Umstead was in office only a little more than twenty-two months. His death has no precedents since the death of Governor Daniel G. Fowle in 1891, Fowle being succeeded by the capable Lieutenant Governor Thomas M. Holt. Back of this was the death of Governor John W. Ellis in 1861 as war boiled across the Southern states.

During his twenty-two months, however, Governor Umstead kept North Carolina on its progressive course of half a century. Under gubernatorial guidance the 1953 General Assembly put through bond issues for schools and for permanent improvements of educational and mental institutions, and increased the appropriation for public schools. Mr. Umstead revised the Highway Department and greatly strengthened the conservation and development program through his own active participation in

[1] *The Asheville Citizen,* November 8, 1954.

soliciting new industry. He was on his way to being a "conservation Governor." Many of his appointments were sound and considered. A staunch Democrat and middle-of-the-roader, he bucked up against problems in the last months of his life that must have hastened his untimely death.

These problems that furrowed the brow of a dedicated man pass to Lieutenant Governor Luther H. Hodges. North Carolina will miss Bill Umstead. It would miss him more were it not for the fact that Luther H. Hodges, a tyro in politics, came out of nowhere in 1952 to win the Lieutenant Governorship handily against the lobbyists and serve the No. 2 role with consummate distinction.

The problems, the burdens, that must weigh down Governor-designate Hodges are ponderous. Even at his death Bill Umstead was reconciled to the unpopular prospect of some sort of tax adjustment upward in 1955 if the schools were to be preserved. He had wrestled, and with distinctive dignity, with the hard-grappling matter of public school desegregation, and had helped North Carolina keep its head. The weight is now on Luther Hodges, a happy refugee from the business world free to offer his talents undivided to the governing of his State. The offer now will be accepted in a fullness he never suspected, and in its sorrow North Carolina must surely come to count itself fortunate that an Umstead was backed up by a Hodges.

UMSTEAD: DEATH TAKES A STATESMAN AT CAREER'S CLIMAX [1]

Governor William B. Umstead's record of service to his State and Nation speaks for itself. In view of this record, it goes without saying that North Carolina suffered a grievous loss when death took its Chief Executive Sunday.

Umstead's death came as no surprise to those who had seen him carry on his duties meticulously despite a serious heart attack which struck him shortly after his inauguration in 1953 and left him weakened in body but still strong in spirit. It is quite possible

[1] *The Fayetteville Observer,* November 8, 1954.

that Umstead, too, realized that his days were numbered. But if so, he refused to allow the hovering shadow of death to deflect his mighty effort to meet and solve the problems confronting the State.

Our Governor's death, coming as it did at the halfway mark in his career as Chief Executive, was not only a loss for the people he served but was something of a personal tragedy for the man himself.

Umstead faced tremendous problems concerning the State's tax structure relative to a readjustment of lowered state revenues and necessary expenditures. He faced the task of maintaining adequate schools despite these lowered revenues and the delicate situation caused by the U. S. Supreme Court's desegregation decision. His determination to meet these problems at any cost to his health was evidenced less than a week ago when he left a hospital bed to plunge into fatiguing discussions with the Advisory Budget Commission.

A governor's true mettle is tested, not only when the Ship of State sails on placid waters, but when dangerous currents are felt which call for a firm hand on the wheel. As the shadows slanted on his career of public service, Umstead exhibited a courageous will to guide his people and overcome obstacles which loomed in the course ahead. But death, with its grim impartiality between the high and the lowly, cut short a notable career just as it reached its climax.

In a sense, it might be said that Umstead "died with his boots on." He did not possess a flair for the dramatic or the spectacular, but his courageous devotion to duty and his intense concern for the welfare of his State now looms as a glowing example for Lieutenant Governor Luther H. Hodges, who will assume the governorship.

APPENDIX III

ADDRESS DELIVERED AT THE JOINT SESSION OF THE GENERAL ASSEMBLY HONORING THE MEMORY OF GOVERNOR UMSTEAD

WILLIAM B. UMSTEAD—THE MAN [1]

By R. Percy Reade

RALEIGH

March 15, 1955

Your Excellency, Mr. President, Mr. Speaker, Mr. Chief Justice, and Associate Justices of the Supreme Court, Members of the Council of State, Members of the General Assembly, Ladies and Gentlemen:

We have assembled here tonight to pay tribute to the memory of a fallen Chief, who succumbed in a struggle with the Grim Reaper while undertaking to secure for his beloved State "a better tomorrow." It is fitting that the Members of this General Assembly, many of whom have heretofore been closely allied with him and who gave him unstinted support in carrying out his program, should pause in your deliberations to sponsor these exercises.

While I am deeply sensible of my inability to command language to portray adequately his fine qualities and his many contributions to the State and Nation, I deeply appreciate the privilege you have afforded me to pay feeble tribute to a great American, one of North Carolina's favorite sons, who for many years was my devoted and understanding friend.

William Bradley Umstead was born on the 13th day of May, 1895, on a farm in Mangum Township in Durham County. He was fortunate in his parents. His mother, Lulie Lunsford Umstead, was the daughter of a prosperous farmer in Mangum Township and was educated in private and public schools in Durham County and at Greensboro Female College. She was a school teacher, church organist, and a civic and religious leader in her community. His father, John W. Umstead, was a Confederate soldier, a

---

This address was delivered in the House of Representatives on March 15, 1955 where a joint session of the Senate and House was held in response to a resolution passed January 7, 1955. The joint session honored the memory of Governor Umstead. The program consisted of the Invocation by Reverend Charles S. Hubbard, pastor of the Chapel Hill Methodist Church, a brief address by Governor Luther H. Hodges, the address of R. Percy Reade, Governor Umstead's former law partner, and the Benediction by Dr. Howard P. Powell, pastor of the Edenton Street Methodist Church, Raleigh, North Carolina.

successful farmer, a legislator, and was likewise a civic and religious leader in the community. For more than twenty years he was a member of the Board of Education of Durham County, most of which time he served as its chairman. Both he and his wife contributed greatly to the religious, cultural, and educational life of their section of the county.

The atmosphere of their home was conducive to right living and high thinking.

Young Umstead spent his early childhood on a farm and performed all of the duties incident to the life of the average country boy. He owned his own horse which he had raised from a colt. She later played a prominent role in his career and as a reward for her faithful service, was kept by him until she died at the ripe old age of thirty-three years, long after her young master had left the farm and had assumed responsible and important public duties.

After completing the ninth grade at Mangum School, William attended high school in the City of Durham, after which he entered the University of North Carolina. In the summer months he raised tobacco to defray his expenses for the succeeding year. Weather conditions were so unfavorable in the spring of his junior year, he was unable to have a crop planted that summer. After reaching home and having no crop, he immediately sought and obtained employment at a sawmill. After working there for a few days, he entered into a contract with a bridge builder to furnish the sand needed in the construction of a bridge over Flat River near his home. In the performance of this task, his horse, Robbie, stood him in good stead. By the time college opened, his contract with the bridge builder had been performed and he returned to Chapel Hill that fall and was graduated with his class in June, 1916.

While a student at the University he became an outstanding debator and student leader. He participated in intercollegiate debates and upon graduation won the coveted Mangum Medal, a prize awarded for the best oration delivered by a member of the graduating class.

Four years as a student at Chapel Hill broadened his vision and stimulated and encouraged in him a desire and determination to live a dedicated life. Passing years never diminished his love for his Alma Mater or his devotion to the memory of helpful, understanding professors who pointed the way in the search for Truth.

He loved the University of North Carolina with a passion and was never happier than when in its service. In later years, in recognition of his interest in it, he was elected president of the Alumni Association of the University of North Carolina; and in 1945 was elected a member of the Board of Trustees of the Consolidated University of North Carolina; and when elected Governor he became ex officio chairman of the Board of Trustees.

He is recognized by the University as one of the brightest jewels in the crown placed upon it by its many distinguished and illustrious sons and daughters.

The fall after his graduation he taught school in Kinston, North Carolina, until our entry into World War I, when he responded to the call to arms and entered the First Officers Training Camp at Fort Oglethorpe, Georgia, where he was commissioned a second lieutenant. He was assigned to the 317th Machine Gun Battalion, a part of the 81st or "Wild Cat" Division, and served overseas. He was separated from the service in March, 1919.

After his discharge from the army he studied law at Trinity College (now Duke University) under Dean S. F. Mordecai, and was licensed to practice law by the Supreme Court in August, 1920. In July 1921, he began to practice in Durham and soon took high place with the leaders in the profession.

In 1922, he made his first entry into politics. In the spring of that year he and two other young lawyers engaged in a spirited contest for the nomination of prosecuting attorney of the Durham County Recorder's Court. Umstead was an easy winner and was elected that fall and again in 1924. In his bid for public office he early demonstrated his popularity with the voters of Durham County.

So well did he perform the duties of the office of prosecuting attorney that when he sought the nomination for solicitor of the Tenth Judicial District, the voters rewarded him by nominating and electing him to a new position of trust and responsibility. He brought to the office of solicitor rare ability. He was skillful and adroit in the examination of witnesses and in his argument before the jury he was forceful and convincing. He was loved and respected by the judges, and was popular with court officials and jurors, and his brethren of the Bar had implicit confidence in every word he said.

He was happily married to Miss Merle Davis of Rutherfordton, North Carolina, on the 5th day of September, 1929. This union was blessed with a beautiful daughter, Merle Bradley, who from her birth was an ever-increasing source of pleasure and inspiration to her parents.

In 1932, Umstead was elected to the House of Representatives from the Sixth Congressional District. He soon took high rank in Congress. He was a tireless and indefatigable worker. No detail of his office, however insignificant, escaped his individual attention. He was vitally interested in legislation as it affected the A. A. A., Farm Home Administration, Rural Electrification, and Soil Conservation.

He succeeded in obtaining appropriations for greatly enlarging the facilities at the Tobacco Experiment Station at Oxford, North Carolina, for the study of tobacco diseases. As a direct result of the studies made at the Experiment Station at Oxford, a new variety of wilt-resisting tobacco has been developed, which has resulted in restoring millions of dollars in value to the farms infected with tobacco wilt.

Probably the most conspicuous and outstanding service rendered by him while in Congress was as chairman of the Subcommittee on Appropriations for the Navy Department. In 1936, after the bill providing for appropriations for the Navy had been prepared and introduced, Glover H. Carey, Congressman from Kentucky, who was then chairman of the Subcommittee, died. Within two days thereafter Umstead was asked to handle the bill on the floor of the House. He immediately familiarized himself with the intricate and involved provisions of the bill and secured its passage. For two succeeding terms he served as chairman of the Subcommittee on Appropriations for the Navy, had charge of the preparation and introduction of bills, and led the fight on the floor of the House for their passage.

After serving in Congress for six years he voluntarily retired from public life and returned to Durham, where he again engaged in the practice of law.

In the spring of 1944 former Governor R. Gregg Cherry persuaded him to manage his campaign for Governor. In the primary, Cherry was nominated and Umstead then was asked to accept the Chairmanship of the State Democratic Executive Committee, which position he held until his resignation in November, 1946.

When Senator Josiah William Bailey died in December 1946, Governor Cherry appointed Umstead United States Senator to fill Senator Bailey's unexpired term, and once more he resumed the role of legislator, and his services in the Senate were characterized by the same qualities of statesmanship he had exhibited while a member of the House.

He was a candidate to succeed himself in the spring of 1948. He was opposed for the nomination by the Honorable J. Melville Broughton, a greatly beloved former Governor. After a spirited and hotly contested campaign, conducted by both candidates in keeping with the dignity of the office to which they aspired, Governor Broughton won by a relatively small majority. This was the first and only defeat Umstead ever met with in his political career.

In the campaign no bitterness was engendered. Umstead gracefully bowed to the will of the majority of the Democratic voters in the primary, and entered into the campaign in the fall of 1948 with as much enthusiasm, and campaigned as vigorously for Broughton's election, as if he himself had been the candidate. He had lost the nomination for the Senate in the spring of 1948, but he captured the hearts of the Democrats of North Carolina in the fall of 1948. He had exhibited that fine spirit of sportsmanship that challenges the admiration of friend and foe alike.

When Congress adjourned in the fall of 1948, Senator Umstead resumed the practice of law in Durham. He was, however, not to remain in private life long.

In the spring of 1952, the Democrats of North Carolina chose him their candidate for Governor. His nomination for Governor was overwhelmingly ratified by the people in the fall of 1952. More than 700,000 voters chose William Umstead to chart the course of the State for the next four uncertain years. They did so because of their confidence in his vision, his sincerity, and his incorruptible integrity.

People rejoiced that he had again been called to high service. They knew he would take office, free and uncommitted, and that when the commission as Governor of the State of North Carolina and the Great Seal of the Commonwealth were delivered to him they would be received by clean hands. They knew also that when the term of his office to which he had been elected had expired, they would be returned untarnished to the people who gave them.

He was inaugurated Governor on the 8th day of January, 1953. The transition from plowboy and driver of a sand wagon to prosecuting attorney of the Recorder's Court of Durham County, solicitor of the Tenth Judicial District, Member of the House of Representatives of the United States, United States Senator, and Governor of North Carolina, came as a deserved reward for arduous, patient, intelligent, unremitting toil.

Within two days after Governor Umstead's inauguration he was stricken with a serious heart attack. For nearly two years, against ever-increasing odds, he carried on, part of the time from a sickbed in Watts Hospital at Durham, and part of the time from a sickroom in the Mansion in Raleigh. Twice after his first attack he was hospitalized. Against the advice of physicians and friends, a dogged determination drove him to the continued discharge of his duties and responsibilities as Governor. Although he was under the constant threat of death, he continued his fight to carry out the promises he had made to the people of the State of North Carolina. Finally his frail body broke under the continued strain, and early Sunday morning, November 7, 1954, he quietly passed into the Great Beyond. He had answered the call, "Come unto Me, all ye that labour and are heavy laden, and I will give you rest." He had literally given his life in the performance of the duties he had assumed on becoming Governor.

His death came as a stunning blow and cast a shadow over the entire State; men and women from every walk of life mourned the loss of North Carolina's First Citizen. Flags were at half-mast all over the State. North Carolina wept. Beautiful funeral services conducted from Trinity Methodist Church in Durham were attended by vast throngs of friends from throughout the State. Streets and highways were crowded with men, women, and children who stood with bowed heads and heavy hearts as they watched in silence the long funeral procession as it wound its way to the last resting place of Durham County's favorite son. He was buried in the Cemetery at Mount Tabor Methodist Church, in Mangum Township, near his father and mother, on an elevation overlooking the scenes of his early childhood.

The story of William Umstead's life is not told by a recital of the number of offices he held or the honors he received; it is only partially told by the things that he did in the public view. Many beautiful things have been written, and many beautiful things have been spoken of him, but nothing has been written and nothing has been said that is more beautiful than the life he lived.

It is worth while to live the kind of life William Umstead lived. His life was one of devoted service. It will always be an example and inspiration to generations yet unborn. He had a sublime Christian faith that found expression in his early connection with the Church, his constant attendance upon its services and his interpretation of the Bible as Sunday School teacher, his service to the Church as steward and as chairman of its official Board. This faith was the compass by which he charted his course, his anchor when the storms of life beat about him. It sustained and comforted him in all the vicissitudes of life.

By nature he was modest and retiring. He never claimed credit for things done by others. He was open, frank, and fair in all his relations in life. He adopted and applied to his own conduct the principle announced in the Golden Rule. The same high standards that governed his private life were strictly adhered to by him in public life. He was a man of charming and engaging personality, a delightful companion with a keen sense of humor and warmth of friendship that bound men to him. At times he was stern, severe, and exacting, but only in regard to obligations to be discharged and duties to be performed. He applied the same rigid rule to his own conduct with respect to these matters that he exacted of others.

Governor Umstead was a man of the finest character and ability. He was sincere, courageous, loyal, dependable, honest, just, genuine, and patriotic. He worked unceasingly at whatever his hands found to do. He never sought to avoid the hard places or shift to the shoulders of others unpleasant duties. He hated sham and pretense and despised hypocrites and demagogues. He regarded men who would stoop to mislead the people for political advantage as public enemies. He would have chosen defeat at any time in preference to compromise. His public and private life was unblemished.

He had a great capacity for friendship, the lives of many have been enriched by the charm of his friendship, and in their hearts his immortality will abide.

His death has brought to those of us who loved and labored with him through the years that are gone an aching void that cannot be filled.

The Commonwealth is richer that he lived; it is poorer that he is gone.

While it is true that a man's life and the measure of its usefulness are not gauged by the length of days that he lives, it would seem to those of us who knew and loved him best that his going was all too soon.

> The broken shaft stands by the wayside; from the base to the point of cleavage the chiseling is that of a master hand, and the size and the perfect workmanship tells to the passer-by how tall and beautiful it would have been if the years had bidden to place the crown and capital upon the completed column.

Able lawyer, wise counselor, conscientious public servant, Christian statesman—affectionate, dependable, golden-hearted friend—God rest his gentle soul.

A

B

H

I

J

N

O

P

Q

R

T

U

Y

Z